BACK TO THE FUTURE

Back to the Future
Legacies, Continuities and Changes in Educational Policy, Practice and Research

Edited by

Maria Assunção Flores
University of Minho, Portugal

Ana Amélia Carvalho
University of Coimbra, Portugal

Fernando Ilídio Ferreira
University of Minho, Portugal

and

Maria Teresa Vilaça
University of Minho, Portugal

SENSE PUBLISHERS
ROTTERDAM / BOSTON / TAIPEI

A C.I.P. record for this book is available from the Library of Congress.

ISBN 978-94-6209-238-9 (paperback)
ISBN 978-94-6209-239-6 (hardback)
ISBN 978-94-6209-240-2 (e-book)

Published by: Sense Publishers,
P.O. Box 21858, 3001 AW Rotterdam, The Netherlands
https://www.sensepublishers.com/

Printed on acid-free paper

TABLE OF CONTENTS

Section 4: Pedagogy and Tutoring in Higher Education

ACKNOWLEDGEMENTS

Back to the future is both a celebration and the outcome of the hard work and generosity of many people. Our thanks go to all our colleagues of the conference organising committee who helped us in putting together an enjoyable and professionally rewarding ISATT Conference in 2011 in Braga, Portugal. We are grateful to the keynote speakers, presenters of papers and participants for their willingness to share thoughts, ideas, and research findings related to the conference theme. The keynote addresses and the selected papers included in this volume illustrate well the wide range and the quality of the contributions made during the conference.

We are also indebted to the international scientific committee of the 2011 ISATT conference and the international reviewers of the chapters who generously contribute to blind review the proposals and whose contribution has made the high quality level of the papers possible. Their comments and suggestions helped the editors to make decisions about the chapters to be included in this book. Special thanks go to Patrícia Santos and Eva Fernandes for their help in compiling and editing the chapters. We also would like to thank Michel Lokhorst of Sense Publishers whose help and guidance throughout the editing process of this book was of paramount importance. We are also grateful to the authors who made the edition of this book possible.

Finally, a special word of gratitude goes to Professor Cheryl Craig, Secretary of ISATT, for her support, guidance and insightful suggestions for the conference organisation and for her foreword to this book.

FOREWORD

ISATT's 15th biennial conference held in Braga, Portugal was aptly titled "Back to the Future: Legacies, Continuities and Changes in Educational Policy, Practice and Research." Edited by Maria Assunção Flores (Braga Conference Organizer), Ana Amélia Carvalho, Fernando Ilídio Ferreira and Maria Teresa Vilaça (Planning Committee Members), this book, which bears the same title as the conference, presents a rich sampling of the international scholarship featured at Braga. As readers browse the Table of Contents, they will quickly see chapters authored by researchers dotted around the globe: Australia, Brazil, Iceland, Palestine, South Africa, to name but a few. This is fully reflective of ISATT's diverse, international character. ISATT members currently hail from 45 nations, an increase of 21 countries since 2008.

Not only does this important volume address the 2011 ISATT conference theme and the global nature of the organization's membership, it will be released at the 16th biennial conference in Ghent, Belgium in 2013. There, ISATT's 30th Anniversary will be celebrated. There, ISATT's grassroots emergence from members focusing on Teachers and Teaching Thinking to a full-fledged international organization centered on Teachers and Teaching will be remembered. This book metaphorically captures the looking backward to the past – pressing forward to the future that typically takes place on celebratory occasions. It causes us to pause and remember even as we race toward a time unknown to us. In a sense, the authors featured in this book serve as tour guides pointing out legacies, continuities and changes in teaching and teacher education. For example, Braga keynote speakers, Linda Darling-Hammond, Christopher Day, Geert Kelchtermans, António Nóvoa, Ciaran Sugrue and Flávia Vieira cause us to consider "how long until the future" (António Nóvoa), "the Janus head" of leadership (Geert Kelchtermans), "adverse settings" (Flávia Vieira) and the "new lives of teachers" (Christopher Day). The full complement of chapter authors offer different apertures of the educational lens, ranging from teachers and teachers' voices to leaders and leadership, and from overarching perspectives and challenges in teacher education to a discussion of pedagogy and tutoring in higher education. At the core, however, ISATT's purpose remains unchanged. Insights into a myriad of relevant topics are sought and the enhancement of the quality of education is of foremost importance.

I strongly urge readers not only to peruse the chapters that follow, but to distill them to their essences and to glean what is of value to be learned from them. In conclusion, the ISATT Executive especially thanks the co-editors of this volume who have compiled a superb collection of chapters on a timely and relevant topic.

Cheryl J. Craig.
Secretary, ISATT

PREFACE

This book reflects the key theme of the 15th Biennial ISATT conference 2011, Back to the Future: Legacies, Continuities and Changes in Educational Policy, Practice and Research, and it focuses attention on a set of concerns that apply to efforts worldwide to meet current challenges through research which contribute to the improvement of the quality of teaching and learning at all levels of education.

Schools and teachers are facing various challenges in a rapidly changing world. In such circumstances, discussing and sharing concerns of mutual interest regarding policy, practice and research is crucial to creating more sophisticated understandings of the various challenges as a first step in the improvement of education. While the future should not be imprisoned in the past, the past does provide valuable lessons that will undergo new iterations in constructing the future. The future will be multi-faceted and complex and the different chapters included in this book are intended to provide important contributions from which to build the future of education.

Recent changes in educational policy worldwide have affected teachers' work and life in all kinds of intended and unintended ways, while research evidence is conflicted regarding many of these influences. Evidence of this contested terrain has implications for teacher education, including initial preparation and continuing professional development understood as a lifelong continuum. What are the continuities and changes in teacher professionalism? To what extent have policies on teacher career and evaluation impacted upon teaching quality in schools and classrooms? What lessons can be learned from the past in order to enhance teacher professional learning?

Societal and cultural changes, locally, nationally and globally, impact in many ways upon teachers' work and educational leadership. What are the implications of these for policy, practice and research? What is the role of school leaders, teachers and other stakeholders in improving education for all in contexts of increasing diversity?

In addition, networks and partnerships have been increasing in number and variety as a means of meeting new and emerging challenges to education professionals. In addressing these trends in contemporary societies, a sense of community and democracy emerges as possible responses to working in uncharted terrain, and as a means of building capacity and creating some situated certainty. What kind of partnerships in education may be built amongst universities, schools and working professional organisations? What is the role of learning and practice communities for equity and inclusion? In what ways may these communities be created and nurtured?

Also, Higher Education has been made more accessible to an increasing number of students. Such developments represent considerable challenges to established and traditional institutional structures, cultures, curricula and pedagogies. What are the significant policies and trends in Higher Education nationally and internationally? What is the role of teacher educators in this new scenario? How can the scholarship of teaching and learning be enhanced in Higher Education institutional environments, both virtual and real?

This book has been written to address these questions and to provide an international forum of what can be learned from the past and how lessons learned from the past can be useful to face and respond to current challenges and to envisage ways of looking forward to the future.

The chapters included in this book result from a set of keynote addresses and refereed papers given at the 2011 International Study Association on Teachers and Teaching (ISATT) Conference, held in Braga, Portugal. The conference was attended by 400 delegates from more than 40 countries from all the continents.

This book has been developed so that it reflects the wide range of contexts and issues discussed during the conference. It is presented in four sections, each one encompassing a key dimension of current challenges and trends in teaching and teachers' work and lives, in leadership and school curriculum, in teacher education and learning and in pedagogy and tutoring in higher education. They draw upon the diverse social, historical, cultural and professional contexts of the different authors and they reflect different ways of looking at the questions identified above from diverse stances and research methodologies.

The first section, Teachers and the teaching profession, discusses the current challenges and directions of teaching as a profession and it analyses teachers' work and lives from an international perspective. The five chapters included in it provide theoretical reflections and compelling empirical evidence of the ways in which teaching and teachers may be enhanced. Chapter 1 – Building a Profession of Teaching – by Linda Darling-Hammond, looks at global lessons that support teaching in order to enhance teacher quality and student learning. The author argues that if teaching is to be a profession that supports effective instruction attention must be paid to building capacity across the entire system including universal high-quality preparation, mentoring, and support and well-designed schools that allow and enable good practice. In Chapter 2 – Teachers: How Long Until the Future? – António Nóvoa critically analyses the distance between discourses about teachers and the tensions and dilemmas that the teaching profession has been facing. He argues for central themes that may redirect the development of the teaching profession, namely the importance of a professionality that is built from inside the profession, the development of professional knowledge through reflection and experience, the relevance of professional collaboration and the implications of the public space of education with a redefinition of schools and teachers and the celebration of a social contract for education. In Chapter 3 – Teachers' Lives and Work: Back to the Future? – Ciaran Sugrue looks at teachers' lives and work internationally and argues that their identities have been a continuous dance between the individual and collective, the prevailing social conditions or policy contexts that at once colour teachers' lives and work while simultaneously characterising the profession of teaching. He discusses autonomy and accountability in teaching and argues for the need to re-construct a sense of professional responsibility that recognises contemporary realities and seeks to loose constraints in the service of others as well as the professional of teaching. In

Chapter 4 – The New Lives of Teachers – Christopher Day, drawing upon an empirical study, looks at teachers' professional phases in which commitment, well being, identity and effectiveness varied within and between these phases. He discusses key influences on teacher identity namely biography, experience, life outside the school as well as social and policy expectations, workplace conditions and relationships and the educational ideals of the teacher. He concludes with the analysis of the role of teacher educators as researchers as part of their commitment to learning and argues for activism in giving voice to the connection between policy, research and practice at all levels. Chapter 5 – Teachers' Voices: Learning from Professional Lives – by Hafdís Guðjónsdóttir and Sólveig Karvelsdóttir, deals with the changing nature of teachers' professionalism, focusing on the work, lives, knowledge and ethics of the teachers. The authors present teachers' stories as they discuss their experiences as teachers, and their hopes and beliefs, which are potentially useful for the development of teacher education. They call for a new professionalism with strong knowledge in pedagogy and subject matter along with a passion for teaching, responsibility, and a commitment to children and to the profession.

The second section, Leadership and school curriculum: contexts and actors, provides conceptual frameworks and empirical analyses of the role of school leaders, curriculum developers and teachers in developing better teaching and learning in schools and classrooms. In Chapter 6 – Living the Janus Head: Conceptualising Leaders and Leadership in Schools in the 21st Century – Geert Kelchtermans and Liesbeth Piot, drawing upon a review of the literature about school leadership, develop a model of leadership which integrates the merits of concentrated and distributed leadership and acknowledges the emotional dimension of school leadership. The model provides an integrated picture of the different and dynamic elements of school leadership and their interconnectedness. In Chapter 7 – Development of a New Curriculum Leadership Model with a Focus on Its Relation to the Professional Learning Communities – Toshiyuki Kihara, Hirotoshi Yano, and Hisayoshi Mori based upon three case studies in North America and Japan present a model of curriculum leadership in which professional learning communities allow teachers to learn and improve their competencies through curriculum leadership. The authors develop the idea of networked learning communities and they discuss their potential for curriculum development. Chapter 8 – Advancing Equity and Inclusion in Schools: an Awareness-Action Framework – by Jude Butcher, Colleen Leathley and Kristin Johnston, presents an empirical study on schools' perceptions of people who are 'poor' and the strategies that schools are using to engage with them and other strategies schools may employ to actively connect with them. Findings provide evidence that may inform how schools can appropriately engage with the communities in order to increase equity and inclusion. The authors develop an 'awareness-action matrix' as a tool for facilitating engagement, assessment and action in a relational context in which awareness and action are intertwined with equity and inclusion. In Chapter 9 – Cognitive Skills in Palestinian Curricula and Textbooks – Shukri Sanber and Irene Hazou look at curriculum and textbooks used in the three stages of schooling in

Palestine. They analyse the learning objectives of the curricula and the content of the textbooks, their learning activities and their end-of-chapter and end-of-unit exercises. They contend that curricula and textbooks under analysis address and support a variety of thinking skills, although the degree of emphasis on higher thinking skills was found to be stronger in the science textbooks than in the social studies textbooks.

The third section, Perspectives and challenges in teacher education and learning, includes five chapters from different countries and contributors who draw attention to key influences and contexts in teacher education and learning. In Chapter 10 – Learning in Professional Development Schools: Perspectives of Teacher Educators, Mentor Teachers and Student Teachers – Joke Daemen, Els Laroes, Paulien C. Meijer and Jan Vermunt present findings from research aimed at examining learning in Professional Development Schools from the perspective of various stakeholders – teacher educators, mentor teachers and student teachers. The authors analyse the ways in which the participants describe their own personal learning, their personal development and how participating in Professional Development Schools influences their professional development. In Chapter 11 – Teacher Professional Learning in Digital Age Environments – Catherine McLoughlin stresses the advantages of Web 2.0 applications for professional learning. The author highlights emerging learning theories, focusing on the revised framework of teacher knowledge: technological pedagogical content knowledge (TPCK) and on communities of learners and of practice. Finally, she reports on a study conducted with 19 pre-service teachers during their four week practicum, taking advantage of Web 2.0 tools. In Chapter 12 – Developing Experienced-based Principles of Practice for Teaching Teachers – Tom Russell and Shawn Michael Bullock, drawing upon their own experience within the context of collaborative self-study, identify six principles of practice for teaching teachers. The authors use the concept of the authority of experience as a central perspective to develop principles of practice for teaching future teachers. They argue that the characteristics of self-study, such as critical friendship and reflection-in-action, make sustained collaborative self-study an important tool to help teacher educators to examine the assumptions underlying their practices and critical features of their pedagogy. In Chapter 13 – Challenges to Promoting Quality in Preservice Practicum Experiences – Tom Russell and Andrea K. Martin, based upon their own experience as supervisors, look at the importance of practicum as the single most important and valuable element of preservice education. They argue for ways to enhance its quality and they conclude with an agenda for an action plan to improve the quality of practicum learning experience. In Chapter 14 – Professional Identity: A Case Study of Pre-service Mathematics Teachers in South Africa – Sonja van Putten, Gerrit Stols and Sarah Howie present findings from an empirical study of the development of pre-service Professional Mathematics Teacher's Identity. The authors highlight the strongest influence of student teachers' personal background, followed by their experiences both at university and during teaching practice.

The fourth section, Pedagogy and tutoring in higher education, provides a set of examples of initiatives in higher education from a diversity of perspectives. In Chapter 15 – The Scholarship of Pedagogy in Adverse Settings: Lessons from Experience – Flávia Vieira, based upon lessons from her own experience with colleagues, looks at the scholarship of pedagogy as a multifaceted practice that involves a reconfiguration of professional identities. The author argues that it is a transitional and risky practice that challenges prevalent cultures regarding teaching and research, raising issues about professionalism and merit in higher education. In Chapter 16 – Tutors' and Students' Views of Tutoring: A Study in Higher Education – Sandra Fernandes and Maria Assunção Flores discuss existing literature on tutoring and present an empirical study of tutoring in project-led education at a university. The authors highlight its contribution to student learning and motivation and they analyse its implications for teaching, learning and faculty professional development. In Chapter 17 – Online Programme to Prepare Teacher Tutors: an Experience Involving a University-School Partnership – Renata Portela Rinaldi, Maria Iolanda Monteiro, Aline Maria de Medeiros Rodrigues Reali, Rosa Maria Anunciato de Oliveira describe a Brazilian online programme to prepare 45 K-4 school teacher tutors, during two modules of 120 hours, indicating its strengths and weaknesses.

The chapters included in this book provide readers with international perspectives, frameworks and empirical evidence of legacies, continuities and changes in educational policy, practice and research in teaching, teacher education and learning. We hope that they inspire the readers to build the future and to change their own professional realities.

SECTION 1

TEACHERS AND THE TEACHING PROFESSION

LINDA DARLING-HAMMOND

BUILDING A PROFESSION OF TEACHING[i]

INTRODUCTION

The experience of [high-performing] school systems suggests that three things matter most: 1) getting the right people to become teachers; 2) developing them into effective instructors and; 3) ensuring that the system is able to deliver the best possible instruction for every child. (Barber & Mourshed, 2007)

As equality of opportunity comes to rest more squarely on the need for quality instruction, issues of how to enhance the professional competence of educators become more important. To ensure equal opportunity in today's context means enhancing, not limiting, the professional nature of teaching, and for that task state policy as it has been conceived in the past is hardly the best instrument ... We need new ways of conceiving the state role and of the strategies at the state's disposal. (Elmore & Fuhrman, 1993, p. 86)

Nations that have steeply improved their students' achievement attribute much of their success to their focused investments in teacher preparation and development (Darling-Hammond, 2010). Such investments, in nations like Finland and Singapore, have been organized to create an infrastructure that can routinely recruit and prepare teachers effectively and can support successful teaching at scale.

These nations realize that, without a comprehensive framework for developing strong teaching, new resources in the system are less effective than they otherwise would be: Reforms are poorly implemented where faculty and leaders lack the capacity to put them into action; districts and schools are often unable to develop and maintain comprehensive training opportunities at scale, and scarce professional development dollars are wasted where teachers leave regularly. Furthermore, when a profession's knowledge is not organized and made available to the practitioners who need it most, advances in the state of both knowledge and practice are slowed.

Good teachers create little oases for themselves while others who are less well-prepared adopt approaches that are ineffective or harmful – sometimes seeking knowledge that is not readily available to them; other times battening down the hatches and eventually becoming impermeable to better ideas. Schools are vulnerable to vendors selling educational snake oils when educators and school boards lack sufficient shared knowledge of learning, curriculum, instruction, and research to make sound decisions about programs and materials. Students experience an instructional hodge-podge caused by the failure of the system to provide the knowledge and tools needed by the educators who serve them.

M.A. Flores et al. (eds.), Back to the Future: Legacies, Continuities and Changes in Educational Policy, Practice and Research, 3–27.

These counterproductive conditions will continue until teaching becomes a profession like medicine, architecture, accounting, engineering, or law in which every practitioner has the opportunity and the expectation to master the knowledge and skills needed for effective practice, and makes the moral commitment to use this knowledge in the best decisions of their clients. Teaching is today where medicine was in 1910, when Abraham Flexner conducted the famous study of medical education that eventually led to its overhaul. At that time, doctors could be prepared in a three-week training program in which they memorized lists of symptoms and cures or, at the other extreme, in a graduate program of medicine at Johns Hopkins University that included extensive coursework in the sciences of medicine along with clinical training in the newly invented teaching hospital.

In his introduction to the Flexner Report, Henry Pritchett, president of the Carnegie Foundation for the Advancement of Teaching, noted that, although there was a growing science of medicine, most doctors did not get access to this knowledge because of the great unevenness in medical training. He observed that, "(V)ery seldom, under existing conditions, does a patient receive the best aid which it is possible to give him in the present state of medicine, … (because) a vast army of men is admitted to the practice of medicine who are untrained in sciences fundamental to the profession and quite without a sufficient experience with disease" (Flexner & Pritchett, 1910, p. x).

In 1910, there were many who felt medicine could best be learned by following another doctor around in a buggy, learning to apply leeches to reduce fevers and selling tonics that purported to cure everything from baldness to cancer. Flexner's identification of universities that were successful in conveying new knowledge about the causes and treatment of disease and in creating strong clinical training for medical practice was the stimulus for the reform of medical education. Despite resistance from weaker training sites, the enterprise was transformed over the subsequent two decades through the efforts of state, and later national, accrediting and licensing bodies that ensured doctors would get the best training the field had to offer.

Creating a strong profession in education is not a task that can be tackled school by school or district by district. And creating uniformly strong schools cannot be accomplished without a strong profession. Ultimately, it is essential to develop a well-designed state and national infrastructure that ensures that schools have access to well-prepared teachers and to knowledge about best practices.

GLOBAL LESSONS

Around the world, there is growing recognition that expert teachers and leaders are the key resource for improving student learning, and the highest-achieving nations make substantial investments in teacher quality.[ii] In top-ranked nations, supports for teaching have taken the form of:
— *Universal high-quality teacher education*, completely at government expense, featuring extensive clinical training as well as coursework;

- *Mentoring for all beginners* from expert teachers, coupled with a reduced teaching load and shared planning time;
- *Ongoing professional learning*, embedded in 15 to 25 hours a week of planning and collaboration time at school, plus additional professional learning time to attend institutes and seminars, visit other schools and classrooms, conduct action research and lesson study, and participate in school retreats;
- *Leadership development* built on opportunities that engage expert teachers in curriculum and assessment development, mentoring and coaching, and professional development, as well as pathways that recruit strong teachers into programs that prepare school principals as instructional leaders;
- *Equitable, competitive salaries*, sometimes with additional stipends for hard-to-staff locations, which are comparable with other professions, such as engineering.

Strong Beginnings

High-achieving nations have overhauled teacher education to ensure stronger programs across the enterprise, and to ensure that able candidates can afford to become well-prepared as they enter the profession. In Scandinavia, for example, teacher candidates in Finland, Sweden, Norway, and the Netherlands now receive two to three years of graduate-level preparation for teaching, completely at government expense, *plus* a living stipend. Typically, this includes at least a full year of training in a school connected to the university, like the model schools in Finland. Programs also include extensive coursework in content-specific pedagogy and a thesis researching an educational problem in the schools.

This is also the practice in Asian nations like Singapore and Korea, and in jurisdictions like Hong Kong and Chinese Taipei, where most teachers prepare in 4 year undergraduate programs, although graduate programs are growing more common. Unlike the United States, where teachers either go into debt to prepare for a profession that will pay them poorly or enter with little or no training, these countries invest in a uniformly well-prepared teaching force by overhauling preparation, recruiting top candidates, and paying them to go to school. Slots in teaching programs are highly coveted in these nations, and shortages are virtually unheard of.

Once teachers are hired, resources are targeted to schools to support mentoring for novices. Generally, induction programs in high achieving nations include: (1) release time for new teachers and mentor teachers to participate in coaching and other induction activities, and (2) training for mentor teachers. In a model like that found in a number of Asian nations, the New Zealand Ministry of Education funds 20 percent release time for new teachers and 10 percent release time for second-year teachers to observe other teachers, attend professional development activities, work on curriculum, and attend courses (Britton, 2006; Clement, 2000). Mentor teachers also have time to observe and meet with beginning teachers. In places like Singapore, mentor teachers receive special training and certification and additional compensation in the salary schedule.

5

Countries like England, France, Israel, Norway, Singapore, and Switzerland also require formal training for mentor teachers (OECD, 2005). Norwegian principals assign an experienced, highly qualified mentor to each new teacher and the teacher education institution then trains the mentor and takes part in in-school guidance (OECD, 2005). Through its National Literacy and Numeracy Strategies, England trains coaches for new teachers about both effective pedagogies for students and the techniques to get teachers to employ them (Barber & Mourshed, 2007). In some Swiss states the new teachers in each district meet in reflective practice groups twice a month with an experienced teacher who is trained to facilitate their discussions of common problems for new teachers (Stansbury & Zimmerman, 2000). In Singapore, master teachers who have received training from the Institute of Education are appointed to lead the coaching and development of new and veteran teachers in each school (Barber & Mourshed, 2007).

Support for Collaboration and Inquiry

There is also a continuous effort to improve the practice of both teaching and teacher development. For example, the many articles that have been written about the "secret" to Finland's success point to its dramatic overhaul of teacher education and teaching since the early 1990s, in a serious of reforms based on ongoing evaluations of its teaching systems – ranging from preparation programs to school and classroom practices, where teachers are centrally involved in the process. The government invests substantial funding in both teacher education and in research on teaching and teacher education, in order to improve them regularly (Mikkola, 2000).

All new Finnish teachers complete a masters' thesis that involves them in research on practice. Programs aim to develop "highly developed problem solving capacity" that derives from teachers' deep understanding of the principles of learning and allows them to create "powerful learning environments" which continually improve as they learn to engage in a "cycle of self-responsible planning, action and reflection/evaluation" (Buchberger & Buchberger, 2004, p. 210). Leaders are drawn from among these highly skilled and reflective teachers, and receive additional support to thinking organizationally about improvement. The entire teaching and schooling system is also continually evaluated as part of the reflective cycle. This is a key element of what Pasi Sahlberg calls "intelligent accountability" in a context where external student testing is rare, but analysis of practice and student learning is pervasive (Sahlberg, 2009).

These practices are widespread. For example, OECD reports that more than 85% of schools in Belgium, Denmark, Finland, Hungary, Ireland, Norway, Sweden, and Switzerland provide time for professional development in teachers' work day or week (OECD, 2004). This time is frequently focused on the kind of action research that catalyzes change in teaching practice (Cochran-Smith & Lytle, 2003). In Denmark, Finland, Italy, and Norway, teachers participate in collaborative research on topics related to education both in their preservice preparation and in their ongoing work on the job (OECD, 2004). Similarly,

England, Hungary, and Ontario (Canada) have created opportunities for teachers to engage in school-focused research and development. Teachers are provided time and support for studying and evaluating their own teaching strategies and school programs and in sharing their findings with their colleagues, and through conferences and publications (OECD, 2005).

Inquiry about practice is also pervasive in Asian nations, made possible by the extensive time that teachers have to work with colleagues on developing lessons, participating in research and study groups, observing each other's classrooms, and engaging in seminars and visits to other schools. Lesson study is a popular approach, which involves teachers in jointly crafting a lesson, observing while a colleague teaches it, and studying student responses and learning evidence to refine the lesson further. When engaged in lesson study, groups of teachers observe each other's classrooms and work together to refine individual lessons, expediting the spread of best practices throughout the school (Barber & Mourshed, 2007).

In Japan, for example, *kenkyuu jugyou* (research lessons) are a key part of the learning culture. Every teacher periodically prepares a best possible lesson that demonstrates strategies to achieve a specific goal (e.g. students becoming active problem-solvers or students learning more from each other) in collaboration with other colleagues. A group of teachers observe while the lesson is taught and record the lesson in a number of ways, including videotapes, audiotapes, and narrative and/or checklist observations that focus on areas of interest to the instructing teacher (e.g., how many student volunteered their own ideas). Afterwards, the teachers, and sometimes outside educators, discuss the lesson's strengths and weakness, ask questions, and make suggestions to improve the lesson. In some cases the revised lesson is given by another teacher only a few days later and observed and discussed again (Barber & Mourshed, 2007; Fernandez, 2002; Pang, 2006).

The research lessons allow teachers to refine individual lessons, consult with other teachers and get colleagues' observations about their classroom practice, reflect on their own practice, learn new content and approaches, and build a culture that emphasizes continuous improvement and collaboration. Some teachers also give public research lessons, which expedites the spread of best practices across schools, allows principals, district personnel, and policymakers to see how teachers are grappling with new subject matter and goals, and gives recognition to excellent teachers (Fernandez, 2002).

These lessons, which become the joint property of the teaching community, have been compared to "polished stones" because they have been so carefully worked on. In their study of mathematics teaching and learning in Japan, Taiwan, and the US, Jim Stigler and Harold Stevenson noted that:

> Asian class lessons are so well crafted [because] there is a very systematic effort to pass on the accumulated wisdom of teaching practice to each new generation of teachers and to keep perfecting that practice by providing teachers the opportunities to continually learn from each other. (Stigler & Stevenson, 1991)

Systems for Professional Development

In addition to supporting ongoing work to improve practice within schools, many high-achieving nations, such as Singapore and Sweden, fund and require as much as 100 hours of professional development time for focused study using resources beyond the school. A number of countries have organized very intensive, systematic professional development that disseminates successful practices in much more effective ways than publishing articles in research journals that practitioners don't read, or describing ideas in bulleted lists to hand out on professional development days.

England, for example, instituted a national training program in 'best-practice' teaching strategies, which led to the percentage of students meeting the target standards in literacy increasing from 63 to 75% in just three years (Barber & Mourshed, 2007). The training program is part of the National Literacy Strategy (NLS) and National Numeracy Strategy (NNS), which provide resources to support implementation of the national curriculum frameworks. These include packets of high quality teaching materials, resource documents, and videos depicting successful practices. A 'cascade' model of training – similar to a trainer of trainers' model – is structured around these resources to help teachers learn and use productive practices.

The National Literacy and National Numeracy Centres provide leadership and training for teacher training institutions and consultants, who train school heads, lead math teachers and expert literacy teachers, who in turn support and train other teachers (Earl, Watson, & Torrance, 2002; Fullan, 2007). As more teachers become familiar with the strategies, expertise is increasingly located at the local level with consultants and leading mathematics teachers and literacy teachers providing support for teachers (Earl et al., 2002). In 2004, England began a new component of the Strategies designed to allow schools and local education agencies to learn best practices from each other by funding and supporting 1,500 groups of six schools each to engage in collaborative inquiry and knowledge-sharing together (Fullan, 2007).

Similarly, since 2000, the Australian government has been sponsoring the Quality Teacher Programme, a large scale program that provides funding to update and improve teachers' skills and understandings in priority areas and enhance the status of teaching in both government and non-government schools. The Programme operates at three levels: (1) Teaching Australia (formerly the National Institute for Quality Teaching and School Leadership); (2) National Projects; and (3) State and Territory Projects. Teaching Australia facilitates the development and implementation of nationally agreed upon teaching standards, conducts research and communicates research findings, and facilitates and coordinates professional development courses. The National Projects have a national focus and include programs designed to identify and promote best practice, support the development and dissemination of professional learning resources in priority areas, and develop professional networks for teachers and school leaders. The State and Territory Projects fund a wide variety of professional learning activities for teachers and school leaders under agreements with state and territory education authorities, allowing professional development activities to be tailored to local needs. These projects include school-based action research and learning, conferences, workshops, on-line or digital media, and training of trainers, school project and team leaders (Atelier Learning Solutions, 2005; Skilbeck & Connell, 2003).

Western Australia's highly successful Getting it Right (GiR) Strategy provides specialist teaching personnel, professional development, and support to select primary schools to improve literacy and numeracy outcomes of high needs students, with a focus on Aboriginal and other at-risk students (Meiers, Ingvarson, Beavis, Hogan, & Kleinhenz, 2006). Each school selects a highly regarded teacher with interest and expertise in numeracy or literacy to be a Specialist Teacher (ST), who is then trained through a series of seven three-day intensive workshops over the course of their initial two-year appointment. The Specialist Teachers work "shoulder to shoulder" with teachers in their schools, for about half a day each week for each teacher. The Specialist Teachers monitor and record student learning, help teachers analyze student learning, model teaching strategies, plan learning activities to meet the identified needs of students, assist with the implementation of these activities, and provide access to a range of resources, sharing expertise and encouraging teachers to be reflective about their practice (Ingvarson, 2005; Meiers et al., 2006). Teachers show greatly enhanced knowledge about how students' learn reading, writing, and mathematics and much stronger teaching and assessment skills, including their ability to use data to identify and diagnose students' learning needs and to plan explicit teaching approaches to address these needs (Meiers et al., 2006).

BUILDING AN INFRASTRUCTURE FOR QUALITY TEACHING

Clearly, if students are to achieve 21st century learning standards, we can expect no less from their teachers and from other educators. Furthermore, teachers need to know a lot more to teach today's diverse students to more challenging learning standards than ever before – including how to teach much more ambitious disciplinary content and cross-disciplinary skills and how to teach special needs learners, new immigrant students, and others who require specialized learning supports.

Developing Strong Initial Preparation Programs

Evidence suggests that some preparation programs are much more effective than others, based both on their employers' ratings of their effectiveness and on their graduates' contributions to student learning gains (Boyd, Grossman, Lankford, Loeb, & Wyckoff, 2008; Darling-Hammond, 2006). In a New York City study that evaluated the contributions to value-added student achievement of beginning elementary teachers from different programs, for example, several preservice programs had much stronger outcomes than any of the other traditional or

alternative routes.[iii] The researchers examined the features of these programs, and found that, in addition to strong faculty, they had:
- More coursework in content areas (e.g. math and reading) and in content-specific methods of teaching;
- A focus on helping candidates learn specific practices that they apply in classrooms where they are practice teaching alongside their coursework;
- Carefully-selected student teaching experiences, well-matched to the contexts in which candidates will later teach;
- Opportunities to study the local district curriculum;
- A capstone project – typically a portfolio of work done in classrooms with students.

Other studies of highly effective teacher education programs reinforce these same features and identify other critical elements, such as coursework and clinical work that are interwoven and pointed at a common conception of good teaching; emphasis on understanding curriculum, learning, and assessment, as well as methods of teaching; and use of case methods, action research, and performance assessments to develop skills for reflecting on teaching in relation to learning (Darling-Hammond, 2006; Darling-Hammond & Bransford, 2005).

In another study of highly effective teacher education programs, I found that their ability to develop new teachers who can teach with the assurance and skill of more experienced, very thoughtful veterans is achieved through several features (Darling-Hammond, 2006). They create a tightly coherent set of learning experiences grounded in a strong vision of good teaching represented both in coursework and clinical placements where candidates can see good teaching modelled and enacted. These programs focus on developing teaching strategies and skills that can be successful with a wide range of learners, for without such skills, beliefs that "all children can learn" soon devolve into little more than rhetoric. They engage candidates in intensive study of learning, child development, curriculum, assessment, cultural contexts, and subject specific teaching methods. This study is connected to at least a full year of student teaching and practicum experiences in carefully selected placements with expert teachers who model excellent teaching in diverse urban classrooms. Candidates' experiences in these classrooms are linked to guided discussions and readings that help them interpret what they are seeing, learning, and doing as they gradually take on more responsibility for teaching.

Like the internships and residencies doctors experience, such apprenticeships with great teachers are critical for learning to teach effectively, especially where students have a wide range of needs that require sophisticated skills from their teachers. In this way, prospective teachers can grow roots on a more complex form of practice that will allow them to teach diagnostically, rather than from scripts or by merely plowing through the text, insensitive to student learning. They learn to adapt their lessons based on ongoing assessment of students' needs, and they acquire a wide repertoire of practices, which they can apply judiciously based on what is needed for different students and different goals in different circumstances.

This is critically important because teaching cannot be learned from books or even from being mentored periodically. Teachers must see expert practices modelled and must practice them with help. However, such experiences are rare for urban teachers in the US, since many traditional and most alternative programs fail to provide the opportunity to learn under the direct supervision of expert teachers working in schools that serve high-need students well. Student teaching is often conducted in classrooms that do not model expert practice, or it is in classrooms that do not serve high-need students – and what is learned does not generalize to other schools. In alternative programs, it is too often reduced or omitted entirely. This fundamental problem has to be tackled and solved if we are to prepare an adequate supply of teachers who will enter urban or poor rural classrooms competent to work effectively with the neediest students and confident enough to stay in teaching in these areas.

It is not just the availability of classroom experience that enables teachers to apply what they are learning. The experience must be well-guided, allowing teachers to learn to use specific *tools* in the classroom, such as assessment protocols, guided reading strategies, writers' workshop techniques, and others. Teachers need tools ranging from knowledge of curriculum materials and assessment strategies to techniques for organizing productive group work and planning well-structured projects and inquiries – and they need opportunities to *practice* with these tools in specific subject areas and with real students. In this way, prospective teachers learn to connect theory to practice in a well-grounded fashion, developing the adaptive expertise they will need to meet the specific classroom contexts they later encounter.[iv]

Candidates also learn to become skilled and analytical teachers by analyzing student work and learning, teachers' plans and assignments, videotapes of teachers and students in action, and cases of teaching and learning, which – as they do in law and medicine – help teachers draw connections between generalized principles and specific instances of teaching and learning (Ball & Cohen, 1999; Hammerness, Darling-Hammond, & Shulman, 2002). In these powerful programs, candidates developed case studies on individual students – including English language learners, special education students, and others – and on specific aspects of schools, teaching, curriculum, families and communities by observing, interviewing, examining students' approaches to learning, and analyzing these data.

In all of these ways, successful programs foster standards-based teaching that helps students learn challenging content successfully. They also support teaching that is culturally and individually responsive, providing teachers with concrete tools for learning about students' lives and contexts – tapping what Luis Moll calls the "funds of knowledge" that exist in their homes and communities (Moll, Amanti, Neff, & Gonzalez, 1992)[v] – and turning that information into resources that can be tapped for learning. This includes learning to work with parents as partners who can provide insights about their children's interests and needs, and who can work collaboratively on supporting learning at home. Thus, successful programs help teachers structure the interaction between students and subject matter that must be intertwined, like the double helix of a DNA chain, if learning is to occur.

The Importance of Developing "Teaching Schools." Finally, all of the exemplary programs we studied had developed strong relationships with local schools – some of which were formal professional development schools (PDS) that partnered closely with the university. Some colleges even helped to start new schools that were models of practice. For example, Bank Street College, a large, internationally renowned teacher education institution, maintains strong connections with many public schools in New York City, partnering with at least a dozen new and existing reform-oriented schools, some of them populated almost entirely by graduates of the College's teaching and leadership programs. All of these schools serve racially, ethnically, linguistically, and economically diverse student populations and are committed to experiential and project-based learning. Similar relationships have been developed by Trinity University with schools in San Antonio, the University of Southern Maine with schools in Portland and surrounding communities, and Alverno College with schools in Milwaukee, as well as many other universities across the country.

Since settings that are beacons of excellent education for low-income students of colour simply do not exist in large numbers, they must be created if practice is to change on a wide scale. Seeking diversity by placing candidates in schools serving low-income students or students of colour that suffer from the typical shortcomings many such schools face can actually "work to strengthen pre-service teachers' stereotypes of children, rather than stimulate their examination, and ultimately compromise teachers' effectiveness in the classroom" (Gallego, 2001, p. 314). For this reason, a growing number of universities – including Clark University, Stanford University, the University of Chicago, the University of Pennsylvania, and others – have actually created new urban schools and developed partnerships that support and help transform existing schools to demonstrate state-of-the-art practices and to serve as training grounds for teachers.

These kinds of relationships, which simultaneously transform schools and teacher preparation, are critical to long-term reform, because it is impossible to teach people how to teach powerfully by asking them to imagine what they have never seen or to suggest they "do the opposite" of what they have observed in the classroom. It is impractical to expect to prepare teachers for schools as they should be if teachers are constrained to learn in settings that typify the problems of schools as they have been – where isolated teachers provide examples of idiosyncratic practice that rarely exhibits a diagnostic, assessment-oriented approach and infrequently offers access to carefully selected strategies designed to teach a wide range of learners well. No amount of coursework can, by itself, counteract the powerful experiential lessons that shape what teachers actually do.

In highly-developed professional development school partnerships, faculty from the school and university work together to develop curriculum, improve instruction, and undertake school reforms. They work together teaching children and prospective teachers, making the entire school a site for learning and feedback for all of the adults, as well as the students (Abdal-Haqq, 1998, pp. 13-14; Darling-Hammond, 2005). In many such schools, they actively pursue an equity agenda, confronting the inheritances of tracking, poor teaching, inadequate curriculum, and unresponsive systems (e.g. Darling-Hammond, 2005; Guadarrama, Ramsey, & Nath, 2002). In these schools, student teachers or interns are encouraged to participate in all aspects of school functioning, ranging from special education and support services for students to parent meetings, home visits, and community outreach to faculty discussions and projects aimed at ongoing improvement in students' opportunities to learn. This kind of participation helps prospective teachers understand the broader institutional context for teaching and learning and begin to develop the skills needed for effective participation in collegial work around school improvement throughout their careers.

Studies of highly-developed PDSs have found that new teachers who graduate from such programs feel better prepared to teach and are rated by employers, supervisors, and researchers as stronger than other new teachers. Veteran teachers working in such schools describe changes in their own practice as a result of the professional development, action research, and mentoring that are part of the PDS. Studies have documented gains in student performance tied to curriculum and teaching interventions resulting from PDS initiatives (Darling-Hammond & Bransford, 2005, pp. 415-416).[vi] Having centres of support for continuous professional learning is essential for turning around schools that serve the students most often left behind because their teachers are left behind.

Beginning Teacher Mentoring. Mentoring for beginning teachers is also important, both for developing teachers' competence and reducing attrition. Many high-achieving countries invest heavily in structured induction for beginning teachers: they fund schools to provide released time for expert mentors and they fund other learning opportunities for beginners, such as seminars, visits to other teachers' classrooms, and joint planning time.

Beginners stay in teaching at much higher rates when they have had strong initial preparation and when they have a mentor in the same subject area and/or grade level, common planning time with teachers in the same subject, and regularly scheduled collaboration with other teachers (Cheng & Brown, 1992; Fuller, 2003; Ingersoll & Kralik, 2004; Odell & Ferraro, 1992; Spuhler & Zetler, 1995). Their practice is enhanced further when their mentors also receive formal training and have release time to provide one-to-one observation and coaching in the classroom, demonstrating effective methods and helping them solve immediate problems of practice (Bartell, 1995; Olebe, 2001; Smith & Ingersoll, 2004).

Evaluating Effective Teaching

Developing good teaching on a wide scale requires not only opportunities for teacher learning but also a shared conception of what effective teachers do, and assessment tools that reflect and develop that kind of practice. Such a shared conception is reflected in professional standards that can guide preparation and professional development. Standard-setting for licensing, certification, and accreditation represents "professional policy," used as an alternative to governmental regulation in fields where knowledge is always growing and its appropriate application is contingent on many different factors. Professional standards hold members of a profession accountable for developing shared expertise and applying it appropriately, rather than imposing standardized prescriptions for practice that would fail to meet clients' different needs (Darling-Hammond, Wise, & Klein, 1999; Thompson & Zeuli, 1999). As Richard Elmore and Susan Fuhrman (1993) note:

> As equality of opportunity comes to rest more squarely on the need for quality instruction, issues of how to enhance the professional competence of educators become more important. To ensure equal opportunity in today's context means enhancing, not limiting, the professional nature of teaching, and for that task state policy as it has been conceived in the past is hardly the best instrument .... We need new ways of conceiving the state role and of the strategies at the state's disposal. (p. 86)

In recent years in the United States, performance-based assessments of teaching have been designed that not only detect aspects of teaching that are significantly related to teachers' effectiveness, but also help develop more effective teaching. These assessments have high leverage as policy tools, as they can help shape who enters and remains in teaching, as well as who should be recognized as expert for purposes of compensation and selection as potential mentors and coaches for other teachers. Furthermore, participation in these assessments has been found to support learning both for teachers who are being evaluated and educators who are trained to serve as assessors, thus growing greater competence in the teaching force and focusing the efforts of educators on common practices.

A standards-based approach to assessing teachers was initially developed through the work of the National Board for Professional Teaching Standards, launched in 1987 and comprised of expert teachers and other members of the public. The Board developed standards for accomplished teaching in each major subject area and then developed an assessment of accomplished teaching that assembles evidence of teachers' practice and performance in a portfolio that includes videotapes of teaching, accompanied by commentary, lesson plans, and evidence of student learning. These pieces of evidence are scored by trained raters who are expert in the same teaching field, using rubrics that define critical dimensions of teaching as the basis of the evaluation. Designed to identify experienced accomplished teachers, a number of states and districts use National Board Certification as the basis for salary bonuses or other forms of teacher recognition, such as selection as a mentor or lead teacher.

A number of recent studies have found that the National Board Certification assessment process identifies teachers who are more effective in raising student achievement than others who have not achieved certification.[vii] Equally important, many studies have found that teachers' participation in the National Board process supports their professional learning and stimulates changes in their practice.

Teachers note that the process of analyzing their own and their students' work in light of standards enhances their abilities to assess student learning and to evaluate the effects of their own actions, while causing them to adopt new practices that are called for in the standards and assessments (Athanases, 1994). Teachers report significant improvements in their performance in each area assessed – planning, designing, and delivering instruction, managing the classroom, diagnosing and evaluating student learning, using subject matter knowledge, and participating in a learning community – and observational studies have documented that these changes do indeed occur (Chittenden & Jones, 1997; Sato, 2000; Sato, Wei, & Darling-Hammond, 2008).

These standards, along with the performance assessments that have been developed to evaluate them, greatly raise the expectations for teachers. They incorporate deep understanding of content and how to teach it, a strong appreciation for the role of culture and context in child development and learning, and an insistence on ongoing assessment and adaptation of teaching to promote learning for all students. By examining teaching in the light of learning, these new standards put considerations of effectiveness at the centre of practice – a shift from the behaviourist approach which has viewed teaching as the implementation of set routines, whether or not they actually produce success.

Because of this, National Board participants often say that they have learned more about teaching from their participation in the assessments than they have learned from any other previous professional development experience (Areglado, 1999; Bradley, 1994; Buday & Kelly, 1996; Haynes, 1995). David Haynes' statement is typical of many:

Completing the portfolio for the Early Adolescence/Generalist Certification was, quite simply, the single most powerful professional development experience of my career. Never before have I thought so deeply about what I do with children, and why I do it. I looked critically at my practice, judging it against a set of high and rigorous standards. Often in daily work, I found myself rethinking my goals, correcting my course, moving in new directions. I am not the same teacher as I was before the assessment, and my experience seems to be typical. (Haynes, 1995, p. 60)

Following on the work of the National Board, a consortium of more than 30 states, working under the auspices of the Council of Chief State School Officers, created standards for beginning teacher licensing. Most states have now adopted these into their licensing systems, and the National Council for Accreditation of Teacher Education (NCATE) incorporated the standards into a new performance-based approach for accrediting teacher education programs.

In the study of exemplary teacher education programs reported earlier, my colleagues and I witnessed the importance of these standards in shaping practice, as they were translated into courses, performance tasks, and assessment tools used to guide prospective teachers in developing much stronger teaching skills for a much wider range of students than was previously expected (Darling-Hammond, 2006). We also saw how the new performance-based accreditation standards drove important institutional changes that created greater coherence, reshaped courses and clinical work, and secured greater resources for supervising and supporting teachers-in-training.

In a few pioneering states, performance assessments for new teachers, using these INTASC standards and modelled on the National Board assessments, are being used either in teacher education as a basis for the initial licensing recommendation (as in California and Oregon), or in the teacher induction period, as a basis for moving from a probationary to a professional license (as in Connecticut).

These performance-based assessments of teaching ability have also proved to be critically important in driving more effective training and practice. The assessments require teachers to document their plans and teaching for a unit of instruction, videotape and critique lessons, and collect and evaluate evidence of student learning. Like the National Board assessments, beginning teachers' ratings on the Connecticut BEST assessment and the California PACT assessment have been found to significantly predict their students' achievement gains on state tests (Wilson & Hallum, 2006).

When combined with mentoring, such assessments also help teachers improve their practice. The BEST system requires districts who hire beginning teachers to provide them with mentors who are also trained in the state teaching standards and portfolio assessment system. Studies in Connecticut have reported that teacher education and induction programs have improved because of the feedback from the assessment; beginning teachers and mentors also feel the assessment has helped them improve their practice as they become clearer about what good teaching is and how to develop it. Thus, the program enhances teacher competence and effectiveness as it shapes and improves preparation and mentoring. A beginning teacher who participated in the assessment described the power of the process, which requires planning and teaching a unit, and reflecting daily on the day's lesson to consider how it met the needs of each student and what should be changed in the next day's plans. He noted:

> Although I was the reflective type anyway, it made me go a step further. I would have to say, okay, this is how I'm going to do it differently. It made more of an impact on my teaching and was more beneficial to me than just one lesson in which you state what you're going to do ... The process makes you think about your teaching and reflect on your teaching. And I think that's necessary to become an effective teacher.

The same learning effects are recorded in research on the very similar PACT (Performance Assessment for California Teachers) assessment used in California teacher education programs. Launched by the University of California campuses with Stanford University, Mills College, San Jose State University, and San Diego State University, and now used by 32 universities, the assessment requires student teachers or interns to plan and teach a week-long unit of instruction mapped to the state standards; to reflect daily on the lesson they've just taught and revise plans for the next day; to analyze and provide commentaries of videotapes of themselves teaching; to collect and analyze evidence of student learning; to reflect on what worked, what didn't and why; and to project what they would do differently in a future set of lessons. Candidates must show how they take into account students' prior knowledge and experiences in their planning. Adaptations for English language learners and for special needs students must be incorporated into plans and instruction. Analyses of student outcomes are part of the evaluation of teaching.

Faculty and supervisors score these portfolios using standardized rubrics in moderated sessions following training, with an audit procedure to calibrate standards. Faculties use the PACT results to revise their curriculum. In addition, both the novice teachers and the scoring participants describe benefits for teacher education and for learning to teach from the assessment and scoring processes. For example:

> For me the most valuable thing was the sequencing of the lessons, teaching the lesson, and evaluating what the kids were getting, what the kids weren't getting, and having that be reflected in my next lesson...the 'teach-assess-teach-assess-teach-assess' process. And so you're constantly changing – you may have a plan or a framework that you have together, but knowing that that's flexible and that it has to be flexible, based on what the children learn that day. (Prospective teacher)

> This [scoring] experience ... has forced me to revisit the question of what really *matters* in the assessment of teachers, which – in turn – means revisiting the question of what really *matters* in the *preparation* of teachers. (Teacher education faculty member)

> [The scoring process] forces you to be clear about "good teaching;" what it looks like, sounds like. It enables you to look at your own practice critically, with new eyes. (Cooperating teacher)

> As an induction program coordinator, I have a much clearer picture of what credential holders will bring to us and of what they'll be required to do. We can build on this. (Induction program coordinator)

In addition to selecting teachers who can, indeed, teach well, these kinds of standards and assessments can help teachers learn to teach more effectively, improve the quality of preparation programs, and create standards and norms that are widely shared across the profession so that good teaching is no longer a magical occurrence.

Standards-Based Evaluations of Teaching. Similarly, standards-based teacher evaluations used by some districts have been found to be related to student achievement gains for teachers and to help teachers improve their practice and effectiveness (Milanowski, Kimball, & White, 2004). Like the teacher performance assessments described above, these systems for observing teachers' classroom practice are based on professional teaching standards grounded in research on teaching and learning. They use systematic observation protocols, based on well-articulated standards of practice, to examine teaching along a number of dimensions. In a study of three districts using standards-based evaluation systems, researchers found positive correlations between teachers' ratings and their students' gain scores on standardized tests (Milanowski et al., 2004).

Standards-based evaluation systems have been used to evaluate beginning teachers for continuation and tenure and to identify struggling teachers for additional assistance and potential dismissal. The most long-standing evaluation systems that have successfully supported evaluation and personnel actions for both beginning and veteran teachers are those that have used Peer Assistance and Review Programs that rely on highly expert mentor teachers to conduct evaluations and provide assistance to teachers who need it. The systems in Rochester, New York; Cincinnati, Columbus, and Toledo, Ohio; and Seattle, Washington have all been studied and found successful in identifying teachers for continuation and tenure as well as intensive assistance and personnel action.[viii]

Key features of these systems include not only the instruments used for evaluation but also the expertise of the evaluators – skilled teachers in the same subject areas and school levels who have released time to serve as mentors to support their fellow teachers – and the system of due process and review that involve a panel of both teachers and administrators in making recommendations about personnel decisions based on the evidence presented to them from the evaluations.

In these systems, beginning teachers have been found to stay in teaching at higher rates because of the mentoring they receive, and those who leave (generally under 5%) are usually those the district has chosen not to continue rather than those who have quit. Among veteran teachers identified for assistance and review (usually 1-3% of the teaching force), generally about half improve sufficiently with intensive mentoring to be removed from intervention status and about half leave by choice or by district request. Because teacher associations have been closely involved in designing and administering these programs in collaboration with the district, the union does not bring grievances when a teacher is discontinued.

In Rochester and Cincinnati, which have developed career ladders that extend beyond the beginning years of teaching, the accomplished teachers identified through more advanced evaluations of practice serve as mentors for these beginning teachers, among other leadership roles. These evaluations depend both on standards-based assessments of teaching – through local evaluations and/or National Board Certification – and, in Rochester's career ladder, evidence of student learning assembled by the teacher in a portfolio.

Arizona's career ladder program – which encourages local districts to design their own systems – requires evidence from both standards-based evaluations of practice and student assessments, assembled by teachers, that illuminate teachers' effectiveness. One study of the Arizona career ladder programs found that, over time, participating teachers demonstrated an increased ability to create locally-developed assessment tools to assess student learning gains in their classrooms; to develop and evaluate pre- and post-tests; to define measurable outcomes in "hard to quantify areas" like art, music, and physical education; and to monitor student learning growth. They also showed a greater awareness of the importance of sound curriculum development, more alignment of curriculum with district objectives, and increased focus on higher quality content, skills, and instructional strategies (Packard & Dereshiwsky, 1991). Thus, the development and use of standards-based evaluations of practice combined with student learning evidence seem to be associated with improvements in practice.

Studies on standards-based teacher evaluation suggest that the more teachers' classroom activities and behaviours are enabled to reflect professional standards of practice, the more effective they are in supporting student learning – a finding that would appear to suggest the desirability of focusing on such professional standards in the preparation, professional development, and evaluation of teachers. Many studies also find that teachers involved in assessing other teachers using standards-based tools also improve their own understanding of teaching, thus spreading good practice.

These kinds of results led one analyst to conclude in his review of teacher pay systems that tying teachers' advancement and compensation to their knowledge and skills and using evaluation systems that help develop those skills, as these systems do, may ultimately produce more positive change in practice than evaluating teachers based primarily on student test scores (Hassell, 2002). Indeed, studies of merit pay plans that have sought to reward teachers based on their students' scores confirm this view. A major experimental study in the US recently found no positive effects on achievement from bonuses tied to student test scores (Springer et al., 2010), and another study of Portugal's efforts to tie teacher pay to student test scores found that the system appeared actually to decrease student achievement. The researcher hypothesized that this form of merit pay likely reduced teacher collaboration to the detriment of student learning (Martins, 2009).

Certainly, knowing what teachers are doing that is leading to improvements in student learning is more valuable than merely watching scores go up or down without clues to the practices that are associated with these changes. When individual teachers, collegial groups of teachers, and schooling systems examine how practices are related to student learning, they can develop efforts to improve teaching throughout the profession as a whole.

Enabling Teachers to Continue to Improve.   A strong system of teacher learning must provide not only a solid foundation of knowledge for entering the profession and clarity about teaching goals and practices, but also ongoing opportunities for learning throughout the career.

Over the last two decades, a new paradigm for professional development has emerged from research that has distinguished approaches that impact teachers' practices and student outcomes from the typically ineffective traditional one-day workshops that proliferate. Among other things, effective professional development is sustained, ongoing, content-focused, and embedded in professional learning communities – where teachers work over time on problems of practice with other teachers in their subject area or school (Darling-Hammond, Wei,

Richardson, Andree, & Orphanos, 2009). Furthermore, it focuses on "concrete tasks of teaching, assessment, observation and reflection," (Darling-Hammond & McLaughlin, 1995, p. 598.) looking at how students learn specific content in particular contexts, rather than emphasizing abstract discussions of teaching. Equally important, it focuses on student learning, including analysis of the skills and understandings that students are expected to acquire and what they are in fact learning (Carpenter, Fennema, Peterson, Chiang, & Loef, 1989; Cohen & Hill, 2001; Lieberman & Wood, 2002; Merek & Methven, 1991; Saxe, Gearhart, & Nasir, 2001; Wenglinsky, 2000).

The Design of Effective Professional Learning Opportunities.   Research has found that teachers are more likely to try classroom practices that have been modelled for them in professional development settings. And teachers judge professional development to be most valuable when it provides opportunities to do "hands-on" work that builds their knowledge of academic content and how to teach it to their students, and when it takes into account the local context (including the specifics of local school resources, curriculum guidelines, accountability systems, and so on) (Carpenter et al., 1989; Cohen & Hill, 2001; Desimone, Porter, Garet, Yoon, & Birman, 2002; Garet, Porter, Desimone, Birman, & Yoon, 2001; Penuel, Fishman, Yamaguchi, & Gallagher, 2007; Saxe et al., 2001; Snow-Renner & Lauer, 2005; Supovitz, Mayer, & Kahle, 2000). Equally important, professional development that leads teachers to define precisely which concepts and skills they want students to learn, and to identify the content that is most likely to give students trouble, has been found to improve teacher practice and student outcomes (Blank, de las Alas & Smith, 2007; Carpenter et al., 1989; Cohen & Hill, 2001; Lieberman & Wood, 2002; McGill-Franzen, Allington, Yokio, & Brooks, 1999; Merek & Methven, 1991; Saxe et al., 2001; Wenglinsky, 2000). To this end, it is often useful for teachers to be put in the position of studying the very material that they intend to teach to their own students.

For example, one well-known study focused on elementary science teachers who participated in a 100-hour summer institute, during which they actively engaged in a standard science "learning cycle" that involved exploring a phenomenon, coming up with a theory that explained what had occurred, and applying it to new contexts. After going through this process, teachers went on to develop their own units and teach them to one another before returning to their classrooms. Later, the researchers tested randomly selected students in those classrooms and found they scored significantly higher in their reasoning ability than did a control group of students taught by teachers who had not had this experience (Merek & Methven, 1991).

Similarly, David Cohen and Heather Hill distinguished successful from less successful approaches to professional development in their study of California's decade long effort to reform the teaching of mathematics (Cohen & Hill, 2001). The new curriculum required elementary teachers and students to understand complex concepts of mathematics, not simply computational algorithms. Of the many professional development opportunities that were offered to support this reform, only two contributed to changes in teachers' practices and increases in student achievement.

The first of the two successful approaches was organized around new curriculum units developed to teach these new standards. An ongoing set of workshops engaged teachers themselves in using the mathematics strategies students were expected to learn and then on developing strategies for teaching the units well. Teachers taught the units and returned to debrief their experiences with other teachers and to problem solve next steps, while preparing to teach subsequent units. Over time, these teachers reported more reform-oriented practices in their classrooms, and their schools showed larger gains in achievement.

The second effective approach involved teachers evaluating student work on assessments directly linked to the reform curriculum. While assessing student work, which showed students' problem solving strategies and reasoning, teachers examined conceptual roadblocks students faced on the assessments and became knowledgeable about how to anticipate these misunderstandings and address them in their classrooms. Student achievement was ultimately higher for these teachers as well.

In another study that compared professional development for mathematics teachers, researchers found large gains in conceptual understanding for students whose teachers had focused on looking at student work and learning through the Integrated Mathematics Assessment (IMA) program. These teachers attended a 5 day summer institute and then met 13 times, once every two weeks, throughout the year. During the workshops teachers looked at samples of student work or videotapes of problem solving; learned to assess student motivation, interests, goals, and beliefs about abilities; and developed specific pedagogies, including how to lead whole class discussions, assess student works with rubrics, and use portfolios. They discussed their practice and solved problems collaboratively. Ultimately, they piloted assessment tools of their own and publicly shared their work. This propelled extensive changes in practice that led to significant student learning gains; meanwhile, researchers found no gains for students whose teachers received traditional workshops, or who participated in a professional community without a strong focus on curriculum content and student learning.

Many studies have found it useful for groups of teachers to analyze and discuss student-performance data and samples of students' course work (science projects, essays, math tests, and so on), in order to identify students' most common errors and misunderstandings, reach common understanding of what it means for students to master a given concept or skill, and find out which instructional strategies are or are not working, and for whom (Ball & Cohen, 1999; Dunne, Nave, & Lewis, 2000; Little, 2003.). Notably, studies of high-achieving or steeply-improving schools have found that student gains were associated with teachers' regular practice of consulting multiple sources of data on student performance and using those data to inform discussions about ways to improve instruction.[ix]

Contexts for Effective Professional Learning. Professional development is also more effective when it is a coherent part of the school's overall efforts, rather than the traditional "flavour of the month" one-shot workshop (Cohen & Hill, 2001; Garet et al., 2001; Supovitz et al., 2000). Teachers are unlikely to apply what they have learned if it is at odds with the demands of their local school context. Curriculum, assessment, standards, and professional learning opportunities need to be seamlessly integrated to avoid disjunctures between what teachers learn in professional development and what they are required to do in their classrooms and schools.

When schools are strategic in creating time and productive working relationships within and across academic departments or grade levels, the benefits can include greater consistency in instruction, more willingness to share practices and try new ways of teaching, and more success in solving problems of practice (Friedlaender & Darling-Hammond, 2007; Hord, 1997; Joyce & Calhoun, 1996; Louis, Marks, & Kruse, 1996; McLaughlin & Talbert, 2001; Newman & Wehlage, 1997). For example, a comprehensive five-year study of 1,500 schools undergoing major reforms found that in schools where teachers formed active professional learning communities, achievement increased significantly in math, science, history, and reading while student absenteeism and dropout rates were reduced. Particular aspects of teachers' professional communities – including a shared sense of intellectual purpose and a sense of collective responsibility for student learning—were associated with a narrowing of achievement gaps in math and science among low- and middle-income students (Newman & Wehlage, 1997). A number of large-scale studies have confirmed that professional community-building can deepen teachers' knowledge, build their skills, and improve instruction (Bryk, Camburn, & Louis, 1999; Calkins, Guenther, Belfiore, & Lash, 2007; Goddard, Goddard, & Tschannen-Moran, 2007; Louis & Marks, 1998; Supovitz & Christman, 2003).

CONCLUSION

Teaching can only become a profession that supports effective instruction if societies construct systems of universal high-quality preparation, mentoring, and support – including well-designed schools that allow and enable good practice. Rather than short-term incentives and quick fixes, policy making must focus on building capacity across the entire system. Reforms must couple thoughtful standards and meaningful assessments with resources that enable educators to acquire deep knowledge and develop high-quality practice. When combined with serious efforts to develop equitable schools, it is possible to create classrooms in which all educators have the opportunity to become expert and all children have the opportunity to be well-taught.

NOTES

[i] This article draws in substantial part on Darling-Hammond, L. (2010). *The flat world and education: How America's commitment to equity will determine our future*. New York: Teachers College Press.
[ii] This section draws on Darling-Hammond (2005) and Wei, Andree, and Darling-Hammond (2009).

iii Boyd et al. (2006) found that, on average, holding student and school characteristics equal, beginning teachers who came through college preservice programs produced stronger achievement gains than those who entered through alternative programs and temporary licenses. In 2008, the same team examined the contributions to student learning gains of graduates from these preservice programs and identified the features of programs whose graduates produced the strongest value-added gains.

iv The concept of adaptive expertise and how it is acquired is described in Darling-Hammond and Bransford (2005).

v Luis Moll, re: funds of knowledge.

vi For a summary see Darling-Hammond and Bransford (2005, pp. 415-416).

vii See, for example, Bond, Smith, Baker, and Hattie (2000); Cavaluzzo (2004); Goldhaber and Anthony (2005); Smith, Gordon, Colby, and Wang (2005); Vandevoort, Amrein-Beardsley, and Berliner (2004).

viii See, for example, NCTAF (1996); Van Lier (2008).

ix See, for example, Strahan (2003).

REFERENCES

Abdal-Haqq, I. (1998). *Professional development schools: Weighing the evidence*. Thousand Oaks, CA: Corwin Press.

Areglado, N. (1999, Winter). *I became convinced: How a certification program revitalized an educator*. National Staff Development Council, pp. 35-37.

Atelier Learning Solutions Pty Ltd. (2005). *An evaluation of the Australian Government Quality Teacher Programme 1999 to 2004*. Canberra: Department of Education, Science and Training.

Athanases, S. (1994). Teachers' reports of the effects of preparing portfolios of literacy instruction. *Elementary School Journal, 94*(4), 421-439.

Ball, D., & Cohen, D. (1999). Developing practice, developing practitioners: Toward a practice-based theory of professional education. In L. Darling-Hammond & G. Sykes (Eds.), *Teaching as the learning profession: Handbook of policy and practice* (pp. 3-32). San Francisco, CA: Jossey-Bass Publishers.

Barber, M., & Mourshed, M. (2007). *How the world's best-performing school systems come out on top*. London: McKinsey and Company.

Bartell, C. (1995). Shaping teacher induction policy in California. *Teacher Education Quarterly, 22*(4), 27-43.

Blank, R. K., de las Alas, N., & Smith, C. (2007). *Analysis of the quality of professional development programs for mathematics and science teachers: Findings from a cross-state study*. Washington DC: CCSSO.

Bond, L., Smith, T., Baker, W., & Hattie, J. (2000). *The certification system of the National Board for Professional Teaching Standards: A construct and consequential validity study*. Greensboro, NC: Center for Educational Research and Evaluation.

Boyd, D., Grossman, P., Lankford, H., Loeb, S., & Wyckoff, J. (2006). How changes in entry requirements alter the teacher workforce and affect student achievement. *Education Finance & Policy, 1*(2), 176-216.

Boyd, D., Grossman, P., Lankford, H., Loeb, S., & Wyckoff, J. (2008). *Teacher preparation and student achievement*. NBER Working Paper No. W14314. National Bureau of Economic Research. Available at SSRN: http://ssrn.com/abstract=1264576.

Bradley, A. (1994, April 20). Pioneers in professionalism. *Education Week, 13*, 18-21.

Britton, T. (2006). Mentoring in the induction system of five countries: A sum is greater than its parts. In C. Cullingford (Ed.), *Mentoring in education: An international perspective* (pp. 110-123). Aldershot, England: Ashgate Publishing.

Bryk, A., Camburn, E., & Louis, K. (1999). Professional community in Chicago elementary schools: Facilitating factors and organizational consequences. *Educational Administration Quarterly, 35*(5), 751-781.

Buchberger, F., & Buchberger, I. (2004). Problem solving capacity of a teacher education system as a condition of success? An analysis of the "Finnish case." In F. Buchberger & S. Berghammer (Eds.), *Education policy analysis in a comparative perspective* (pp. 222-237). Linz: Trauner.

Buday, M., & Kelly, J. (1996). National Board certification and the teaching profession's commitment to quality assurance. *Phi Delta Kappan, 78*(3), 215-219.

Calkins, A., Guenther, W., Belfiore, G., & Lash, D. (2007). *The turnaround challenge: Why America's best opportunity to dramatically improve student achievement lies in our worst-performing schools.* Boston, MA: Mass Insight Education & Research Institute.

Carpenter, T., Fennema, E., Peterson, P., Chiang, C., & Loef, M. (1989). Using knowledge of children's mathematical thinking in classroom teaching: An experimental study. *American Educational Research Journal, 26*, 499-532.

Cavaluzzo, L. (2004). *Is National Board Certification an effective signal of teacher quality?* (National Science Foundation No. REC-0107014). Alexandria, VA: The CNA Corporation.

Cheng, M., & Brown, R.S. (1992). *A two-year evaluation of the peer support pilot project: 1990-1992.* Toronto, Ontario, Canada: Toronto Board of Education, Research Department.

Chittenden, E., & Jones, J. (1997, April). *An observational study of National Board candidates as they progress through the certification process.* Paper presented at the annual meeting of the American Educational Research Association, Chicago, IL.

Clement, M. (2000). Making time for teacher induction: A lesson from the New Zealand model. *The Clearing House, 73*(6), 329-330.

Cochran-Smith, M., & Lytle, S. (1993). *Inside/outside: Teacher research and knowledge.* New York: Teachers College Press.

Cohen, D. K., & Hill, H. C. (2001). *Learning policy.* New Haven, CT: Yale University Press.

Darling-Hammond, L. (2005). Teaching as a profession: Lessons in teacher preparation and professional development. *Phi Delta Kappan, 87*(3), 237-240.

Darling-Hammond, L. (2006). *Powerful teacher education: Lessons from exemplary programs.* San Francisco: Jossey-Bass.

Darling-Hammond, L., & Bransford, J. (2005). *Preparing teachers for a changing world: What teachers should learn and be able to do.* San Francisco: Jossey-Bass.

Darling-Hammond, L., & McLaughlin, M. W. (1995). Policies that support professional development in an era of reform. *Phi Delta Kappan, 76*(8), 597-604.

Darling-Hammond, L., Wei, R.C., Richardson, N., Andree, A., & Orphanos, S. (2009). *Professional learning in the learning profession: A status report on teacher development in the US and abroad.* Washington, DC: National Staff Development Council.

Darling-Hammond, L., Wise, A., & Klein, S. (1999). *A license to teach: Building a profession for 21st century schools.* San Francisco: Jossey-Bass.

Desimone, L., Porter, A., Garet, M., Yoon, K., & Birman, B. (2002). Effects of professional development on teachers' instruction: Results from a three-year longitudinal study. *Education Evaluation and Policy Analysis, 24*(2), 81-112.

Dunne, F., Nave, B., & Lewis, A. (2000). Critical friends: Teachers helping to improve student learning. *Phi Delta Kappa International Research Bulletin (CEDR), 28*, 9-12. Retrieved September 11, 2008, from http://www.pdkintl.org/edres/resbul28.htm.

Earl, L, Watson, N., & Torrance, N. (2002). Front row seats: What we've learned from the National Literacy and Numeracy Strategies in England. *Journal of Educational Change, 3*(1), 35-53.

Elmore, R., & Fuhrman, S. (1993). Opportunity to learn and the state role in education. In *The debate on opportunity-to-learn standards: Commissioned papers.* Washington, DC: National Governors Association.

Fernandez, C. (2002). Learning from Japanese approaches to professional development: The case of lesson study. *Journal of Teacher Education, 53*(5), 393-405.

Flexner, A., & Pritchett, H.S. (1910). *Medical education in the United States and Canada: A report to the Carnegie Foundation for the Advancement of Teaching.* New York: Carnegie Foundation for the Advancement of Teaching.

Friedlaender, D., & Darling-Hammond, L. with the assistance of Andree, A. Lewis-Charp, H., McCloskey, L., Richardson, N., & Vasudeva, A. (2007). *High schools for equity: Policy supports for student learning in communities of color.* Stanford, CA: School Redesign Network at Stanford University, 2007. Available at http://www.srnleads.org/resources/publications/hsfe.html.

Fullan, M. (2007). *The new meaning of educational change,* 4th edition. NY: Teachers College Press.

Fuller, E. (2003). *Beginning teacher retention rates for TxBESS and non-TxBESS teachers.* Unpublished paper. State Board for Educator Certification, Texas.

Gallego, M.A. (2001). Is experience the best teacher? The potential of coupling classroom and community-based field experiences. *Journal of Teacher Education, 52*(4), 312-325.

Garet, M., Porter, A., Desimone, L., Birman, B., & Yoon, K.S. (2001). What makes professional development effective? Results from a national sample of teachers. *American Educational Research Journal, 38*(4), 915-945.

Goddard, Y.L., Goddard, R.D., & Tschannen-Moran, M. (2007). Theoretical and empirical investigation of teacher collaboration for school improvement and student achievement tin public elementary schools. *Teachers College Record, 109*(4), 877-896.

Goldhaber, D., & Anthony, E. (2005). *Can teacher quality be effectively assessed?* Seattle, WA: University of Washington and the Urban Institute.

Guadarrama, I. N., Ramsey, J., & Nath, J. L. (Eds.) (2002). *Forging alliances in community and thought: Research in professional development schools.* Greenwich, CT: Information Age Publishing.

Hammerness, K., Darling-Hammond, L., & Shulman, L. (2002). Toward expert thinking: How curriculum case writing prompts the development of theory-based professional knowledge in student teachers. *Teaching Education, 13*(2), 221-245.

Hassell, B.C. (2002). *Better pay for better teaching: Making teacher compensation pay off in the age of accountability.* Progressive Policy Institute 21st Century Schools Project. Retrieved November 18, 2004, from http://www.broadfoundation.org/investments/education-net.shtml.

Haynes, D. (1995). One teacher's experience with National Board assessment. *Educational Leadership, 52*(8), 58-60.

Hord, S. (1997). *Professional learning communities: Communities of continuous inquiry and improvement.* Austin, TX: Southwest Educational Development Laboratory.

Ingersoll, R., & Kralik, J. M. (2004). *The impact of mentoring on teacher retention: What the research says.* Denver, CO: Education Commission of the States.

Ingvarson, L. (2005). Getting professional development right. In Australian Council for Educational Research *Annual Conference Proceedings 2005 – Getting Data to Support Learning Conference* (pp. 63-71). Retrieved June 28, 2008, from http://www.acer.edu.au/documents/RC2005_Ingvarson.pdf.

Joyce, B., & Calhoun, E. (1996). *Learning experiences in school renewal: An exploration of five successful programs.* Eugene, OR: ERIC Clearinghouse on Educational Management.

Lieberman, A., & Wood, D. (2002). From network learning to classroom teaching. *Journal of Educational Change, 3*, 315-337.

Little, J.W. (2003). Inside teacher community: Representations of classroom practice. *Teacher College Record, 105*(6), 913-945.

Louis, K. S., Marks, H. M., & Kruse, S. (1996). Professional community in restructuring schools. *American Educational Research Journal, 33*(4), 757-798.

Louis, K.S., & Marks, H.M. (1998). Does professional learning community affect the classroom? Teachers' work and student experiences in restructuring schools. *American Journal of Education, 106*(4), 532-575.

Martins, P. (2009). *Individual teacher incentives, student achievement and grade inflation* (Paper No. 4051). London, UK: Queen Mary, University of London, CEG-IST and IZA.

McGill-Franzen, A., Allington, R.L., Yokio, L., & Brooks, G. (1999). Putting books in the classroom seems necessary but not sufficient. *The Journal of Educational Research, 93*(2), 67-74.

McLaughlin, M. W., & Talbert, J. E. (2001). *Professional communities and the work of high school teaching.* Chicago: University Of Chicago Press.

Meiers, M., Ingvarson, L, Beavis, A., Hogan, J., & Kleinhenz, E. (2006). *An evaluation of the getting it right: Literacy and numeracy strategy in western Australian schools.* Victoria: Australian Council for Educational Research.

Merek E., & Methven, S. (1991). Effects of the learning cycle upon student and classroom teacher performance. *Journal of Research in Science Teaching, 28*(1), 41-53.

Mikkola, A. (2000). Teacher education in Finland. In C. Paiva (Ed.), *Teacher education policies in the European Union* (pp. 179-193). Lisbon: INAFOP.

Milanowski, A. T., Kimball, S. M., & White, B. (2004). *The relationship between standards-based teacher evaluation scores and student achievement.* University of Wisconsin-Madison: Consortium for Policy Research in Education.

Moll, L. C., Amanti, C., Neff, D., & Gonzalez, N. (1992). Funds of knowledge for teaching: Using a qualitative approach to connect homes and classrooms. *Theory into Practice, 31*(1), 132-141.

National Commission on Teaching and America's Future (NCTAF) (1996). *What matters most: Teaching for America's future.* New York: Author.

Newman, F., & Wehlage, G. (1997). *Successful school restructuring: A report to the public and educators by the Center on Organization and Restructuring of Schools.* Madison, WI: Document Service, Wisconsin Center for Education Research.

Odell, S. J., & Ferraro, D. P. (1992). Teacher mentoring and teacher retention. *Journal of Teacher Education, 43*(3), 200-04.

Olebe, M. (2001). A decade of policy support for California's new teachers: The beginning teacher support and assessment program. *Teacher Education Quarterly, 10*(2), 9-21.

Organisation for Economic Cooperation and Development (OECD) (2004). *Completing the foundation for lifelong learning: An OECD survey of upper secondary schools.* Paris: OECD.

Organisation for Economic Cooperation and Development (OECD) (2005). *Education at a Glance: OECD Indicators, 2005.* Paris: OECD.

Packard, R., & Dereshiwsky, M. (1991). *Final quantitative assessment of the Arizona career ladder pilot-test project.* Flagstaff: Northern Arizona University.

Pang, M. (2006). The use of learning study to enhance teacher professional learning in Hong Kong. *Teaching Education, 17*(1), 27-42.

Penuel, W., Fishman, B., Yamaguchi, R., & Gallagher, L. (2007, December). What makes professional development effective? Strategies that foster curriculum implementation. *American Educational Research Journal, 44*(4), 921-958.

Sahlberg, P. (2009). Educational change in Finland. In A. Hargreaves, M. Fullan, A. Lieberman, & D. Hopkins (Eds.), *International Handbook of Educational Change* (pp. 1-28). Dordrecht: Kluwer Academic Publishers.

Sato, M. (2000, April). *The National Board for Professional Teaching Standards: Teacher learning through the assessment process.* Paper presented at the Annual Meeting of American Educational Research Association. New Orleans, LA.

Sato, M., Wei, R. C., & Darling-Hammond, L. (2008). Improving teachers' assessment practices through professional development: The case of National Board Certification. *American Educational Research Journal, 45*, 669-700.

Saxe, G., Gearhart, M., & Nasir, N. S. (2001). Enhancing students' understanding of mathematics: A study of three contrasting approaches to professional support. *Journal of Mathematics Teacher Education, 4*, 55-79.

Skilbeck, M., & Connell, H. (2003). *Attracting, developing and retaining effective teachers: Australian country background report.* Canberra: Commonwealth of Australia.

Smith, T. M., & Ingersoll, R. M. (2004). What are the effects of induction and mentoring on beginning teacher turnover? *American Educational Research Journal, 41*(3), 681-714.

Smith, T., Gordon, B., Colby, S., & Wang, J. (2005). *An examination of the relationship of the depth of student learning and National Board Certification status.* Office for Research on Teaching, Appalachian State University.

Snow-Renner, R., & Lauer, P. (2005). *Professional development analysis.* Denver, CO: Mid-Content Research for Education and Learning.

Springer, M., Ballou, D., Hamilton, L., Le, V., Lockwood, V., McCaffrey, D., Pepper, M., & Stecher, B. (2010). *Teacher pay for performance: Experimental evidence from the project on incentives in teaching.* Nashville, TN: National Center on Performance Incentives, Vanderbilt University.

Spuhler, L., & Zetler, A. (1995). *Montana beginning teacher support program: Final report.* Helena, MT: Montana State Board of Education.

Stansbury, K., & Zimmerman, J. (2000), *Lifelines to the classroom: Designing support for beginning teachers.* San Francisco: WestEd.

Stigler, J. W., & Stevenson, H. W. (1991, Spring). How Asian teachers polish each lesson to perfection. *American Educator,* 12-20, 43-47.

Strahan, D. (2003). Promoting a collaborative professional culture in three elementary schools that have beaten the odds. *The Elementary School Journal, 104*(2), 127-133.

Supovitz, J. A., & Christman, J. B. (2003, November). *Developing communities of instructional practice: Lessons from Cincinnati and Philadelphia* (CPRE Policy Briefs RB-39). Pennsylvania: University of Pennsylvania, Graduate School of Education.

Supovitz, J. A., Mayer, D. P., & Kahle, J. B. (2000). Promoting inquiry based instructional practice: The longitudinal impact of professional development in the context of systemic reform. *Educational Policy, 14*(3), 331-356.

Thompson, C. L., & Zeuli, J. S. (1999). The frame and the tapestry: Standards-based reform and professional development. In L. Darling-Hammond & G. Sykes (Eds.), *Teaching as the learning profession: A handbook of policy and practice* (pp. 341-375). San Francisco: Jossey-Bass.

Van Lier, P. (2008). *Learning from Ohio's best teachers.* Cleveland, OH: Policy Matters.

Vandevoort, L. G., Amrein-Beardsley, A., & Berliner, D. C. (2004). National Board Certified teachers and their students' achievement. *Education Policy Analysis Archives, 12*(46), 117.

Wei, R.C., Andree, A., & Darling-Hammond, L. (2009). How nations invest in teachers. *Educational Leadership, 66*(5), 28-33.

Wenglinsky, H. (2000). *Teaching the teachers: Different settings, different results.* Princeton, NJ: Policy Information Center, Educational Testing Service.

Wilson, M., & Hallum, P. J. (2006). *Using student achievement test scores as evidence of external validity for indicators of teacher quality: Connecticut's beginning educator support and training program.* Berkeley, CA: University of California at Berkeley.

AFFILIATIONS

Linda Darling-Hammond
School of Education
University of Stanford, USA

ANTÓNIO NÓVOA

TEACHERS: HOW LONG UNTIL THE FUTURE?

INTRODUCTION

Teachers have become central in societies claiming to be "knowledge societies" and that have expanded their education systems in a manner considered unthinkable not long ago.[i]

In this chapter I develop thoughts under the title *Teachers: How Long until the Future?* to critically analyse the distance between discourses about teachers and the tension and dilemmas that the teaching profession faces. This chapter is written in essay form that takes into account the original meaning of the term, which is a trial or an attempt to answer a question using personal perspectives.

According to Aldous Huxley "the essay is a literary device for saying almost everything about almost anything" (1971, p. v). The intent of this paper is not to build a scientific argument, but instead to share personal views arising from my own historical and philosophical location. These issues have been with me for a long time, and "all this fricassee that I am scribbling here is nothing but a record of the essays of my life" (1968, p. 826), as stated by the first essayist, Montaigne, in the sixteen century.

There is too much talk about the future and there is not enough critical thinking to enable us to build this future. Therefore, this paper suggests the following four theses that expound, at the same time, problems of the present and intentions for the future, which is referred to here as the *future present*.

− From inside the profession;
− Activity is the road to knowledge;
− The risks of dialogue;
− Education as a public space.

I attempt to avoid the usual language when talking about teachers and teaching, and work on these four ideas mainly through the eyes of historians and philosophers that dedicated a part of their lives to educational matters.

PERPLEXITIES AND FAMILIARITIES

Please allow me to begin with two educationalists who are part of my personal library, one from the past and the other from the present: Gabriel Compayré and David Labaree.

The French educator Gabriel Compayré was one of the most influential thinkers and reformers at the end of the 19th century. His work has been widely diffused, not only in Europe but also around the world. In his well-known *Cours de Pédagogie,*

M.A. Flores et al. (eds.), Back to the Future: Legacies, Continuities and Changes in Educational Policy, Practice and Research, 29–37.

he wrote, "As an educator, I spent half of my life fighting for some ideals, and the other half fighting against the false assumptions of these ideals and the way how they are wrongly applied" (1889, p. 43).

My academic experience is full of the same perplexities as the work of Gabriel Compayré. How many times was I warned of the misuse of concepts for which I had struggled? For an educationalist, each portion of hope needs to be balanced with a portion of scepticism, not cynically but critically. Fashion is the worst way to deal with educational issues because it entails magical solutions that are always false. They are false not only because they are necessarily wrong, but because they dispense us from thinking.

In education, nothing can replace our own awareness, our own decisions and our own judgments. Marcel Proust says that no one can avoid his or her own journey with dilemmas and turbulence: "the only true voyage of discovery would be not to visit strange lands but to possess other eyes" (1923, p. 109). There is no knowledge without a process of personal appropriation, but this process is not complete without a dialogue and a conversation with others.

The second remark is related to the work of David Labaree. In the article, *Life on the Margins*, he explains that "although progressive rhetoric is everywhere, progressive practice is much harder to find," concluding that evidence "shows the dominance of progressivism over teacher talk rather than teacher practice" (2003, p. 1).

David Labaree asks a very important question: Why have teacher educators been so ineffective at shaping policy in their own domain? He also provides some answers. One problem is that teacher education programmes occupy a low status in the hierarchy of higher education. Another factor that undermines our influence is that teaching is an extraordinarily difficult form of professional practice that looks easy. A third reason relates to the fact that we are too predictable. Finally, he points out that, in the mind of the public and despite all of our railing against the traditional system of schooling, we are seen as inveterate defenders of the status quo in public education.

These problems are very prejudicial for the field of teacher education and for the credibility of educationalists:

> We are in the unlovely position of being seen both as pillars of the establishment and as zealots of the constructivist insurrection and, thus, we find ourselves defending the indefensible while also demanding the unrealizable. (Labaree, 2003, p. 5)

I share the perplexities of these two authors. There is a strange familiarity to how educational issues are discussed around the world. One of our main tasks is to deconstruct these "evidences," showing that the obvious is not so obvious. We need to isolate "the systems of thought that have now become familiar to us, that appear evident to us" and "to work in common with practitioners, not only to modify institutions and practices but to elaborate forms of thought" (Foucault, 1996, pp. 424-425).

FROM INSIDE THE PROFESSION

My first thesis is about the need to avoid excessive talk about teachers without the participation and the presence of the teachers themselves. I argue that we need to build an educational perspective from inside the profession. During the last three or four decades, several groups and professional communities have developed around the teaching profession: teacher educators, international experts, educational researchers, curriculum experts, "the teaching industry," educational administrators, educational technologists, etc.

The 1970s saw the scientific rationalization of teaching, an effort to plan and control the work of teachers. Throughout the 1980s, major educational reforms were launched with the main focus on curriculum. In the 1990s, special attention was given to school management and to quality and international comparisons. The sign at the beginning of this century is the growing interest in digital technologies.

All of these groups and movements have been extremely important in fostering new ideas and in rendering visible the complexity of educational issues. Yet, at the same time, paradoxically – even when their intention was to "empower teachers" – they inevitably contribute to the depreciation of teachers. We need to understand the paradox if we want to overcome this problem.

In fact, most of these developments related to the science of teaching, including the expansion of educational research, the teacher professional movement and the reflective practitioner, to mention a few, led to a definition of the teaching profession "from outside." This definition inevitably entails a reduction in the professional and political space of teachers.

In a certain sense, the useless sociological concept of teaching as a semi-profession or a quasi-profession – a concept that has been very harmful for teachers – has never been so true as it is today, ironically, after thirty years of elaborating on the professionalization and empowerment of teachers. That is why I am calling for the coming back of teachers, a provocative expression intended to illuminate the role of teachers in the debates about their own profession "from inside," to expand (and not reduce) their professional space.

I am addressing a crucial change in the manner in which we place our thinking and ourselves in the educational arena. This change is essential to rebuilding new strategies for the recruitment and training of teachers and, at the same time, to strengthen the autonomy and the forms of organisation of the teaching profession.

First, let me underline the need for teachers to have a predominant place in the training of their peers. Nothing will be achieved if the "teacher education community" and the "teachers' community" do not become more permeable and overlapping. Writing text after text about *praxis* and *practicum*, about *phronesis* and *prudentia* as bases for teaching knowledge is not possible if teachers do not reach a greater presence in training their future colleagues. These proposals cannot be mere rhetorical declarations. They only make sense if they are constructed within the profession and if they are appropriated by the teachers themselves. If they remain injunctions from outside, the changes within the teaching profession will be rather useless.

Second, most of our proposals become unrealistic and unworkable if the profession continues to be distinguished by ingrained individualist traditions or by rigid external regulations. The paradox is well known among historians: the more one talks of teacher autonomy, the more teachers are controlled in various ways, leading to a reduction in their margins for freedom. Professional collegiality, sharing and collaborative cultures cannot be imposed through administrative means or decisions from above. Pedagogic movements or communities of practice consolidate a feeling of belonging and professional identity that are essential for teachers to appropriate processes of change and transform them into concrete practice.

Currently, despite many ambiguities, teachers have seemed to acquire a new centrality, as recognised in an interesting OECD report published in 2005, *Teachers Matter*. Teachers tend to reappear as irreplaceable elements, not only in the promotion of learning, but also in the development of the process of integration that responds to the challenges of social inclusion, diversity and cultural dialogue.

ACTIVITY IS THE ROAD TO KNOWLEDGE

My second thesis is formulated in a peculiar way – activity is the road to knowledge. Explaining why I choose this title is easy. In *Maxims for Revolutionists* published a century ago, Bernard Shaw wrote the famous aphorism: "He who can, does. He who cannot, teaches" (1971, p. 784). This shameful aphorism has been repeated throughout the last century as a criticism and denigration of teachers. I will not go back to this discussion because Lee Shulman provided an excellent response: "We reject Mr. Shaw and his calumny. With Aristotle we declare that the ultimate test of understanding rests on the ability to transform one's knowledge into teaching. Those who can, do. Those who understand, teach" (1986, p. 14).

I would like to draw attention to the following sentence of Bernard Shaw, which has been unnoticed: "Activity is the only road to knowledge," as well as another aphorism, a little further, on experience: "Men are wise in proportion, not to their experience, but to their capacity for experience. If we could learn from mere experience, the stones of London would be wiser than its wisest men" (1971, p. 792).

Underlining the importance attached by Bernard Shaw to activity, to experience and primarily to the "capacity for experience" is very interesting. In doing so, he points out the importance of two dimensions for teaching.

First, consider the idea of travelling or crossing over to the other border. Teaching carries on a principle of activity, and that is why one of my recent papers had the title of a tale by the Brazilian writer Guimarães Rosa, *Pedagogy – The Third Bank of the River*. The third bank is the river itself, it is the river flow. The true path takes place in the middle.

I end this text with a reference to one of the most influential authors in my academic life, the French philosopher Michel Serres. His book *Le tiers-instruit* underlines the importance of travelling for learning:

Who doesn't move doesn't learn.

Without travelling there is no learning.

All learning involves a journey with the other and towards alterity. (1991, pp. 28, 86)

The analogy with the teaching activity is inspiring. Teachers' reflection must be conceived as a sequence of ideas and thoughts arising from the activity and with consequences in their practice. To say that this process needs rules and needs to be systematic and organised, or cannot be realised without interaction and cooperation between teachers and between teachers and academics is unnecessary. In contrast, the capacity for experience, the capacity to nourish theoretically the experience, is what best define the teaching profession.

Travelling should lead us to ways of estrangement (*distancing from practice*) and entrenchment (*immersion into practice*) because we cannot remain prisoners neither of theory built outside the profession nor of a practice that is routine and repetitive without creation.

The process of reflection needs to avoid the "capitalization of the self" present in the languages and policies of the teacher as a lifelong learner, but also in the salvation narratives that look at teachers as a kind of social redeemers. We need to avoid the social undervaluing of teachers and a discourse that puts enormous pressure on the profession through redemption narratives. The distance between teachers as heroes and teachers as the guilty ones for all of our social problems is often very short.

As modest as our job can be, it should focus on the ability to reveal the richness and complexity of teaching through a "knowledgeable activity." Maybe it is a modest task, but it is certainly the most ambitious one that an educationalist can accomplish.

THE RISKS OF DIALOGUE

The work that I have been arguing for cannot be done in isolation, which is why teachers need to engage in dialogue and primarily in professional dialogue. My intention is not to sing the praises of collaboration as a kind of magical solution for all problems. Undoubtedly, networks, communities of practice, school cooperation and partnerships are important initiatives to enrich the educational field. However, the worst service that we can provide to collaboration is to transform it into a litany without rules and without consequences.

Adapting to our field an argument developed by the anthropologist Arjun Appadurai (2006) would be useful, an argument in which he talks about the risks of dialogue between cultures and civilizations.

The first risk of dialogue is that the other party may not understand what you mean. The risk of misunderstanding is inherent in all human communication.

The second risk of dialogue is that we may in fact be understood clearly – exactly the opposite. This paradox is partly based on the concern that the other party may see through our surface expressions and understand the motives or intentions that we prefer to conceal. But the deeper risk of being fully understood is the risk that the other party will actually see our deepest convictions, our foundational opinions and even our doubts.

Dialogue cannot be seen as a kind of rhetoric or a mere declaration of goodwill. Saying the words does not make it so. Dialogue is not about everything and anything. It needs to have solid grounds and lead to collective action. Dialogue is an inspiration for the future of education because it liberates new meanings and entails new understandings of communalities and differences.

All dialogue is a form of negotiation, and negotiation cannot be based on complete mutual understanding or a total consensus across any sort of boundary or difference. To be effective, dialogue must be, to some extent, about shared ground, selective agreement and provisional consensus. Appadurai (2006) suggested a strategy of selectivity to build a contingent and evolving framework for conviviality.

These ideas are very intriguing and, at the same time, inspiring for teachers. A dialogical approach to education is about *presences*, which is about recognising differences and building a space for dialogue and to enter into conversation. One of the most important consequences is the construction of entirely new institutions for teacher education, overcoming the traditional division between schools and schools of education.

Looking at the history of teacher education, it is possible to identify three major phases:
- In the mid-nineteenth century, there were no training programmes and teachers learned their craft in schools along with a more experienced teacher through the logic of apprenticeship;
- Between the late nineteenth and early twentieth centuries, teacher education acquired a separate institutional status and came to be held in normal schools, prevailing logic of a theoretical and pedagogical preparation that ends with practical training in schools;
- From the last decades of the twentieth century, teacher training progressively acquired a university status, with a gradual distancing from the profession even when initiatives were undertaken to build strategies of cooperation and partnership between teacher education programmes and schools.

Today, we face a new challenge with enormous consequences: the merging of schools and teacher training institutions. In recent years, the field of medicine developed academic medical centres, bringing together the provision of health services, medical education and scientific research. Medical facilities are a good example for the kind of institutions we need to create in the area of education, which are academic centres of education bringing together schools, teacher training institutions and educational research. The success of such an initiative requires two fundamental conditions: the unified leadership of the spaces of practice, training and research and the reduction of disparities between the professional status of university professors and schoolteachers.

These academic centres of education must be capable of relating personal biographies with social contexts, life histories with political processes and the individual with the social. They must be open to politics of collaboration that bring new levels and dimensions, connecting teachers and schools with social and political debates and commitments.

EDUCATION AS A PUBLIC SPACE

"Knowledge societies" are inevitably societies of the unknown, not because we know less than in the past, but because we do not know enough and we do not have the intellectual tools to answer the questions that we ask (Innerarity, 2006).

In historical moments of transition, like the one in which we are living in at present, two tendencies must be avoided: prophecies of the past and prophecies of the future.

In education, the past always strikes back. We do not need more past, with an inescapable nostalgic vision of education and teachers. The past has no lesson to give us. We need more history, more historical consciousness and more historical understanding because history invites us to be prudent and raises our awareness.

History helps us avoid a vision of schools as a place where all problems of "knowledge societies" will be answered. Prophecies of salvation through the school tend to enclose teachers in unreasonable ambitions and blame them for all of the failures of school reforms.

Avoiding prophecies of the past and the future help us to understand the importance of education as a public space or, to be more precise, the importance of building the public space of education.

Differently from societies of the last two centuries, contemporary societies enormously expanded social institutions for education, culture, arts and science. At the same time, families and communities are much more educated than in the past. There is no reason for teachers and schools to take responsibility for a huge quantity of educational and social missions.

I am calling for a redefinition of schools as institutions focused on learning, in the broader sense of the term, avoiding an excessive view of their missions and possibilities. Paradoxically, this place, which seems more modest, will allow schools to play a more important role in contemporary societies. Schools are revitalised around a strong "knowledge" agenda; this focus needs to be well understood by the public and avoids the risk of ever-widening social remits, making impossible demands on schools. The teacher corps will be reinforced as a more distinct profession (OECD, 2001, p. 89).

My point is that this scenario will not be achieved if other agencies and institutions of society do not accept their responsibilities in a wide range of educational matters. Adapting the well-known concept of public sphere (Habermas, 1989) to education, I have been talking about the development of the "public space of education," a space for debate and civic participation but also for deliberation and collective decision making.

The public space of education is broader than public school and brings together institutions, associations and social movements in promoting education. *In the school what belongs to the school; in the society what belongs to society*. This approach avoids stifling the school by excessive missions, and calls all of society to the educational mission, which is a major shift for the teaching profession and for the organization of public school systems.

Around this theme, imagining a series of new possibilities, a way out for current crises and dilemmas, is possible. The centrality of knowledge in contemporary societies grants new responsibilities for teachers and for families and communities. The strengthening of *presences* in the educational field is crucial for the reinvention of societies based on democracy and participation.

FINAL COMMENTS

In a very simple manner, these four ideas attempt to open new lines of reflection for teachers. They can redirect our attention to central themes for the future of the profession by:
- Firstly, pointing out the importance of a professionality that is built inside, and not outside, the teaching corps;
- Secondly, underlining the meaning of professional knowledge that is elaborated through a pedagogical journey, where reflection on activity and experience assume a prominent role;
- Thirdly, emphasising the significance of practices of professional collaboration, not as a rhetorical statement but as a new way of organising the teaching profession;
- Fourthly, stressing the implications of the public space of education with a redefinition of schools and teachers and the celebration of a new social contract for education.

These ideas are crucial in order to foster an educational project from different and even contradictory influences. Sometimes we remember too much, which leads us to nostalgia. Sometimes we forget too much, frustrating the inscription of our action in the course of history. A wise balance between remembering and forgetting is a precondition to think critically, to avoid the burning of the present in the mirage of the future.

Teachers: How Long Until the Future? My answer is that the future is now; it is being defined through our ideas and commitments, through our voices and silences:

> To be at the same time an academic and an intellectual is to try to engage a type of knowledge and analysis that is taught and received in the university in a way so as to modify not only the thought of others but one's own as well. This work of modifying one's own thought and that of others seems to me to be the intellectual's reason for being. (Foucault, 1996, p. 461)

Please allow me to end with a tribute to Michel Serres. For a long time, I have been reading his book *Le tiers-instruit*, probably the book that has greatly influenced my way of thinking about education. Each time that I read the book, I find new ideas, new meanings and new connections that have been absent from my first readings.

On the last page of the book is a blank space and, after that, two lines that I had not noticed for a long time:

Reborn, he knows, he takes pity.
Finally, he can teach. (1991, p. 249)

Now, I think that maybe these lines are the key to the book and, in a sense, the key to the teaching profession.

- *Reborn*: to be teacher is to reborn, to do a work about ourselves and about our relationship with others;
- *S/he knows*: to be teacher is always a dialogue with knowledge and with the ways that knowledge changes our perceptions of the world;
- *S/he has pity*: in the philosophical assertion of dedication and generosity, to be a teacher is to take care, to assume our own responsibilities towards the other. *Finally, s/he can teach.*

NOTES

[i] This text is the transcription of the keynote address given at 15th Biennial of the International Study Association on Teachers and Teaching (5 July 2011). I would like to thank the organisers for this invitation, and mainly to Maria Assunção Flores for her friendly insistence to participate in this Conference.

REFERENCES

Appadurai, A. (2006). The risks of dialogue. In *New stakes for intercultural dialogue*. Seminar conducted at UNESCO (pp. 33-37). Paris, France : UNESCO.

Compayré, G. (1889). *Cours de pédagogie théorique et pratique*. Paris: Librairie Classique Paul Delaplane.

Foucault, M., & Lotringer, S. (Eds.) (1996). *Foucault live (interviews 1961–1984)*. New York: Semiotext.

Habermas, J. (1989). *The structural transformation of the public sphere*. Cambridge: Polity Press.

Huxley, A. (1971). *Collected essays*. New York: Harper & Row.

Innerarity, D. (2006). *El nuevo espacio publico*. Madrid: Espasa.

Labaree, D. (2003). Life on the margins. *Journal of Teacher Education, X*(10), 1-6.

Montaigne, M. (1968). *The complete essays of Montaigne* (edited by Donald Frame). Stanford: Stanford University Press.

OECD. (2001). *What schools for the future?* Paris: OECD.

OECD. (2005). *Teachers matter*. Paris: OECD.

Proust, M. (1923). *Remembrance of things past* (1981 Ed.,Vol. V). New York: Random House.

Serres, M. (1991). *Le tiers-instruit*. Paris: Éditions François Bourin.

Shaw, B. (1971). *Collected plays with their prefaces*. (1900, 1st ed.). London: The Bobley Head.

Shulman, L. (1986). Knowledge growth in teaching. *Educational Researcher, 15*(2), 4-14.

AFFILIATIONS

António Nóvoa
Institute of Education
University of Lisbon, Portugal

CIARAN SUGRUE

TEACHERS' LIVES AND WORK:
BACK TO THE FUTURE?

INTRODUCTION

With such a large canvas to paint on, choosing an appropriate starting point when embarking on an account in broad brushstrokes of teachers' lives and work is challenging. I've chosen work rather than 'career' since for many, myself included, who entered into teaching, especially in smaller jurisdictions, career – in the sense of prospects for advancement, opportunities for planned promotional trajectories were extremely limited. Rather, part of the attractiveness of teaching was its 'permanent and pensionable' conditions, at a time when being a public servant was respected rather than pilloried, though there is considerable variation in this regard from one jurisdiction to another, as evidence presented below indicates. In jurisdictions, such as my own, with high annual levels of emigration, a necessity that has returned in the austerity induced by prevailing economic conditions in post-Celtic Tiger Ireland, permanent and pensionable take on heightened significance, create conditions that are largely protective of status and respect, aspects of collective professional identities that have been eroded elsewhere. A recent study in the Irish context summarises its findings as follows:

> Overall, there was a high level of satisfaction with the way teachers do their jobs with almost one in four (24%) very satisfied1 with the way teachers do their jobs and a further 40% satisfied2. By contrast, only 12% were dissatisfied3 or very dissatisfied4 with the way teachers do their jobs. When compared with the other occupations and professions, they ranked second only to nurses. (Council, 2009, p. 1)

Though formal schooling as we have come to recognise it, and the profession of teaching are relatively recent phenomena, it is difficult to avoid the notion that teaching has been an essential element of our survival and evolutionary kit from time immemorial. Even before we came down from the trees, or indulge a glance at our near relatives who continue to populate such habitats, such rear view perspectives suggest that parenting, passing on the 'wisdom' of troop, pride or tribe have been integral and essential to our survival as a species. Though often not included, teaching and learning are integral to the ingenuity that has fuelled and continue to fuel evolution. From the outset then it is important to recognise that "past, present and future [are] fundamentally ambiguous" and, as a consequence, "there is no single right or correct interpretation of the world around us" and the

M.A. Flores et al. (eds.), Back to the Future: Legacies, Continuities and Changes in Educational Policy, Practice and Research, 39–56.

teaching profession is no different in this regard (Homer-Dixon, 2001, p. 389). This is part of our past history. Thus, even if we claim to speak with some authority on teachers' lives and work, it is important that spaces and opportunities are created and left available for the voices of others to be heard, particularly those who currently labour in the world's schools and classrooms.

With varying degrees of formality and informality the teaching-learning process has been with us from pre-history. For the most part however, it was in the 19th century, primarily spawned by the industrial revolution in the Western world and the plight of the new urban poor that systems of mass schooling were created. Within this general mass movement there were tensions between those of a reformist bent who saw education as a vehicle for enlightenment and advancement for all, and those who saw it as a means of controlling the (unruly) masses – rendering them literate to serve the dual purpose of – saving their souls by reading the Bible, while being able to take or follow instructions while knowing their place, thus perpetuating the status quo; a literacy of compliance rather than a liberating literacy (Eggleston, 1977), a struggle that has considerable contemporary resonance, but perhaps construed in more technical-rational language such as 'closing the achievement gap' (Ferguson, 2007). As a general statement therefore it may be asserted that at the heart of mass schooling and the teaching profession as they have been continuously re-shaped during the past century, there has been a persistent tension between a tendency towards emancipatory enlightenment and a more oppressive penchant favouring indoctrination and social control. Such oppressive socialisation has been variously described as a 'pedagogy of the oppressed' (Freire, 1970/2001) or alternatively – 'teaching as a conserving activity' (Postman, 1979), or even more oppressively – 'education as enforcement' (Saltman, 2003). Within this cauldron of contradiction and conflict teachers too have sought to serve the public interest, or greater good, while seeking to create a professional identity; an appropriate professional formation and conditions of service that enhance social status and remuneration while simultaneously enhancing professional formation at various career stages as well as serving the public good. The major external stakeholders who have sought in various ways to 'regulate' the professional autonomy sought by teachers have been church/ religious bodies, state and public – all of whom claim to be pursuing the 'best' interests of society.

Not surprisingly therefore, different periods since the 19th century have borne witness to different emphases, as the pendulum swings of policy-makers have shaped and buffeted the contexts in which teachers live and work. For example, teacher educators and educational researchers have sought to (re-) shape discourses around the profession of teaching as indicated by Harvard Professor Josiah Royce who, writing in the first *Educational Review* (1891) advocated that "teachers should have 'a scientific training for their calling" (quoted in Condliffe Langemann, 2000, p. ix). Persistent and contemporary tensions are already evident in his choice of words. There is implicit technicisation in his privileging of 'training' over education, while his use of 'calling' is redolent with vocational overtones, called to fulfil a particular and largely pre-determined role – a conserving activity. There are implicit tensions too between a conceptualisation of teacher formation as a 'science' or as craft knowledge, when he describes initial teacher education programmes as "opportunities to learn to reflect on their craft," a form of phronesis (practical wisdom) with a pedigree that can be traced back to Aristotle (Aristotle, 1999; see also Dunne, 1993; B. Green, 2009; J. Green, 2010). This tension is reinforced further by his refusal to espouse the perspective that there is a "universally valid science of pedagogy ... capable of complete formulation and ... direct application to individual pupils and teachers" (p. ix). Such tensions between scientifically based and craft knowledge or artistry continue to have resonance in contemporary discourses surrounding the art and science of teaching with consequences also for professional formation, continuing professional learning, as well as professional identity – particularly regarding professional autonomy and regulation. Such tensions in more recent times have calcified around two competing logics – the logic of accountability and the logic of professional responsibility – the former largely determined by policy-makers and regulating bodies that specify standards against which teacher 'performance' will be measured, as opposed to internal regulation whereby professions and professionals take on the moral mandate assigned by society whereby they act in the best interest of learners and profession thus contributing to the common good (Englund & Dyrdal Solbrekke, 2011), a more 'ecological professionalism' (Barnett, 2011). Within the logic of professional responsibility, there is an obligation on professionals to:

> ... embed the responsibility for professionals' discretionary specialisation with regard to both individual clients and the public interest, and it requires professionals to base their judgements in both science and experience-based knowledge and professional ethics. (Englund & Dyrdal Solbrekke, 2011, p. 61)

By contrast, the logic of accountability demands conformity and compliance with a set of externally determined standards, with an additional necessity to render organisations 'auditable' (Power, 1999).

As the policy pendulum has arced towards autonomy or control, a persistent constant has been the centrality of teachers as reflected in the recent White Paper published in England when it states: "no education system can be better than the quality of its teachers" (Education, 2010, p. 3). The second important 'truth' this document identifies is

> ... world class education systems ... devolve as much power as possible to the front line, while retaining high levels of accountability. The OECD has shown that countries which give the most autonomy to head teachers and teachers are the ones that do best. (Education, 2010, pp. 3-4)

Regarding the first 'truth' however, it too is reductionist as well as being de-contextualised, thus regardless of context, education is reduced to a set of transactions between teacher and learner, and success or failure is capable of being predicted and measured with reference to a set of competencies and learning outcomes. Nevertheless, as Finland continues to remain on or near the top of the international comparative data generated by PISA (OECD, 2010), the view that professional autonomy is necessary for education systems to flourish gains further traction, yet commentators on the Finnish system draw attention also to a creeping managerialism, one that owes more to the logic of accountability and attendant performativity than to professional responsibility. They say:

> The movement towards large-scale reform in the latter part of the twentieth century, with its accompanying emphases on more detailed government intervention and high stakes testing, turned leadership which inspired communities to achieve and improve upon their purposes, into management that emphasized delivering the short-term policies and purposes of others (Fink & Brayman, 2006; Hargreaves & Goodson, 2006). (Hargeaves, Halasz, & Pont, 2007, p. 6)

Without wishing to be essentialist, my contention is that throughout the period of mass schooling, the lives and work of teaches have laboured under the twin-towers of autonomy and various external accountability mechanisms or 'technologies of control' (Ball, 2008). Within this panopticon of autonomy and accountability the agency of teachers (coupled with teacher educators and educational researchers) capture the salient struggles in the forging of teachers' professional identities. I will show, and anticipate that the empirical evidence provided in Chris Day's contribution to this volume, will vindicate the perspective that it is necessary to revitalise and reconceptualise in appropriate ways for our times, the concept of professional responsibility if 'making a difference' is to entail bringing about a more equitable and just interdependent world, rather than vindicating individual autonomy in ways that perpetuate the status quo. Rather, a more engaged teaching profession, one that takes its professional responsibility seriously in a vigilant proactive manner, is a necessity in the process of 'creating capabilities' (Nussbaum, 2011) that promote dignity and respect while simultaneously seeking "genuine opportunity for secure functionings" for the most disadvantaged (Wolff & De-Shalt, 2007/2010, p. 168).

However, all of this may appear as a significant remove from the real lives of teachers. Let me begin therefore by providing some initial theoretical perspectives on autonomy, accountability and professional responsibility, before turning to particular testimony regarding the lives and work of teachers to illustrate the presence of these internal and external shaping influences – to illuminate the larger canvas, the presence of international 'social movements' (Castells, 2004) that become integral to the creation of professional identities and responsibilities, to teachers' lives and work. This approach is inspired by the view that "professional work cannot and should not be divorced from the lives of professionals" (Goodson, 2001), but should also include "contextual commentary on issues of time and space" (p. 17). This life history approach offers "a way of exploring the relationship between the culture, the social structure and individual lives" (Ibid.) My intention is to indicate and illustrate that, in broad brush strokes, the identity projects of teachers have been a continuous dance between the individual and collective, the prevailing social conditions or policy contexts that at once colour teachers' lives and work while simultaneously characterising the profession of teaching. I will conclude by drawing together some threads of this extensive tapestry and weave then into a tentative fabric of professional responsibility—a contemporary confluence where past, present and future meet, that continues to command attention, but too often is neglected.

AUTONOMY, ACCOUNTABILITY AND PROFESSIONAL RESPONSIBILITY

I am in agreement with Appiah when he asserts that "personal autonomy seems to entail a lot more than just being left to your own devices" (Appiah, 2007, p. 37) but this begs the question from a real world perspective, and in the context of the teaching life, what is professional autonomy and how much of it is apposite for a thriving teaching profession? There is considerable disagreement regarding individual autonomy let alone when it comes to the latitude accorded professionals to determine principles by which their actions will be governed. Additionally, while there are many autonomies, Western liberal versions of autonomy can have very different outcomes. Consequently, because value pluralism exists, "autonomy is not a still point in the turning world of values" (Appiah, 2007, p. 44). How autonomy is conceptualised therefore has been subjected to revision over time, thus the necessity to keep such matters under constant review – an inherent part of professional responsibility. If it is accepted that autonomy is a matter of degree, then it opens up the possibility that professionals are not entirely free to choose the principles by which they will conduct their affairs, but rather are obliged to accommodate a diversity of perspectives within their own deliberations. Nevertheless the autonomous person does not merely exercise agency in the sense of pursuing "projects, plans, values" but is rather "part author of his life" (Appiah, 2007, pp. 38-39). It may be suggested therefore that the autonomous professional carries a communitarian responsibility to act in the interests of others rather than singular pursuit of self-interest; such autonomous agency is exercised in the interest of solidarity (Dews, 1986/1992). The professional, though acting alone, is always also acting within a 'web of commitments' (May, 1996). In this regard, rather than pursue an abstract ideation of autonomy, the notion of 'relational autonomy' is particularly fit for purpose. Such an approach points to the necessity to "think of autonomy as a characteristic of agents who are emotional, embodied, desiring, creative, and feeling, as well as rational creatures" (Mackenzie & Stoljar, 2000, p. 21).

For Archer, on the other hand, 'active agents' are those "who can exercise some governance in their own lives ... develop and define their ultimate concerns;" what she calls "those internal goods that they care about most" (Archer, 2007, p. 6). However, from a professional perspective, with its connotations of acting in the interest of others, while serving and enhancing one's profession, there is the suggestion that 'professional responsibility' puts a restraining order on mere pursuit of 'ultimate concerns' as part of a more collective oriented agenda. It is important therefore to distinguish between individual autonomy that enables active agents to pursue their interests and moral autonomy which necessitates that "a good society ... create the conditions by which its members can become agents, and foster a sense of justice" (Appiah, 2007, p. 38). It may be suggested therefore that professional responsibility includes a degree of self-regulation that sets limits to the pursuit of 'ultimate concerns,' thus seeking to balance and re-calibrate the competing interests of personal and moral agency. Such balancing also permits states and governing agencies to regulate, specify rules that are intended to promote benefits for society in general while leaving adequate autonomy and discretionary judgement to professionals to act in that larger interest.

Pervasive contemporary policy rhetorics and practices of accountability are a set of elaborate restraining mechanisms that sets limits to and asserts control over professional autonomy while selling autonomy and professional responsibility short. Such shortcomings become immediately apparent if attention is focused on contemporary realities for teachers. Consider the following:

> A very common experience in teaching ... is the conflict between forms of accountability that necessitate spending time reporting on classroom activities and students' results, and the form of professional responsibility that entails engaging with and teaching the students (Becher et al., 1979). (Englund & Solbrekke, 2011, p. 64)

Such scenarios give rise to what Wellard and Heggen (2011) have identified as a privileging of 'paper care' over professional care and when such practices become commonplace, they create a 'cult of efficiency' whereby 'efficiency' is privileged, professional autonomy and agency eroded, and a sense of professional responsibility hollowed out. Such situations are described thus:

> In our avowedly secular age, the paramount sin is now inefficiency. Dishonesty, unfairness, and injustice – the sins of the past – pale in comparison with the cardinal transgression of inefficiency. (Gross Stein, 2001, p. 2)

This emphasis on accountability, at the expense of responsibility, promotes compliance and the language of New Public Management (NPM), its technical-rationality, privileges or coerces individuals into compliance rather than encourage them to exercise professional responsibility. Gross Stein captures the impact of the language of NPM on both thought and action when she says:

> *Efficere* translates ... as 'to bring about,' to accomplish, to effect. Only in modern times do we separate effectiveness, efficacy and efficiency and our public conversation is consequently fractured – and impoverished. (Gross Stein, 2001, p. 2)

Similarly, the lives and work of teachers is hollowed out when efficacy is marginalised and efficiency privileged through regimes of accountability. In such circumstances, the moral obligation to do 'good work' (Gardner, 2007; Gardner, Csikszentmihalyi, & Damon, 2001) is reduced to a set of standards and targets, with more emphasis on compliance than on providing a public service, of contributing to the common good. Since "education and health care do not meet only our personal needs; they are the core of our relationship as citizens to our governments, and they reflect the ways we think about ourselves as citizens in society" (Gross Stein, 2001, p. 4). Professional responsibility includes a sense of agency, to act in the interest of the profession and the common good – there is a collective responsibility on the individual professional. At a time of rampant individualism; what has been labelled "the age of selfishness: the credo of self, inextricably entwined with the gospel of the market, has hijacked the fabric of our lives" (Gerhardt, 2011, p. 11), it is worth recalling that the latter half of the 19th Century and the heyday of the British Empire, payment by results became a policy priority, the contemporary equivalent of which is national testing, and performance related pay. In language redolent of the US legislation No Child Left Behind (2001) the annual report of the chief inspector in Ireland in 1858 in response to poor pupil attendance he decreed:

> The only remedy for this defect is to have one thorough and scrutinising examination annually of every child undergoing the continuous process of education; and this examination ... should be held in the most formal manner possible. (quoted in Coolahan, 2009, pp. 40-41)

Such externally imposed standards were lent further coercive force with the threat that unless all pupils were in attendance "forfeit of a continuance grant or of some other advantage or privilege" would result. As the scheme evolved through implementation, teachers could supplement their salaries depending on the performance of their pupils, a system that did much to promote attention on the most able, to the detriment of other learners.

In large measure, the changing professional identities of teachers and the profession of teaching have been buffeted and re-shaped continuously by the internal struggle to establish and promote professional autonomy, as a space in which to act with a sense of responsibility that seeks to balance professional interests with social, communitarian interests, while Governments and State Agencies have sought through various mechanisms of control to regulate teacher autonomy and professional discretion. Although this historical trajectory has been marked in particular ways by the contributions of 'great educators'(Sagakian & Sahakian, 1966), and frequently also by 'outstanding' schools, these are not of primary concern here. Rather, my focus is on the ordinary lives and work of the generality of teachers, while exceptionality too paints aspects of teachers' lives and work in high relief.

PROFESSIONAL RESPONSIBILITY: IN THE SHADOWS OF AUTONOMY AND ACCOUNTABILITY

It may be useful to think of the work and lives of teachers in three major phases – pre-industrial, industrial and, in contemporary parlance – post-industrial societies; the latter contemporary phase frequently described as teaching in and for the knowledge economy/society (Hargreaves, 2003). The pre-industrial is not our concern here, thus I confine attention to teachers' lives and work in modern and post-modern societies. In a more general sense, we cannot separate teachers' lives and work from large 'social movements' and major changes in society over the past 150 years or so. The re-shaping of identity within contemporary realities is captured in the following:

> A new identity is being constructed, not by returning to tradition, but by working on traditional materials in the formation of a new godly, communal world, where deprived masses and disaffected intellectuals may reconstruct meaning in a global alternative to the exclusionary global order. (Castells, 2000, pp. 21-22)

Re-creating a sense of teachers' identities over time is the focus of the remainder of this section. By way of illustration, inspectors' reports in Ireland during the 1860s indicated:

> The majority of teachers are very poor, and find it hard to keep up a respectable exterior, such as becomes their profession .... The wonder is not that teachers are not more respectably dressed, but that they are able to appear at their work with anything like becoming decency at all. (quoted in Coolahan, 2009, p. 39)

A number of comments seem justified and appropriate. There is recognition that a profession requires a standard of living that enables its members to act professionally, that there is an obligation on the state to provide appropriate conditions – in terms of salary, surroundings of service and workplace environments. While such conditions until recently have been largely taken-for-granted in Western context, but are by no means secure, 150 years later it is still far from being universally the case. To illustrate this point, the conditions of work of primary teachers in a 'poor' area of Dar es Salaam are indicated while signalling also that even within such challenging contexts there is considerable variation. Nevertheless, the following is indicative and commonplace – Aziza's life and work:

Aziza: a biographical sketch

Aziza is a 27 year old single parent, mother of a four year old boy. She teaches English to the three standard 7 classes in the school. She completed her primary schooling in her home district in the north west. Her aunt provided financial assistance to enable her to complete private secondary schooling in the capital, having failed to gain entry to a state secondary school. Subsequently, she qualified as a primary teacher and began her teaching career in 2005. She transferred to her current school in 2008. Her salary is roughly the equivalent of $100 USD per month and she sends a proportion to her elderly parents. Her monthly rent is a fifth of her salary. She struggles to make ends meet and child-care is a particular challenge. She employs a house girl for this purpose, but these young girls (12-13 year olds) are often unreliable or sometimes run away. Consequently, we met Aziza's son in the school on a number of occasions during fieldwork. She supplements her income through petty trading. (Sugrue & Fentiman, 2012, p. 104)

It does not require much imagination to arrive at the view that Aziza's life and work may have more in common with Irish teachers in mid-19th century than a typical teacher in a Western context today. In a globalised, interdependent world, to what extent should such conditions be of concern to teacher-professionals everywhere? If it is the case that within this globalised world, where national boundaries are significantly more porous then incorporating human rights, with dignity, autonomy and agency calls for a new reinvigorated sense of professional responsibility that moves beyond the following which urges that teachers:

> Become part of a national social movement in which teachers individually and collectively develop skills, competencies and dispositions of mind that will contribute to the enhancement of teaching and the improvement of student learning outcomes. (Sachs, 2004, p. 35)

While such exhortations seek to be a rallying call they need to be international in their ambition, while "placing responsibility before accountability" (Hargeaves, 2009, p. 109).

What such evidence and sentiment suggest is that the struggles around autonomy-agency, regulation-responsibility have been the major contours, the ensuing struggles have been dominated by various oppressive regulations- not always the current dominance of 'efficiency.' Take for example, an account from the oral testimony provided in '*Hill Country Teachers*' – female Texas teachers in the 1930s and 1940s. This first vignette is illustrative of how times have changed in terms of 'norms' and alerts us to the necessity to keep under review what is considered appropriate—professional, responsible and the identification of commitments and how 'making a difference' is construed. The backdrop to this vignette is a struggle by young women to get an education (an appropriate professional qualification) and the conditions in which such 'freedoms' were hard won. Sibyl describes her accommodation as she pursued a degree having been teaching for a few years. She says:

> I didn't stay in a dorm. I never stayed in one in my life. I stayed at boarding houses where the ladies had rooms – like seven or eight rooms. They would keep maybe fourteen girls, or boys, as the case may be – but never mixed. It was cheaper to stay in a boarding house than a dorm. We had four together in a room with two double beds. It was cheaper for there to be four in a room than for two in a room. I know our big bedroom had two double beds in it. Here again I slept with someone and found it difficult. (Manning, 1990, p. 15)

This testimony reports on taken-for-granted gender segregation – a technology of control and regulation that has been eroded considerably. This evidence strongly suggests that moral aspects of the teaching role have been more explicit in the past, prior to the foregrounding of 'expert' knowledge whereas earlier formulations of teacher identities made this explicit – being of good character and religious were deemed more significant that classroom craft (Dyrdal Solbrekke & Sugrue, 2011). As Karseth (2011, p. 165) has recently pointed out drawing on historical evidence in the Norwegian context:

> Baune (2001) argues that the teacher in the 1850s still was a pious minded man who in life and living was a true Christian example for his students. In fact all activities and all that took place at the teacher training seminaries [colleges] were prepared and arranged to fulfil this purpose. According to regulations a strict selection procedure for accepting students was demanded from the seminaries and material should be handled in a way consistent with their religious and moral aims. The teacher training seminaries consequently were more like religious institutions more so than educational institutions. The students should be educated – not only to become pious and moral Christians – but also to become good and obedient members of the common people's class of society. (Baune, 2001, p. 86, author's translation)

These 'seminaries' were total institutions, in many respects modelled on monastic life, where there was a strong sense of 'formation' as moulding for conformity, for perpetuation of the established order rather than any sense of the transformative potential of education. More explicitly this experience was very definitely intended to be 'training' rather than transformation. It provides evidence that professional autonomy has had to be fought for over time, and as the pendulum of larger 'social movements' has swung in opposite directions, discretionary judgement, one of the hallmarks of being professional has been narrowed or expanded while continuously being re-negotiated.

In more contemporary liberal post-Christian European environments it is frequently forgotten that such requirements were also a means of controlling teachers' lives and work, but they are important reminders also of the moral dimensions of teaching, of being a professional. As Biesta (2010, p. 71) points out: "the postmodern doubt about the possibility for ethical rules and systems is the beginning of responsibility, not its end." Similarly, Bauman urges that individually we must take 'responsibility for our responsibility' – suggesting that we are condemned by the human conditions to act responsibly (Bauman, 1993).

Individually and collectively these various technologies of control – from selection criteria, conditions for learning, the nature of professional preparation programmes exert influence on the dispositions of teachers and the extent to which they are 'obedient servants' or more autonomous active agents pursuing professional and social agenda. Such struggles to create better futures have amusing moments too event if they also signal lurching disjunctures with the past, as the following vignette from Rural Texas of the 1930s relates:

> When I was staying ... out at the Divide, where this lake was, one day I washed my underwear and put it out on the line to dry. And here came the lady of the house all out of breath. 'Barney's coming! I know you'll want to

take your things in so he won't see them. You won't want him to see your underwear. Run get it off the line real quick" I blinked and said more or less, "I don't mind it being out there." She said, "I've lived with Mr. Klein all these years, and he never say my underwear. Six or seven children, I'm sure he saw her underwear sometime, somewhere in there. I thought that was just hilarious. I guess it's just the way people are brought up. (Manning, 1990, p. 11)

This woman's vignette provides further evidence of the shifting boundaries mentally, morally and socially that require constant revisiting, revision etc. Such incidents draw attention to the relationship more generally between teachers and the communities they serve – another constraint on professional responsibility. It reminds contemporary readers of the gendered nature of teacher's identities, the social demand to be a role model with all that entails rendering autonomy relative. As Waller asserts: "teachers are paid agents of cultural diffusion. They are hired to carry light into dark places. To make sure that teachers have some light, standard qualifications for teachers have been evolved" (Waller, 1932, p. 40). The evocation of light and darkness has Evangelical overtones that continue to resonate while signalling the moral responsibilities of teachers. What the vignette barely touches on is the extent to which her thinking is different from the preceding generation and that for such changes to emerge, an activism is necessary, individually and collectively as such incremental changes have to be fought for. One generation's legacy is another's barrier to professional autonomy and the forging of appropriate professional identity. Such evidence provides testimony of the struggles entailed in taking leave of the past, and this was captured most succinctly and aptly recently when the Queen of England made a historic visit to Ireland, the first such visit since 1911. In the only formal speech made during a four-day state visit she observed that we should "bow to the past but not be bound by it" implicitly acknowledging that the ongoing process of forging a professional identity is a work in progress with uncertain outcomes, while recognising also that formation is a struggle between past and present in the construction of the future (II, 2011).

Professional Preparation: Sites for Professional Formation

Another important struggle for teachers' professional identities continues to be what is entailed by way of appropriate preparation, the formation of the next generation of teachers; struggles with particular poignancy and contemporary resonance in the context of very recently proposed reforms in various jurisdictions, strongly suggestive also that the struggles continue even if the terrain on which advance and retreat are hard fought have altered in significant ways. To illustrate this, I return to another US text in a chapter entitled 'those who train the young,' some insight into preparation is provided in the following:

All teachers today [1929] must have graduated from high school and have spent at least nine months in a recognized teacher-training college, while at least two years more of normal school training or a college degree are necessary to teach in the high school. (Lynd & Lynd, 1929, p. 206)

This commentary marks another differentiation within the teaching profession, namely the struggle by primary teachers and their representatives for more adequate formal preparation – to become a graduate profession. However, significant distinctions remain in terms of professional identities around pedagogical rather than subject-matter expertise. With increasing contemporary emphasis on self-directed learning and learning how to learn in order to become a life-long learners such tensions, distinctions and demarcations may be eroded.

Nevertheless, the quotation immediately above very definitely favours 'training' rather than education. In more general terms, what is also significant in this 'study in American Culture' is the positioning of teachers within society- in contemporary parlance – in an entrepreneurial culture where risk-taking is lauded, and the key to unlocking such enterprise is small government and reduced taxes, seems to suggest that the class and social positioning of teachers is to be disparaged and despised. Rather like those 19th century teachers described by Karseth above – who should belong to a 'common class of people,' in a more competitive globalised world and the knowledge economy, claims to expertise have become a more definitive dimension of professional identity formation, thus the old order of moral formation struggles to retain an appropriate place within teacher professional formation narratives. As the 'social anthropology' of 'Middletown' asserts:

The whole situation is complicated by the fact that these young teachers go into teaching in many cases not primarily because of their ability or great personal interest in teaching; for very many of them teaching is just a job. The wistful remark of a high school teacher, "I just wasn't brought up to do anything interesting. So I'm teaching!" possibly represents the situation with many. (Lynd & Lynd, 1929, p. 207)

Such pejorative comments are culture bound, and contrast sharply with evidence from other jurisdictions where the calibre and commitment of entrants to teaching are significantly different (Sugrue, 2005). In the competitive arena of PISA international comparative league tables, the high status, high calibre and highly qualified teaching profession in Finland is continuously cited as a major contributing factor to student performance (Hargreaves, Halász, & Pont, 2007). Such glowing testimony however is far from universal, and in sharp contrast to evidence provided by an entrant to teacher education in Lesotho when he stated: "I am ashamed to say I am a student teacher" because it is evidence of failure to gain entry to any other higher education programme (see Sugrue, 2012). Struggles around professional identity and what professional responsibility entails are far from uniform and continue to be shaped significantly by local and national circumstance.

In the land of the free and the home of the brave, teachers continue to struggle in a climate of intense regulation that tends to rob the soul of passion, purpose and commitment. In a recent account, Lasky indicates the impact on teachers' lives and work of the NCLB legislation and its disproportionate impact on schools serving the poor. In such circumstances, 'warehousing the schoolhouse' restricts the autonomy of teachers to preoccupation with test scores where: "Teachers were keenly aware of where their schools stood in the state and district accountability rankings as evidenced by the statements: "If we don't meet AYP [annual yearly progress], the state will come in" (Lasky, 2012, p. 80). More generally, such pervasive accountability measures lead to the following conclusion:

> In theory, schools had been given devolved responsibility for budgets and implementation. In practice, the restricted scope for autonomous action amounted in many cases to displacement of blame from governments to schools when results were poor. (Hargeaves & Shirley, 2009, p. 10)

From a practitioner perspective, such controls run counter to their sense of professional responsibility, and contribute to low morale and teacher attrition. Such mechanisms require sustained critique and renewed rebuttal. However, ingenuity and agency may be found in the strangest of places, sometimes when oppression is at its most acute, individual and collective action find the resources to rise above adversity. One of the principles espoused by the South African Teachers' League in their struggle during the Apartheid era was "you must rise above your circumstances. You must find the ways and means to circumvent what the state wanted you to do" (Wieder, 2003, p. 45).

Teaching in Extremis

The example provided here, what I've called 'teaching in extremis' is a vindication of Ayers' perspective:

> Teacher biographies and biographical research in education can provide examples of possible lives – dynamic portraits of teachers working and making choices in an imperfect world, living in landscapes of fear and doubt, holding to a faith in the craft of teaching and in the three-dimensional humanity of their students that allows them to reach a kind of greatness against the grain. (Ayers, 1998, p. 230)

In the contemporary cauldron of tension between devolved responsibility and increasing control through mechanisms of accountability, 'resilience' has been identified as a major hallmark of teacher identity, something that is "both a product of personal and professional dispositions and values, and socially constructed" (Day, Sammons, Stobart, Kingston, & Gu, 2007, p. 198). It is characterised as the 'ability to bounce back' and quickly in the face of adversity (Day & Gu, 2010). Nevertheless, in the same manner that it may be legitimately posited that there are limits to professional responsibility, there are limits too to resilience, as evidenced by the Inspectors' comments cited above. There are legitimate concerns regarding the sustainability of resilience or indeed professional responsibility when working conditions are less than conducive. Nevertheless, though 'heroes' and 'heroines' in teaching are increasingly disparaged in leadership literature in particular (Gronn, 2003, 2009; Haslam, Reicher, & Platow, 2011) there is something uplifting and instructive also about recognising 'ordinary heroes' and their indomitable struggle to 'make a difference' (Zimbardo, 2007).

Sedick (Dickie) Isaacs, a teacher, spent thirteen years on Robben Island as student and teacher. His contribution was enormous, and it can only be touched upon here. However, two vignettes are worth recording as they are a tribute to human agency, a thirst for learning and an indomitable spirit that engenders solidarity and trust, characteristics that appear as necessary building blocks in the forging of professional identities and standards (Day & Gu, 2010; Day et al., 2007).

> We had to look for writing materials. A few people were already studying, and they were allowed to buy writing materials. You must remember that anybody misusing these studies had study privileges withdrawn, and misconduct included sharing papers and pens. But we did share. And at that time they were building the prison so there was cement around and the cement bags had three layers. And we were able to cut out those three layers, clean off the brown paper and stick it together into a type of loose flat book. And whenever possible, pencils were broken and halved or quartered and shared out. And many of us started writing small in order to conserve space. My writing is still extremely small. (Waider, 2003, p. 66)

Teaching in extremis too required innovative pedagogies, while breach of any of the technologies of control resulted in deprivations – including solitary confinement, denial of food and physical torture. Yet, they persisted, as Isaacs indicates:

> I taught mathematics and I taught physical sciences. And I thought one of the ways for me to make it as interesting as possible was to give them exercises. When you go to the island, you'll see that there's a door leading to the bathroom. There were no doors at that time. You come back from the quarry, you're all dusty and so on and you rush to get a shower. My students who were interested in their mathematical problems came with me. I sometimes think I lived very non-conventional. Have you ever taught a class standing completely naked while you're in the shower? In the shower, having helped people with tutorials while sitting on the toilets. I had a friend in the next-door cell and he wanted to study mathematics. So I wrote him a textbook of mathematics on toilet paper. I had a small study kit and half a ballpoint pen, which I managed to bring in. … In any case I wrote this textbook and he did exercises on it, but they discovered it. And then they rationed toilet paper – one sheet per day. (p. 67)

Needless to say, such learning was undertaken despite the physical, mental and emotional demands of each day, but there was community and solidarity too as evidenced by the following: "and all my comrades knew that I came from the universities. And they used to make extra stones for me and bring it along and give a donation to me in order to make that pile" (p. 67).[1]

In such extreme circumstances, education was a liberation, while outside, among other teachers in the struggle against apartheid as well as among high school students, liberation was often given priority over education. From the perspective of a professionally responsible teaching profession, it is possible to salvage inspiration from among these heaps of stones, while being simultaneously convinced that continuing to re-think professional responsibility and what it entails is both a necessity and an individual and collective obligation into the future in building possible professional lives while being open to a plurality of circumstances and activities.

PROFESSIONAL RESPONSIBILITY, POSSIBLE FUTURES?

My thesis throughout is that forging a professional identity since the advent of formal or national systems of schooling has been constantly buffeted between the twin-towers of autonomy and accountability, while readily recognising that how both autonomy and accountability are construed have also continued to evolve, a choreography that remains simultaneously: fluid and uncertain, constraining and liberating, empowering and disempowering. In order to re-construct a sense of professional responsibility that simultaneously recognises contemporary realities and seeks to loose constraints in the service of others as well as the professional of teaching, it is important to recognise, perhaps even 'bow to the past' while being inspired to do better in the interests of others. The ingredients identified here are part of the picture only though I suggest how we interrogate the past is an important means of building a secure future (Sugrue, 2008). This is an individual and collective responsibility that requires the combined attention of practitioners, teacher educators and researchers, while policy-makers and public too need to be draw into this discourse. Re-claiming rather than romanticising the lost heritage of previous generations of teachers provides important 'bricolage' for constructing the future. Securing a better educational future for all depends on it, and that future is now! In the words of one celebrity celluloid teacher – Carpe Diem. In the current context however, this exhortation might be refashioned as 'seize Day' (Chris that is!) to render more complete the emerging tapestry of teachers' lives and work.

NOTES

[i] Comrades broke extra stones to ensure that Isaacs met his daily quota, thus enabling him to be fed and to avoid possible additional deprivations.

REFERENCES

Appiah, K. A. (2007). *The ethics of identity*. Princeton & London: Princeton University Press.
Archer, M. S. (2007). *Making our way through the world: Human reflexivity and social mobility*. Cambridge: Cambridge University Press.

Aristotle. (1999). *Nicomachean ethics* (2nd edition, translated, with introduction, Notes and Glossary, by Terence Irwin). Indianapolis/Cambridge: Hackett Publishing Company.

Ayers, W. (1998). I search, you search. In C. Kridel (Ed.), *Writing educational biography* (pp. 235-244). New York: Garland.

Ball, S. (2008). The legacy of ERA, privatization and policy ratchet. *Educational Management Administration & Leadership, 36*(2), 185-199.

Barnett, R. (2011). Towards an ecological professionalism. In C. Sugrue & T. Dyrdal Solbrekke (Eds.), *Professional responsibility: New horizons of praxis* (pp. 29-41). London/New York: Routledge.

Bauman, Z. (1993). *Postmodern ethics.* Oxford: Blackwell.

Biesta, G. (2010). *Good education in an age of measurement ethics, politics, democracy.* Boulder/London: Paradigm Publishers.

Castells, M. (2000). *The information age: Economy, society and culture. Volume III. End of millennium* (second ed.). Oxford: Blackwell Publishers.

Castells, M. (2004). *The information Age aconomy, society and culture. Volume II. The power of identity* (second ed.). Oxford: Blackwell Publishing.

Condliffe Langemann, E. (2000). *An elusive science: The troubling history of educational research.* Chicago: University of Chicago Press.

Coolahan, J., with O'Donnovan, P. F. (2009). *A history of Ireland's school inspectorate 1831-2008.* Dublin: Four Courts Press.

Council, T. (2009). *Evaluation of public attitudes to the teaching profession summary of findings from iReach market.* Research, Maynooth Teaching Council.

Day, C., & Gu, Q. (2010). *The new lives of teachers.* London & New York: Routledge.

Day, C., Sammons, P., Stobart, G., Kingston, A., & Gu, Q. (2007). *Teachers matter connecting lives, work and effectiveness.* New York: McGraw HIll and Open University Press.

Dews, P. (Ed.). (1986/1992). *Autonomy & solidarity interviews with Jurgen Habermas.* London: Verso.

Dunne, J. (1993). *Back to the rough ground 'Phronesis' and 'Techne' in modern philosophy and in Aristotle.* Notre Dame: University of Notre Dame Press.

Dyrdal Solbrekke, T., & Sugrue, C. (2011). Professional responsibility – Back to the future. In T. Dyrdal Solbrekke & C. Sugrue (Eds.), *Professional responsibility: New horizons of praxis* (pp. 10-28). London/New York: Routledge.

Education, D. D. o. (2010). *The importance of teaching the schools.* White Paper. London: The Stationary Office (HMSO).

Eggleston, J. (1977). *The sociology of the school curriculum.* London: Routletdge, and Kegan Paul.

Englund, T., & Dyrdal Solbrekke, T. (2011). Professional responsibility under pressure? In C. Sugrue & T. Dyrdal Solbrekke (Eds.), *Professional responsibility: New horizons of praxis* (pp. 59-73). London/New York: Routledge.

Ferguson, R. F. (2007). *Towards excellence with equity: An emerging vision for closing the achievement gap.* Cambridge, MA: Harvard Educational Publishing Group.

Freire, P. (1970/2001). *Pedagogy of the oppressed* (Introduction by Donaldo P. Macedo and translated by Myra Bergman Ramos). London: Continuum.

Gardner, H. (2007). *Responsibility at work. How leading professionals act (or don't act) responsibly.* San Francisco: John Wiley & Sons.

Gardner, H., Csikszentmihalyi, M., & Damon, W. (2001). *Good work when excellence and ethics meet.* New York: Basic Books.

Gerhardt, S. (2011). *The selfish society. How we all forgot to love one another and made money instead.* London/New York: Simon & Schuster.

Goodson, I. F., & Sikes, P. (Eds.). (2001). *Life history research in educational settings.* Buckingham/Philadelphia: Open University Press.

Green, B. (Ed.). (2009). *Understanding and researching professional practice.* Rotterdam: Sense Publishers.

Green, J. (2010). *Education, professionalism and the quest for accountability hitting the target by missing the point.* London: Routledge.

Gronn, P. (2003). *The new work of educational leaders changing leadership practice in an era of school reform.* London: Thousand Oaks & New Delhi: Paul Chapman Publishing.

Gronn, P. (2009). Hybrid leadership. In K. Leithwood, B. Mascall, & T. Strauss (Eds.), *Distributed leadership according to the evidence* (pp. 17-40). London/New York: Routledge.

Gross Stein, J. (2001). *The cult of efficiency*. Toronto: Anansi Press.

Hargreaves, A. (2003). *Teaching in the knowledge society*. Buckingham: Open University Press.

Hargeaves, A. (2009). The fourth way of change: Towards an age of inspiration and sustainability. In A. Hargeaves & M. Fullan (Eds.), *Change wards*. Bloomington: Solution Tree.

Hargeaves, A., & Shirley, D. (2009). *The fourth way the inspiring future for educational change*. Thousand Oaks: Sage.

Hargeaves, A., Halasz, G., & Pont, B. (2007). *School leadership for systemic improvement in Finland. A case study report for the OECD activity improving school leadership*. Paris: OECD.

Haslam, S. A., Reicher, S. D., & Platow, M. J. (2011). *The new psychology of leadership identity, influence and power*. Hove: Psychology Press.

Homer-Dixon, T. (2001). *The ingenuity gap*. Toronto: Vintage Canada.

II, Q. E. (2011). The Queen's speect at the Irish State Dinner, 18th May 2011. Retrieved 010512 from www.royal.gov.uk/.

Karseth, B. (2011). Teacher education for professional responsibility: What should it look like? In C. Sugrue & T. Dyrdal Solbrekke (Eds.), *Professional responsibility: New horizons of praxis* (pp. 159-174). London & New York: Routledge.

Lasky, S. (2012). Warehousing the schoolhouse: Impact on teachers' work and lives? In C. Day (Ed.), *Routledge international handbook on teacher and school development* (pp. 73-83). Abingdon/New York Routledge.

Lynd, R. S., & Lynd, H. M. (1929). *Middletown: A study in modern American culture*. New York: Harcourt, Brace & World Inc.

Mackenzie, C., & Stoljar, N. (Eds.). (2000). *Relational autonomy feminist perspectives on autonomy, agency, and the social self*. New York/Oxford: Oxford University Press.

Manning, D. (1990). *Hill Country teachers oral histories from the one-room schools and beyond*. Boston: Twayne Publishers.

May, L. (1996). *The socially responsive self. Social theory and professional ethics*. Chicago: Chicago University Press.

Nussbaum, M. C. (2011). *Creating capabilities: The human development approach*. Cambridge, MA: The Belknap Press of Harvard University Press.

OECD. (2010). *PISA 2009 Results: What students know and can do – Student performance in reading, mathematics and science*. Paris: OECD.

Postman, N. (1979). *Teaching as a conserving activity*. New York Delacorte Press.

Power, M. (1999). *The Audity Society rituals of verification*. Oxford: Oxford University Press.

Sachs, J. (2004). *The activist teaching profession*. Buckingham/Philadelphia: Open University Press.

Sagakian, W. S., & Sahakian, M. L. (1966). *The ideas of the great philosophers*. New York: Barnes & Noble Books.

Saltman, K. J., & Gabbard, D. A. (2003). *Education as enforcement: The militarization and corporatization of schools*. New York & London: Routledge Falmer.

Sugrue, C. (2005). Revisiting student teachers' lay theories and cultural arcetypes of teaching. In D. Beijaard, P. Meijer, G. Morine-Dershimer, & H. Tillema (Eds.), *Teacher professional development in changing conditions*. Dordrecht: Springer.

Sugrue, C. (2008). Epilogue: The future of educational change? In C. Sugrue (Ed.), *The future of educational change. International perspectives*. London/New York: Routledge.

Sugrue, C. (2012). Conjuncture and disjuncture in teachers' work and lives: Introduction. In C. Day (Ed.), *Routledge International handbook on teacher and school development*. Abingdon/New York: Routledge.

Sugrue, C., & Fentiman, A. (2012). Teachers' work and lives in sub-Saharan Africa: Outsider perspectives In C. Day (Ed.), *The Routledge international handbook of teacher and school development* (pp. 108-120). Abingdon/New York: Routledge.

Waller, W. (1932). *Sociology of teaching*. New York/London/Sydney: John Wiley and Sons (reprinted 1993 by University Microfilms International, Ann Arbor).

Wieder, A. (2003). *Voices from Cape Town classrooms: Oral histories of teachers who fought Aparteid*. New York: Peter Lang Publishers.

CIARAN SUGRUE

Wolff, J., & De-Shalt, A. (2007/2010). *Disadvantage*. Oxford: Oxford University Press.
Zimbardo, P. (2007). *The Lucifer effect how good people turn evil*. New York: Random House.

AFFILIATIONS

Ciaran Sugrue
School of Education
University of College Dublin, Ireland

CHRISTOPHER DAY

THE NEW LIVES OF TEACHERS[i]

INTRODUCTION

It is almost a truism to note, from reflecting upon experiences and a range of largely small scale qualitative research internationally, that personal biographies and the contexts in which these are played out influence who we are and how we behave as professionals – our motivations, beliefs, aspirations; and that our identities and our practices are in part influenced by these and in part by the personal, workplace and socio-cultural contexts in which we work – what Ivor Goodson calls 'genealogies of context.' In my own case, had it not been for the encouragement of a parent, the impact of a teacher educator and a lucky escape from delinquency, I would not have become a teacher. But the teacher I was is not the teacher I am. I, like most people, have been affected by a host of people, events, environments and unanticipated personal and professional experiences.

During my career first as a classroom teacher, then a teacher educator, local authority schools adviser (superintendent) and finally a university researcher and teacher, I have experienced life in education from a variety of perspectives. I published my first piece when I had been teaching for two years and I continue to learn though my own writing and through that of others. There are many across the world from whose work and colleagueship I have learned; and it is through such self study, learning from others throughout my career and a determination that all children and young people are entitled to the best education that have caused me to remain passionate about the quality of education and, therefore, the work of teachers upon which this largely, though not exclusively, depends.

THE NEW LIVES OF TEACHERS

The Depending upon our own ontological and epistemological positioning we may believe that it is: i) the meganarratives or grand stories (Cohen & Garet, 1975) of broader performativity, results driven, contexts which determine the changes in nature, shape and direction of the new work and lives of teachers; or ii) that the accumulation and persistence of what are sometimes called "small stories" (Georgakopolou, 2004) show that these only influence and thus may be mediated by individual and collective agency aided by a strength of vocation, the passion of moral purpose. Some researchers position themselves in a critical sociological perspective, often using Bourdieu (1970) or Foucault (1976) as their theoretical mentors. These researchers tend to write about teachers and schools as victims of policy driven imperatives as bureaucratic surveillance and new pervasive forms of

M.A. Flores et al. (eds.), Back to the Future: Legacies, Continuities and Changes in Educational Policy, Practice and Research, 57–74.

contractual accountability which (wrongly) assume a direct causal link between good teaching, good learning and measurable student attainments persist and increase. I see research evidence of this but research evidence, also, of teachers who remain skilful, knowledgeable, committed and resilient regardless of circumstance

I subscribe to what Judyth Sachs identifies as the "activist professional" (Sachs, 2003). By a predisposition to hope, persistence in believing that I can make a difference to the lives of those who I teach, knowledge of a range of research and by conducting research which keeps me close to teachers, for example, through a networked learning community of schools in one city in England, now about to celebrate a decade of teacher inquiry endeavours, I am persuaded that, like me, many teachers, despite some 'bumpy moments,' also maintain their commitment to teach to their best across a career and in changing, sometimes challenging, circumstances. We see this in the in-depth work of Susan Moore Johnson and her colleagues (2004) with new teachers, in Nieto (2003) and Hansen's (2001) writings, in the professional learning communities reported by Ann Lieberman and Bob Bullough's recent writings of happiness, hope and hopefulness.

New Lives, Old Truths

The work and lives of teachers have always been subject to external influence as those who are nearing the end of their careers will attest, but it is arguable that what is new over the last two decades is the pace, complexity and intensity of change as governments have responded to the shrinking world of economic competitiveness and social migration by measuring progress against their position in international league tables. This is in part the reason I have called this address the 'New Lives of Teachers.' Parallel to these are the growing concerns with the new generation of 'screen culture' children who, suggests one author (Greenfield, 2008), spend more time interacting with technology than with family or at school and whose attention span and sense of empathy are diminishing alongside real and potential conflicts in increasingly heterogeneous societies.

As a result, there are regularly repeated claims that teacher educators are failing to prepare their students well enough and so, as in my own country, governments promote apprenticeship models of training (not education) (Donaldson Review, 2011; Hobson et al., 2009; Holmes Report, 1986). 'Teach for America' is one of the models borrowed by my own current government. Schools are encouraged to become 'Teaching Schools' which buy in teacher educators, who themselves are subject to new functionalist performativity demands. In these forms of teacher education students spend most of their time in schools learning the craft of teaching but not necessarily developing their thinking, capacities for reflection and their emotional understandings; for teaching at its best is an intellectual and emotional endeavour.

In the new lives of teachers, schools and classrooms have become, for many, sites of struggle as financial self-reliance and pressure for ideological compliance have emerged as the twin realities. Externally imposed curricula, management innovations and monitoring and performance assessment systems have been introduced but have often been poorly implemented, and resulted in periods of destabilisation, increased workload, intensification of work and a crisis of professional identify for many teachers who perceive a loss of public confidence in their ability to provide a good service.

Governments seem not quite to realise the results of a range of robust, well documented research that tell us: i) teachers' commitment to their work will increase student commitment (Bryk & Driscoll, 1988; Louis, 1998; Rosenholtz, 1989); and ii) enthusiastic teachers (who are knowledgeable and skilled) who have a sense of vocation and organisational belonging work harder to make learning more meaningful for students, even those who may be difficult or unmotivated (Day & Leithwood, 2007; Guskey & Passaro, 1994). While governments in different countries of the world have introduced reforms in different ways at different paces, change is nevertheless not optional but, it is said, is a part of the "post-modern" condition, which requires political, organisational, economic, social and personal flexibility and responsiveness (Hargreaves, 1994). Little wonder that the postmodern condition for many teachers represents more of a threat than a challenge, or that many are confused by the paradox of decentralised systems (i.e. local decision-making responsibilities), alongside increased public scrutiny and external accountability, and the associated bureaucratic burdens.

There are many other examples worldwide and educational researchers continue to critique policy and its consequences for recruitment, quality and retention. However, it is important, having set the scene, to look more closely at what a range of research tells us about the new lives of teachers in terms of their continuing capacity to teach to their best.

Lessons from Michael Huberman's Research

More than 30 years ago, Huberman conducted a preliminary study (1978-79) with 30 teachers followed by an extended study (1982-85) with 160 secondary level teachers of all subjects in Geneva and Vaud two cantons (districts) of Switzerland. Roughly two-thirds taught at lower secondary and the rest at upper secondary. There were slightly more women than men. Four 'experience groups' were chosen: 5-10 years of experience, 11-19 years of experience, 20-29 years of experience, and 30-39 years of experience. During a series of 5-hour interviews, informants were asked to review their career trajectory and to see whether they could carve it up into phases or stages, each with a theme and identifiable features.

The career development 'process' that Huberman's research revealed, filled as it is with "plateaux, discontinuities, regressions, spurts and dead ends" (1995, p. 196), has become the touchstone for researchers in this field world-wide.

Writing in 1995 about professional careers and professional development, Huberman (1995) stated:

The hypothesis is fairly obvious: Teachers have different aims and different dilemmas at various moments in their professional cycle, and their desires to reach out for more information, knowledge, expertise and technical competence will vary accordingly ... A core assumption here is that there will be commonalities among teachers in the sequencing of their professional lives and that one particular form of professional development may be appropriate to these shared sequences ... (p. 193)

He suggested that we:

can begin to identify modal profiles of the teaching career and, from these, see what determines more and less 'successful' or 'satisfactory' careers ... identify the conditions under which a particular phase in the career cycle is lived out happily or miserably and, from these, put together an appropriate support structure. (Huberman, 1995, p. 194)

However, in a typical self critical note – a characteristic worthy of the best researchers – he warned of the ways in which ontogenetic, psychological research underestimates, as he had the organisational effects and the importance (and influence) of social and historical factors. In addition, there continues to be is a need to conduct empirical research on teachers' professional life trajectories in all countries, for, as he acknowledged, his own work was limited by the cultural effect of a homogeneous teaching population and did not take place in times of turbulence in teaching.

Huberman was not afraid to speak to policy makers directly with the power of his findings:

Minimally, sustaining professional growth seems to require manageable working conditions, opportunities – and sometimes demands – to experiment modestly without sanctions if things go awry, periodic shifts in role assignments without a corresponding loss of prerequisites, regular access to collegial expertise and external stimulation, and a reasonable chance to achieve significant outcomes in the classroom. These are not utopian conditions. It may just be the case, in fact, that they have not been met more universally because policy and administrative personnel have not deliberately attended to them. (1995, p. 206)

Michael Huberman's (1995) research provided a springboard for much of my own and others. Until recently, however, there have been few large scale longitudinal studies of teachers' lives and work and even those have tended to focus upon the first 0-5 year period of teaching, perhaps since this is where traditionally there has been considerable attrition (Moore-Johnson, 2004). The 'VITAE' project was a four year national mixed methods study of 300 primary and secondary teachers in 100 schools in seven regions of England who were in different phases of their professional lives (Day, Sammons, Stobart, Kington, & Gu, 2007). That study, which I was privileged to lead, was designed to investigate variations in teachers' effectiveness over their careers. Effectiveness was defined as that which was both perceived by teachers themselves and by student progress and attainment which was measured in terms of attainment results over a three year consecutive period. It is complemented by the work of my colleagues in the International Successful School Principals Project (ISSPP), a 14 country, highly collaborative research network of researchers which now has the largest international collection of now more than 100 case studies of principals who have built and sustained success in different contexts and sectors (Day & Leithwood, 2007; Moos, Day, & Johansson, 2011); and by the findings of a national, three year mixed methods project in England which focussed upon associations between effective school principals and pupil outcomes (Day et al., 2011). The findings of these and other recent research in this area (e.g. Robinson, Hohepa, & Lloyd, 2009) are profoundly important for their contributions to knowledge of conditions which contribute to teacher quality, retention and achievement (for example, values, democratic leadership, collegiality, professional learning, learning communities, and forms of distributed leadership and trust) in ways which go far beyond those available to Michael Huberman (1995). The leadership literature tells us much about school environments in which teachers flourish and in which they are likely to sustain commitment as well as competence, a sense of well being and positive professional identity; and teachers over the years are consistent in telling us that where they experience sustained support, both personally outside and professionally inside their workplace, they are able not only to cope with but also positively manage adverse circumstances - in other words, to be resilient.

It is this close connection between teachers' lives, their work, its contexts and its effectiveness for students and school leadership which marks the focus of my own work over the last decade in particular. 'New Lives, Old Truths' is the title of the final chapter of the second book which arose from the VITAE project. Whereas the first, "Teachers Matter: Connecting Work, Lives and Effectiveness"(Day et al., 2007), reported on and discussed the mixed methods project design and findings about variations in teachers' perceived and measured effectiveness and the reasons for this, the second, 'The New Lives of Teachers' (Day & Gu, 2010) draws primarily upon new qualitative data drawn from the project in order to tell the stories of teachers in what my co-author, Qing Gu, and I identified as teachers' 'professional life phases' (PLPs) in order to distinguish these from career phases, a term usually associated more with role changes.

What we learnt about teachers who experience these PLPs enabled us to identify generic similarities and differences within each phase. It also allowed the identification of critical incidents or phases and, through these, provided new insights into positive and negative variations in personal, workplace and socio-cultural and policy conditions which teachers experience across a career and the consequences for teacher and students if support is not available. We found that teachers' ongoing capacities, commitment and passion to teach to their best for the benefit of their students relate to:

− *professional life phase;*
− *the relative instability and stability of their sense of identity − so important to their sense of self-efficacy and agency;*
− *a passion for teaching: commitment, wellbeing and effectiveness.*

Professional life phases. We identified six professional life phases. We found that teachers' commitment, well being, identity and effectiveness varied within and between these and that, within each phase, there were those whose commitment was rising, being sustained despite challenging circumstances, or declining (see Figure 1).

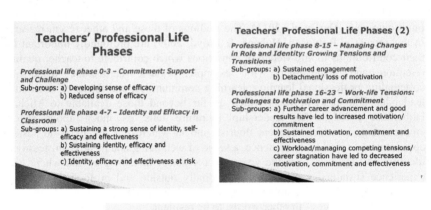

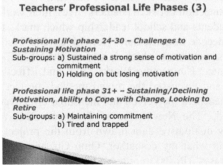

Figure 1. Professional life phases

The majority of teachers in the VITAE research maintained their effectiveness but did not necessarily become more effective over time. Indeed, we found that the commitment of teachers in late professional life phases, though remaining high for many, is more likely to decline than those in early and middle years (see Figure 2).

It is especially important to note also that the commitment and resilience of teachers in schools serving more disadvantaged communities where relational ties are the "sources of reservoirs of resilience" (Tonnies, 2001, p. 27), are more persistently challenged than others. One implication of this is that schools, especially those which serve disadvantaged communities, need to ensure that their CPD provision is relevant to the commitment, resilience and health needs of teachers in each of their professional life phases.

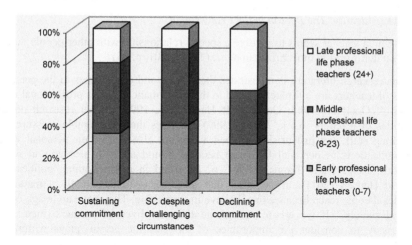

Figure 2. Teachers' commitment by professional life phase (Day et al., 2007)

Given the nature of teaching, particularly in inimical reform contexts, this is, perhaps unsurprising. An implication of this finding is that national organisations and schools need to target strategies for professional learning and development to support teachers in the later phases of their careers. Teachers will move backwards and forwards within and between phases during their working lives for all kinds of reasons concerning personal history, psychological, social and systemic change factors. Taking on a new role, changing schools, teaching a new age group or new syllabus or learning to work in new ways in the classroom will almost inevitably result in development disruption, at least temporarily. It is clear from this that there are problems, in a changing world, with assuming that the acquisition of expertise through experience marks the end of the learning journey. Huberman's (1995) work also provides an important in principle critique of linear, 'stage' models of professional development which ignore the complexity and dynamic of classroom life, the discontinuities of learning; and points to the importance of continuing regular and differentiated opportunities for deliberative, systematic reflection 'on' and 'about' experience as a way of locating and extending understandings of the broad and narrow contexts of teaching and learning, and reviewing and renewing commitment and capacities for effectiveness.

Becoming an expert does not mean that learning ends – hence the importance of maintaining the ability to be a lifelong inquirer. Experienced teachers who are successful, far from being at the end of their learning journeys, are those who retain their ability to be self-conscious about their teaching and are constantly aware of and responsive to the learning possibilities inherent in each teaching episode and individual interaction.

Teacher Identity: The Person in the Professional.

> Being a teacher seems to involve a special relationship with other people that
> you don't find in most professions … (Trier, 2001, p. 35)

Much research literature demonstrates that events and experiences in the personal
lives of teachers are intimately linked to the performance of their professional roles
(Ball & Goodson, 1985; Goodson & Hargreaves, 1996). In her research on the
realities of teachers' work, Acker (1999) describes the considerable pressures on
teaching staff, not just arising in their work but also from their personal lives.
Complications in personal lives can become bound up with problems at work.
Woods, Jeffrey, and Troman (1997, p. 152) and in a forthcoming publication,
David Hansen (2011), argue, also, that teaching is fundamentally a matter of
values. People teach because they believe in something. They have an image of the
'good society.' If we are to understand the new lives of teachers, then, it is
necessary to consider the importance of the part the person plays within the
professional. This is essential because a raft of literature points to teaching as an
essentially human endeavour in which who the teacher is as important as what she
teaches (Beijaard, 1995; Bullough & Knowles, 1991; Hamachek, 1999;
Kelchtermans, 2009; Korthagen, 2004; Nias, 1989; Palmer, 2007; Russell, 2007).

> … paying attention to the connection of the personal and the professional in
> teaching … may contribute to educational goals that go far beyond the
> development of the individual teacher. (Meijer, Korthagen, &Vasalos, 2009,
> p. 308)

Several researchers (Hargreaves, 1994; Nias, 1989, 1996; Nias, Southworth, &
Campbell, 1992; Sumsion, 2002) have also noted that teacher identities are not
only constructed from the more technical aspects of teaching (i.e. classroom
management, subject knowledge and pupil test results) but, as Van Den Berg
(2002) explains:

> … can be conceptualised as the result of an interaction between the personal
> experiences of teachers and the social, cultural and institutional environment
> in which they function on a daily basis. (p. 579)

It matters enormously what kind of person the teacher is because:

> … those of us who are teachers cannot stand before a class without standing
> for something … teaching is testimony. (Patterson, 1991, p. 16)

There is, then, an unavoidable interrelationship between the personal and the
professional if only because the overwhelming evidence is that teaching demands
significant personal investment. So when we think of the importance to good
teaching of a positive, stable identity, it is necessary to construe such identity as
being made up of these elements.

Dimensions of Identity. Professional identity is influenced by biography and
experience, life outside the school and reflects social and policy expectations of

what a good teacher is, workplace conditions and relationships and the educational ideals of the teacher. The VITAE project found that professional identity was, for the three hundred participating teachers, a composite of the interaction in different work scenarios between socio-cultural/policy, workplace, and personal dimensions and that it was not always stable or positive (Day & Kington, 2008; Day et al., 2011).

Interviews with these teachers over a three year period revealed four scenarios or sites of struggle which reflected different relationships between the three dimensions of identity:
- The first was holding the three in balance. The dominant characteristics of this group of teachers included being highly motivated, committed, and self-efficacious;
- In the second scenario, one dimension was dominant, for example, immediate school demands dominating and impacting on the other two;
- In the third scenario two dimensions dominated and impacted on the third;
- The fourth scenario represented a state of extreme fluctuation within and between each dimension.

Teachers from across the professional life phases who expressed a positive sense of agency, resilience and commitment in all scenarios spoke of the influence of in-school leadership, colleague and personal support. The supporting factors mentioned most frequently by teachers who expressed a positive, stable sense of identity (67%) were:
- *Leadership (76%)*. It is good to know that we have strong leadership who has a clear vision for the school (Larissa, year 6);
- *Colleagues (63%)*. We have such supportive team here. Everyone works together and we have a common goal to work towards (Hermione, year 2). We all socialize together and have become friends over time. I do not know what we'd do if someone left (Leon, year 9);
- *Personal (95%)*. It helps having a supportive family who do not get frustrated when I'm sat working on a Sunday afternoon and they want to go to the park (Shaun, year 9).

Teachers who judged their effectiveness to be at risk or declining (33%) spoke of negative pressures. Those mentioned most frequently were:
- *Workload (68%)*. It never stops, there is always something more to do and it eats away at your life until you have no social life and no time for anything but work (Jarvis, year 6). Your life has to go on hold – there is not enough time in the school day to do everything (Hermione, year 2);
- *Student behaviour (64%)*. Over the years, pupils have got worse. They have no respect for themselves or the teachers (Jenny, year 6). Pupil behaviour is one of the biggest problems in schools today. They know their rights and there is nothing you can do (Kathryn, year 9);
- *Leadership (58%)*. Unless the leadership supports the staff, you are on your own. They need to be visible and need to appreciate what teachers are doing (Carmelle, year 2). I feel as if I'm constantly being picked on and told I'm doing something wrong (Jude, year 9).

65

An implication of this finding is that strategies for sustaining commitment in initial and continuing professional development programs should differentiate between the needs of teachers in different phases of their professional lives and experiencing different sites of struggle which may threaten their sense of positive stable identity and sense of wellbeing.

A Passion for Teaching: Commitment, Wellbeing and Effectiveness. A lesson from the VITAE project and a range of research internationally (Day, 2004) is that passion for teaching, a commitment to understand and educate every learner, is necessary if teachers are to teach to their best, but that this may grow or die according to changes in personal and work circumstances. Being passionate about others' learning and achievement creates energy and fuels determination, conviction and commitment. Yet passion should not be regarded only as a disposition – people are not born, nor do they die, passionate. Whilst many teachers enter the profession with a sense of vocation and with a passion to give their best to the learning and growth of their pupils, for some, these become diminished with the passage of time, changing external and internal working conditions and contexts and unanticipated personal events. They lose their sense of purpose and well-being which are so intimately connected with their positive sense of professional identity and which enable them to draw upon, deploy and manage the inherently dynamic emotionally vulnerable contexts of teaching in which they teach and in which their pupils learn.

Without organisational support, bringing a passionate and resilient self to teaching effectively every day of every week of every school term and year can be stressful not only to the body but also to the heart and soul, for the processes of teaching and learning are rarely smooth, and the results are not always predictable. Thus, the commitment, hope and optimism with which many teachers still enter the profession, unless supported within the school, may be eroded over time as managing combinations of low level disruption from those who don't wish to learn or cannot, or interfere with others' opportunities to learn, increasing media criticisms and lack of work-life balance take their toll on professional wellbeing.

Teacher well-being is both a psychological and social construct:

> … a dynamic state, in which the individual is able to develop their potential, work productively and creatively, build strong and positive relationships with others, and contribute to their community. (Foresight Mental Capital and Wellbeing Project, 2008, p. 10)

To achieve and sustain a healthy state of well being, teachers need to manage successfully a range of cognitive and emotional challenges in different, sometimes difficult sites of struggle which vary according to life experiences and events, the strength of relationships with pupils and parents, the conviction of educational ideals, sense of efficacy and agency and the support of colleagues and school leadership. As Moore Johnson (2004) reminds us:

... anyone familiar with schools knows that stories about the easy job of teaching are sheer fiction. Good teaching is demanding and exhausting work, even in the best of work places ... (p. 10)

Experience and research, then, suggest that, in terms of nurturing well being, a dichotomy between promoting technical competence and personal growth among teachers is a false economy. Rather, teachers at their best combine their professional craft expertise with their personal commitment, experience and values in their work in the knowledge that teaching cannot be devoid from an interest in and engagement with the learner. In other words, it is the extent to which both learner, teacher and teaching content are all fully 'present' which will influence, in interaction with the internal and external environments, the quality of the process and its results. This journey of the personal and the professional in the here and now of teaching is what Csikszentmihalyi (1990) calls 'flow' and Rodgers and Raider-Roth (2006) term, 'presence':

Presence from the teacher's point of view is the experience of bringing one's whole self to full attention so as to perceive what is happening the moment. (Rodgers & Raider-Roth, 2006, p. 267)

Many writers on teacher education focus on the role and presence of the teacher in the classroom (Meijer et al., 2009), emphasising the need for personal strengths or core qualities such as care, courage, fairness, kindness, honesty, perseverance (Frederickson, 2002; Noddings, 2003; Palmer, 2004; Seligman, 2002; Sockett, 1993). Others have combined this with research on the nature, purposes and forms of reflection in, on and about education (Schön, 1983), and developed humanistic pedagogies of teacher education which emphasise the importance to good teaching practice of understanding and interrogating teachers' own belief systems (Loughran, 2004) and the interchange between these teaching contexts and purposes (Korthagen & Vasalos, 2005).

Teacher presence, whilst a necessary condition for successful teaching, is, however, not sufficient to achieve optimal learning. Students themselves must also be willing and able to be present. At this point, it is worth once again bringing to the attention of policy makers the observation that there is no necessary direct cause and effect relationship between high quality teaching and student learning (Fenstermacher & Richardson, 2005).

Five key observations about the qualities evident in good teaching and teachers have been made by researchers across the world:

– Good teaching is recognised by its combination of technical and personal competencies, deep subject knowledge and empathy with the learners (Hargreaves, 1998, 2001; Palmer, 1998). Teachers as people (the person in the professional, the being within the action) cannot be separated from teachers as professionals (Nias, 1989). Teachers invest themselves in their work. Teaching at its best, in other words, is a passionate affair (Day, 2004);

– Good teachers are universally identified by students as those who care. They care for them as part of their exercise of their professional duty and their care about them is shown in the connectiveness of their everyday classroom

interactions as well as their concern for their general wellbeing and achievement (Ashley & Lee, 2003; Fletcher-Campbell, 1995; Noddings, 1992);
- Teachers' sense of identity and agency (the means by which they respond, reflect upon and manage the interface between their educational ideals, beliefs, work environments and broader social and policy contexts) are crucial to their own motivation, commitment, wellbeing and capacity to teach to their best. It is how they define themselves as 'teacher' (Day & Lee, 2011; Schutz & Zembylas, 2010);
- The extent to which teachers are able to understand emotions within themselves and others is related to their ability to lead and manage teaching and learning. Good teaching, "requires the connection of emotion with self-knowledge" (Denzin, 1984; Harris, 2007; Zembylas, 2003, p. 213);
- To be a good and effective teacher over time requires hopefulness and resilience, the ability to manage and lead in challenging circumstances and changing contexts (Bullough, 2011; Day & Gu, 2010; Gu & Day, 2007).

THE ROLE OF TEACHER EDUCATOR RESEARCHERS

Finally, I want to grasp a difficult nettle which continues to be a source of discussion in universities and colleges. It concerns the role, influence and impact of teacher educators who are also researchers as part of their commitment to learning. In his paper in Teacher Education Quarterly (Fall, 2008) Bob Bullough wrote that in the current political context, researchers have, as Goodson (1992) earlier argued, a special obligation: "to assure that 'the teacher's voice is heard, heard loudly, heard articulately" (p. 112). It would be difficult not to agree with Bob Bullough that, "... At this moment in time, as we research teachers' lives there may be no more important task before us than championing the cause of teachers and making clear the ineluctable connection between their well-being and the well-being of children" (Bullough, 2008, p. 23).

However, in involving ourselves in research with teachers and schools, as university researcher educators and researchers we also need appropriate competencies:

> ... the competence to cross borders, cultures and dialects, the learning and translating of multiple languages (the political, the everyday, the academic) and the courage to transgress when faced with social injustices ... How we practice our authority is then the issue, not what we claim or profess: if we believe in something then we have to practice it. (Walker, 1996)

Finley's (2005) metaphor of 'border crossings,' together with Becher's (1989) metaphor of 'tribes and territories' provide vivid illustrations of the persisting separation cultures both between university researchers and between researchers and teachers. In addition, the environments in which teachers teach and in which our research is conducted have become more problematic. So called neo liberal, 'performativity,' results driven agendas have invaded and changed our worlds of work, threatening hard won and treasured practices and professional identities. In academia, we see this especially through the creeping erosion of time to conduct research, as bureaucratic procedures continue to increase; through the rise of research funding which is tied to short term government agendas in some countries; and, in others, the imposition of national research assessment exercises associated with league tables and increases or decreases in finance, social citation indexes and judgements of research worthiness based upon evidence of impact on the user communities.

The implications of drawing lines of separation between policy makers, professional researchers (from the academy) and 'other' researchers (in schools) without considering their complementarity and respective development need to be carefully considered, lest continuing separation does a disservice to all. The evidence still points to a lack of use by teachers of much research where they themselves have not been involved in the research process. We know well that, 'the gap between educational research and practice is a more complex and differentiated phenomenon than commonly assumed in the international literature' (Vanderlinde & van Broakk, 2010, pp. 311-312).

The separation between the school teaching, policy-making and academic communities which exists partly because of history, partly because of function and partly because of collusion *need not continue*. Worlds which emphasise the systematic gathering of knowledge, the questioning and challenge of ideology, formal examination of experience, professional criticism and seemingly endless discussion of possibilities rather than solutions, need not necessarily conflict with those dominated by unexamined ideology, action, concrete knowledge and busyness. Although it is interesting to observe that as researchers from universities and other agencies seek to work more closely with teachers and schools, policy formulation becomes more distant, there are examples of growing understandings of the possibilities for their complementarity. Research needs to be more open, more amenable to those interest groups which seek to influence policy. Part of higher education's responsibility is to use our 'room to manoeuvre,' to critique policy where it flies in the face of research, to be rigorous in our own research, whether separate from or in collaboration with teachers; and to communicate with rather than colonise the voices of practitioners. In order to do this we need to maintain and develop critical engagement with policy-makers, interest groups and practitioners.

Ball and Forzani (2007) claim that:

> At the centre of every school of education must be scholars with the expertise and commitment necessary to study educational transactions … (and that) … if they do not work actively to disseminate that knowledge among policy makers and members of the public, then educational problem solving will be left to researchers and professionals without the requisite expertise … Educational researchers must also arm themselves with the special analytical skills that will allow them to usefully bridge the alleged divide between theory and practice. It is along this divide that educational researchers have special expertise. (p. 537)

Essentially, Ball and Forzani (2007) are identifying what we call in England, 'the elephant in the room,' something so obvious that we often overlook its huge importance. In this case, there are two elephants: researcher independence and moral purpose. Whilst all of us would support Ivor Goodson's articulation of the researcher as independent, "a public intellectual, not a servant of the state" (Goodson, 1999), I would argue that alongside independence is moral purpose, a sense of deep responsibility of contributing to the 'betterment' of society though our work on, about, with and for teachers. As researchers, we do need to acknowledge what research tells us about ourselves, our endeavours and our influence (or lack of it). There are sceptics among teachers and policy makers – and even researchers of different ontological and epistemological dispositions – about the intrinsic value of research and about its relevance, language and applicability. However, there are also examples of research which does lead to greater educational understandings, which influences policy and practice, which, ultimately, makes a difference to the contexts and quality of teachers' and childrens' experiences in schools and classrooms.

No single model of research will necessarily be best fitted to bridge the gap. However, whether research is constructed and conducted primarily for the purpose of furthering understanding or for more direct influence on policy makers and practitioners, whether it is on, about or for education, the obligation of all researchers is to reflect upon our broader moral purposes and measure the worth of our work against their judgement of the extent to which we are able to realise this as we continue to develop our work.

THE CHALLENGE TO BE THE BEST

The challenge for university faculties, schools and departments of education, then, is to engage in strategic planning in which our capacity to respond to schools' agendas as well as to take forward those of the academy can be heightened. In developing new kinds of relationships with schools and teachers, we will be demonstrating a service-wide commitment in which traditional expertise (e.g. in research and knowledge production) is combined with new expertise in cooperative and collaborative knowledge creation, development and consultancy that are part of a more diverse portfolio that connects more closely with the needs of the school community at large. Such a portfolio would demonstrate the commitment of university educators to improving teaching and learning in collaboration with schools and teachers through capacity-building partnerships through, for example, participatory forms of research, in addition to an ongoing commitment to producing knowledge about education and generating knowledge for education (Carr & Kemmis, 1986), through more traditional forms of outsider research which could be utilised and tested by the system for which it has been produced, both directly and indirectly. Currently perceived problems of credibility, relevance of research and fitness for purpose of programmes of study would thus be minimised.

The challenge to be the best, then, not only applies to teachers, but also to us as researchers whose work aims to further understandings of their work and lives in their personal, work place and policy-related contexts and, in some cases, to influence them. To be the best ourselves requires us to be partisan (we are for teachers) but dispassionate, to be both close up and distant to our work and, like teachers at their best, to monitor and reflect on the efficacy, processes and impact of our work upon the policy and practice communities we seek to influence. Like Michael Huberman (1995), to whom the work of all who are engaged in research on the work and lives of teachers owes a lasting debt, I urge us all to be active always in checking out and giving voice to the connections, at all levels, between policy, research and practice, and most of all to become and remain, with integrity and passion, as he was and I remain, 'recklessly curious.'

NOTES

[i] This paper was first published in the Winter 2012 issue of Teacher Education Quarterly.

REFERENCES

Acker, S. (1999). *The realities of teachers' work: Never a dull moment*. London: Cassell.

Ashley, M., & Lee, J. (2003). *Women teaching boys: Caring and working in the primary school*. Stoke on Trent: Trenthan Books.

Ball, D. L., & Forzani, F. M. (2007). What makes education research 'educational'? *Educational Researcher, 36*(9), 529-540.

Ball, S. J., & Goodson, I. (1985). *Teachers' lives and careers*. Lewes: Falmer Press.

Becher, T. (1989). *Academic tribes and territories. Intellectual enquiry and the cultures of disciplines*. Milton Keynes: The Society for Research into Higher Education and Open University Press.

Beijaard, D. (1995). Teachers' prior experiences and actual perceptions of professional identity. *Teachers and Teaching: Theory and Practice, 1*, 281-294.

Bourdieu, P. (1970). *La reproduction. Elements pour une theorie du systeme d'enseignement* (Paris, Editions de iinuit) (with J. C. Passeron). Translated by R. Nice as *Reproduction in education, society, and culture* (1977) (Second edition, 1990, with a new preface by Bourdieu). London/ Beverley Hills: Sage Publications.

Bryk, A., & Driscoll, M. (1988). *The high school as community: Contextual influences and consequences for students and teachers*. Madison: University of Wisconsin, National Center on Effective Secondary Schools.

Bullough, R. V. (2008). The writing of teachers' lives – Where personal troubles and social issues meet. *Teacher Education Quarterly*, Fall, 2008.

Bullough, R. V. (2011). Hope, happiness, teaching and learning. In C. Day & J. C. K. Lee (Eds.), *New understandings of teacher's work: Emotions and educational change* (pp. 17-32). New York: Springer.

Bullough, R. V. Jr., Knowles, J. G., & Crow, N. A. (1991). *Emerging as a teacher*. London: Routledge.

Carr, W., & Kemmis, S. (1986). *Becoming critical. Education, knowledge and action research*. Lewes: Falmer.

Cohen, D. K., & Garet, M. S. (1975). Reforming educational policy with applied social research. *Harvard Educational Review, 45*(1), 17-43.

Csikszentmihalyi, M. (1990). *Flow: The psychology of optimal experience*. New York: Harper & Row.

Day, C. (2004). *A passion for teaching*. London: Routledge Falmer.

Day, C. (Ed.). (2011). *International handbook of teacher and school development*. London: Routledge.

Day, C., & Gu, Q. (2010). *The new lives of teachers*. London: Routledge.

Day, C., & Kington, A. (2008). Identity, well-being and effectiveness: The emotional contexts of teaching. *Pedagogy, Culture & Society, 16*(1), 7-23.

Day, C., & Lee, J. C. K. (Eds). (2011). *New understandings of teacher's work: Emotions and educational change*. Dordrecht: Springer.

Day, C., & Leithwood, K. (Eds.). (2007). *Successful principal leadership in times of change: International perspectives.* Dordrecht: Springer.

Day, C., Sammons, P., Leithwood, K., Hopkins, D., Gu, Q., Brown, E., & Ahtaridou, E. (2011). *School leadership and student outcomes: Building and sustaining success.* Maidenhead: Open University Press.

Day, C., Sammons, P., Stobart, G., Kington, A., & Gu, Q. (2007). *Teachers matter: Connecting lives, work and effectiveness.* New York: McGraw Hill.

Denzin, N. (1984). *On understanding emotion.* San Francisco: Jossey-Bass.

Donaldson, G. (2011). *Teaching Scotland's future: Report of a review of teacher education in Scotland.* Scottish Government, January 2011.

Fenstermacher, G. D., & Richardson, V. (2005). On making determinations of quality in teaching. *Teachers College Record, 107*(1), 186-213.

Finley, A. (2005). Arts-based inquiry: Performing revolutionary pedagogy. In N. K. Denzin & Y. S. Lincoln (Eds.), *Handbook of qualitative inquiry* (3rd edition) (pp. 681-694). Thousand Oaks, CA: Sage Publications.

Fletcher-Campbell, F. (1995). Caring about caring? *Pastoral Care,* September, 26-8.

Foresight Mental Capital and Wellbeing Project (2008). *Final Project Report.* London: The Government Office for Science.

Foucault, M. (1976). *The history of sexuality. Volume 1, The will to knowledge.* London: Penguin Books.

Fredrickson, B. L. (2002). Postive emotions. In C. R. Snyder & S. J. Lopez (Eds.), *Handbook of positive psychology* (pp. 120-134). Oxford: Oxford University Press.

Georgakopoulou, A. (2004, May). *Narrative analysis workshop: How to work with narrative data.* Paper presented at Narrative Matters 2004: An Interdisciplinary Conference on Narrative Perspectives, Approach, and Issues across the Humanities and Social Sciences. Fredericton, New Brunswick, Canada.

Goodson, I. F. (1992). Life histories and the study of schooling. *Interchange, 11*(4), 62-76.

Goodson, I. (1999). The educational researcher as a public intellectual. *British Educational Research Journal, 25*(3), 277-297.

Goodson, I., & Hargreaves, A. (Eds.). (1996). *Teachers' professional lives.* London: Falmer Press.

Greenfield, S. (2008). *Autonomy, creativity and social relationships in early learning.* Researcher-Practitioner Seminar, Oxford Brookes University.

Gu, Q., & Day, C. (2007). Teachers' resilience: A necessary condition for effectiveness. *Teaching and Teacher Education, 23*(8), 1302-1316.

Guskey, T. R., & Passaro, P. D. (1994). Teacher efficacy: A study of construct dimensions. *American Educational Research Journal, 31*(3), 627-643.

Hamachek, D. (1999). Effective teachers: What they do, how they do it, and the importance of self-knowledge. In R. P. Lipka & T. M. Brinthaupt (Eds.), *The role of self in teacher development* (pp. 189-224). Albany, NY: State University of New York Press.

Hansen, D. T. (2001). *Exploring the moral heart of teaching: Toward a teacher's creed.* New York: Teachers College Press.

Hansen, D. (2011). *Teacher and the world.* London: Routledge.

Hargreaves, A. (1998). The emotional practice of teaching. *Teaching and Teacher Education, 14*(8), 835-854.

Hargreaves, D.H. (1994). The New Professionalism: The synthesis of professional and institutional development, *Teaching and Teacher Education, 10*(4), 423-438.

Harris, B. (2007). *Supporting the emotional work of school leaders.* London: Sage Publications.

Hobson, A., Malderez, A., Tracey, L., Homer, M., Ashby, P., Mitchell, N., McIntyre, J., Cooper, D., Roper, T., Chambers, G., & Tomlinson, P. (2009). *Becoming a teacher: Final report.* London: Department for Children, Schools and Families.

Holmes Group. (1986). *Tomorrow's teachers: A report of the Holmes Group.* East Lansing, MI.

Huberman, M. (1995). Networks that alter teaching. *Teachers and Teaching: Theory and Practice, 1*(2), 193-221.

Kelchtermans, G. (2009). Career stories as gateways to understanding teacher development. In M. Bayer, U. Brinkkjaer, H. Plauborg, & S. Rolls (Eds.), *Teachers' career trajectories and work lives.* London: Springer.

Korthagen, F. A. (2004). In search of the essence of a good teacher: towards a more holistic approach in teacher education. *Teaching and Teacher Education, 20*, 77-97.

Korthagen, F., & Vasalos, A. (2005). Levels in reflection: Core reflection as a means to enhance professional growth. *Teachers and Teacher Education, 19*, 787-800.

Loughran, J. J. (2004). Learning through self-study. In J. J. Loughran, M. L. Hamilton, V. K. LaBoskey, & T. L. Russell (Eds.), *The international handbook of self-study of teaching and teacher education practices* (Volumes 1 & 2, pp. 151-192). Dordrecht: Kluwer Academic Publishers.

Louis, K. S. (1998). Effects of teacher quality worklife in secondary schools on commitment and sense of efficacy. *School Effectiveness and School Improvement, 9*(1), 1-27.

Meijer, P. C., Korthagen, F. A. J., & Vasalos, A. (2009). Supporting presence in teacher education: The connection between the personal and professional aspects of teaching. *Teaching and Teacher Education, 23*(2), 297-308.

Moore Johnson, S. (2004). *Finders and keepers: Helping new teachers survive and thrive in our schools.* San Francisco, CA: John Wiley & Sons.

Moos, L., Day, C., & Johansson, O. (Eds.) (2011). *How school principals sustain success over time: International perspectives.* Dordrecht: Springer.

Neito, S. (2003). *What keeps teachers going?* New York: Teachers College Press.

Nias, J. (1989). *Primary teachers talking: A study of teaching as work.* London: Routledge.

Nias, J. (1996). Thinking about feeling: the emotions in teaching. *Cambridge Journal of Education, 26*(3), 293-306.

Nias, J., Southworth, G., & Campbell, P. (1992). *Whole school curriculum development in primary schools.* London: Falmer Press.

Noddings, N. (1992). *The challenge to care in schools.* New York: Teachers College Press.

Noddings, N. (2003). *Happiness and education.* New York: Cambridge University Press.

Palmer, P. J. (1998). *The courage to teach: Exploring the inner landscape of a teachers' life.* San Francisco: Jossey-Bass.

Palmer, P. (2004). *A hidden wholeness.* San Francisco, CA: Jossey-Bass.

Palmer, P. (2007). *The courage to teach: Exploring the inner landscape of a teacher's life.* San Francisco, CA: John Wiley & Sons.

Paterson, L. J. (1991). *An evaluation of the Scottish pilot projects in the technical and vocational education initiative.*

Robinson, V., Hohepa, M., & Lloyd, C. (2009). *School leadership and student outcomes: Identifying what works and why. Best Evidence Synthesis Iteration (BES).* Auckland, New Zealand: New Zealand Ministry of Education.

Rodgers, F. R., & Raider-Roth, M. B. (2006). Presence in teaching. *Teachers and Teaching: Theory and Practice , 12*(3), 265-287.

Rosenholtz, S. J. (1989). *Teachers' workplace: The social organization of schools.* New York, NY: Longman.

Russell, T. (2007). How experience changed my values as a teacher educator. In T. Russell & J. Loughran (Eds.), *Enacting a pedagogy of teacher education: Values, relationships and practices* (pp. 182-191). London: RoutledgeFalmer.

Sachs, J. (2003). *The activist teaching profession.* Buckingham: Open University Press.

Schon, D. A. (1983). *The reflective practitioner.* London: Jossey-Bass.

Schutz, P. A., & Zembylas, M. (Eds.). (2011). *Advances in teacher emotion research: The impact on teachers' lives.* Dordrecht: Springer.

Seligman, M. (2002). *Authentic happiness.* New York: Free Press.

Sockett, H. (1993). *The moral base for teacher professionalism.* New York: Teachers College Press.

Tonnies, F. (2001). *Community and civil society.* Cambridge: Cambridge University Press.

Trier, J. D. (2001). The cinematic representation of the personal and professional lives of teachers. *Teacher Education Quarterly*, Summer, 127-142.

Van Den Berg, R. (2002). Teacher's meanings regarding educational practice. *Review of Educational Research, 72*(4), 577-625.

Vanderlinde, R., & van Broak, J. (2010). The gap between educational research and practice: Views of teachers, school leaders, intermediaries and researchers. *British Educational Research Journal, 36*(2), 299-316.

73

Walker, P. J. (1996). Taking students by surprise: Some ideas on the art of inspiring students. *New Academic, 5*, 12-16.

Woods, P., Jeffrey, B., & Troman, G. (1997). *Restructuring schools, reconstructing teachers.* Buckingham: Open University Press.

Zembylas, M. (2003). Emotional teacher identity: A post structural perspective. *Teachers and Teaching: Theory and Practice, 9*(3), 213-38.

AFFILIATIONS

Christopher Day
University of Nottingham, England

HAFDÍS GUÐJÓNSDÓTTIR AND SÓLVEIG KARVELSDÓTTIR[†]

TEACHERS' VOICES: LEARNING FROM PROFESSIONAL LIVES[i]

INTRODUCTION

Teaching is an open-ended activity that never leaves you alone. After school or in your car on the way home you constantly think about your students. You try to figure out what you need to do for them to be more successful or you look around your home to see what can be useful at school. I believe teaching is a lifestyle. (Guðjónsdóttir, 2000)

These words, articulated just before the end of the twentieth century by an Icelandic teacher, illustrated the passion and commitment of many teachers worldwide. They also remind us of the importance of learning with teachers as we move further into the challenges of the twentieth-first century.

The overall purpose of this study was to collaborate with teachers as they reflected on their practice and gained a better understanding of: a) teachers' response to these demands, b) their resilience and commitment, and c) their use of support and professional development. Qualitative research methods were used in partnership with nine teachers to create opportunities for reiterated cycles of interviews. Working together we aimed to reveal and document their perspective of the changing nature of their work and professionalism, including their work, lives, knowledge and ethics, plus the interpretation of the consequent information about the nature and dimension of their work in schools. We were thus able to develop and map new understandings of the professional lives of teachers. We used the results to introduce the changing profession of teachers from the perspective of teachers themselves and to identify where, what kind, and how teachers need support.

International research reports changes in both teachers' work and teaching environments. Despite local variations, common factors can be seen across many countries: government intervention, increasing teachers' workloads, little attention to teachers' identities or the importance of teacher wellbeing (Day & Gu, 2010; Guðjónsdóttir, 2005; Jóhannsson, 2006). While we know a great deal about teachers' work, we also know that the profession is diverse and extensive. We hear from teachers that the work and expectations are constantly changing and becoming more and more challenging (Guðjónsdóttir, 2000; Jóhannsson, 1999).

Some are concerned about the teaching profession and point out that constancy is missing, that the "best" university students don't become teachers, or after

M.A. Flores et al. (eds.), Back to the Future: Legacies, Continuities and Changes in Educational Policy, Practice and Research, 75–89.
© 2013 Sense Publishers. All rights reserved.

having gone through teacher education programs students do not return to the field and that a number of those who begin their career, particularly subject teachers, do not last very long in the profession (Darling-Hammond, Berry, Haselkorn, & Fideler, 1999; Van Kraayenoord, 2001). Others, such as Halperin and Ratteree (2003) cited research demonstrating that "a silent problem" was emerging – namely that a growing shortage of teachers across the world was appearing in response to inadequate support of teachers' human and professional roles.

Yet, in spite of these changing conditions and the demands of the work, many people do make it their lifelong profession and become successful teachers. Hargreaves' (1994) assumption is that it is not the salary, expanded reputation, or promotion that keeps teachers going, instead it is the passion and the reward that is built into the profession, the joy of working with children, to care for and support them. He believes teachers feel their importance. Teachers are pleased when they think about certain incidents although they admit to having experienced frustration, inequity or difficult situations (Gose, 2007). Brunetti's (2001) conclusion from research findings was that working with young people and seeing them learn and grow is a principal motivator for teachers. Stanford (2001) came to a similar conclusion, to make a difference in students' lives and learning was a prominent reason to stay in the profession.

SITUATING PROFESSIONAL PRACTICE IN THE REAL LIVES OF TEACHERS

As noted above, changes in society affect teachers' work. Over the last decades radical changes have taken place around the world as well as in Icelandic society. The growth of migration is leading to increased diversity in student groups (e.g. language, culture, and religion). At the same time the strong implementation of the policy of inclusive education has welcomed previously excluded students into schools (Guðjónsdóttir & Karlsdóttir, 2009; Jóhannesson, 2006). Technological advances are constantly growing and the accessibility of information has rapidly changed. Women's participation in the work force is more than 80% in Iceland, which is among the highest in Europe. Children spend longer hours in school and teachers report that these factors are increasing the cost of academic work (Jóhannesson, 1999; Karvelsdóttir, 2004). In addition to these changes the increase in government intervention into the teachers' role and the work in schools has lead to a number of changes that affect their professionalism, such as increased workload for teachers, little attention to teachers' identities, or the importance of teacher wellbeing are all factors (Day & Gu, 2010; Jóhannesson, 2006). Hargreaves (1994) reports teachers' responsibilities are more extensive and their roles more diffuse than before. He wonders what these changes mean, how to understand them, and if the job is getting better or worse. In his studies with teachers in Iceland Jóhannesson (2006) learned that these teachers feel that the way children express themselves, behave and learn has changed and teachers find that this makes their work more difficult. Teachers reported a need to gain specialized knowledge of teaching methods and assessment strategies. In addition, gaining efficiency in problem solving is important in order to deal with many problems at once, both didactical issues as well as special educational needs (Jóhannesson, 1999).

Day and Gu (2010) indicate that teacher professionalism continues to be associated with a strong knowledge base, ethical commitment to students, professional responsibility and the management of classroom practice. They also point out that teachers who are committed to their work and to their students are also ready to learn, to develop, and to change. Students' learning relies on what teachers think, believe and do at the classroom level (Hargreaves, 1994) and therefore the teacher is a key person in education. Effective teachers are passionate about their work, their students, their subject, and believe that the way they teach can make a difference in students' lives. This is not a choice between knowledge, pedagogy or art as all are necessary (Cameron, 2007). While a strong knowledge of pedagogy and particular disciplines is important, a strong feeling for the work, including passion, responsibility and commitment will engage both students and teachers as lifelong learners. However, support and encouragement to sustain this commitment and energy are essential. Teachers recognize that their work, and the conditions and requirements, are changing, along with the rest of the world. Nevertheless, if teachers are left responding to these complex and rapid changes in isolation it may create more overload, guilt, uncertainty, distrust, and burnout (Hargreaves, 1994). Support from school leaders and colleagues can make a difference, but also the respect of politicians and policy makers, adequate professional remuneration, attention so that the lives and work of teachers are intertwined, and that the focus must also be on the physical condition, and the psychological, emotional, and social environment (Day & Gu, 2010). Commitment and engagement is the key for good teaching and effective learning and is related to the feeling for the individual and a holistic perspective of wellbeing, self-efficacy, agency and professional identity (Day, 2004).

The changes in society and teachers' work raise questions concerning the professional roles and identity of teachers. By exploring the literature the following characterizations of the teaching profession can be found:

– Practical Professionalism: the personal practical knowledge that teachers develop, use and share with other educators (Clandinin & Connelly, 1995; Cochran-Smith & Lytle, 1993; Hargreaves & Goodson, 1996);
– Reflective Professionalism: thoughtful and informed professional reflection as the basis of improved professional practice, judgment and decision-making (Beck & Kosnik, 2000; Hargreaves & Goodson, 1996; Loughran & Northfield, 1996; Schön, 1983);
– Responsive Professionalism: incorporating practical and reflective professionalism with the added dimensionalities of mediation of theory, practice and ethics, incorporation of holistic perspectives, awareness of broader socio-cultural contexts, and contribution to educational inquiry and knowledge creation (called "extended Professionality" by Hargreaves and Goodson, 1996, p. 14) (Dalmau & Guðjónsdóttir, 2002; Guðjónsdóttir, 2000);
– Shared Professionalism: developing and contributing to pedagogy (the complex nature of teaching and learning, "continually being developed, refined and

articulated within the profession") in partnership with teacher educators (Loughran & Russell, 1997).

Circumstances that are related to situations in the life of each individual, especially events that are related to personal or professional challenges, affect teachers' commitment and their abilities to be resilient. An understanding of why some teachers have the resilience that is necessary to stay in teaching, a job that is continuously developing and becoming more and more complex, is the key to supporting teachers to develop the competence needed for good teaching and to further professionalism. To Lortie (2002) continuous education has supported teachers' development and professionalism, and resulted in teacher reflection, which means teachers spend more time thinking about their decisions and responses and the outcome is better and more careful decision-making.

Studying the professionalism of teachers through the observation and analysis of teachers' practice in diverse classrooms involved extensive descriptions by the teachers of the phenomena of their practice, participant observation, and shared analysis and interpretation with the teachers. From this process, Guðjónsdóttir (2000) was able to identify six different roles performed by the teachers as a basis for her holistic description of "Responsive Professional Practice."

- Pedagogues and experts in teaching and learning. Teachers share a body of knowledge about teaching and learning. Whenever teachers meet they continue the "never ending" professional dialogue with their colleagues;
- Reflective and critical problem solvers. In the classroom teachers continuously respond to students in the process of teaching and supporting learning for each individual. Outside the classroom, independently and in collegial groups, teachers reflect more formally on events of the school day and plan action;
- Researchers and change agents. When teachers wish to understand a practice in more depth or plan systematic or long term change they use a variety of assessment, evaluation and practitioner/action research processes to collect data, analyse and interpret findings and plan action;
- Creators of knowledge and theory builders. In the process of reflective practice and educational research, teachers build new understandings of learning and teaching and educational change;
- Writers and adult educators. Teachers publish and provide adult education both formally and informally. They publish their research in professional journals, write curriculum texts, speak at conferences, and develop educational programs for parents and other teachers;
- Authoritative voices in the community. Teachers' voices are heard in their local communities and beyond. Formally and informally teachers' opinions are sought about educational issues, learning, and educational improvement. Teachers provide the "good news" about student learning – often in pessimistic and critical environments (Dalmau & Guðjónsdóttir, 2002; Guðjónsdóttir, 2000).

Although these six professional roles varied in both range and commitment they were common and served to articulate and systematically analyse teachers' professional identities and practice (Guðjónsdóttir, 2000, 2005). Cochran-Smith and Lytle (1999) identified four critical elements for consideration in future discourse on teacher professionalism: (a) emphasis on the teacher as knower and agent of change, (b) creation of new ways to theorize practice, (c) participation of teachers and colleagues in intellectual discourse about critical issues, (d) linking teaching and curriculum to wider political and social issues, and (e) the creation of inquiry communities that focus on the positive, rather than negative, aspects of what teachers know.

The Professional Working Theory

The "personal pedagogy," "practical theory" or "living theory" of teachers is based on theory, practice, and ethics that lie behind everything they do (Handal & Lauvås, 1987; Muchmore, 2001; Whitehead, 1993). Professional Working Theory (PWT), as developed by Dalmau and Guðjónsdóttir (2002), supports teachers to enhance understandings based on the constant interplay of professional knowledge, practice, reflection, and ethical or moral principles. Thus PWT processes offer teachers (and academics) opportunities to frame their reflection on the living theories implicit in their practice. Explicit PWT is developed through systematic and comprehensive critical reflection, collegial dialogue and continuous action. Over time these practices contribute to the construction of professional identity, the creation of professional knowledge, and the development of collegial approaches to practice (Dalmau & Guðjónsdóttir, 2002).

The PWT is divided into three interwoven components:
– Practice relates to teachers' experience of their teaching, the strategies they use to teach, and their relationships with students, other teachers, staff and parents;
– Theory focuses on the knowledge each teacher brings into their work and explores the way they understand and explain their teaching practice and how they relate these understandings to educational theories. It relates their self-understanding and their reflective practice to theory;
– Ethics and the moral reasoning that lie behind teachers' work provide space for teachers to explore the reasons behind their decisions and reflections on who they are becoming and who they want to be as teachers.

Three levels of reflective questions are introduced to encourage the inclusion of perspectives from beyond the classroom. For example, in the first component "Practice" the three levels and the matching reflective questions covered:
– Close/local: What users see in their daily work;
– Medium distance: Factors that directly affect the working environment;
– Broad/societal: Broad societal connections, which affect practice.

Detailed reflective questions are included for each of these levels, in each of the three components (Practice, Theory and Ethics). The "three level" framework enabled connection-building between implicit and explicit or formal theory, and between lived experience and socio-cultural and political influences.

Using the PWT and listening to stories of many teachers gives an opportunity to gain a picture of their professional lives and see the similarities and differences between teachers (Guðjónsdóttir, 2005). Thus we believe that it can be useful to receive information from teachers and learn about their profession, attitude, ethics, and vision. Many researchers and scholars have recognized the importance of researching teachers' work and learning about their profession from teachers themselves. In Sólveig Karvelsdóttir's (2004) research about teachers' work and feelings in a challenging school neighbourhood, the teachers sincerely discuss their work, their workload, worries and emotions. Reporting the conclusion can inform others about teachers' work and build up understanding for the profession. It can influence the schools, the policymakers, and teacher education, and it can strengthen it and improve (Jóhannesson, 1999).

SHARED INQUIRY: METHODOLOGY AND DATA SOURCES

To understand teachers' professional lives, it is critical to work collaboratively with teachers themselves and listen to their stories and their perspective of the profession. Thus it is critical to create an opportunity for teachers to reflect on their practice and report stories from their professional lives (Loughran & Northfield, 1998). Qualitative research methods provide the opportunity to adapt the questions to the particular experiences of each teacher. The cyclical approach of critical research offers space for clarification and deeper discussion (Kincheloe, 2005). The purpose of this research was to understand what it means to the participant in this study to be a teacher. The main research question is related to their personal and practical practice, and how they relate their practice to educational theories and how they ground it in their ethics.

The overall purpose of this study was to collaborate with teachers as they reflected on their practice and gain a better understanding of a) the changes in their environment and how teachers respond to the changes and demands, b) their way to keep resilient and committed, and c) what supports their professional development. The goal was to gain a picture of the new professional lives of the participants, how it is changing and what can support the sustainability. These are the main research questions: (1) How are teachers' practices affected by their knowledge, ethics, and educational changes? (2) What impacts their work and commitment? (3) What supports their professional development and resilience?

Data was collected through semi-structured interviews with nine teachers. The participant sample was purposeful and to maximize the participant differences, novice and experienced teachers, men and women, teachers who teach young children as well as teachers teaching adolescence, were invited to participate. Their teaching experience varies from 3 to 35 years. This small number of participants doesn't give us all the variance we would like but the group is as mixed as possible.

Each teacher was given two opportunities in an interview to reflect on their practice. The teachers decided where the interview would take place, and chose either their school or to come to our workplace. Each interview took between an hour and an hour and a half. To support the teachers through their critical reflection we used the Professional Working Theory Instrument (PWTI) that provides a framework for reflection and dialogue on teachers' professional working theory (Dalmau & Guðjónsdóttir, 2002). The questions were open-ended, inviting the teachers to fully elaborate their own lines of response. As we discussed the work and lives of teachers we learned that the PWT approaches extended the theoretical dialogue with teachers. Even though it was difficult to move beyond the parameters of the classroom, framing the discussion (PWT instrument) and supporting the dialogue (process) effectively extended the scope of our discussions. The quality of the discourse did not reside in the PWT instrument itself, but in how and why it was used.

We audiotaped the interviews, listened to them and transcribed them. The PWTI was used as a framework for data analysis, looking for inductive and deductive themes within and across different data sources in order to address the research questions. The data was grouped into the three main categories according to the PWT, i.e. practice, theories and ethics, but also by the themes and repeated patterns that emerged. The aim of the analysis process was to identify and describe teachers' practices on how they respond to the changes in their work environment and conditions and how they explain the teaching profession. To seek verification the participants had several opportunities to respond to our report.

TEACHERS' PROFESSIONAL LIVES

Teachers' stories, their voices as they discuss their experiences as teachers, and their hopes and beliefs form the basis of the findings introduced in this chapter. The process using the PWTI enabled the teachers and our selves to participate in situated theoretical dialogue. The ensuing discussions began a shared process of knowledge generation related to (a) identification of critical elements in the dialogic process, and (b) understanding the professionalism of teachers. The teachers reported to us that they did not find this easy: "I never would have thought about my teaching this way if I had not participated in this project. I feel that with this digging into my personal and professional life I have complied with my being and now I can get rid of them and begin new digging. Thank you for asking me to participate. Another reported: I would like to say that I find it hard to get the hang of shorting between theories and ethics." The chapter is divided into the three components: practice, theory and ethics. The quotes are verbatim from the teachers but the translation to English is by the authors.

Practice

The teachers talked about their practice, told us about a typical day or a typical teaching period. They found it hard to think of typical days, because they felt they are all different but they also said that is one of the reasons they stay in the job. The diversity makes the teaching interesting. Teaching is never boring, it is hard, demanding, and challenging but not boring. Discussing the change a teacher of 28 years said:

If I compare teaching at present to my first years it has changed a great deal.
In the beginning we were teaching students, but we were not necessarily

aware of students' status or situation, at that time discussion about diagnosis had not really begun. Our students either managed themselves or not. We had a group of students we supervised but we really didn't know their background nor did anyone expect us to do so. If we had challenging students we learned little by little how to work with them, but parent collaboration was minimal, only twice a year unless something really huge happened. This has changed a lot.

While teachers spoke of their first years of teaching it was common that they felt that the course books controlled their teaching and the main goal was to teach their subject. If the students "didn't get it" the teacher couldn't do anything about it because she needed to go through the subject material in time.

Before I taught a lot each week, about 43 class hours for at least 15 years, and in addition to that I was occupied with politics, curriculum writing, was a committee chairperson and spoke about teaching as my hobby! I was very well organized, my teaching plans had to work whatever happened.

As we can see here teachers have different roles, they don't only teach. Even though 30 years ago more and more attention was being paid to students' wellbeing, their feelings and their rights to have something to say about their learning were maybe more in the dialogue than the actual practice in the classroom.

These last years so many things have been added to the teacher's job, the teaching is more student-focused, we view student status and check if they have been diagnosed. We try to understand his or her cries, ask ourselves how we can encounter each student and this calls for much, much more time on the job. We think about different teaching strategies and that takes time also.

The teachers take notice of the National curriculum and the individual school curriculum as they plan teaching and learning. They use basic materials and add to them according to the students' needs and interest. "I check the goals my students need to work towards and then I check if the main material covers that, if not I bring in exercises or mathematic problems from other resources. I also try to use something from students' daily lives."

In some of the classes the students create their individual learning plan along with their teachers. All the teachers find it important that their students become independent and responsible in their learning.

I use individualized learning in two subjects, Icelandic and mathematics. The students receive a plan for the whole week. In there I put in what is to be done in the other subjects but they decide themselves what to do in Icelandic and mathematics. I have a minimum requirement, a basic material that everyone has to cover ... and then they set up their own plan. They are very clever in doing it.

The teachers find it fundamental to show interest in and care for the children.

I believe it to be critical and fundamental for learning that children feel good in school and that they feel secure when they are around the teacher and among their schoolmates. I find it critical that children can, without feeling afraid, state their opinions and that they learn that it is possible to discuss different opinions without being judged for the difference.

In addition, again and again, they talk about the importance that the students are assured that they wish them to succeed in their learning. "To motivate them I make them feel that they have some responsibility, that they can control things themselves, and they can for example postpone the boring pages until later if they wish to do so. This makes them interested and passionate. The teachers find it important to manage their class, the behaviour, the learning, and the social interference. I want to manage my class and I discuss with the children what we need to do so everyone will feel good in the classroom."

According to the teachers that have a lot of teaching experience, classes or student groups have become more and more diverse. This calls for differentiating the teaching and responding to students' abilities, interests and experience.

I had four girls in one of my groups last year that had difficulties with learning, reading, and Icelandic. They were 10th graders and were sick of school. It was a challenge to get them going, to help them build their confidence, to realize their abilities. If they were going to literature class, I read to them because it was hard for them; we discussed the content and wrote together. I would write the text on the blackboard and they would copy it. It mattered a lot to them to have the spelling right. We read a book together and then they did a collage to illustrate the content. We used the computers and they created a webpage with a focus on their interest. In the end they had to take the same test as everyone else and you know they did very well and got high grades. The content was similar but they learned it in a very different way.

Here the challenge for the teacher was to find different strategies for the students to approach their learning, by making sure to not lower standards but at the same time open up for differentiation and creative approaches.

Those teachers believe that it is important to collaborate with parents, they believe the teacher should manage this collaboration and they respect that families can participate in different ways. "I try to keep good relationships with parents and respond to their demands around their child's learning. I find parents to be too neutral and I would like to see more of them in the school. I am becoming more confident, as I get older and the parents younger."

Teachers' stories from the classroom are endless; they talk about students learning, about success, but also about disappointment. They find it rewarding when students with learning difficulties succeed or begin to believe in themselves.

Theory

Discussing what lies behind teachers' pedagogical decisions we learned that it doesn't only differ but it is often a tacit knowledge. One teacher said she had used theories to back up her decisions at the beginning of her teaching career, but theories "come and go, and come again." Now she relies more on her experience. However, she also points out that teachers must be able to discuss theories and debate them to be at an equal level with those who consider themselves to be specialists in education. "You must have good knowledge of theories, if only to be taken seriously..." Another teacher said: "What I learned during my teacher education affects my teaching but I am not always sure from where I take things." We found it common that these teachers refer to what they learned during their teacher education when discussing the theories and knowledge that lay behind their practice.

> In my studies I learned about Piaget and Dewey. That opened my eyes that to get the best results for learning the students must have a chance to experience and practise, be active in their own learning and in so doing gain experience that relates new knowledge to old ... Ericson's theories hit my heart because it builds on so much humanity. ... Later I learned about multiple intelligence, 4MAT, cognitively guided instruction and inclusive education. All these theories and ideas affect my teaching and ideas of teaching and learning.

These teachers say that they rely on well-known theorists.

> First when I began my teaching I favoured Piaget and Vygotsky, then I discovered Tomlinson and she appealed to me, but now I look to Bruner's theory that one has to know the child's cultural background. I find it extremely interesting to step into the child's world.

In discussing theories one notices the emphasis on the child and on theories that focus on the child. "It is necessary to learn to know the child and it is a part of meeting the individual need," one of the teachers said. The teachers find it difficult to discuss these things and tell us that they don't really build on theories, it is more their experience that they take into account. However participating in this research and having the chance to reflect on their experience and to discuss their job professionally one of the teachers reports:

> When I finished my teacher education I did a final project on how to work with students. I kept my project but did not read it until a few days ago I fetched it from my attic and read it again. It was very interesting because I am learning that the theories I wrote about in my final project are the theories that have been very strong and evident in my pedagogy through the years. Of cause literature theories are there since that is my subject, but Thomas Gordon, and from the Scandinavia countries Sverre Asmervik, Böe and Hilling are all theorists that I studied and as I read about their ideology again I realized where my pedagogy came from.

The teachers reported that they found it difficult to discuss theories. As they gained experience they relied on their experience and not on theories that they learned in school. They also confessed that they are not used to discussing this matter. "It's not what we talk about at my school," one of them repeated as we asked about theories they rely on. Some of the teachers told us about theories and practice that was forced upon them from the outside community. Education authorities in their communities had decided to build behavioural management on certain theories and they found it difficult to discuss or respond to the request because they lacked the theoretical knowledge.

Ethics

All the teachers place emphasis on the students being happy at school. They say their emotional wellbeing is important and it sets the foundation for education to grow. "How can we NOT start by fostering systematically their mentality, their feelings and wellbeing?" The teachers realize that they are role models for their students. "It is important for me to smile. I have a picture of a big smile on my desktop to remind me to begin each day by smiling to the children." They find it very important how they respond to students and what comes about on the job, what they do and how. "I find it very important that my students come to class on time, that they turn in their assignments on time and therefore I must do the same myself." They sometimes find it hard to be allowed to be human, to make mistakes or show their emotions.

> During my first years of teaching it was expected that I was tough and had a hard shell, I went through huge deprivation the first two years. I felt I had to change myself as a human being. I am very sensitive but I had to move away from my emotions and put on a mask and play to get through.

Teachers with experience told us that they are more ready to get close to the children and allow themself to care for them and be friendly. They are not as distant as they were before or as they experienced as schoolchildren themselves.

Sometimes teachers have to teach something they don't agree with, something that is in the curriculum or they know students will be tested on in standardized testing. This they find frustrating. Other times they experience conflicts because they feel they need to cover certain knowledge in a certain time but at the same time they have the feeling the students are not really learning.

Teachers discussed what kind of teachers they want to be or become.

> When I decided to become a teacher, which was not until close to my graduation, I started thinking of my values and what I felt was important for me as a teacher. I came to the conclusion that I wanted to become a teacher who cares, who shows empathy. I began my teaching career with one thing in mind and that was to make my children enjoy school.

Another teacher said: If I can make my students leave my class with the feeling of being able or the feeling of "I can" and "we all can," then I feel I have succeeded.

Teachers' practice, theories and ethics don't stand alone, they are interlocked and make the holistic picture of the new lives of teachers, the new professionalism. Hearing from the experienced teachers how their jobs have developed and changed, and how the newcomers bring in different perspectives of what they think teaching is, provided us with rich insights of teachers' professional lives.

LEARNING IN PARTNERSHIP WITH TEACHERS

Learning in partnership with teachers about their professional lives was the fundamental basis of this research. The teachers taught us about the unique knowledge and contributions of the teaching profession in their communities. We learned that the profession is complicated and teachers take on different roles, both in their schools and their communities (Dalmau & Guðjónsdóttir, 2002). Teaching is not only about delivering knowledge but it is also about caring, wellbeing, creating pedagogical knowledge, and sharing it, among many other challenges.

The teachers found their job fulfilling and working with the children delightful. They emphasized the children's wellbeing and success in the school. This is in accordance with Brunetti (2001) and Stanford (2001) who reported that the main motivator for teachers is working with their students and making a difference in their lives. Or as one of the teachers said: The attitude towards the students comes first, number two is the teaching methods you choose, that you know them, and you need theories to justify your choice of teaching. These stories show that the teachers have a great knowledge of how children learn, the environment that is necessary for learning, and how to work with children so they will succeed.

From the teachers' stories we can also see that the teachers have a definite plan for their teaching and stretch individualization in their practice. They use theories and some mention specific theories or theorists. Others have created their own professional working theory. We wondered if they build on these theories with awareness or if they are so common that they can mention them without deep knowledge or relation to practice. It sounded like relating theory and practice was a bit murky; they were not used to discussing educational theories and found it difficult to talk about this part. They said that as they gained experience they relied on their personal knowledge and not on theories they learned in school. Teachers' knowledge is not always recognized and is often tacit and stays with each individual teacher. However, it is important to value it, make it known, and increase understanding for the teacher profession. It can influence and strengthen teachers' positions and teacher education. The results can also be useful for policymakers.

Teachers with long teaching experience discuss the changes they have gone through and state that teaching was more subject oriented when they began their teaching but that now it is more student oriented. They find that this can also be seen in the responsibilities that society has added to schools and teachers. Teachers are not only teaching certain subjects but caring is becoming a greater part of the curriculum, as is participating in bringing the children up (Cameron, 2007). Teaching is more student-focused but at the same time it has become more centralized with a national curriculum with defined goals and objectives as a framework for evidence-based teaching. This makes teaching complicated and calls for a new professionalism with strong knowledge in pedagogy and subjects, but also a passion for teaching, responsibility, and a commitment to children and the profession (Day & Gu, 2010). According to Reeves (2009) the new professionalism focuses on learner-centred practice, clarity about moral and social purpose, evidence-informed practice, critical reflection, collegiality, collaboration, and commitment to professional development and knowledge creation. This is in accordance with the professional roles teachers take on (Guðjónsdóttir, 2000) and could be seen within the professional lives of these teachers. In this research we learned about teachers who have the resilience needed (Day & Gu, 2010; Hargreaves, 1994; Lortie, 2002) to stay in this complex and ever-changing job that teaching is. Working with children and seeing them grow, develop, and learn matters but for teachers to be able to do so attention must be paid to their working condition and the environment (Day & Gu, 2010). Through partnership with teachers, the teacher education community can learn about and understand why some teachers have the resilience necessary to stay in teaching, and the encouragement needed to become a teacher and to sustain this commitment and energy. Doing that we might learn what kinds of working conditions are needed for the new professionalism to develop and grow, and how to support teachers through teacher education.

NOTES

[i] The research was a collaborative work between Hafdís Guðjónsdóttir and Sólveig Karvelsdóttir and the paper is written in honour of Sólveig who passed away in January 2011.

REFERENCES

Beck, C., & Kosnik, C. (2000). Associate teachers in preservice education: Clarifying and enhancing their role. [Electronic Version]. *Journal of Education for Teaching, 26*(3), 207-225.

Brunetti, G. J. (2001). Why do they teach? A study of job satisfaction among long-term high school teachers. *Teacher Education Quarterly, 28*(3), 49-74.

Cameron, L. (2007). Using LAMS to facilitate an effective program of ICT instruction. In *Proceedings of the 2007 European LAMS Conference: Designing the future of learning* (pp. 39-49).

Clandinin, J., & Connelly, M.F. (1995). *Teachers' professional knowledge landscapes.* New York: Teachers College Press.

Cochran-Smith, M., & Lytle, S. L. (1999). The teacher research movement: A decade later. *Educational Researcher, 28*(g), 15-25.

Cochran-Smith, M., & Lytle, S. M. (1993). *Inside outside: Teacher research and knowledge.* New York: Teachers College Press.

Dalmau, M., & Guðjónsdóttir, H. (2002). Framing professional discourse with teachers: Professional working theory. In J. Loughran & T. Russell (Eds.), *Improving teacher education practices through self-study* (pp. 102-129). London/New York: Routledge/Falmer.

Darling-Hammond, L., Berry, B. T., Haselkorn, D., & Fideler, E. (1999). Teacher recruitment, selection, and induction: Policy Influences on the supply and quality of teachers. In L. Darling-

Hammond & G. Sykes (Eds.), *Teaching as the learning profession. Handbook of policy and practice*. San Francisco: Jossey-Bass.

Day, C. (2004). *A passion for teaching*. London: Routledge Taylor & Francis Group.

Day, C., & Gu, Q. (2010). *The new lives of teachers*. London: Routledge Taylor & Francis Group.

Gose, M. (2007). *What it means to be a teacher: The reality and gift of teaching*. Lanham: Rowman & Littlefield Education.

Guðjónsdóttir, H. (2000). *Responsive professional practice: Teachers analyze the theoretical and ethical dimensions of their work in diverse classrooms*. Unpublished doctoral thesis. University of Oregon, Eugene, Oregon.

Guðjónsdóttir, H. (2005). Researching with teachers: Making responsive professional practice visible (and viable). In F. Bodone (Ed.), *What difference does research make and for whom?* (pp. 161-176). New York: Peter Lang.

Guðjónsdóttir, H., & Karlsdóttir, J. (2009). "Látum þúsund blóm blómstra." Stefnumörkun um skóla án aðgreiningar [Policy on inclusion]. *Uppeldi og menntun [Icelandic Journal of Education]*, *18*(1), 61-78.

Halperin, R., & Ratteree, B. (2003). Where have all the teachers gone? The silent crisis. *Prospects*, *33*(2), 133-138.

Handal, G., & Lauvås, P. (1987). *Promoting reflective teaching: Supervision in action*. London: The Society for Research into Higher Education and Open University Press.

Hargreaves, A. (1994). *Changing teachers, changing times: Teachers' work and culture in the postmodern age*. New York: Teacher College Press.

Hargreaves, A., & Goodson, I. (Eds.). (1996). *Teachers' professional lives*. London: Falmer Press.

Jóhannesson, I. Á. (1999). Sérhæfð þekking kennara. [Teachers' professional knowledge]. [Icelandic Journal of Education]. *Uppeldi og menntun: Tímarit Kennaraháskóla Íslands, 8*, 71-89.

Jóhannesson, I. Á. (2006). Different children – A tougher job. Icelandic teachers reflect on changes in their work. *European Educational Research Journal*, *5*(2), 140-151.

Karvelsdóttir, S. (2004). Kennsla við erfiðan grunnskóla. Hvað segja kennarar um störf sín og líðan [Teaching at a challenging school. What do teachers say about their work and feelings]. *FUM Tímarit um menntarannsóknir [Journal of Educational Research]*, *1*, 103-114.

Kincheloe, J. L. (2005). *Critical pedagogy*. NY: Peter Lang.

Lortie, D.C. (2002). *Schoolteacher: A sociological study*. Chicago: University of Chicago.

Loughran, J., & Northfield, J. (1996). *Opening the classroom door: Teacher research learner*. London: Falmer Press.

Loughran, J., & Northfield, J. (1998). A framework for the development of self-study practice. In M. L. Hamilton, S. Pinnegar, T. Russell, J. Loughran, & V. LaBoskey (Eds.), *Reconceptualizing teaching practice: Self-study in teacher education* (pp. 7-18). London: Falmer Press.

Loughran, J., & Russell, T. (1997). *Teaching about teaching: Purpose, passion and pedagogy in teacher education*. London: Falmer Press.

Muchmore, J. A. (2001). The story of "Anna": A life history study of the literacy beliefs and teaching practices of an urban high school English teacher. *Teacher Education Quarterly*, *28*(3), 89-110.

Reeves, J. (2009). Inventing the chartered teacher. In S. Gewirtz, P. Mahony, I. Hextall, & A. Cribb (Eds.), *Changing teacher professionalism: International trends, challenges and ways forward* (pp. 106-116). London: Routledge Taylor & Francis Group.

Schön, D. (1983). *The reflective practitioner. How professionals think in action*. London: Temple Smith.

Stanford, B. H. (2001). Reflections of resilient, persevering urban teachers. *Teacher Education Quarterly*, *28*(3), 75-87.

Whitehead, J. (1993). *The growth of educational knowledge: Creating your own living educational theories*. Bournemouth: Hyde Publications.

Van Kraayenoord, C. (2001). Wanted-teachers! *International Journal of Disability, Development and Education*, *48*(2), 125-128.

AFFILIATIONS

Hafdís Guðjónsdóttir and Sólveig Karvelsdóttir[†]
School of Education
University of Iceland

SECTION 2

**LEADERSHIP AND SCHOOL CURRICULUM:
CONTEXTS AND ACTORS**

GEERT KELCHTERMANS AND LIESBETH PIOT

LIVING THE JANUS HEAD: CONCEPTUALIZING LEADERS AND LEADERSHIP IN SCHOOLS IN THE 21ST CENTURY

INTRODUCTION

Leadership in schools changes. Traditionally leadership in schools was about "the man in the principal's office" as Wolcott (1973) labelled it in his seminal work about four decades ago. The formal leaders –principals, head teachers, directors, ... whatever their name was- were people who did not hang around in classrooms, but had an office, a separate space to perform their separate duties. That place as well as the character of their duties made them "different" from teachers –the other professional group in schools- who worked in classrooms. That traditional view of leadership and the division of labour it implies, still exists and is relevant (see a.o. Day & Leithwood, 2007).

Yet at the same time, leadership in schools has dramatically changed recently. We only mention two important changes. First of all many countries saw the birth of forms of school clusters where several schools joined forces in a particular form of structural collaboration, without actually merging into a new organization. In the collaborative clusters schools remain entities of their own, while at the same time also creating an extra layer of governance. At that level the group of individual principals collectively "leads" the school. This form of leadership creates opportunities for collaboration –among professionals who by the nature of their job used to work relatively isolated and on their own. At the same time this level of governance deeply affects the power relationships and therefore the possible form and content of leadership.

A second phenomenon is the diversification of leadership in schools, in the different forms of teacher leadership: mentors of beginning teachers, heads of subject departments, remedial teachers, curriculum developers, ... all of them new roles and accompanying practices in which former or still part-time teachers can demonstrate particular expertise or perform particular responsibilities. This raises questions about how school leadership takes place in contemporary educational organizations and which conceptual framework would be appropriate to study leadership in school organizations that are getting bigger and becoming more complex.

In this chapter we will address these two questions. In the first part we present the outcomes of a literature review in which we have tried to map the swampy area of leadership in schools.[i] The results of that review are threefold:

M.A. Flores et al. (eds.), Back to the Future: Legacies, Continuities and Changes in Educational Policy, Practice and Research, 93–114.

- The literature shows two main categories in the conceptualization of leadership: on the one hand the concentrated views of leadership (leadership is concentrated in the person of the formal leader) and on the other the distributed view of leadership (where leadership is shared by several members of the organization);
- One can observe a stalemate between both views on leadership;
- The literature on leadership in schools has almost exclusively focused on the task dimension of leadership –what do leaders need to do in order to make schools effective and functional? Only recently one can see a growing interest in the emotional dimension of leadership.

In response to these findings, we outline in the second part a model of leadership in schools that tries to a) move beyond the stalemate between concentrated and distributed approaches and to integrate the merits of both, and b) acknowledge the emotional dimension in educational leadership.

The review was designed to develop a framework that allows us to study leadership in contemporary school organizations that are becoming more complex, gain more autonomy, while at the same time operating in a policy climate in which performativity and accountability have become the taken for granted frames (see Day & Leithwood, 2007; Kelchtermans, 2007a, 2007b).

TERMINOLOGY ISSUES AND DEFINITIONS

Providing a single and generally accepted definition of school leadership is a difficult task. There is no single, general or widely accepted definition available in the literature (Bush, 2003; Bush & Glover, 2003; Coleman & Early, 2005; Leithwood & Duke, 1999; Vandenberghe, 2008). Rather, there is a plethora of definitions. However, there are some points of agreement between most authors. Firstly, there is some agreement about a distinction between the related concepts of school leadership, management and administration. Secondly, there are some key dimensions that are part of most definitions of school leadership. After we have elaborated more on these distinctions and key dimensions, we present our working definition of school leadership (and management).

Leadership, management and administration are related concepts that are often used interchangeable in our daily talking about school leadership and so on. In the Dutch literature 'leadership' and 'management' are used to refer to leading and managing school organizations, while in some English literature (in particular in the USA, the UK, Canada and Australia) 'administration' is also used.

'Administration' refers to the supporting services and activities (e.g. preparing and executing policies) at central (e.g. the central government and its administration), regional or local level (e.g. school secretaries). In Flanders the notion 'administration' is mostly used in the context of the Flemish government and its administration, for instance the administration at the department of education. From now on, we will preserve the term 'administration' to refer to specific supporting services and activities in the context of local executive tasks (e.g. the tasks of the secretaries of schools and school clusters). As such, administration is part of the management of an organization.

School leadership and management are regarded as two distinct, but complementary notions. The idea that school leaders and members of the middle management should be both good leaders and effective managers is also stressed (Bolman & Deal, 1991; Bush, 2003; Cuban, 1988). In general, it is widely acknowledged that *leadership* is about vision and change (influencing organizational members and initiating changes to achieve (new) desirable organizational goals), while *management* is about implementing and executing decisions and preserving the effective functioning of the organization (Bush, 2003; Cuban, 1988; Hopkins, 2001).

> Leadership is a process of influence leading to the achievement of desired purposes. It involves inspiring and supporting others towards the achievement of a vision for the school which is based on clear personal and professional values. Management is the implementation of school policies and the efficient and effective maintenance of the school's current activities. Both leadership and management are required if schools are to be successful. (Bush & Glover, 2003, p. 10)

Bush and Glover (2003; see also Day & Leithwood, 2007) describe three dimensions of school leadership that are present in many definitions of the concept. '*Leadership as influence*' refers to leadership as a social influence process where a person or group influences another person or group intentionally in order to structure the activities and relations in a group or organization. '*Leadership and values*' stresses the task of leaders to unite people around core values. '*Leadership and vision*' points to vision being regarded an essential characteristic of effective leadership by most definitions.

While it is acknowledged in the literature that leadership and management are distinct qualities and that principals should be both leaders and managers, both are most often referred to with the notion of 'leadership.' Therefore, from now on we will use the term 'leadership' to refer to both school leadership and management.[ii] This way, management is considered to be one dimension of leadership, next to building a vision, uniting organizational members around core values and initiating change (see also Spillane, Halverson, & Diamond, 2004). This becomes clear in the following *working definition of school leadership*, which also summarizes the above mentioned aspects of school leadership (and management) that are common in the literature:

School leadership refers to a process of social influence enacted by one or more organizational members. It involves activities aimed at achieving desirable and necessary organizational goals. Therefore, leadership comprises at least:

– *Building a vision (alone or together with others) about what is necessary and desirable in order for the school organization to provide 'good education.' In other words, determining what organizational goals are to be strived for and what needs to be done in order to achieve them, as well as the organization's core values and vision;*

- *Efforts to unite the organizational members around this vision, the core values and organizational goals and to influence these members and motivate them to do what is necessary to achieve those purposes;*
- *Managing or keeping in order the existing organizational arrangements, structures, activities, etc. that are required to achieve the desired organizational goals. This is often referred to as 'school management';*
- *Initiating changes to achieve the desired goals and thus improve the organization. This involves determining (alone or together with others) which changes are necessary and desirable, engaging in activities to achieve these changes and influencing and motivating others to do so.*

This definition conceives of leadership as an *organizational construct* (Greenfield, 1991). This means that it can be enacted by both formal leaders and teachers. This is also underlined by (recent) theories on distributed and shared leadership (see e.g. Gronn, 2000, 2002a, 2002b; Spillane, 2006; Spillane, Halverson, & Diamond, 2001, 2004). Moreover, leadership as an organizational construct explicitly relates leadership to the effective functioning of the organization.

> [...] leadership is an *organizational* [original emphasis] construct referring to processes and activities that increase a school's effectiveness in accomplishing its goals. The principal and teachers alike engage in a range of actions that serve to stimulate, guide, develop, and sustain organizational leadership processes and activities. In this sense, both the principal and teachers act as leaders. While the school principal holds an office that is assigned formal responsibility for school leadership, many teachers do foster leadership in the school, albeit informally. (Greenfield, 1991, p. 162)

The term '(school) leadership' is used in the literature to refer to the position of school administrators as well as leadership activities. Moreover, with the introduction of shared and distributed leadership, the term 'leader' is used not only to point to school administrators or principals, but also to organizational members that enact leadership tasks or take on leadership activities, regardless of their position within the school. This may also cause conceptual confusion about what a certain term is referring to. To avoid this, from now on, we will use the following concepts in a particular way.
- 'Leadership tasks,' 'leadership activities' and 'leadership' refer respectively to tasks and activities associated with leadership (mentioned in the previous working definition) and the enactment of leadership tasks and activities;
- 'Leader' refers to a member of the organization who exerts leadership and is recognized as such by other members of the organization;
- 'Principal,' 'formal (school) leader(s),' '(coordinating) principal,' 'manager,' 'middle management,' 'upper-school management,' 'head teacher,' 'administrator' refer to (the occupants of) positions within the organization with regard to its governance. These persons are often expected to exert leadership and are accountable for the effective functioning of the school organization.

CONCEPTUALIZATIONS OF LEADERSHIP IN SCHOOLS: A LITERATURE REVIEW

In our analysis of the literature we focused on definitions, conceptualizations and research on school leadership in general and school leadership in a context of scale enlargement and collaborations and networks of schools in particular.[iii]

A stalemate between concentrated and distributed approaches of school leadership

Reviews of the literature show that there exists a multitude of competing theories rather than a conceptual integration. Most models are formulated as alternatives for previous ones, that are blamed for having little explanatory value and a lack of empirical corroboration. This has installed a sort of paradigm war (Waite, 2002) between different approaches of school leadership. One of the most prominent oppositions in contemporary writings on school leadership is what we call the stalemate between "concentrated" and "distributed" approaches of school leadership. The concentrated approaches (e.g. the spectre of instructional, transactional and transformational leadership theories) focus on the central role and capacities of one or more formal school leaders. Traditionally this is the solo or stand-alone principal of a school. Recently, a second group of approaches has come up, the distributed approaches. Distributed models state that leadership is not exclusively related to the formal school leader(s) – as is suggested by the concentrated approaches – but is distributed over different organizational members. However, recently, these approaches have been criticized as well. Below we present the core characteristics of both the concentrated and the distributed approaches. Next, we describe the stalemate between them. Finally, we propose an integrated leadership approach as a way out of the stalemate.

Critical analysis of concentrated leadership approaches. What we call 'the concentrated leadership approaches' are present in the major part of the literature about theories and research on school leadership. Examples are instructional, transactional and transformational leadership models. They all presume that leadership is the result of the role, the capacities and the actions of formal school leaders, traditionally the school principal.[iv]

Several authors have formulated some critical remarks on these concentrated approaches. First of all, there appears to be a lack of conceptual clarity. The concepts and models of instructional, transactional and transformational leadership have a different meaning and are used in different ways by diverse authors (Bush, 2003; Hallinger, 2003; Harris, 2005; Hopkins, 2001; Leithwood & Duke, 1999). Harris (2005), for example, concludes that it is difficult to provide an unequivocal description of instructional leadership because of the massive amount of meanings that are attributed to it. This lack of clarity and differences in use are also manifest in the literature on transactional and transformational leadership (see, e.g., Leithwood & Duke, 1999).

As a result it has become unclear what empirical reality is actually being referred to by these concepts (Bush, 2003; Hallinger, 2003; Harris, 2005). This can be (partly) explained by the often vague and general descriptions of these leadership concepts. An example is the dimension 'modelling best practices and important organizational values,' an essential characteristic of transformational leadership (Leithwood, 1994). Thus, to judge whether a leader is a transformational one, one needs to take into account (amongst other things) to what extent he or she models best practices and important organizational values. However, what is considered 'best practice' or 'important organizational goals' in educational organizations is subject to discussion and negotiation (Hargreaves, 1994). There are no objective grounds to determine which goals and practices in education are 'best' or 'important.' Hence, it is a rather ambiguous endeavour to decide whether or not a leader models best practice and important organizational values.

The second criticism concerns a number of assumptions of the concentrated approaches of school leadership that are untenable: a leader-centrism, a static dualism between 'leaders' and 'followers,' and an overestimation of the role of formal leadership (see Gronn, 2003a).

Most of the research on school leadership is based on a 'leader-centrism' (Bennett, Wise, Woods, & Harvey, 2003; Day & Leithwood, 2007; Gronn, 2000, 2002a, 2002b, 2003a, 2003b, 2003c; Harris, 2003; Leithwood & Duke, 1999; Ogawa & Bossert, 1995; Spillane et al., 2004). It is assumed that only formal leaders are able to exert influence on the thinking and acting of members of the organization. Emphasis is placed on

the concentrated leadership of high status, formally positioned individuals. (Gronn, 2002a, p. 662)

Yukl (2006) refers to this as 'the heroic leadership paradigm.' However, the explanatory value attributed to the role and actions of formal leaders to account for an organization's functioning seems to be overrated, since power and influence in an organization are distributed over multiple individuals and processes (Gronn, 2002a, 2002b, 2003b; Gronn & Hamilton, 2004). Because every member of the organization has the possibility to influence others, every organization member (theoretically) is able to exert leadership and can be recognized as such by others (see also Altrichter & Salzgeber, 2000; Ball, 1994; Blase, 1998; Blase & Anderson, 1995; Hoyle, 1982; Kelchtermans, 2007a, 2007b, 2007c). This, however, is often neglected by the concentrated approaches because they almost exclusively attribute the possibility to influence others and thus to exert leadership to those who occupy formal leadership positions.

Next – and following from the leader-centrism- the concentrated leadership approaches presume that leadership will manifest itself in a static relationship between two abstract categories of people:

a leader (although sometimes leaders) and her or his followers, into either of which categories an organization's entire membership may be grouped. (Gronn, 2003a, p. 23)

However, dualisms such as 'leader-follower' and 'leadership-followership' presume that there is an a priori division of labour within an organization.

Leadership approaches that are based on such an assumption thus prescribe a specific division of labour rather than allowing descriptions of the actual divisions of labour within an organization. This basic assumption of the concentrated approaches becomes more and more irreconcilable with the increasing complexity of educational organizations (e.g. the formation of school clusters) that affects the ways in which work is divided and completed: the division of labour continually changes, complex tasks are completed by different people who depend on each other, there is an increasing need for coordination of different tasks and groups, and it has become almost impossible for the formal school leader to complete the broad range of management and leadership tasks on his own. In other words, executing tasks and functions in schools is increasingly becoming a distributed process

in which a number of persons coordinate their joint endeavours to accomplish work. (Gronn, 2003b, p. 279)

Third, concentrated approaches consider leadership as the most important factor explaining how work is divided and executed in an organization. Kerr and Jermier (1978; see also Gronn, 2003b; Jermier & Kerr, 1997; Tosi & Kiker, 1997), however, present examples of situations in which leadership is not needed to explain the events in a working environment. Next to leadership, there are a number of other factors that can explain how work is being done in an organization: characteristics of the context (e.g. the nature of the tasks that need to be done), personal characteristics (e.g. the motivation and personal beliefs of teachers), and group processes (e.g. feedback by colleagues). Therefore, Gronn (2003b) advocates to start from the work that actually takes place in an organization and analyze it from there, rather than presuming in advance that leadership is (one of) the most or sole explanatory variable of the work, division of labour and events occurring in schools (see also Jermier & Kerr, 1997).

The previously mentioned assumptions are central elements of the concentrated leadership approaches. Gronn (2003a) refers to them as having an "elixir view of leadership" (p. 24): it is assumed that the formal leader has the privilege and capacity to change the actions of his/her followers, as if he/she has got some extraordinary skills or characteristics as one might have after drinking an elixir or magical drink. This vision not only creates the illusion that a formal leader, by nature or by holding a leadership position, possesses extraordinary capacities and is capable of influencing others in a desirable direction without much effort. This image also forces an unrealistic and compelling causal model onto reality. This way injustice is done to organizations in which formal leaders not only influence so-called 'followers,' but where at the same time followers influence formal leaders and others, and where formal leaders sometimes struggle to lead teachers and the school. This criticism was one of the reasons why several authors have developed distributed leadership models, stressing that other organizational members take part in leadership practices as well. We will elaborate on this in the next section.

99

Critical Analysis of the Distributed Leadership Approach. As an alternative for a concentrated approach, some authors have suggested to use a conceptualization of leadership that allows to describe leadership practices as they actually take place in schools (see e.g. Gronn, 2000, 2002a, 2002b, 2003a, 2003b; Spillane, 2006; Spillane et al., 2001, 2004). This way 'distributed leadership' has come up as a new concept and perspective in theory and research on school leadership. According to its proponents, it allows to investigate the actual divisions of labour and leadership practices in organizations. A distributed approach also rejects the assumption that leadership -influencing organization members in order to reach organizational goals- is primarily or even exclusively related to formal leaders. As such, the dualistic vision on leaders-followers is also rejected.

Even though the distributed approaches offer an alternative for problems posed by the concentrated approaches, they have themselves also been criticized recently. First, there remains confusion about the exact meaning of the term 'distributed leadership.' Second, this approach also falls prey to a similar bias as the concentrated views of leadership, since it tends to underestimate the unique role, capacities and actions of single formal or informal leaders for understanding actual leadership practices. In other words, a distributed approach runs the risk of being at the opposite end of the concentrated approaches by underestimating or ignoring the role and influence of individuals. As a result, the opposition between the two approaches creates a stalemate in the research and literature on school leadership. Although distributed leadership has become very prominent in the theory, research and practice of school leadership, there is at the same time a growing in confusion and ambiguity about its precise meaning (Woods, Bennett, Harvey, & Wise, 2004). Analyzing the research literature, brought Mayrowetz (2008) to identify four usages of the concept 'distributed leadership,' respectively one theoretical and four normative ones: (1) distributed leadership as a theoretical lens for looking at the activity of leadership, (2) distributed leadership for democracy, (3) distributed leadership for efficiency and effectiveness, and (4) distributed leadership as human capacity building. The first usage is purely theoretical and entails primarily the basic writings on distributed leadership in school organizations by Spillane (2006; see also Spillane et al., 2001, 2004) and Gronn (2000, 2002a, 2002b, 2003a, 2003b). Each of these authors has developed a theoretical framework that can be used to describe and analyze leadership practices. Other authors often start from this framework. However, sometimes the framework is not only used to analytically describe leadership practices, but also to make normative statements about what leadership practices should look like. For example, Storey (2004, p. 252) states:

> The fundamental premise advanced by proponents of the concept of distributed leadership is that leadership activities should not be accreted into the hands of a sole individual but, on the contrary, they should be shared between a number of people in an organization or team.

This leads towards a problematic intertwinement between descriptions, theorizing and empirical research on the one hand and normative statements about how leadership should be exerted on the other. Examples of such normative models of and statements about distributed leadership are the other usages that Mayrowetz (2008) distinguishes: distributed leadership for democracy, for efficiency and effectiveness, and as human capacity building. What is problematic about them is that they often are not presented as being normative. Therefore, there is a risk that they are received as if they were results of scientific research, while the empirical evidence for these models and statements is often scarce or contradictory (Bennett et al., 2003; Hopkins, 2001; Mayrowetz, 2008; see also Gronn, 2008).

The second critique on the distributed models considers their assumption that the collective action of organization members or the interaction between leaders, followers and the situation will determine leadership practices in schools.[v] For example, Gronn (2000, p. 331) posits:

> In the relations between organizational heads and their immediate subordinates or between executives and their personal assistants for example, couplings form in which the extent of conjoint agency resulting from the interdependence and mutual influence of the two parties is sufficient to render meaningless any assumptions about leadership being embodied in just one individual.

However, by doing so, they risk neglecting the role of individual (formal) leaders in the analysis of leadership practices in schools and in a sense make a similar mistake as the concentrated approaches. Where the latter relate leadership almost exclusively to the thinking and acting of the (individual) formal leader, the distributed approaches relate leadership almost exclusively to the actions of teams. For example, Yukl (2006, pp. 292-293) states:

> The leadership actions of any individual leader are much less important than the collective leadership provided by members of the organization.

This way, however, the distributed approaches may neglect the role of individual (formal) leadership. Gronn (2008), one of the advocates of the distributed leadership approach, recently pointed to this shortcoming of the distributed approaches himself:

> Thus, even though I allowed originally for distributed leadership to encompass [...] the idea of a potentially large number of leaders in schools (e.g. 1 + leaders), this possibility may well underplay the significance of the contributions of highly influential individuals working in parallel with collectivities. That is, an emphasis on quantity may ignore qualitative variations. Consider a hypothetical case in which schools with numerous solo performers, each of whom might fit a classic charismatic or transformational prototype, to which might be added a couple of teams and teacher networks, all of which adds up to a critical mass of leaders. To characterize such an overall leadership configuration as 'distributed,' would not necessarily be an accurate representation of reality. In hindsight, it may have been better to

confine 'distributed' to instances of conjoint agency (Gronn, 2002a, p. 431). (Gronn, 2008, p. 152)

Opening up the Stalemate: Towards an Integrated Conceptual Framework. The literature and research on school leadership, or at least a major part of it, seems to be trapped in a stalemate. Gronn (2008) also describes this opposition between 'focused' and 'distributed' views on leadership. He posits that because of this injustice is done to the changing patterns of influence and leadership in schools, where the 'locus' of influence can be situated both in individuals and groups, for example depending on the moment and leadership task at stake.

There is also some empirical evidence that leadership practices result from concentrated or individual as well as collective or conjoint agency. For example, Gronn (2008) describes studies of leadership practices in educational organizations where there is "a mixed pattern of solo and shared leading" (p. 151).

Timperley (2005) illustrates, based on multiple case studies, that leadership practices aimed at improving students' literacy, were determined by the interaction between teams of teachers and the principal, i.e. distributed leadership. However, this interaction and conjoint agency was initiated by individual leadership by expert-teachers. This form of concentrated leadership "spanned the boundaries between principals and teacher teams" (Timperley, 2005, p. 410).

These studies stress the interplay of forms of individual and distributed leadership. In order to be able to describe and analyze actual leadership practices and the changing locus of influence and leadership (between individual leaders, followers, and/or groups), we suggest there is a need for an integrated leadership approach. Such an approach should consider leadership as an organizational function (Greenfield, 1991) that is shaped by the individual and/or collective agency of organization members, situated in the particular context of the organization. This way such an approach[vi] may overcome the stalemate between concentrated and distributed approaches of school leadership.

Almost a decade before the renewed interest in distributed leadership, Greenfield (1995) stated that leadership is a 'multifaceted phenomenon.' This implies that leadership can be a function of an individual, a group or an entire organization. In the past, researchers have often neglected to make such a distinction and/or have situated leadership exclusively with one of these elements. This is, according to Greenfield (1995), one of the reasons why there is so little research about the actual practices of school leadership.

Therefore, and joining Greenfield (1995) and Gronn (2008), we state there is a need for radical empirical descriptions of leadership practices in schools. This should be done starting from an integrated framework that makes it possible to map both concentrated and distributed forms of leadership, as well as their interaction. This way, theory and research on school leadership can further develop, taking into account and building on previous conceptualizations and empirical findings of school leadership. This is even more important given the increasing complexity of school organizations and the growth of collaborations, partnerships and networks of schools. On the one hand, distributed forms of leadership are increasingly emerging in contemporary educational organizations, since formal school leaders are no longer capable to execute the plethora of leadership tasks on their own (Harris, 2005). On the other hand, and at first sight paradoxically, such forms of distributed leadership in complex organizations are often based on strong individual and/or formal leadership (Crawford, 2005).

Acknowledging Both the Task Dimension and the Emotional Dimension of School Leadership

Analyzing the literature, we found that the studies on leadership in school, both from the concentrated and distributed perspectives, primarily and often exclusively address the task dimension of school leadership: what should school leaders do? How can school leaders act effective and efficiently? Which characteristics and strategies provide the best results? Which approach 'works' best? However, descriptions of what it means and how it feels for people to engage in leadership practices and/or occupy leadership positions are largely absent in the literature (Wolcott's (1973) *The man in the principal's office* being an important exception[vii]). Even though most of the studies acknowledge the interactive and relational aspects of school leadership, these elements are mostly looked at exclusively from a functionalist point of view (what should a leader do in order for the followers to actually do what is necessary to achieve organizational goals?). Yet – as is shown from the literature on sensemaking (see e.g. Coburn, 2001, 2005; Weick, 1995) and teachers' work lives (see e.g. Ballet & Kelchtermans, 2009; Bayer, Brinkkjær, Plauborg, & Rolls, 2009; Kelchtermans, 2009; Piot, Kelchtermans, & Ballet, 2010) – the way organization members experience their working conditions is highly relevant to properly understand their attitudes and actions. This, however, remains underestimated in most of the literature on school leadership.

However, recently – and parallel with research on the role of emotions in teaching (see e.g. Nias, 1996; Schutz & Zembylas, 2009; Van Veen & Lasky, 2005) – several authors started to explicitly include the emotional dimension in their studies on leadership (Ackerman & Maslin-Ostrowski, 2004; Beatty, 2000, 2002; Beatty & Brew, 2004; Blackmore, 1996, 2004, 2009; Crawford, 2007a, 2007b, 2009; Gronn, 2009; Gronn & Lacey, 2004; Hargreaves & Fink, 2004; Leithwood, Begley, & Cousins, 1992; Loader, 1997; Samier & Schmidt, 2009; Solomon, 1998). These authors show that emotionality is no side-effect of school leadership, but constitutes an essential part of it. They criticize management approaches of leadership for (solely) stressing rational goals and decision making, technical skills, and the efficiency and effectiveness of school leaders (Beatty, 2000; Loader, 1997). This dominant 'management discourse' makes it difficult for principals to accept emotionality as an inherent part of their profession. As a result, emotions are often regarded as idiosyncratic, accidental, temporary and annoying side-effects of school leadership, that need to be avoided and controlled (Beatty, 2000; Beatty & Brew, 2004).

The central role of emotions in school leadership has been described in some recent empirical studies. Emotions are regarded as socially constructed, embedded in social interactions and triggered by the context (Samier & Schmidt, 2009). Therefore, they should not be regarded as merely the characteristics of an individual, but also as contextualized, relational and even political phenomena (see also Hargreaves, 1998).

Crawford (2007b) concludes that an inherent emotional dimension is present in the experiences and actions of principals. This manifests itself in (1) the concern of the principals to balance between 'being professional' and 'being human'; (2) a personal vulnerability of the principals; and (3) the conclusion that 'rational' behaviour often is based on personal emotions that reflect values that are regarded as important by the principals. In other words, rationality and emotionality inevitably intertwine in the professional experiences of principals. Principals often struggle with this because they feel obliged to hide their emotions in order to look professional. At the same time, however, they feel that this is not possible, since the principal's self is often put on the line in his/her acting.

Beatty (2000, 2002) describes positive (e.g. feelings of enthusiasm and flow, support, acknowledgement, and self-esteem) and negative emotions (e.g. feelings of disappointment, discouragement or threat) which principals experience and also analyses how these emotions arise. Not only principals' own feelings, but also feelings of others (for example teachers) have an impact on the ways principals fulfill and experience their job, as have emotional conflicts of interest that principals might experience.

Based on a secondary analysis of qualitative-interpretive studies in Flemish primary schools, we have argued that the metaphor of the gatekeeper captures some of the particular complexities of principals' emotional experience of themselves and their working conditions (Kelchtermans, Piot, & Ballet, 2011). In particular, two themes appeared prominently in principals' experience of the position of the gatekeeper. First, the principal as gatekeeper is caught in a web of conflicting loyalties. The principal finds him/herself between different groups inside and outside the school, which often have different and even conflicting expectations and normative educational agendas, for example parents and teachers (see also Devos, 2000; Vandenberghe, 2008). Second, principals often struggle between loneliness and belonging (see also Vandenberghe, 2008). The formal position of the principal is – especially in primary schools – structurally lonely. There are almost no organization members that find themselves in a similar position. As such, principals struggle between on the hand dealing with the structural loneliness and, on the other hand, being part of the school team.

These studies show that leaders' experiences and actions are intertwined and that drawing a line between the (emotional) experiences and actions of school leaders is not only impossible, but also not desirable. Therefore, it is crucial to acknowledge this intertwinement between an emotional dimension and a task dimension of school leadership. Both dimensions can be considered as two sides of the same coin. It is neither possible nor desirable to separate them from each other.

CONCLUSION: AN INTEGRATED CONCEPTUAL FRAMEWORK
OF SCHOOL LEADERSHIP

In the rest of this chapter we sketch a conceptual framework that allows one to overcome the stalemate between concentrated and distributed views of leadership as well as the negligence towards the emotional dimension in leadership practices. It aims at providing an integrated picture of the different constitutive elements of school leadership and their interconnectedness. The framework also serves as a map to navigate through theories and research on school leadership. Put differently, it is a model that helps to situate relevant factors and dimensions of school leadership. Important is that these factors and dimensions are considered as related (like for example the relationship between the emotional and the task dimension). By using the map, both researchers and practitioners (for example people designing courses or training for school leaders) can question, design and/or use theories, research, and training programs for school leadership, while being aware of the different relevant factors and processes and their connections.

General Overview

The central frame of the figure entails the general overview of the framework. It represents the three constitutive or basic elements of leadership practices in school organizations: leader(s), follower(s), and context. It is largely inspired by the model of Spillane and colleagues (2004). Leadership practices are the result of the interaction between leader(s) and follower(s) and this interaction is always a contextualized one. The context is not merely the background or the stage on which leadership practices take place, but is an essential constitutive element of it. It shapes leadership practices and, in return, is also influenced by those practices. The left and the right frame of the figure are more detailed representations of respectively the context and the actors (leaders and followers). It is important to take the different elements of the figures and their relations into account.

We also want to stress the dynamic nature of school leadership and leadership practices. The central element of the framework is the actual leadership practices that take place in a school. By describing and reconstructing the actual leadership practices it is possible to map the different factors and processes that have influenced the leadership practices and/or are a result of the practices. Our conceptual framework gives an overview of possible relevant factors and processes, based on previous theorizing and research on school leadership. As such, it may help to unravel the elements that have contributed to leadership practices in schools. Is thus allows us to see 'the whole picture' or at least a more comprehensive picture than in the majority of the research.

We will now discuss the different elements of the conceptual framework or the different factors and processes that might influence how leadership practices are enacted in schools or school clusters. These are possible explanations for the way leadership practices actually take place in school organizations.

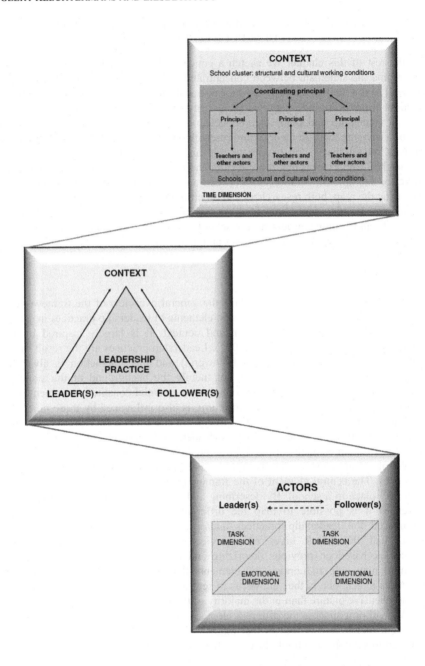

Figure 1. General overview of the conceptual framework

First, we discuss the context and its different components. The central idea is that the context is at the same time constitutive of and constituted in leadership practices (see also Spillane et al., 2004). Second, we pay attention to the interaction between leaders and followers and the related task and emotional dimension. This way, the conceptual framework becomes an instrument that can be used to describe and analyze leadership practices.

Context

This element of the conceptual framework stresses the contextualized nature of school leadership. Leadership practices arise from the interaction between leaders and followers and this interaction is always situated in time and in space (see also Spillane et al., 2004). The spatial dimension of the context refers to the structural and cultural characteristics of the organization, in the way that they constitute the actual conditions for teachers and principals to live their professional lives.

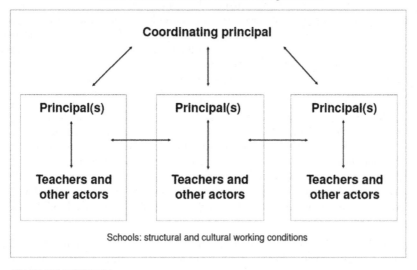

CONTEXT

School cluster: structural and cultural working conditions

Coordinating principal

| **Principal(s)** | **Principal(s)** | **Principal(s)** |

| **Teachers and other actors** | **Teachers and other actors** | **Teachers and other actors** |

Schools: structural and cultural working conditions

TIME DIMENSION

Figure 2. Detail of the conceptual framework: context

Structural working conditions are relatively stable. Examples are formal positions, management structures and hierarchies, formal and explicit rules and procedures or the legislation schools have to follow.

107

Cultural working conditions are less tangible than structural ones. They refer to the normative ideas about 'how we do things in our school (cluster)' or 'the school (cluster) we want to be' and arise from the individual and collective processes of sensemaking in schools (Stoll, 2000, p. 9). Therefore, we argue that if we want to describe and reconstruct leadership practices, it is necessary to take into account the shared knowledge, beliefs, values and norms of the school members as well as the processes of social construction, negotiation or struggle that constitute them.

The context also entails a temporal dimension. In a sense, just like human beings in general, schools as organizations are characterized by historicity: they have a past as well as expectations about the future. This situatedness in time impacts sensemaking and actions in the present. For example, often schools that are now part of a school cluster have a history of competition and rivalry in attracting students. This past might hinder the collaboration and trust between schools and their representatives (De Wit, Devos, & Verhoeven, 1998-1999; Kelchtermans, Janssen, & Vandenberghe, 2003).

The structural and cultural working conditions as well as elements from the past determine which actions actors can take. As such, context influences and determines leadership practices. Put differently, context is constitutive of leadership practices (see also Spillane et al., 2004). However, at the same time, in turn leadership practices also influence the context. Context is also constituted through leadership practices, since structures only determine the actual practices if they are acknowledged by and maintained in the actions of the actors, the agents in the organization. As such, structure is both the medium and the outcome of action or agency (see also Altrichter & Salzgeber, 2000; Giddens, 1979/2007; Spillane et al., 2004). It both enables and constrains actions, but never fully determines them.

> The concept of structuration involves that of the duality of structure, which relates to the fundamentally recursive character of social life, and expresses the mutual dependence of structure and agency. By the duality of structure I mean that the structural properties of social systems are both the medium and the outcome of the practices that constitute those systems. [...] The identification of structure with constraint is also rejected: structure is both enabling and constraining [...] Structure thus is not to be conceptualized as a barrier to action, but as essentially involved in its production [...]. (Giddens, 1979/2007, p. 238)

Also with regard to organizational culture there is a similar interaction with agency. Organizational cultures exist and are relatively stable. As such, they partly determine organization members' actions. At the same time, however, these cultures are only meaningful as long as they are acknowledged and maintained in the actions of organization members. In other words, understanding leadership practices demands an awareness of the complex interplay of the sense-making agents who live and work in schools on the one hand and the influence of structures on the other. With regard to this, Schein (2004) stresses the importance of taking mutual interaction between leadership and culture into account when studying organization's functioning and the role of leadership:

In an age in which leadership is touted over and over again as a critical variable in defining the success or failure of organizations, it becomes all the more important to look at the other side of the leadership coin – how leaders create culture and how culture defines and creates leaders. (p. xi)

This relationship between structure and culture on the one hand and actors on the other, brings us to the second central building block of the conceptual framework: the actors, namely leaders and followers.

Actors: Leaders and Followers as Appearing in Practices

With regard to the actors relevant to leadership practices we distinguish between leaders and followers. Conceptually such a distinction is valuable because a leader, because of his/her mandate, is responsible for the execution of a certain leadership task. This formal responsibility has an impact on the social influence processes that form the base of leadership practices. Empirically this distinction makes it possible to describe both concentrated and distributed forms of leadership and their possible interaction. Which organization members are considered leader or follower depends on the leadership task or practice at stake. Moreover, with regard to a specific task there can be one or more leaders and/or one or more followers. And the actual division of these roles shifts over time.

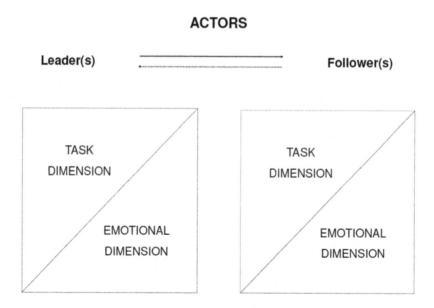

Figure 3. Detail of the conceptual framework: actors

A leader is an organization member that occupies a leadership position at a certain moment in time with regard to a specific task. In other words, a leader receives a formal or informal mandate from other organization members. Followers, then, are the other organization members who are involved in a specific leadership task, but who do not have such a mandate. This however does not mean that they are not able to have influence and thus contribute to leadership practices. Both leaders and followers are constitutive of leadership practices (see also Spillane et al., 2004). And both leaders and followers can influence each other. Thus, there is a changing 'locus' of influence. As such, leaders and followers together shape leadership practices. Leaders influence followers and/or each other. Because of their mandate and formal responsibility they have certain possibilities for influencing others that followers do not possess. This is represented by the difference between the 'full' and the 'dotted' arrow. This way, the conceptual framework recognizes insights from both concentrated and distributed models of leadership.

Finally, the content of the enacted leadership or the leadership practices always involves at the same time issues of the task as well as the way they are being experienced by the people involved. Task dimension and emotional dimension are to be acknowledged as both relevant and present in any leadership practice.

NOTES

[i] From June to August 2009 (with a limited follow up November 2011) we searched the literature for definitions, conceptualizations and studies on school leadership in general and school leadership in a context of scale enlargement and collaborations and networks of schools in particular. We looked for relevant articles in peer reviewed journals, international handbooks and national and international edited volumes, using the search engines 'Librisource Plus: Education Sciences' and 'Google scholar.' Journals listed in 'Social Sciences Citation Index' (SSCI), 'Arts and Humanities Citation Index,' 'Web of Science,' 'Academic Search Premier,' 'Educational Resources Information Center' (ERIC), 'FRANCIS,' and 'Sociological Abstracts' were included in our search. Because of the often very numerous results (sometimes 20000 search results) we narrowed them down, using the following criteria: 1) the key word had to be mentioned in the title; 2) published since 1999. Older publications were not excluded per se. Such articles or books were still included if they were mentioned (repeatedly) in existing reviews and/or often cited in other publications.

[ii] The term 'management' is mainly used in the United Kingdom and Europe, whereas in the United States 'administration' is also common (Bush, 2003). Management refers to activities aimed at the preservation of the organization, while administration points more specifically to the lower-order tasks that are required to do this. Nevertheless, 'school administration' is also used to refer to school leadership (see, e.g., Leithwood, 1992). Therefore, to avoid confusion we will only use the terms 'leadership' and 'management' from now on (management including the lower-order tasks that are sometimes referred to by the term 'administration').

[iii] For detailed information on the analysis and selection of the literature, see Kelchtermans and Piot (2010); Piot & Kelchtermans (submitted).

[iv] Transformational leadership is sometimes an exception, since transformational processes can also be initiated by other individuals or groups than the formal leader(s) (Gronn, 2002b; Hallinger, 2003; Leithwood & Duke, 1999). However, the plethora of the literature on transformational leadership focuses on the formal leader. Therefore, de facto, transformational leadership mainly proposes a concentration of influence from formal leaders.

[v] This is however less the case for the writings of Spillane and colleagues (2001, 2004). They never explicitly state that the conjoint agency of organizational members is more important than the actions of single leaders.

^{vi} Gronn (2008) refers to this as 'hybrid leadership.'
^{vii} The dissertation of West (2010) is another – more recent – exception to the trend.

REFERENCES

Ackerman, R. H., & Maslin-Ostrowski, P. (2004). The wounded leader. *Educational Leadership, 67*(1), 28-32.

Altrichter, H., & Salzgeber, S. (2000). Some elements of a micro-political theory of school development. In H. Altrichter & J. Elliott (Eds.), *Images of educational change* (pp. 99-110). Buckingham: Open University Press.

Ball, S. J. (1994). Micropolitics of schools. In T. Husen & T. N. Postlethwaite (Eds.), *The international encyclopedia of education* (2nd ed., Vol. 7, pp. 3821-3826). Oxford: Pergamon.

Ballet, K., & Kelchtermans, G. (2009). Struggling with workload. Primary teachers' experience of intensification. *Teaching and Teacher Education, 25*, 1150 -1157.

Bayer, M., Brinkkjær, U., Plauborg, H., & Rolls, S. (2009). (Eds.). *Teachers' career trajectories and work lives.* Professional learning and development in schools and higher education, Vol. 3. Dordrecht: Springer.

Beatty, B. (2000). The emotions of educational leadership: Breaking the silence. *International Journal of Leadership in Education, 3*, 331-357.

Beatty, B. (2002). *Emotional epistemologies and educational leadership: A conceptual framework.* Paper presented at the Annual Meeting of the American Educational Research Association, New Orleans.

Beatty, B., & Brew, C. (2004). Trusting relationships and emotional epistemologies: A foundational leadership issue. *School Leadership and Management, 24*, 329-356.

Bennett, N., Wise, C., Woods, P., & Harvey, J. A. (2003). *Distributed leadership. A review of literature. Full report.* Oxford: National College for School Leadership. Retrieved September 4, 2007, from http://www.ncsl.org.uk/media/7B5/67/distributed-leadership-literature-review.pdf.

Blackmore, J. (1996). Doing 'emotional labour' in the education market place: Stories from the field of women in management. *Discourse: Studies in the Cultural Politics of Education, 17*, 337-349.

Blackmore, J. (2004). Leading as emotional management work in high risk times: The counterintuitive impulses of performativity and passion. *School Leadership and Management, 24*, 440-459.

Blackmore, J. (2009). Measures of hope and despair. Emotionality, politics, and education. In E. A. Samier & M. Schmidt (Eds.), *Emotional dimensions of educational administration and leadership* (pp. 109-124). London: Routledge.

Blase, J. (1998). The micropolitics of education change. In A. Hargreaves, A. Lieberman, M. Fullan, & D. Hopkins (Eds.), *International handbook of educational change* (pp. 544-557). Dordrecht: Kluwer Academic.

Blase, J., & Anderson, G. L. (1995). *The micropolitics of educational leadership: From control to empowerment.* London: Cassell.

Bolman, L. G., & Deal, T. E. (1991). *Reframing organizations. Artistry, choice, and leadership.* San Francisco: Jossey-Bass.

Bush, T. (2003). *Theories of educational leadership and management* (3rd ed.). London: Sage.

Bush, T., & Glover, D. (2003). *School leadership: Concepts and evidence. Full report.* Oxford: National College for School Leadership. Retrieved September 13, 2007, from http://www.ncsl.org.uk/media/761/CE/randd-what-leaders-read-education-summary.pdf.

Coburn, C. E. (2001). Collective sensemaking about reading: How teachers mediate reading policy in their professional communities. *Educational Evaluation and Policy Analysis, 23*, 145-170.

Coburn, C. E. (2005). Shaping teacher sensemaking: School leaders and the enactment of reading policy. *Educational Policy, 19*, 476-509.

Coleman, M., & Earley, P. (2005). *Leadership and management in education. Cultures, change and context.* Oxford: Oxford University Press.

Crawford, M. (2005). Editorial. Distributed leadership and headship: A paradoxical relationship? *School Leadership and Management, 25*, 213-215.

Crawford, M. (2007a). Emotional coherence in primary school headship. *Educational Management, Administration and Leadership, 35*, 521-534.

Crawford, M. (2007b). Rationality and emotion in primary school leadership: An exploration of key themes. *Educational Review, 59*(1), 87-98.

Crawford, M. (2009). The leader and the team: Emotional context in educational leadership. In E. A. Samier & M. Schmidt (Eds.), *Emotional dimensions of educational administration and leadership* (pp. 186-197). Londen: Routledge.

Cuban, L. (1988). *The managerial imperative and the practice of leadership in schools*. Albany: State University of New York Press.

Day, C., & Leithwood, K. (Eds.). (2007). *Successful principal leadership in times of change. An international perspective*. Dordrecht: Springer.

Devos, G. (2000). *School management. Een reflectie op de praktijk van de schoolleider*. Diegem: Kluwer.

De Wit, K., Devos, G., & Verhoeven, J. C. (1998-1999). Op weg naar samenwerking. Vier case-studies uit het secundair onderwijs. *Tijdschrift voor Onderwijsrecht en Onderwijsbeleid, 10*(1), 53-64.

Giddens, A. (1979/2007). Agency, structure. In C. Calhoun, J. Gerteis, J. Moody, S. Pfaff, & I. Virk (Eds.), *Contemporary sociological theory* (2nd ed.) (pp. 239-242). Malden: Blackwell. (Original work published 1979.)

Greenfield, W. D. (1991). The micropolitics of leadership in an urban elementary school. In J. Blase (Ed.), *The politics of life in schools. Power, conflict, and cooperation* (pp. 161-184). Newbury Park: Sage.

Greenfield, W. D., Jr. (1995). Toward a theory of school administration: The centrality of leadership. *Educational Administration Quarterly, 31*, 61-85.

Gronn, P. (2000). Distributed properties: A new architecture for leadership. *Educational Management, Administration and Leadership, 28*, 317-338.

Gronn, P. (2002a). Distributed leadership. In K. Leithwood & P. Hallinger (Eds.), *Second international handbook of educational leadership and administration* (pp. 653-696). Dordrecht: Kluwer Academic.

Gronn, P. (2002b). Distributed leadership as a unit of analysis. *The Leadership Quarterly, 13*, 423-451.

Gronn, P. (2003a). Leadership's place in a community of practice. In M. Bundrett, N. Burton, & R. Smith (Eds.), *Leadership in education* (pp. 23-35). Londen: Paul Chapman.

Gronn, P. (2003b). Leadership: Who needs it? *School Leadership and Management, 23*, 267-290.

Gronn, P. (2003c). *The new work of educational leaders. Changing leadership practice in an era of school reform*. London: Paul Shapman.

Gronn, P. (2008). The future of distributed leadership. *Journal of Educational Administration, 46*, 141-158.

Gronn, P. (2009). Emotional engagement with leadership. In E. A. Samier & M. Schmidt (Eds.), *Emotional dimensions of educational administration and leadership* (pp. 198-211). Londen: Routledge.

Gronn, P., & Hamilton, A. (2004). 'A bit more life in the leadership': Co-principalship as distributed leadership practice. *Leadership and Policy in Schools, 3*(1), 3-35.

Gronn, P., & Lacey, K. (2004). Positioning oneself for leadership: Feelings of vulnerability among aspirant principals. *School Leadership and Management, 24*, 405-424.

Hallinger, P. (2003). Leading educational change: Reflections on the practice of instructional and transformational leadership. *Cambridge Journal of Education, 33*, 329-351.

Hargreaves, A. (1994). *Changing teachers, changing times: Teacher's work and culture in the postmodern age*. London: Cassell.

Hargreaves, A. (1998). The emotional politics of teaching and teacher development: With implications for educational leadership. *International Journal of Leadership in Education, 1*, 315-336.

Hargreaves, A., & Fink, D. (2004). The seven principles of sustainable leadership. *Educational Leadership, 61*(7), 8-13.

Harris, A. (2003). Teacher leadership as distributed leadership: Heresy, fantasy or possibility? *School Leadership and Management, 23*, 313-324.

Harris, A. (2005). Leading from the chalk-face: An overview of school leadership. *Leadership. 1*, 73-87.

Hopkins, D. (2001). *School improvement for real*. London: Routledge Falmer.

Hoyle, E. (1982). Micropolitics of educational organizations. *Educational Management and Administration, 10*, 87-98.

Jermier, J. M., & Kerr, S. (1997). "Substitutes for leadership: Their meaning and measurement." Contextual recollections and current observations. *The Leadership Quarterly, 8*, 95-101.

Kelchtermans, G. (2007a). Teachers' self-understanding in times of performativity. In L. F. Deretchin & C. J. Craig (Eds.), *International research on the impact of accountability systems. Teacher education yearbook XV* (pp. 13-30). Lanham: Rowman & Littlefield Education.

Kelchtermans, G. (2007b). Professional commitment beyond contract. Teachers' self-understanding, vulnerability and reflection. In J. Butcher & L. McDonald (Eds.), *Making a difference: Challenges for teachers, teaching, and teacher education* (pp.35-53). Rotterdam: Sense.

Kelchtermans, G. (2007c). Macropolitics caught up in micropolitics. The case of the policy on quality control in Flanders. *Journal of Education Policy, 22*, 471-491.

Kelchtermans, G. (2009). Who I am in how I teach is the message. Self-understanding, vulnerability and reflection. *Teachers and Teaching: Theory and Practice, 15*(2), 257-272.

Kelchtermans, G., Janssen, V., & Vandenberghe, R. (2003). *Structuurverandering of schoolontwikkeling? Over schaalvergroting in basisscholen*. Mechelen: Wolters Plantyn.

Kelchtermans, G., & Piot, L. (2010). *Schoolleiderschap aangekaart en in kaart gebracht*. Leuven: Acco.

Kelchtermans, G., Piot, L., & Ballet, K. (2011). The lucid loneliness of the gatekeeper: Exploring the emotional dimension in principals' work lives. *Oxford Review of Education, 37*, 93-108.

Kerr, S., & Jermier, J. M. (1978). Substitutes for leadership: Their meanings and measurement. *Organizational Behavior and Human Performance, 22*, 375-403.

Leithwood, K. A. (1992). The move toward transformational leadership. *Educational Leadership, 49*(5), 8-12.

Leithwood, K. (1994). Leadership for school restructuring. *Educational Administration Quarterly, 30*, 498-518.

Leithwood, K., Begley, P., & Cousins, J. (1992). *Developing expert leadership for future schools*. London: Falmer.

Leithwood, K., & Duke, D. (1999). A century's quest to understand school leadership. In J. Murphy & K. Louis (Eds.), *Handbook of research on educational administration* (pp. 45-72). San Francisco: Jossey-Bass.

Loader, D. (1997). *The inner principal*. London: Falmer.

Mayrowetz, D. (2008). Making sense of distributed leadership: Exploring the multiple usages of the concept in the field. *Educational Administration Quarterly, 44*, 424-435.

Nias, J. (1996). Thinking about feeling: The emotions in teaching. *Cambridge Journal of Education, 26*, 293-306.

Ogawa, R. T., & Bossert, S. T. (1995). Leadership as an organizational quality. *Educational Administration Quarterly, 31*, 224-243.

Piot, L., Kelchtermans, G., & Ballet, K. (2010). Beginning teachers' job experiences in multi-ethnic schools. *Teachers and Teaching: Theory and Practice, 16*, 259-276.

Samier, E. A., & Schmidt, M. (Eds.). (2009). *Emotional dimensions of educational administration and leadership*. Londen: Routledge.

Schein, E. H. (2004). *Organizational culture and leadership* (3rd ed.). San Francisco: Jossey-Bass.

Schutz, P. A., & Zembylas, M. (2009). *Advances in teacher emotion research. The impact on teachers' lives*. Dordrecht: Springer.

113

Solomon, R. C. (1998). Ethical leadership, emotions, and trust: Beyond "charisma." In J. B. Ciulla (Ed.), *Ethics, the heart of leadership* (pp. 83-102). Westport: Praeger.

Spillane, J. P. (2006). *Distributed leadership.* San Francisco: Jossey-Bass.

Spillane, J. P., Halverson, R., & Diamond, J. B. (2001). Investigating school leadership practice: A distributed perspective. *Educational Researcher, 30*(3), 23-28.

Spillane, J. P., Halverson, R., & Diamond, J. B. (2004). Towards a theory of leadership practice: A distributed perspective. *Journal of Curriculum Studies, 36,* 3-34.

Stoll, L. (2000). School culture. *Professional Development, 3,* 9-14.

Storey, A. (2004). The problem of distributed leadership in schools. *School Leadership and Management, 24,* 249-265.

Timperley, H. S. (2005). Distributed leadership: Developing theory from practice. *Journal of Curriculum Studies, 37,* 395-420.

Tosi, H. L., & Kiker, S. (1997). Commentary on "Substitutes for leadership." *The Leadership Quarterly, 8,* 109-112.

Vandenberghe, R. (2008). *Beginnende directeurs basisonderwijs.* Antwerpen: Garant.

Van Veen, K., & Lasky, S. (2005). Emotions as a lens to explore teacher identity and change: Different theoretical approaches. *Teaching and Teacher Education, 21,* 895-898.

Waite, D. (2002). The 'paradigm wars' in educational administration: An attempt at transcendence. *International Studies in Education Administration, 30*(1), 66-81.

Weick, K. E. (1995). *Sensemaking in organizations.* Thousand Oaks: Sage.

West, D. L. (2010). *The daily lives of principals: Twenty-one principals in the 21st century.* Unpublished dissertation, University of North Carolina, Faculty of the Graduate School, Greensboro. Supervisor: Dr. U. C. Reitzug.

Wolcott, H. F. (1973). *The man in the principal's office. An ethnography.* New York: Holt, Rinehart and Winston.

Woods, P. A., Bennett, N., Harvey, J. A., & Wise, C. (2004). Variabilities and dualities in distributed leadership. Findings from a systematic literature review. *Educational Management, Administration and Leadership, 32,* 439-457.

Yukl, G. A. (2006). *Leadership in organizations* (6th ed.). Upper Saddle River: Prentice-Hall.

AFFILIATIONS

Geert Kelchtermans
Centre for Educational Policy, Innovation and Teacher Training
The Education and Training Research Unit
Faculty of Psychology and Educational Sciences
KU Leuven, Belgium

Liesbeth Piot
PhD Fellow FWO Vlaanderen
Centre for Educational Policy, Innovation and Teacher Training
The Education and Training Research Unit
Faculty of Psychology and Educational Sciences
KU Leuven, Belgium

TOSHIYUKI KIHARA, HIROTOSHI YANO AND HISAYOSHI MORI

DEVELOPMENT OF A NEW CURRICULUM LEADERSHIP MODEL WITH A FOCUS ON ITS RELATION TO THE PROFESSIONAL LEARNING COMMUNITIES

INTRODUCTION

Since the 1990s, under the strong impacts of the globalization of economy and the shift to knowledge-based society on education, standards and accountability have been demanded in school education in many countries including Japan. In the midst of this situation, the concept of leadership came to be introduced in discussions of how school curriculum should be developed. A growing number of researchers took up discussing the process of curriculum practices, which are defined as an accumulation of creative teaching and learning. And, in their research, more attention was being paid to the role of curriculum leaders in this process, and so on. During these years, we have focused our attention to the theory of curriculum leadership as seen from literature on the subject, and examined its concept. On the other hand, by paying attention to the agents engaged in curriculum leadership, we have realized that curriculum development is a collaborative and inquiring process led by those who act in the form of communities in schools. Curriculum practices are based on partnership and cooperation among administrators, teachers, and practical leaders, where a process of learning is essential because curriculum leadership functions only when those concerned are working in collaboration with one another. It suggests that curriculum leadership in action needs to be supported by the presence of professional learning communities (PLCs), which is another new idea developed in recent educational reforms in countries of North America and Japan. The concept of PLCs is known as a teacher development scheme in recent educational reforms.

THEORETICAL FRAMEWORK

Literature Review on Curriculum Leadership

The attention to curriculum leadership started as an effort to identify the traits school leaders need to share so that they can tackle educational issues. For instance, Glatthorn and Jailall (2009) refer to curriculum leadership in terms of principals' role. They explain that curriculum leadership is "simply one component of effective organizational behaviour" (Glatthorn & Jailall, 2009, p. 42), and

M.A. Flores et al. (eds.), Back to the Future: Legacies, Continuities and Changes in Educational Policy, Practice and Research, 115–128.

introduces five "enabling behaviours": 1) facilitating communication, 2) creating a positive open climate, 3) Building a vision with the staff, 4) Developing staff through involvement, 5) being an effective and positive role model. Although they distinguish four different curriculum levels; state, district, school, and classroom, their attention is mostly paid to a principal's strong and effective leadership role. It is also known from their definition of curriculum leadership: "the exercise of those functions that enable school systems and the schools to achieve their goal of ensuring quality in what students learn" (Glatthorn & Jailall, 2009, pp. 36-37).

On the other hand, with attention still paid to the role of curriculum leaders, there appears to be a trend that views curriculum leadership as a function related to the process of problem solving and decision making for certain solutions because what is needed is something more than helping "educators to select, develop, and implement curricular materials" (Mullen, 2007, p.20). Henderson (2010) distinguishes three different paradigms in terms of curriculum decision-making, the Standardized Management Paradigm, the Constructivist Best Practice Paradigm, and the Curriculum Wisdom Paradigm. The Standardized management paradigm focuses on student performances on standardized tests, Constructivist best practice paradigm is concerned about student performances of subject matter understanding. Admitting the effectiveness of these two paradigms on certain occasions, Henderson (2010) refers to Curriculum wisdom paradigm as benefiting all students thorough the enhancement of students' subject understanding embedded in democratic self and social understanding. It is a perspective that views curriculum practice in a more critical and wider social context (Henderson & Gornik, 2007).

Although there is a rather more traditional view that curriculum leadership is a trait or attribute that school leaders ought to develop in themselves (Glatthorn, 2006), it is more common to see it as a new idea of problem solving for curriculum development, teaching and learning in schools of rapidly changing society (Mullen, 2007). It means that curriculum leadership is a process that involves a wider range of people than school leaders. Curriculum leadership is a term used to describe the process of problem solving in the creation and innovation of school curriculum. It is defined as "problem solving with curriculum wisdom" (Henderson & Gornik, 2007).

Recent discussions on curriculum leadership are shifting away from the attention to the role of school leaders to more non-central leadership functions, e.g. "urge for decentralization" (Hau-Fai Law, Galton, & Wai-Yan Wan, 2007). It is an argument that central agencies alone would not work in designing and planning a new curriculum and that teachers are far more requested to participate in decision making in a democratic way. The similar line can be observed in Leander and his colleagues' (2008) view that the theorization of leadership in recent school improvement debates are searching for a more flexible leadership model, where those concerned with school life play evolving roles (Leander & Osborne, 2008).

Mullen's (2007) summary helps us have an overview of current curriculum leadership discourse. She favourably sees Henderson and Gornik's (2007) modification of curriculum leadership, which is known as "transformative curriculum leadership," for the reason that it has the perspective of challenging current social issues in a democratic way. She also highly estimates Brubaker's (2004) "creative curriculum leadership" for its attention to inner curriculum, an autobiographical aspect of curriculum. Inner curriculum is important because it is regarded as leading to self-reflective, aesthetic and creative activities.

Through a study of curriculum leadership literature, the authors have extracted some common aspects that are regarded as components of curriculum leadership. New trends in curriculum leadership are represented by several key words: transformative (Henderson, 2010; Henderson & Gornik, 2007), creative (Brubaker, 2004; Mullen, 2007), democratic (Henderson, 2010; Henderson & Gornik, 2007; Mullen, 2007), critical (Henderson, 2010; Henderson & Gornik, 2007; Mullen, 2007), collaborative (Glatthorn, 2006; Henderson, 2010; Henderson & Gornik, 2007), and organizational (Brubaker, 2004; Henderson, 2010; Henderson & Gornik, 2007). If categorizing these key words into broader categorical groups, it is possible to summarize the following three adjectives: creative, democratic, and managerial. One of the common aspects in curriculum leadership is being creative. Curriculum development needs to be creative so that students learn to be creative. It ought to be a creative process for innovation in the rapidly changing society. The second aspect is being democratic. Curriculum needs to be designed to match a democratic society. And curriculum development and implementation ought to be put forward as a democratic process where information or an idea is shared by all the people concerned. And the process needs to be in progress as a managerial process as is the case with all other organizational activities in school.

Another finding the authors have obtained, suggested by Henderson (2010), is that it is possible to see a conceptual set, "narrative" and "inquiry," as an analyzing tool for curriculum leadership. According to Henderson (2010), education can be seen as a metaphor of journey. An educational journey is completed through the understanding of "Subject" matter embedded in democratic "Self" and "Social" understanding. He calls them "3S" and thinks that curriculum judgment for the integration of 3S understanding is of vital importance. For the realization of teaching toward 3S understanding, he argues, one needs balanced subject, self, and social inquiry, and also teachers' autobiographical examination embedded in academic knowledge and historical outlook. As a method to study autobiographical narratives and inquiries, he has developed a "currere method," which produces "currere narratives" mediating curriculum development cycle: designing and planning – teaching – evaluating – organizing. He thinks of curriculum development cycle as a process of cultivating reflective inquiry and reconceptualising subject standards.

Based on Henderson's (2010) conceptual set of "narrative" and "inquiry," the authors have developed a model of curriculum leadership. The concept of the model is illustrated as follows (see Figure 1); 1) responding to a constantly changing society (that is, innovating) as *creative* endeavours; 2) when advancing these creative endeavours, the significance of a *democratic* process for decision-making and resolving problems, which is supported by sharing information and

Figure 1. Main leadership groups in curriculum development

ideas (that is, creating networks); and 3) the importance of *management* of curriculum as part of the school's organizational activities (Kihara, Yano, & Mori, 2009; Yano, Kihara, & Mori, 2009).[1]

The Relationship between PLCs and Curriculum Leadership

The concept of PLCs emerged as questions about the quality of students' academic abilities gained momentum in the US from the 1990s. This concept was proposed by Hord (1997a) in her work, Professional Learning Communities: Communities of Continuous Inquiry and Improvement. Influences that led to the proposal of PLCs included research by Rosenholtz (1989) on the teaching profession. He observed the importance of professionalizing teachers from the standpoint of improving students' quality of education and also the importance of sharing what teachers learned and put into practice. He found that 1) teachers who felt "supported" in learning and in teaching had greater levels of enthusiasm and leadership ability; and 2) expanding teacher networks, cooperation among colleagues, and the role of the profession increased teachers' leadership ability. As a result, people became aware that for the teaching profession, which is known as an isolated job, support and networking and community lead to improved job performance.

The introduction of PLCs was also based on the findings by McLaughlin and Talbert (1993). They described teachers created accumulated wisdom through their own experiences and that they were able to share such wisdom through the opportunities to study and learn together as a group. PLCs were also influenced by Darling-Hammond's study (1996). It showed that actual reformation of school curriculum was effective not when it was implemented in a top-down manner, but when it involved all teachers in decision-making and secured time for teachers to train together. This suggested the importance of teachers' participation in school decision-making.

Furthermore, PLCs took ideas from the theory of "the learning organization" proposed by Senge (1990) in the field of organizational management. Learning organizations are "organizations where people continually expand their capacity to create the results they truly desire, where new and expansive patterns of thinking are nurtured, where collective aspiration is set free, and where people are continually learning to see the whole together." These organizations are strong when it comes to developing.

According to Hord (1997b), PLCs have the following five attributes: 1) supportive and shared leadership, 2) collective creativity, 3) shared values and vision, 4) supportive conditions (material, structural conditions; human abilities and qualities), and 5) shared personal practice. In PLCs theory, these five attributes are treated as defining characteristics of PLCs. For example, Hord and Sommers (2008) organized PLCs in the manner shown in Table 1.

Table 1. Components of professional learning communities (Hord & Sommer, 2008, p. 9)

Shared Beliefs, Values, and Vision	Shared and Supportive Leadership	Collective Learning and Its Application	Supportive Conditions	Shared Personal Practice
The staff consistently focuses on students' learning, which is strengthened by the staff's own continuous learning – hence, professional learning community.	Administrators and faculty hold shared power and authority for making decisions.	What the community determines to learn and how they will learn it in order to address students' learning needs is the bottom line.	*Structural factors* provide physical requirements: time, place to meet for community work, resources and policies to support collaboration. *Relational factors* support the community's human and interpersonal development, openness, truth-telling, and focusing on attitudes of respect and caring among the members.	Community members give and receive feedback that supports their individual improvement and that of the organization.

PLCs do not seek to improve schools and curriculum through the powerful leadership of the school administration or a part of the staff. Instead, it does so by involving the entire staff in the leadership process of making decisions (PLCs' democratic aspect), producing creativity that transcends individual power from this collaborative process (PLCs' creative aspect), and improving human relationships together by maximizing usable resources and material conditions

(PLCs' management aspect). Pursing these aspects will promote student learning. However, to create a learning community that includes students, it is essential to have a collaborative organization to unflaggingly nurture learning by teachers who are involved in the leadership process and their professional development. The authors find overlaps between these characteristics of PLCs and the characteristics of curriculum leadership that have been made clear in research up to now. The authors can understand the relationship between the two by viewing PLCs as a developmental tool for making curriculum leadership work.

RESEARCH QUESTION

Following the theoretical framework described above, the authors need to put it in a more specific context from a more realistic perspective. Through a consideration of the two different concepts, curriculum leadership and PLCs, with their mutual connectedness in view, a model of curriculum leadership has been built with a focus on its relation to PLCs. The research question can be raised as follows. Is it possible to identify the relationship between curriculum leadership and PLCs in the actual curriculum practices in schools? If possible, in what way do PLCs as a framework of teacher development contribute to the development of curriculum leadership? This paper is an attempt to verify a theoretical model by describing how it works in the process of curriculum practices, based on the observations made in schools in North America and Japan.

METHODOLOGY

Case studies

To clarify the research questions mentioned above, the authors visited some schools in US, Canada (once in March 2010) and Japan (five times in 2007-2009) where teachers tried to develop their PLCs. They are as follows:

Case 1: School A. School A is the elementary school (grades K-5) which is located in the midtown Memphis, Tennessee in US. It had 22 teachers and 25 support staff and so on when the authors visited there. The Mission Statement of this school is "Children First, Excellence Always" which means that all staff is eager to prepare and equip all students with the knowledge and skills to be productive citizens in an ever-changing global society.

It was famous as the "Science and Technology Optional School" with the computer and science laboratories (see Figure 2). In addition, School A got high mark on the website of school ranking at this region.

120

Figure 2. Computer Laboratory in School A

Case 2: School B. School B is also the elementary school (grades K-8) which is located outside Toronto, Canada. There was 26 staff in this school. The principal was proud of the wonderful parent support and excellent staff. Additionally she took pride in the program the staff offered their students and showed the authors the example named "Roots of Empathy." In the program children meet and communicate with babies in the school, which is an opportunity for them to raise social/emotional competence and increase empathy (see Figure 3 left). Moreover teachers in this school tried to use the rubric for the improvement of learning assessment. They develop rubric and share it with children with the usage of notice board on the wall and so on (see Figure 3 right).

Figure 3. "Roots of Empathy" (left) and Rubrics (right) in School B

121

Case 3: School C. School C is a small rural school located in the east of Hiroshima prefecture in Japan. It is regarded as one of the successful elementary schools in the country in terms of student learning, and has experience as a research school, designated by the Ministry of Education, the prefectural board of education and a non-profit funding organization, and supported by their teachers' high morale. What characterizes this school the most is the teachers' motivation to improve their teaching and their strong research-mindedness in everyday practice. The goal that the teachers have been striving for – it has been a research topic for the last few years – is "the development of teaching that aims at the enhancement of logical thinking skills and expression skills through the effective use of Information & Communication Technology in language art and mathematics." The strategies that have been conceived in order to achieve this goal include the introduction of teaching design to connect thought with expression and the use of ICT for teaching and learning in classrooms (see Figure 4). ICT may be used in a variety of ways not only by the teachers but also by the students; for instance, ICT may be used to visualize the problems that students are to work on and as a tool for rethinking. The teachers occasionally meet for peer lesson observations and also for conferences where reflections on lessons are held through in-depth discussions. All the teachers are required to show their research lessons three times or more every year in this particular school.

Figure 4. The usage of ICT in School C

Data Gathering

In those schools, the authors observed the lessons and interviewed principals and leading teachers about the design and implementation of the school-based curriculum development. In some cases, they collected the documents on the PLCs in the schools.

In addition, in the case of School C, we asked the leading teacher in charge of practical research and teacher development in the school to maintain a journal to periodically record data on the planning and implementation process of their school research.

FINDINGS

Case 1: Curriculum Leadership with PLCs in School A

In Tennessee, due to objectives set by the state superintendent, district boards of education and schools are doing all they can to improve students' academic abilities. Specific activities to accomplish this goal are symbolized by standardized testing and formative assessments.

To cope with these activities, at School A, two types of PLCs were developed. The teacher leaders of each grade and of each subject (language arts, mathematics, science, social studies, and technology) were assigned to PLCs. The first type, which is named "Horizontal Team PLCs," established 1) collaborative lesson planning time (three times per week for all school years, 35-45 minutes per session) and 2) sharing of teaching plans. Also, teams of the second type were assembled to allow teachers in charge of kindergarten children, students from grades 1 to 6, and special classes to work together on the subjects listed above. They called the teams "Vertical Team PLCs."

Additionally, a staff member called the Professional Development School Compliance Coach was placed in the school to handle the planning and steering of all the pluralistic PLCs. She not only planned and steered PLCs, but was also responsible for educating parents of the school's efforts.

Case 2: Curriculum Leadership with PLCs in School B

The term "PLCs" is also heard in School B in Memphis. Teachers in the school district also felt pressure to improve the test results of language and math abilities. Thus PLCs were introduced as a method to meet this goal. For example, in School B, days for PLCs were established. On those days "School Improvement Teams" by the teacher leaders of each school year gave presentations to one another about improving rubric-based lessons (see Figure 5). The teachers also shared ideas among themselves on how to improve lessons with rubrics.[ii]

We interviewed the principal and the leading teacher about the PLC in practice. As a result, we also identified a case of PLC networking that is worthy of mention. This is called TLCP (Teaching and Learning Critical Pathway), which is combined training program that spans schools. Several times a year, teachers from multiple schools gather at a teachers' centre or a school and exchange views on improving education. In short, it is peer assessment among schools. It is a strategy to widely obtain ideas on the suitability and even the possibility of school improvement plans that are decided by each school. In the midst of pressure exerted by standardized academic testing on teachers and their risk of being agitated by competition between schools, this effort contributes to creating an approach for improving students' academic abilities that builds on the unique foundation of each school.

Figure 5. Presentation by school improvement team of School B

Case 3: Curriculum Leadership with PLCs in School C

The descriptions contained in the journal of the leader teacher in School C were analyzed; the journal had chronologically recorded the process of curriculum development and implementation while referring to the activities that had taken place throughout the school. It had also recorded the journal-keepers contributions to those activities, and their achievements and outcomes. In his journal, a variety of activities have been referred to in terms of what he had done for the development of the school curriculum. Attempting a generalization of all such activities described in the journal, the following ten incidents were extracted as being representative of leadership functions: 1) designing staff development programs and workshops, 2) plan-do-check-action cycle for curriculum development, 3) making practical research reports as teaching portfolios, 4) organizing "research conferences" as opportunities for narrative inquiries, 5) building a close relationship with the local board of education, 6) bridging external resources, 7) preparing communication tools, such as newsletters, for sharing practical ideas and information, 8) collecting and sharing practical information on curriculum in other schools, 9) setting up a task force for curriculum development, and 10) being involved in role-rotation among the teachers as part of their "lesson study." For instance, the leading teacher describes the significance of the workshops as follows: "I introduced a workshop approach into the lesson research conferences this year and saw an unprecedentedly high level of participation in discussions in these conferences" (see Figure 6). It is obvious that those ten actions drawn up from the research are founded on the components of PLCs (Hord & Sommers, 2008, p. 9).

Figure 6. Lesson studies at School C

Commonalities among the Three Cases

Comparing the three cases, the authors found the commonalities on curriculum leadership functioning in the three schools. The following three findings are what the authors have drawn from the data analysis, the first of which is the answer to the first research question and the others are the ones to the second research question.

- PLCs promote to the development of curriculum leadership in practice as is seen in School B, where teachers develop how to use rubrics for assessment of student learning through exchanging ideas of using rubrics with teachers in other schools;
- The relationship between PLCs and curriculum leadership is strengthened more as one school is networked with others. It results in active workshops and conferences taking place in School C;
- Some leading teachers (e.g. the Professional Development School Compliance Coach at School A) or groups (e.g. School Improvement Team at School B) in schools play important roles to connect PLCs with curriculum leadership.

CONCLUSION AND DISCUSSION

The staff of the schools the authors visited had sought to develop their own curriculum that contribute to the learning of students, while being involved with diverse members, including the students and parents in the region. Such actions (practices) can be considered to be "School-Based Curriculum Development (SBCD)." Then, through four activities (collaborative lesson planning, securing and using resources, creating a teacher culture in which teachers learn from one another, and acquiring theories and models), leaders of practices, administrators, and teachers develop a specialized learning community within their own school. In such a case, curriculum leadership is a process that creates and grows a community to discuss and explore ways for making students' learning richer. And such a community can be considered to be a collaborative one for exploring ways to continually promote teachers' learning and professional development.

Based on the background described above, the authors made case studies in North America and Japan. Through a comparative review of the three cases, the authors have recognized that in both areas PLCs serve as the foundation of community of narrative inquiries with curriculum leadership for SBCD. In the course of the research, the authors have developed renewal model of curriculum leadership (see Figure 7). In this model, PLCs are regarded as a community that allows teachers to continue learning and improve their competencies through curriculum leadership.

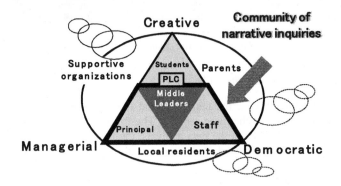

Figure 7. Structural model of curriculum leadership that pays attention to PLCs

In addition, it can be pointed out for further suggestions that a PLC resonates with the growth of other PLCs by becoming networked with one another. The result is the creation of networked learning communities (NLCs), where richer collective wisdom is created, accumulated, and shared among members. Teachers who "connect and learn" develop their capability even further by networking not only with others in their own schools, but with the PLCs of other schools. Such connections with others (other schools) are created not merely for the sake of networking, but for serving as a cultural tool to improve the competencies of teachers.

In this sense, the greatest significance of the model presented here lies not only in the creation and growth of PLCs within schools, but in the possibility of making (School-Based) curriculum development more fruitful by networking with the PLCs of other schools. For example, in Japan, "how the development of school- and classroom-based curriculum, which mainly involve teachers, is established in schools, and how education administrations and teachers' centres support the school- and classroom-based developments, and how this developmental process is researched and generalized, are critical questions that will determine the success or failure of developing future curriculum" (Sato, 2000, p. 122). Related to this observation, questions may have also been raised on the possible closed nature and conservativeness of lesson studies and school-based teacher training program (Abiko, 2009; Kihara, 2006; etc.).[iii]

This chapter argues, to address these questions, that good ideas for curriculum practices can be shared and accumulated (that is, collective wisdom is produced) by collaborative (School-Based) curriculum development among schools. This is accomplished by putting in place a full-powered, dual-oriented PLC, which makes the "uniqueness" of the curriculum of each school conspicuous. Good examples of this proposal include the Teaching and Learning Critical Pathway program mentioned earlier, which is joint teacher training program that encompasses the schools in the district. Other examples are practical research conferences in Japanese schools and collaborative educational activities between Japanese elementary and middle schools including School C. These efforts embody the developmental attitudes of a "community of narrative inquiry."

NOTES

[i] These results are provided in detail in our report Modelling the Role of Leadership Groups in School-Based Curriculum Development (Heisei 18–20 [2006-08] Ministry of Education, Culture, Sports, Science and Technology Grant-in-Aid Report) (March 2009).

[ii] The "school improvement team" in School B's case consisted of ten staff members, namely the principal, vice-principal, and head teachers of each school year. Their role included creating school improvement plans and planning and implementing training inside the school. When asked about the features of this team, they replied that their activities were based on analysis of data from tests given by the provincial government's Education Quality and Accountability Office.

[iii] For example, Kihara (2006) observes that "training and research activities in schools until now have a closed nature." He believes that this is because teachers respect conditions that have formed in the schools they belong to, based on the schools' history of practices. He states that teachers should shirk such exclusiveness and avoid sinking into inertia though the style of lesson studies and curriculum development at their schools are worthy (p. 17). Abiko (2009) states that study groups in Japan currently do not exchange much opinion and information on lesson studies. Therefore, even though what they are engaged in is called 'lesson studies,' what they learned is limited to the group, and their insights do not reach other groups" (p. 19).

REFERENCES

Abiko, T. (2009). Karikyuramu Kenkyuu to Jugyou Kenkyu [Curriculum Study and Lesson Study]. In Nihon Kyouiku Houhou gakkai [National Association for the Study of Educational Methods] (Ed.), *Nihon no Jugyou Kenkyu: Jugyou Kenkyu no Houhou to Keitai* [Lesson Study in Japan: Methods and Styles of Lesson Study] (pp. 11-20). Tokyo: Gakubunsha.

Brubaker, D. L. (2004). *Creative curriculum leadership: Inspiring and empowering your school community*. Corwin Press.

Darling-Hammond, L. (1996). The quiet revolution: Rethinking teacher development. *Educational Leadership, 53*(6), 4-10.

Gratthorn, A. A. (2006). *Curriculum leadership*. Sage Publications.

Gratthorn, A. A., & Jailall, J. M. (2009). *The principal as curriculum leader: Shaping what is taught and tested* (3rd edition). Corwin Press.

Hau-Fai Law, E., Galton, M., & Wai-Yan Wan, S. (2007). Developing curriculum leadership in schools: Hong Kong perspectives. *Asia Pacific Journal of Teacher Education, 35*(2), 143-159.

Henderson, J. G. (2010). Curriculum leadership. In Craig Krides (Ed.), *Encyclopedia of curriculum studies*, Vol. 1 (pp. 891-892). Sage.

Henderson, J. G., & Gornik, R. (2007). *Transformative curriculum leadership* (3rd edition). Pearson Education.

Hord, S. M. (1997a). Professional learning communities: Communities of continuous inquiry and improvement. *Issues about Change, 6*(1), 6-8.

Hord, S. M. (1997b). Professional learning communities: What are they and why are they important? *Issues about Change, 6*(2), 2-5.

Hord, S. M., & Sommers, W. A. (2008). *Leading professional learning communities: Voices from research and practice.* Thousand Oaks: Corwin Press.

Kihara, T. (2006). *Kyosi ga Migakiau Gakkou Kenkyu* [School-based action researches: Teacher collaboration and development]. Tokyo: Gyousei.

Kihara T., Yano, H., & Mori, H. (2009). *Gakko wo Kibantosuru Karikyuramu Kaihatu ni okeru Ri-da-shipugru-pu no Yakuwari no Moderuka* [Modeling the role of leadership groups in school-based curriculum development]. 2006-08 Ministry of Education, Culture, Sports, Science and Technology Grant-in-Aid Report.

Leander, K. M., & Osborne, M. D. (2008). Complex positioning: Teachers as agents of curricular and pedagogical reform. *Journal of Curriculum Studies, 40*(1), 23-46.

McLaughlin, M. W., & Talbert, J. E. (1993). *Contexts that matter for teaching and learning.* Stanford: Center for Research on the Context of Secondary School Teaching, Stanford University.

Mullen, C. A. (2007). *Curriculum leadership development: A guide for aspiring school leaders.* Lawrence Erlbaum Assoc.

Mullen, C. A. (Ed.). (2009). *The handbook of leadership and professional learning communities.* Palgrave Macmillan.

Rosenholtz, S. J. (1989). *Teacher's workplace.* New York: Longman.

Sato, M. (2000). Karikyuramu Kaihatsu [Curriculum development]. In Nihon Kyouiku Koggakai [Japan Society for Educational Technology] (Ed.), *Kyoiku Kougaku Jiten* [Encyclopedia of educational technology]. Tokyo: Jikkyou Shuppan.

Senge, P. M. (1990). *The fifth discipline: The art & practice of the learning organization.* New York: Doubleday Business.

Yano, H., Kihara, T., & Mori, H. (2009). *Development of a viable model for curriculum leadership.* Conference paper presented at the 3rd Triennial Conference of the International Association for the Advancement of Curriculum Studies (IAACS), NH The Lord Charles Hotel, Cape Town, South Africa.

AFFILIATIONS

Toshiyuki Kihara
Faculty of Education
Osaka Kyouiku University, Japan

Hirotoshi Yano
School of Letters
Mukogawa Women's University, Japan

Hisayoshi Mori
Junior College
Ryukoku University, Japan

JUDE BUTCHER, COLLEEN LEATHLEY AND KRISTIN JOHNSTON

ADVANCING EQUITY AND INCLUSION IN SCHOOLS: AN AWARENESS-ACTION FRAMEWORK

INTRODUCTION

Equity and inclusion are ever-present challenges for schools and school systems. Such challenges exist at the individual student level, requiring schools to provide opportunities for all students to participate and learn to their full capacity. The challenges also exist at a broader, systemic level, including having a supportive, inclusive and proactive school community.

Considering the contexts within these challenges occur is integral to raising people's educational aspirations (Lupton & Kintrea, 2011). The contexts within which these challenges are found can be characterised by a diversity of cultures (Keddie & Niesche, 2012). This diversity has been described sometimes in terms of cultural wars, and other times in terms of the "complexity of discourse *between* cultures both within and *between* societies" (Bates, 2005, p. 234). Another dimension of these contexts is seen in the extent of poverty which people experience with its associated impact upon educational attainment (Egan, 2012; Gazeley, 2010). The Australian Council of Social Services (2010) notes that those living in relative poverty in Australia – those whose living standards fall below an overall community standard and who miss out on opportunities and resources that most in the community take for granted – was around 11.1% in the 2006 census and is increasing. The Council notes that child poverty is of particular concern, with around 12% of Australian children living in households with equivalent income less than 50% of the median. They also note that Indigenous Australians are especially vulnerable to poverty.

The Council's findings are endorsed by Stilwell (2006, p. 8), who reports that: In a wealthy nation like Australia, ... particular social groups, such as single-parent families, recent migrants from non-English-speaking countries, and the long-term unemployed, commonly experience unacceptable levels of poverty. Many Aboriginal communities have living standards more typical of poor people in 'third world nations.'

A third dimension of these contexts is the extent and forms of multiple disadvantages which makes accessing the opportunities and benefits of education difficult for many children (Sinclair, McKendrick, & Scott, 2010). This dimension includes people experiencing at least three forms of disadvantage; for example economic in terms of lack of employment and low income, social in terms of lack

M.A. Flores et al. (eds.), Back to the Future: Legacies, Continuities and Changes in Educational Policy, Practice and Research, 129–145.

of support in crisis, and personal in terms of poor health or low educational attainment (Australian Social Inclusion Board, 2010).

Education has long been recognised as an effective tool in helping to break cycles of current or intergenerational poverty and disadvantage (Vinson, 2007). Mastery of even basic literacy and numeracy skills is recognised as being important for reducing poverty and empowering people with the knowledge, skills and confidence to help shape a better future. In recognition of this, 'universal primary education by 2015' has been established as the second Millennium Development Goal (UNESCO, 2011).

The benefits of inclusion and social participation at individual and community levels have also been long established. Maslow (1968) identified a sense of social belonging as one of the more basic human needs, recognising that it was difficult to develop higher-level needs of self-fulfilment without it. Positive parent and peer relationships have been shown to have an important impact upon social and emotional development (Cripps & Zyromski, 2009). Supportive relationships amongst peers, families, teachers and the broader community have also been shown to be helpful in mobilising social and cultural resources to support academic development (Moll, 2010).

Within the school context, positive relationships based on trust, respect and genuine interest, have been shown to positively impact on students' academic orientation and success (Darling-Hammond et al., 2005). 'Networks of exchange,' predicated on trust, are similarly seen to hold 'educational capital' (Moll, 210). In contrast, communities with limited social networks have been linked to limited aspirations among disadvantaged young people (Cuthbert & Hatch, 2009).

Abu El-Haj (2007) defines 'substantive inclusion' in the school community as the capacity to participate fully and to contribute meaningfully to all its activities. She encourages schools and educators to acknowledge, rather than to ignore differences, and to consider these from a relational and educational perspective. This implicates the broader society in the process of change, where everyone is part of the solution to educational inequality.

This recognition of the importance of relationships and networks reinforces that schools do not operate in an educational or social vacuum. Decisions and actions made by the school influence, and are influenced by, the broader community context in which they exist. In this, schools are a community within a community, and have social, educational and cultural parameters and networks in which they operate. However, this community element of education is played out within what has been described as:

> a crucial problematic for schools, for they are sandwiched between system demands for the production of skills required by the competitive economy and cultural demands to respond to the quest for meaning in individual lives through access to sources for the self. (Bates, 2005, p. 236)

While equity and inclusion are important questions for school systems generally, they have particular relevance to Catholic schools for whom it is important that they "ensure participation by all social strata of our community, especially the poor' (Catholic Bishops of NSW and the ACT, 2007, p. 9). Research into factors related to the participation within Catholic schools by communities and families who are "poor" is designed primarily for promoting equity and inclusion in Catholic schools. These findings will in turn inform how schools generally engage with communities and families who are "poor" or marginalised (Butcher, Johnston, & Leathley, 2011).

This paper reports upon an education system's study designed to address the following four research questions:
- What are schools' perceptions of people who are "poor"?
- What are schools' perceptions of their roles in relation to the poor?
- What strategies are schools using in engaging with people who are poor?
- What other strategies could schools employ for engaging with people who are poor?

The results of the study were examined subsequently in terms of a frame of reference which emerged from the data for informing how schools can appropriately engage with the communities to advance equity and inclusion.

METHODOLOGY

The geographical catchment area (diocese) in which the research was undertaken is situated on the outer fringes of Sydney, Australia. The area encompasses some of the wealthier and poorer Local Government Areas in New South Wales.

A total of 25 Systemic schools participated in the research. Of these, 20 (80%) were Primary and 5 (20%) were Secondary. The number of students in the schools ranged from less than 200 to over 1000.

Table 1. School by type and student numbers

Students	Primary	Secondary	Total
0-200	1		1
201-300	4		4
301-400	9*		9
401-500	4		4
501-800	2		2
810-999		2	2
1000+		3	3
Total	20	5	25

* 1 school = combined early childhood and primary

Data collection encompassed surveys, interviews and focus groups, as follows.

Surveys

Parents, teachers, senior school support officers, welfare groups and clergy all received the same survey, seeking their views on:
– their understanding of 'the poor' when applied to members of the school community;
– role(s) Catholic schools should play in caring for the poor;
– factors helping Catholic schools in caring for the poor;
– factors hindering Catholic schools in caring for the poor;
– recommendations or suggestions to help Catholic schools assist the poor; and
– three ways a commitment to people who are poor should influence the life of the school.
The survey also included scope to provide additional comments.

The survey for school principals encompassed the above items, and also asked them to provide additional information on:
– the number of students enrolled in the school;
– percentage of students in the school they considered poor;
– policies and strategies in place to assist the poor; and
– possible exclusion of poor from enrolling or continuing in the school.

Table 2. Survey responses by participant group

Participant group	No. responses
Principals	25
Teachers > 10 years experience	58
Teachers < 10 years experience	34
Parents	30
Senior School Support Officers	17
Clergy	5
CEO Leadership Team	3
Welfare agencies	3
Total:	175

Interviews

A total of 29 individual interviews were conducted, with a cross section of participants from six selected schools (see Table 3). These schools were selected in collaboration with the Diocese's Catholic Education Office and conducted by the researchers. They explored similar themes to those in the survey while providing an opportunity for a more detailed and personalised understanding of key issues.

Table 3. Interviews conducted

Participant group	Number
Principals	6
Teachers > 10 years experience	6
Teachers < 10 years experience	6
Parents	2
Senior School Support Officers	6
Clergy	1
Support staff (e.g. business manager; uniform shop personnel)	2
Total:	29

Focus Groups/Workshops

In addition to one-on-one interviews, information was gained through five focus groups:
– 2 focus groups of secondary school students, with 3-4 students in each group;
– 1 focus group of parents;
– 1 workshop with over 20 Religious Education Coordinators;
– 1 focus group of ten specialists working in the welfare area. This focus group was conducted by a leader of a local welfare agency, with responses collated on a Welfare survey form.

The focus groups provided an opportunity for the researchers to gain a fuller understanding of the issues, opportunities and challenges of responding to the poor, as per the aims of the research. They ranged in duration from one hour (students and parents) to one morning (RECs, welfare). With the exception of the Welfare workers, all focus groups and workshops were conducted by the researchers.

RESULTS

Perceptions of People Regarded as Being 'Poor'

The most common understanding of 'poor' comprised a financial or economic dimension, however nearly two thirds (63%) of participants reported multidimensional features, involving a mixture of material, emotional, spiritual, disability and life style factors. Principals, teachers with over ten years' experience, CEO leaders and welfare groups, in particular, recognised this broader, more complex, perception.

> The predominant word for me is anyone who is disadvantaged – either economically, socially, academically, psychologically, physically and spiritually. (Teacher>10yrs, LB)

> Poor does not necessarily have to refer to poor in wealth, but poor in love and nurturing as well. (Teacher<10 yrs, QE)

133

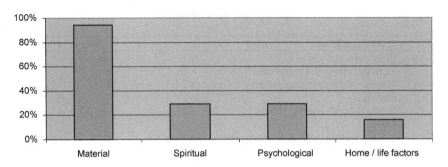

Figure 1. Participants' perceived dimensions of poor

Nearly three quarters (71%) of principals considered that being poor excluded some children from enrolling or continuing in their school. They based their assessment on an inability or difficulty to meet fees, growing enrolments in public schools, and a 'private school' mentality. Groups they deemed most likely to be affected were those from low-SES, Aboriginal and housing commission families.

> People can be spiritually, emotionally, socially and intellectually 'poor.' In my experience, the poor who are in financial difficulty are sometimes just the most obvious. (CEO, #1)

Nearly all principals reported having formal or informal strategies in place for identifying the poor. The most common strategies included information from parents at enrolment, parent-interviews or other discussions, or other referral sources, such as primary feeder schools and established community groups. Other principals were proactive in advertising or inviting families to bring it to the attention of the school.

Role(s) of the school in relation to the poor. There was very strong indication that schools do have, and often are already playing, a significant role in relation to the poor. Participants indicated that the most common roles encompassed practical support, pastoral care or support, and religious education and formation.

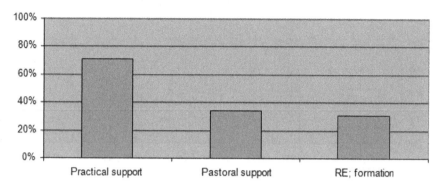

Figure 2. Perceived role of the school in caring for the poor

I think the school's role should be to ensure that children are not missing out on important things or are not seen by others to be missing out. (Parent, LE)

Catholic schools were established to educate the poor and marginalised. All children and families need to have an opportunity for a Catholic education if they wish. (Principal, JD)

In the Catholic school, responsibility is given to all members – teachers, students, parents, clergy, to create social conditions in which the dignity of each person regardless of background is respected and upheld. (Teacher>10yrs, JF)

Factors That Help Schools in Caring for the Poor. The research highlighted a number of resources and networks that are available or could be developed within and outside the school community in caring for the poor. There was strong support to use these resources and networks, including providing practical support and assistance; pastoral support and a sense of community; manifesting Gospel values; and establishing and providing referrals and networks. Having school leaders with the knowledge, compassion and skill to identify and respond to those in need in a discreet and sensitive manner was also considered a major factor.

Catholic schools have the resources and network to play a pivotal role in helping the poor. I am not sure whether the Catholic system pays enough emphasis or priority in assisting the poor on a consistent basis. (Parent, YE)

It is a small school with very supportive parish and parents. School leadership team is also proactive in identifying possible issues. (Principal, LC)

I believe we are committed to helping those in need. It is part of our culture and what we are, stand for and believe in; helping one and all. (SSSO, LF)

135

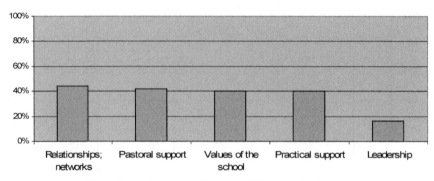

Figure 3. Factors that assist a school in caring for the poor

Factors That Hinder Schools in Caring for the Poor.   Along with the strong basis for providing support, it was evident that pragmatic and personal factors influence the level and nature of support schools can provide. Human and financial resource constraints were particularly highlighted. While economic factors were not the primary driver in running a school, they could not be ignored. Staffing allocations, funding levels, the proportion of non-paying families and competing demands of staff and school time and teaching loads were identified as contemporary realities that influence a school's ability to identify and respond to those in need in a caring manner.

Attitudinal factors also featured highly in hindering both identification of and assistance to the poor. This included pride and embarrassment preventing people from asking for help; perceptions that Catholic schools are private schools or for the middle class; and discrepancy between the 'haves' and 'have nots.' This highlights the need to address broader social and school culture perceptions, where word of mouth and general impressions often have greater influence than policy, practice or advertisements.

Structural and broader system requirements, including policies, reporting requirements, politics, varying agendas, organisational and operational processes, were highlighted as hindering factors, particularly by principals and teachers with more than ten years' experience.

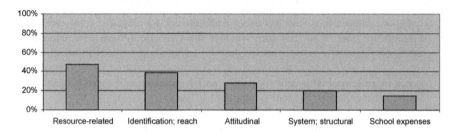

Figure 4. Factors that hinder a school in caring for the poor

Changing role and focus on educators to achieve results and prove academic merit across the diocese. Therefore less of a focus on the needs of individuals or families in the school community. (Parent, JA)

The danger of parents treating the school as a 'private' school rather than a Catholic school wanting all the latest and most expensive resource and facilities – seeing material and intellectual achievements as being the sole reserve of success. (Clergy, #2)

Schools are so busy and crammed with compliance and curriculum ... as well as good agendas that there is no time left. (Principal, ZC)

Suggested Strategies for Better Assisting the Poor. Participants highlighted a number of ideas for building on the 'helping factors' or addressing 'inhibiting factors,' to respond more effectively to those in need. Key ideas included:
– Proactive engagement for increased awareness of the poor and their needs – proactively engaging and identifying areas of need and opportunity, not waiting for them to be presented;
– Providing practical assistance and support – e.g., fee relief, fundraising initiatives, uniform assistance or support networks;
– Providing a pastoral response – promoting a sense of community; modelling the way; a supportive, caring community that provides practical and personal support to its members;
– Promoting a collaborative partnership – recognising the need for schools to work collaboratively with the parishes and broader communities to provide a more integrated, collective response;
– Reviewing policies and procedures – administrative changes to policy, processes or curriculum to increase awareness, understanding and response to the poor.

We have to go out to the poor, not expect them to be able to come ... – school/church must be aware of needs and outreach to them. (Welfare, #3)

Schools need to know what the need is in their area. Need to work as a team – school reps, parents, children and a charitable organisation. (SSSO, JB)

Look beyond the boundaries of the school fence and involve the community in the school. (Parent, YE)

Families who find it difficult to pay for school fees could offer other services in lieu of money. For example, parents could work one day a week in the canteen or assist on working bees for maintenance of the school. (Teacher<10yrs, QE)

DISCUSSION

The research identified varying perceptions between and within schools, in terms of what defines 'the poor' and the school's role in supporting them. The broad range of definitions and perceived incidence of 'the poor' indicates the term is a subjective, multidimensional and complex one and that it is not easy to categorise or distinguish between different types of 'poor.' Recognising and addressing this broader and multidimensional reality of what it means to be 'poor' must be a priority.

While all participants in the research were able to offer a definition of 'the poor,' and saw the school or broader community as having a key role in caring for them, the depth of responses indicated varying levels of awareness or contact with the poor. For parents and teachers with less than ten years' experience, in particular, the responses indicated a largely conceptual or academic response, in contrast to a personal or experience-based understanding. Responses from principals, teachers with more than ten years' experience and welfare agencies tended on the whole to exhibit a more discerning and grounded emphasis and experience, suggesting they "engaged" with the poor on a regular basis and were fluent in their language.

The research highlighted many examples of what can be done within school communities with limited resources but a good community spirit. It also highlighted many examples of unmet need and the significant impact of leadership, community engagement and, at times, conflicting priorities.

The study also identified a number of valuable insights for schools wishing to increase their equity and inclusion agenda. Four key insights, relevant to the subsequent development of a framework, are listed below.

– Schools need to consider many dimensions, including material and non-material, in identifying and responding to the poor in their community;

– Schools need to consider how they can best respond in a way that is appropriate to their unique context, adapting and working effectively within their environment and constructing and applying learning;

– To have a full understanding and appreciation of the poor requires personal encounter – it is not something that can be learned second hand but needs to come from engaging directly with people who are disadvantaged, or socially isolated. This transformative approach must extend beyond a transactional 'doing' or 'giving.' It requires relationships and an engagement, of 'working with' the poor where both the giver and receiver are open to being transformed by the other as part of a collective, caring community. Ultimately, it calls for a conversion of heart and mind;

– Community engagement principles foster a collaborative spirit of mutual transformation and allow for partnerships and relationships to be strengthened and to contribute to the greater good of society. Schools form part of multiple systems, and need to consider the role they can best play, through engaging for mutual benefits, with the broader educational and social systems and networks in their environment.

AWARENESS-ACTION FRAMEWORK

Two main dimensions stood out in the responses and themes from the research in terms of a school's approach to identifying and engaging with those in need:
– Awareness – knowing who and where are those who are in need, and their awareness of the support and services available to them; and
– Action – factors that help or hinder; strategies and recommendations for improving care.

The dimensions are inherently intertwined, in that it is difficult to respond if not first being aware, and that awareness itself is of limited value if no action is taken.

When reviewing participants' comments in relation to survey or interview questions, it was apparent that they varied in the type and level of complexity, engagement and ownership they exhibited. Some responses appeared to be somewhat uni-dimensional in nature, lacking an empathy or exposure to the relevant issue or people. In contrast, some responses exhibited a multidimensional understanding and empathy, indicating the participant had not only personal exposure and engagement with people who are poor, and familiarity with the issue in question, but also a level of efficacy in working with them. They also tended to emphasise a community approach and sense of ownership.

This contrast is evident in the following survey extracts, in relation to the question 'what do you understand 'the poor' to mean when applied to members of our school community?':

Those less fortunate than others. Families experiencing financial hardship. (SSSO, JC)

I believe that 'the poor' in our school community is relating to those families that are grossly affected by extreme difficulties. These difficulties do not necessarily have to do with financial ones, but can be due to dealing with chronic illness, physical, emotional, or a combination of all the above. (Parent, QC)

'The poor' are those members of the school community whose income is at a level where meeting the general financial obligations of school life is a great hardship. This includes uniforms, equipment, fees and excursions. They may also be financially illiterate – unable to prioritise spending appropriately. Families who suddenly find themselves losing income through death or loss of unemployment may also experience great financial difficulty and require emotional assistance during this time as well. (Teacher >10yrs, QF)

The poor within the community can be defined as those who struggle financially but also those who are spiritually poor. Generally, those who are struggling financially are those who pay what they can in terms of fees and school costs but also those who give in other ways, e.g. their time, food, preparation, volunteer assistance. These people are humble yet happy of heart. Those who are spiritually poor are those who are seeking something more in their lives and yet may be at a loss to name or act on it. (Principal, LD)

It was also evident that the comments could be rated on a low-high scale, depending on the level of complexity, understanding and familiarity they exhibited within and between the awareness-action dimensions.

Within the awareness dimension, for example:

– a 'low' level would demonstrate limited (one-dimensional) knowledge or personal experience, and a situation where those in need in the school or community went largely unrecognised. Understanding would be largely conceptual versus personal in nature;

– a 'high' level would demonstrate a more personal knowingness of people and their circumstances, where people in need are recognised in a compassionate, discreet and sensitive manner. Understanding would be largely empirical and personal in nature, demonstrating a high level of familiarity and efficacy.

Similarly, within the action dimension:

– a 'low' level would be one where the response is limited (one-dimensional), or largely transactional in nature. This would include referral to another support agency, anonymous donations or no response at all;

– a 'high' level would be one which is personal and interactive, allowing for mutual transformation and delivered with dignity and compassion.

Given the identified rating schedule and the recognised interplay between the two dimensions, the following awareness-action matrix or framework (see Figure 5) was developed.

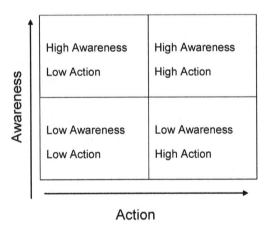

Figure 5. Awareness-action framework

In reviewing the survey and interview responses from participants, it was possible to 'map' them to the matrix, depending on their awareness and action levels. Responses that displayed what could be considered acumen and skill in knowing and responding to the needy in their community, for example, would be more likely to sit at the higher (right hand corner) end of the matrix. In contrast, responses demonstrating a lower level of familiarity or experience, or being uni-dimensional or isolated in nature, would more likely sit at the 'lower' end of the spectrum.

An example of how sample quotes map to the framework is provided in Table 4.

Table 4. Action-awareness framework: Low-high levels

High Awareness; Low Action	In-between:	High Awareness; High Action
Example quote: "The word 'poor' brings to mind 'disadvantaged,' 'need,' 'lacking.' As with any community our school community is unique – affected by demographics, multiculturalism, economics, language and social issues – all members of our school community at some point in time would be 'poor' in these areas" (SSSO, XD).	"There are many dimensions to the notion of 'poor' including spiritual and emotional poverty. Poverty implies a deprivation of something, so people can be poor if they are deprived of services, opportunities or access to reasonable standards of living. In regard to school communities in our Diocese, I believe that these non-material types of poverty have been well identified and targeted to date. They are still problematic but they are, at least, in the general consciousness. The real issue is that of material poverty. Those with little or no money, often fuelled by unemployment and other social issues related to poor education, language, immigration, family breakdown, substance abuse, lack of social support, etc. There are many people with little or no money or assets who need direct intervention and assistance from our school community." (Welfare, #4).	Example quote: "The poor within the community can be defined as those who struggle financially but also those who are spiritually poor. Generally, those who are struggling financially are those who pay what they can in terms of fees and school costs but also those who give in other ways, eg their time, food, preparation, volunteer assistance. These people are humble yet happy of heart. Those who are spiritually poor are those who are seeking something more in their lives and yet may be at a loss to name or act on it. (Principal, LD).
Low Awareness; Low Action		Low Awareness; High Action
Example quote: "Don't support helping those who claim to be poor but don't help themselves or are after handouts – hard to distinguish these though." (Parent, XC).		Example quote: Ability of school to care for its 'poor' has a strong relationship with how it can connect to its community. Need to look outside traditional school structure to provide greater innovation and access to school resources (Parent, YE).

Potential Application of the Framework

While initially intended to act as an organising tool for the data, it became apparent that the framework could also act as a useful tool for assisting schools (or systems or departments) to consider where they currently sit on the framework, the implications of this, and how they might enhance their awareness and action levels.

The tool has both structure and flexibility to identify and assess relevant measures and criteria for 'high' and 'low' dimensions, much as a marking rubric.

This could be applied to just the awareness and action dimensions, or could also encompass sub-dimensions, such as complexity (recognition of single or multiple dimensions); integration (whether strategies are predominantly isolated or linked); attitude (respect and dignity or judgemental); effectiveness (do the strategies seem to be working); and process (transformational versus transactional). Some sample questions that may assist in this process within each dimension are below:

Awareness
− How well do we know the members of our school community;
− If I was a member of the school community, would I feel comfortable approaching the school for help;
− What strategies do we have, or can put in place, to identify those in the school community who are struggling and require assistance from the school community;
− How do, or can, we reach out to the poor in the community who feel excluded from attending or participating in the school;
− Is our perception more inward or outward looking;
− Are we proactive in our approach, or rely on others to come forward with information?

Action
− When we become aware of those in our community needing assistance, how do we respond;
− Is this something we do often and comfortably;
− Are our actions done with respect and promote dignity;
− Whose needs do our strategies really serve;
− Do those who receive our assistance feel supported and welcomed;
− Are we willing to be changed by the encounter;
− Is our action essentially transactional or personal and transformational in nature;
− Where is the potential for a systemic and integrated response;

It is perceived that a key benefit of the framework is in providing a structure and opportunity for honest and healthy dialogue by schools (and departments or systems), in looking at the ways they identify and respond to the needs of 'the poor' in their school.

Using the questions and low-high dimensions as a guide, schools could assess where they currently sit in the framework. This would also entail considering potential 'risks' to the school community in being in the low awareness-low action cell, and strategies for increasing their awareness or actions. The tool could also act as a progress monitor, with schools and the system being able to compare progress across time periods, schools, classes or programs.

It is to be noted that this framework tool has been conceptualised from this research data and will benefit from further development and testing. The following factors also need to be taken into consideration regarding the application of the framework:

– Non-articulation of a sentiment does not mean it does not exist;
– Articulation of a sentiment does not mean it is in place, or is perceived to be effective by those it is designed to serve;
– The process of moving towards a 'higher' cell requires consideration and sensitivity. Rushing or imposing strategies could have adverse and unintended consequences that do not advance inclusion and mutual transformation;
– It is possible to reduce rater bias and increase objectivity by establishing relevant criteria before self-assessing (perhaps using or adapting the items and questions listed above) and by approaching the task with humility and honesty.

CONCLUSION

Schools are microcosms of our broader society. They are communities within communities or communities engaging with wider communities. All schools, irrespective of their economic or demographic base, will have students who are 'poor' or 'in need' and this will often entail multiple disadvantage. The challenge, and the opportunity in many ways, is for schools to identify and engage with these children and families in a timely, respectful and mutually transformative way. The diversity and complexity of the contexts within these challenges and opportunities are to be addressed calls for awareness and action which are proactive and multi-dimensional.

Research cited throughout this paper highlights clear benefits to schools, students and the broader community in adopting a relational, integrated and transformational approach to equity and inclusion. This involves looking beyond individual people or transactions, to a broader community-engagement and collective response. It reflects the difference between a 'walking with,' rather than a 'handing out.' In the process, all are transformed in beneficial ways.

Adopting such an approach requires engagement with and awareness of the other, reflection upon one's own school, and action. It involves assessing how well a school currently engages with and responds to those in need in their school community. It also involves considering future strategies, and an avenue for reviewing progress.

The awareness-action framework deriving from research introduced in this paper is offered as a tool, for facilitating engagement, assessment and action in a relational context. It recognises that awareness and action are intertwined with regards to equity and inclusion – the presence of one necessitates acknowledgement of the other. Its semi-structured nature is designed to provide for both consistency and flexibility of approach. It also encourages schools, and

143

broader systems, to consider the complexity, integration and dignity of their approaches and to consider if they are effectively uni- or multidimensional in their engagement, awareness and action. It can also help schools identify ways to be transformed and proactive in adopting a multidimensional approach to engaging with families for promoting equity and inclusion in education.

Teacher educators could employ the awareness-action framework in the development of teacher education programs and structuring student teachers' school-community experiences. The framework could also be used as a tool for student teachers' self-reflection upon their engagement with and understanding with a school's wider community.

REFERENCES

Abu El-Haj, T. R. (2007). *Equity, difference and everyday practice. Taking a relational approach.* Retrieved 18 March 2011 fromhttp://annenbergchallenge.org/Equity/pdf/Essay_El-Haj.pdf.

Australian Council of Social Services. (2010). *Poverty report.* Retrieved 25 January, 2011, from http://acoss.org.au/images/uploads/ACOSS_poverty_report_October_2010.pdf.

Australian Social Inclusion Board (2010). *Social inclusion in Australia: How Australia is faring.* Australian Government, Canberra.

Bates, R. (2005). An anarchy of cultures: The politics of teacher education in new times. *Asia-Pacific Journal of Teacher Education, 33*(3), 231-241.

Butcher, J., Johnston, K., & Leathley, C. (2011). The poor in Catholic schools: A transformative agenda – Engaging schools and communities. *Journal of Catholic School Studies, 83*(1), 40-53.

Catholic Bishops of NSW and the ACT. (2007). *Catholic schools at a crossroads: Pastoral letter.* Sydney: Catholic Bishops of NSW and the ACT.

Cripps, K., & Zyromski, B. (2009). Adolescents' psychological well-being and perceived parental involvement: Implications for parental involvement in middle schools. *Research in Middle Level Education Online, 33*(4), 1-13.

Cuthbert, C., & Hatch, R. (2009). *Educational aspiration and attainment amongst young people in deprived communities.* Edinburgh: Centre for Research on Families and Relationships.

Darling-Hammond, L., Banks, J., Zumwalt, K., Gomez, L., GarmoranSherin, M., Giesdorn, J., & Finn, L-E. (2005). Educational goals and purposes: Developing a circular vision for teaching. In L. Darling-Hammond & J. Bransford (Eds.), *Preparing teachers for a changing world* (pp. 169-200). San Francisco: Jossey-Bass.

Egan, D. (2012). *Communities, families and schools together: A route to reducing the impact of poverty on educational achievement in schools across Wales.* London: Save the Children Fund.

Gazeley, L. (2010). The role of school exclusion processes in the re-production of social and educational disadvantage. *British Journal of Education Studies, 58*(3), 293-309.

Keddie, A., & Niesche, R. (2012). Productive engagements with student difference: Supporting equity through cultural recognition. *British Educational Research Journal, 38*(2), 333-348.

Lupton, R., & Kintrea, K. (2011). Can community-based interventions on aspirations raise young people's attainment? *Social Policy & Society, 10*(3), 321-335.

Maslow, A. H. (1968). *Toward a psychology of being* (2nd ed.). New York: Harper & Row.

Moll, L. C. (2010). Mobilizing culture, language and educational practices: Fulfilling the promises of Mendez and Brown. *Educational Researcher, 39*, 451-460.

Sinclair, S., McKendrick, J. H., & Scott, G. (2010). Failing young people?: Education and aspirations in a deprived community. *Education, Citizenship and Social Justice, 5*(1), 5-20.

Stilwell, F. (2006). Processes of globalisation: The generation of wealth and poverty. In K. Serr (Ed.), *Thinking about poverty* (pp. 8-23). Sydney: The Federation Press.

Vinson, T. (2007). *Dropping off the edge: The distribution of disadvantage in Australia.* Richmond, Vic: Jesuit Social Services; Curtin, ACT: Catholic Social Services Australia.

AFFILIATIONS

Jude Butcher
Institute for Advancing Community Engagement
Australian Catholic University, Australia

Colleen Leathley
Institute for Advancing Community Engagement
Australian Catholic University, Australia

Kristin Johnston
Institute for Advancing Community Engagement
Australian Catholic University, Australia

SHUKRI SANBER AND IRENE HAZOU

COGNITIVE SKILLS IN PALESTINIAN CURRICULA AND TEXTBOOKS

INTRODUCTION

Since the establishment of the Palestinian National Authority in 1994, efforts have been directed at developing a Palestinian school curriculum to replace the Jordanian and Egyptian curricula used during the Israeli occupation. The first Palestinian curriculum was implemented in 2000 (Ministry of Education and Higher Education, 1998), and new textbooks aligned to the objectives of this new curriculum were released. Textbooks play a vital role in the teaching and learning process in Palestinian schools, because of the paucity of alternative learning resources in most schools. The country has been devastated by several regional wars and long-term occupation, during which minimal effort and resources were employed to modernise its education system. It seems logical that systematic research should be conducted to determine the extent to which these textbooks provide the necessary contexts to allow students to gain targeted knowledge and skills. This study was designed to fill an identified gap in the literature. Analytical instruments reflecting Marzano's (2001) 'new taxonomy of educational objectives' were developed to help determine the thinking levels addressed by the textbooks. Two individual subject curricula and two corresponding textbooks – for science and for social studies, respectively – were purposefully sampled for analysis. The learning objectives of the curricula and the content of the textbooks, their learning activities and their end-of-chapter and end-of-unit exercises were analysed. The results of the study indicate that the sampled curricula and textbooks address and support a variety of thinking skills. However, the degree of emphasis on higher thinking skills was found to be stronger in the science textbooks than in the social studies textbooks.

BACKGROUND TO THIS STUDY

Policymakers and educators advocate the importance of designing learning environments that support the development of learners' cognitive skills. Fischer, Bol, and Pribesh (2011) argue that thinking skills are essential components of modern education, and this emphasis on cognitive skills is reflected in the objective and goal statements of modern movements of curriculum reform. It seems that "the new millennium brought with it a wave of educational goal statements advocating the importance of higher-order thinking" (McEwan, 2008, p. 51). This interest in promoting thinking skills is a worldwide phenomenon, with emphasis on the

M.A. Flores et al. (eds.), Back to the Future: Legacies, Continuities and Changes in Educational Policy, Practice and Research, 147–161.
© *2013 Sense Publishers. All rights reserved.*

acquisition of such skills being promoted in developed countries as well as in developing countries.

For example, Britain's National Curriculum targets thinking skills: as Jones (2010) points out, the "development of pupils' cognitive skills has been a focus of international research interest for decades, and in the UK a specific surge of interest in this area took place in the 1990s" (p. 70). In the United States, interest in thinking skills is embedded within the standards movement. Resnick (2010), who coined the term 'thinking curriculum,' states that "from the 1990s on, the public agenda for raising educational levels for all has been promoted under the banner of the standards movement" (p. 183).

In Palestine in the late 1990s, the Ministry of Education and Higher Education (MEHE) embarked on the development of a national curriculum to be implemented in all Palestinian schools from the year 2000. The First Palestinian Curriculum Plan (Ministry of Education, 1998) was built on seven principles, including the following two.

> Social justice, equality and the provision of equal learning opportunities for all Palestinians, to the limits of their individual capacity must be ensured without discrimination on grounds of race, religion, colour, or sex.

> Opportunities must be provided to develop all Palestinians intellectually, socially, physically, spiritually and emotionally, to become responsible citizens, able to participate in solving problems of their community, their country and the world. (p. 5)

These principles are based on the universal premise that learners need to have opportunities to acquire and develop the knowledge and cognitive competencies they will need to enable them to participate actively in their communities and societies. These principles are not unique to the Palestinian curriculum. Similar aspirations are common globally.

The uniqueness of the Palestinian situation lies in the fact that the land and people of Palestine have been under occupation since 1967. For more than 37 years the military occupation directly administered all aspects of life in Palestine, including education. The occupation maintained the same curricula that were in use in Palestine prior to 1967. Schools in the West Bank, the eastern wing of Palestine, followed the Jordanian curriculum and adopted its textbooks, while schools in Gaza followed the Egyptian curriculum and adopted its textbooks. No efforts or resources were invested in the development of Palestinian learning environments. Therefore, when the Palestinian National Authority was formed in 1994 to administer the people of Palestine as an outcome of the Oslo Accords, the development of a national curriculum was given priority.

Modern education systems routinely review and evaluate their programs, initiatives and functions. Therefore, it seems logical to evaluate the First Palestinian Curriculum Plan. The existing literature involving review of the Palestinian curriculum and textbooks may be grouped under the following three themes.

– Studies designed primarily to monitor the implementation of the Palestinian curriculum and textbooks, whose interest is to ensure that these documents do not foster nationalistic feelings among learners (see, for example, Meridor, 2006). These studies are funded either by Israeli agencies or by US and/or European agencies. The primary interest of the latter group is to observe the extent to which the Palestinian curriculum and textbooks comply with the terms of the Oslo Accords (see, for example, Israel/Palestine Centre for Research and Information, 2004).

– Studies reviewing the treatment of particular social or political issues within the curriculum and textbooks. These studies explore such issues as the portrayal of women, as was the case with the Jarbawi study (Habazi, 2003), or the extent to which the curriculum and textbooks foster a sense of citizenship among learners (see, for example, Abu Zahira, 2004).

– Studies reviewing broader aspects of the curriculum or textbooks, such as those reviewing the foundations of the curriculum and the extent of their alignment with the perceived needs of learners or of society (see, for example, Abu Jamous, 2004).

An obvious gap in the literature is the absence of formal reviews of the emphasis on thinking skills in the Palestinian curriculum. The purpose of this study is to address this gap, by determining the extent of such emphasis. The study also seeks to explore the extent to which these thinking skills are represented in the textbooks.

Textbooks are traditionally important elements in the learning process, both in Palestine and in most other countries of the Middle East. They are the *de facto* curriculum plans. Education authorities in many Middle Eastern countries prescribe the textbooks that are allowed to be used in their schools. They often approve the use of a single textbook per grade level to be used to teach each subject. These textbooks are often the only resources available to support student learning. Therefore, any formal review of the Palestinian curriculum should include a study of the corresponding official textbooks.

This study is motivated primarily by the identified need to evaluate the national curriculum initiative in Palestine. It aims to provide formal feedback that may be of benefit to both policymakers and teachers. The study can also be viewed as a case study that may help in understanding the universal dissatisfaction with the current level of facilitation of cognitive skills in schools (Fischer et al., 2011; Resnick, 2010). Accountability programs involving system-wide assessment are often blamed for this problem (Fischer et al., 2011).

Methodologically, the study provides a viable example of the use of a modern taxonomy of educational objectives to content-analyse the Palestinian curriculum and textbooks.

The main research questions that this study aims to answer are:

– What are the major higher thinking skills that the Palestinian curricula and textbooks target?

– Are the curricula and textbooks congruent in their emphasis on the various levels of thinking skills in Palestine?

THEORETICAL FRAMEWORK FOR CURRICULUM AND TEXTBOOK ANALYSIS

For the purpose of analysing the Palestinian curriculum and textbooks, it was decided to use Marzano's 'new taxonomy of educational objectives' (Marzano, 2001; Marzano & Kendall, 2007). This taxonomy builds on and extends the established taxonomies, such as Bloom's (1956) taxonomy. It incorporates the findings of a large number of studies that have been reviewed by the authors.

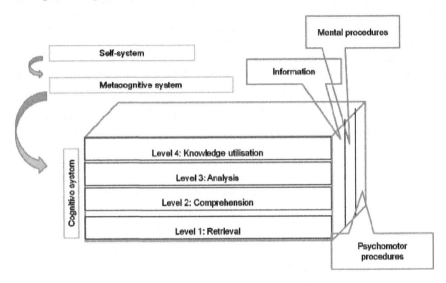

Figure 1. Marzano's 'new taxonomy of educational objectives'
(adapted from Marzano & Kendall, 2007)

The four cognitive levels of the new taxonomy (see Figure 1) are based not on the assumed difficulty of the task but on a qualitative difference in the processing of information. They comprise retrieval, comprehension, analysis, and knowledge utilisation. Each level incorporates a number of processes (see Table 1).

Kendall et al. (2008) used the new taxonomy in their analysis of thinking skills in standards documents from seven states in the US. They reported that the taxonomy 'provides useful definitions of and distinctions among these skills' (p. 1). They further noted that 'the taxonomy is simply a tool for analysis and does not prescribe what students should learn; its value lies in the systematic way it defines a wide variety of skills related to thinking and learning' (ibid.).

Table 1. Marzano's cognitive levels and their related processes
(adapted from Marzano & Kendall, 2007)

Cognitive level	Process (skill)	Description
Retrieval	Recognition	Matching information on a prompt with information in the permanent memory
	Recall	Producing information related to the stimulus
Comprehension	Integrating	Distilling knowledge to its key characteristics
	Symbolising	Creating a symbolic analogue of the knowledge
Analysis	Matching	Identifying similarities and differences
	Classifying	Organising knowledge into meaningful categories
	Analysing errors	Addressing logic, reasonableness or accuracy
	Generalising	Constructing new meanings or principles from what is learned or observed
	Specifying	Generating new applications of known principles or meanings
Knowledge utilisation	Decision making	Selecting one option from a number of alternatives
	Problem solving	Attempting to overcome obstacles
	Experimenting	Generating and testing hypotheses to understand a phenomenon
	Investigating	Employing logical analysis to test a hypothesis or a proposition

METHOD

Definitions

Objectives.   Objectives are statements that describe the learning targets specified in the curriculum and the textbooks. Objectives play a pivotal role in the organisation of the teaching and learning process. This study was limited to the analysis of the cognitive objectives and the cognitive elements of the affective and psychomotor objectives.

Curriculum.   The curriculum is the subject syllabus approved by the education system. It includes objectives, prescribed content, and related learning activities and materials. Students' classroom experience is not included in this study.

Learning activities.   Learning activities are tasks designed to be carried out by students in the learning environment, either individually or in groups.

151

Assessment tasks. Assessment tasks are activities designed to be carried out by students in the learning environment, either individually or in groups, at the end of a lesson or unit of work, for assessment purposes. Each assessment task may include one or more activities.

Sample

The population of the study comprised the curriculum and textbooks used in the three stages of schooling in Palestine. These stages are as follows.
–   Preparatory stage comprises Grades 1 to 4. This is the stage widely known as lower primary school.
–   Empowerment stage comprises Grades 5 to 10. This is the stage widely known as middle school.
–   Secondary stage comprises Grades 11 and 12. This is the stage widely known as senior secondary school.

Due to time and resource limitations it was decided to restrict the study to a sample of two specific subject curricula (science and social studies) and the two corresponding textbooks, representing the Preparatory and Empowerment stages. This sample was purposefully selected to ensure:
–   representation of both primary and secondary schooling (the sample was limited to the compulsory stages, comprising Grades 1 to 10);
–   representation of both science and the humanities;
–   representation of subjects with an emphasis on both literacy and numeracy;
–   representation of subjects that traditionally include ample opportunities for learners to draw on their own resources and experiences.

Given these specifications, the following curricula and textbooks were selected:
–   the Social Studies curriculum for the Preparatory stage;
–   the Civic Education textbook for Grade 4;
–   the Science curriculum for the Empowerment stage;
–   the Science textbook for Grade 9.

Instruments

Three instruments were used in this study. Two were designed to assist the content analysis of the curricula and the textbooks, respectively (see Tables 2 and 3). Each of these had two dimensions, one relating to the cognitive processes (skills) involved (Marzano & Kendall, 2007) and the other to the context of analysis. Each contained 12 cognitive processes (*recognition* and *recall* were combined under *retrieval*).

The third instrument used was an open-response survey (see Appendix 1) administered to the curriculum consultants and authors who had participated in the design and writing of the sampled curricula and textbooks. The survey comprised 10 questions about the thinking skills addressed by the curricula and textbooks. The questions focused on the respondents' evaluations of:

- cognitive skills targeted by the curricula and textbooks;
- congruence between the curricula and the textbooks.

Table 2. Dimensions of analysis of the curricula

Context of analysis	Cognitive process (skill)											
Curriculum domain Cognitive Psycho- motor Affective	Retrieval	Integrating	Symbolising	Matching	Classifying	Analysing errors	Generalising	Specifying	Decision making	Problem solving	Experimenting	Investigating

Table 3. Dimensions of analysis of the textbooks

Context of analysis	Cognitive process (skill)											
Textbook element Learning activities Assessment tasks	Retrieval	Integrating	Symbolising	Matching	Classifying	Analysing errors	Generalising	Specifying	Decision making	Problem solving	Experimenting	Investigating

The survey was designed to gather the views of these consultants and authors in order to validate the findings of the content analyses of these documents. A list of 29 consultants and authors was provided by the MEHE. All were invited to complete the survey. Seven respondents completed the survey.

Procedures

The study was carried out in seven stages, as follows.
1. Review of existing studies directly or indirectly relating to the Palestinian curriculum and textbooks;
2. Construction of research instruments;
3. Selection of sample of subject curricula and textbooks;
4. Analysis of sampled curricula and textbooks;
5. Review of analyses by two experienced teachers in science and social studies;
6. Distribution of open-response survey to nominated curriculum consultants and authors;
7. Analysis of survey responses.

Data Analysis

Analysis of the Curriculum Documents and Textbooks. The content analyses of the curriculum documents and textbooks were conducted by a research assistant with extensive teaching experience. The research assistant and the first author independently analysed one unit of the Science curriculum for the Empowerment phase, and one chapter of the Year 4 Civic Education textbook. They compared the results of their analyses and discussed points of agreement and disagreement. They repeated this process with the next components of the same documents, until they achieved a ratio of agreement of 0.90. The research assistant then carried out the rest of the analyses on her own. The first author reviewed all her analyses and made minor changes. Two other experienced teachers, one in science and the other in social studies, critically and independently examined the content analyses. They testified that the analyses represented the sampled curricula and textbooks.

Analysis of the Survey Responses. The responses were thematically analysed by the first author, and broken down into segments that each contained one idea. These segments were then coded, grouped into categories and aligned with the two analytical questions that the survey was designed to answer. These questions were as follows.
- What are the cognitive skills that the curricula and textbooks target, as viewed by the consultants and authors?
- Do the consultants and authors believe that there is congruence between the curriculum plans and the textbooks that reflect these plans?

FINDINGS AND DISCUSSION

Preparatory Stage Social Studies Curriculum

The analysis of the Social Studies curriculum for the Preparatory stage identified 429 specific objectives. These objectives represented all four of the cognitive levels portrayed in the new taxonomy (retrieval, comprehension, analysis and knowledge utilisation). Specifically, the objectives were distributed as follows:

- Approximately 39% of the objectives targeted retrieval.
- Approximately 16% of the objectives targeted comprehension.
- Approximately 44% of the objectives targeted analysis.
- Approximately 1% of the objectives targeted knowledge utilisation.

The distribution of the objectives across the four levels (see Figure 2) did not vary by grade (chi square = 5.75, df = 9, p > 0.05). The cognitive process most targeted by the identified Social Studies curriculum objectives was *generalising*. Approximately 93% of the objectives called for the

154

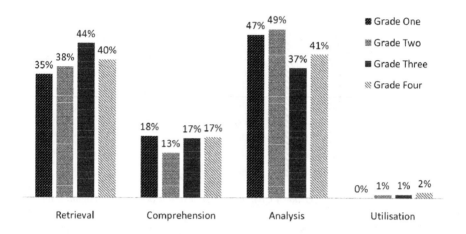

*Figure 2. Distribution of preparatory stage Social Studies curriculum objectives
by grade across the four cognitive levels*

use of generalisation. Other analytical processes, such as *analysing errors* and *classifying*, were not targeted.

These findings show that the objectives identified in the Social Studies curriculum were diverse. They also show a clear imbalance between the levels of comprehension and of analysis. The specific cognitive processes targeted within analysis are quite narrow and limited. This observed imbalance, when considered alongside the paucity of available resources in the country and the long period of stagnation of the educational process due to political conflict and prolonged occupation, should be of concern to policymakers and teachers in Palestine.

Grade 4 Civic Education Textbook

The analyses of the learning activities and assessment tasks in the Civic Education textbook for Grade 4 indicated that they represented all four cognitive levels of the new taxonomy. The learning activities presented in the textbook tended to favour higher thinking levels when compared with the assessment tasks at the end of each chapter or unit (see Figure 3).

Most of the analytical processes targeted by the textbook activities can be classified as *generalising*. Other analytical processes, such as *analysing errors* and *classifying*, were not targeted.

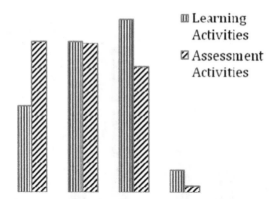

Figure 3. Distribution of Grade 4 Civic Education textbook activities by cognitive level

Empowerment Stage Science Curriculum

The analysis of the Science curriculum for the Empowerment stage identified 485 specific objectives. These objectives represented all four of the cognitive levels portrayed in the new taxonomy (retrieval, comprehension, analysis and knowledge utilisation). Specifically, the distribution of the objectives was as follows:

– Approximately 41% of the objectives targeted retrieval.
– Approximately 40% of the objectives targeted comprehension.
– Approximately 19% of the objectives targeted analysis.
– Approximately 1% of the objectives targeted knowledge utilisation.

The distribution of the outcomes across the four levels related to Grades 5 to 9 (chi square = 54.32, df = 12, p = 0.000). Figure 4 shows clearly that more emphasis on retrieval appears in lower grades, while in the upper grades more emphasis is given to the higher cognitive levels such as comprehension and analysis.

The objectives of the Science curriculum target almost evenly the analytical processes of *matching, classifying, generalising* and *specifying. Analysing errors* is almost not targeted at all by the Science curriculum objectives. Knowledge utilisation was also not strongly emphasised, with approximately 2% of the objectives targeting this cognitive processes.

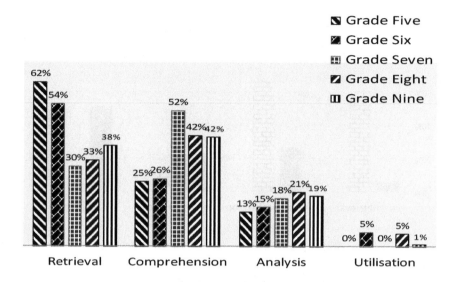

Figure 4. Distribution of Empowerment stage Science curriculum objectives by grade across the four cognitive levels

Grade 9 Science Textbook

The analyses of the learning activities in the Science textbook for Grade 9 indicated that they represented all four of the cognitive levels of the new taxonomy (retrieval, comprehension, analysis and knowledge utilisation). The assessment tasks, on the other hand, focused mainly on retrieval and comprehension.

The learning activities in the Science textbook include discussion stimuli, practical problems and practical and laboratory activities. These activities are designed to stimulate thinking and enhance discovery skills. However, the complexity of the issues discussed and the demands of the learning activities require resource-rich learning environments and well trained teachers able to provide support and feedback in ways that encourage autonomous learning.

The differences between the organisation of the learning activities and that of the end-of-chapter or -unit assessment tasks are quite striking. The latter are presented in formats that encourage retrieval of information. In other words, these two groups of activities seem to represent two different models of student learning. The learning activities seem designed to encourage active learning and student construction of learning, while the assessment tasks seem to promote direct teaching.

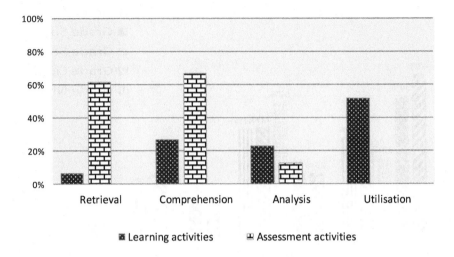

Figure 5. Distribution of Grade 9 Science textbook activities by cognitive level

Congruence between Science Curriculum and Science Textbook

The comparison between the cognitive levels targeted by the specific objectives of the Grade 9 Science curriculum and by the learning and assessment activities in the Grade 9 Science textbook (see Table 4) indicated that they are statistically different (p = 0.000). The main source of discrepancy between the two documents relates to the considerable percentage of activities in the textbook that provide students with opportunities to investigate or experiment.

Table 4. Congruence between Grade 9 Science curriculum and Grade 9 Science textbook

Cognitive level	Curriculum		Textbook		df	χ^2
Retrieval	48	38.4%	75	30.12%	3	20.9
Comprehension	52	41.6%	94	37.75%		
Analysis	24	19.2%	39	15.67%		
Knowledge utilisation	1	0.8%	41	16.47%		
Total	125	100%	249	100%		

Responses to Survey of Curriculum Consultants and Textbook Authors

The results of the survey administered to curriculum consultants and textbook authors should be viewed with caution, as the number of respondents was small.

Furthermore, the purpose of the survey was to validate the findings of the content analysis.

Nevertheless, the respondents did provide rich information. The major themes derived from the responses were as follows.

- Respondents felt that the Palestinian curriculum was consistent with the needs of the people of Palestine and with the available resources and conditions of the learning environments.
- Respondents differed in their perceptions of the extent of emphasis of the Social Studies curriculum and textbook on cognitive skills. Some believed that the Social Studies curriculum and textbook did target higher thinking and cognitive skills, while others did not believe that these documents placed enough emphasis on such skills.
- Respondents seemed to be in agreement that the Science curriculum and textbook did facilitate the development of students' thinking skills. However, they believed that improvement was still needed in this area.
- Respondents seemed to believe that authentic implementation of the curriculum, particularly in Science, required trained teachers. They believed that trained teachers were the link between the curriculum and an emphasis on cognitive skills.

CONCLUSION

This study was conducted to explore the level of emphasis on teaching thinking skills in the Palestinian school curriculum and associated textbooks. A purposeful sample of individual subject curricula and corresponding textbooks was identified and analysed. The analyses used Marzano's 'new taxonomy of educational objectives' (Marzano, 2001; Marzano & Kendall, 2007) as its theoretical framework. The analyses of the curricula focused mainly on the identified learning objectives. The analyses of the textbooks focused on the learning activities within the texts and on the end-of-chapter or end-of-unit assessment tasks and exercises, as applicable.

The analysis of the Social Studies curriculum indicated that the cognitive processes of retrieval, comprehension and analysis were being targeted by the learning objectives. Knowledge utilisation, which is the application of skills and knowledge in authentic or simulated situations, was found to be less well emphasised. This finding is concerning in view of the widely agreed need to emphasise active learning in schools. Nisbet (1993) argued that cognitive skills are constructed by learners. Therefore, students need to have opportunities to experience learning in order to facilitate the construction of knowledge and the development of the targeted skills.

The findings indicate that there is an imbalanced focus on the skill of *generalising* in particular, at the expense of comprehension. The new taxonomy assumes that comprehension is a prerequisite to the achievement of the higher-level cognitive skills. Therefore, this imbalance would restrict the benefits learners may reap from their experience of and involvement in higher-order activities.

This problem was not found to exist in the Science curriculum. Its objectives and activities seemed to represent all four of the cognitive levels in a balanced way. The main issues here were the discrepancy between the learning models represented by the learning activities and by the assessment activities, and the inconsistency of available resources in the learning environments of a country that has been under direct occupation for four decades with minimal effort directed towards improvements and innovation in education.

APPENDIX I

Open-Response Survey Administered to Consultants and Authors of Palestinian Curricula and Textbooks

Please provide below the grade and the subject that you will discuss in your responses to the following questions.

Grade	1	2	3	4	5	6	7	8	9	10
Subject										

– As an author of a textbook or curriculum consultant for the subject and the grade you nominated above, do you believe that the performance standards in the subject curriculum plan are well specified? Why?
– Do the Palestinian curricula, particularly in the nominated subject, target a wide range of cognitive skills? Why?
– Please name some of the skills that are particularly well represented in the curriculum plan of the nominated subject. Elaborate on the factors that helped you formulate your opinion.
– Please name the skills that you believe are missing from the curriculum plan in the nominated subject.
– Why are the skills that you nominated in Question 4 important? Why are they missing from the plan?
– Are the skills that are targeted by the curriculum plan in the nominated subject presented as subject-specific skills? Please explain. Provide examples from the curriculum plan to help me understand your point of view.
– How do you assess the quality of the organisation of the curriculum plan in the nominated subject, in terms of educational objectives, content and learning activities? Is this organisation helpful to authors? Is it helpful to the teachers who are going to implement it?
– How do the Palestinian curriculum plans compare with similar plans in Jordan? How do they compare with international plans that you are familiar with, such as those in the US, Britain or Germany? Please name the country or the region that you are comparing the Palestinian plans with.
– Please assess the degree of alignment between the textbook that you authored or supervised and the curriculum plan. Explain the basis of your assessment. Provide me with one example to illustrate your point of view.

160

- Please evaluate the quality of the learning activities that are included in the textbook that you authored in terms of:
- their clarity;
- their alignment with the content;
- the performance levels they target.

REFERENCES

Abu Jamous, A. (2004). *Palestinian curriculum: Praise and criticism.* Available at www.pcdc.edu.ps/Arabic/ar_menhaj_praise_and_criticism.htm.

Abu Zahira, I. (2004). Atasamoh wal mosawah fi al-minhaj Al-Filestiny: Mawad Asafin Al-Awal wa Asades Al-Asasi [Tolerance and equality in the Palestinian curriculum for grades one and six]. *Journal of Tasamoh, 4,* 69-80.

Bloom, B.S. (Ed.) (1956). *Taxonomy of educational objectives: The classification of educational goals: Handbook I, cognitive domain.* New York: Longman.

Fischer, C., Bol, L., & Pribesh, S. (2011). An investigation of higher-order thinking skills in smaller learning community social studies classrooms. *American Secondary Education, 39*(2), 5-26.

Habazi, M. (2003). *A critical study in response to Dr Jarbawi's study of the Palestinian woman in the curriculum.* Available at www.pcdc.edu.ps/Arabic/critical_study_curricula_Tafida.pdf.

Israel/Palestine Center for Research and Information (2004). *Analysis and evaluation of the new Palestinian curriculum: Review of Palestinian textbooks and tolerance education program.* Jerusalem: Author.

Jones, H. (2010). National curriculum tests and the teaching of thinking skills at primary schools: Parallel or paradox? *Education 3-13, 38*(1), 69-86.

Kendall, J., Ryan, S., Weeks, S., Alpert, A., Schwols, A., & Moore, L. (2008). *Thinking and learning skills: What do we expect of students?* Denver, CO: Mid-continent Research for Education and Learning.

Marzano, R. (2001). *Designing a new taxonomy of educational objectives.* Thousand Oaks, CA: Corwin Press.

Marzano, R., & Kendall, J. (2007). *The new taxonomy of educational objectives* (2nd edition). Thousand Oaks, CA: Corwin Press.

McEwan, R. (2008). Dimensions of learning: teaching students to think. *Teacher, 197,* 50-53.

Meridor, N. (2006). *An examination of Palestinian fifth- and tenth-grade textbooks for the 2004-2005 school year.* Israel: Center for Special Studies, Intelligence and Terrorism Information Center.

Ministry of Education (1998). *First Palestinian curriculum plan.* Ramallah, Palestine: Author, www.pcdc.edu.ps/first_curriculum_plan.pdf.

Nisbet, J. (1993). The thinking curriculum. *Educational Psychology, 13*(3/4), 281-291.

Resnick, L. (2010). Nested learning systems for the thinking curriculum. *Educational Researcher, 39,* 183-197.

AFFILIATIONS

Shukri Sanber
School of Education (NSW), Australian Catholic University
Sydney, Australia

Irene Hazou
Bethlehem University
Bethlehem, Palestine

SECTION 3

PERSPECTIVES AND CHALLENGES IN TEACHER EDUCATION AND LEARNING

JOKE DAEMEN, ELS LAROES, PAULIEN C. MEIJER AND
JAN VERMUNT

LEARNING IN PROFESSIONAL DEVELOPMENT SCHOOLS

*Perspectives of Teacher Educators, Mentor Teachers and
Student Teachers*

INTRODUCTION

Enhancing effectiveness of teacher education programmes and increasing attractiveness of the teaching profession become increasingly important given large teacher shortages and high numbers of teacher attrition. Scientific research focusing on this improvement as yet shows little international consensus (e.g. Brouwer & Korthagen, 2005; Zeichner, 2008). Professional development schools (PDSs), i.e. partnerships between secondary schools and universities, seem promising in this respect. Due to the possibility of integrating theory and practice, PDSs are seen as opportunities to enhance effective teacher education (e.g. Grossman, Hammerness, & McDonald, 2009; Korthagen, Kessels, Koster, Lagerwerf, & Wubbels, 2001). These partnerships are also expected to enhance lifelong teacher learning and stimulate the innovative capacity of teachers and contribute to schools as professional learning communities (e.g. Bransford, Derry, Berliner, & Hammerness, 2005; Darling-Hammond & Hammerness, 2005; Hawley & Valli, 1999; Little, 2006). And the different perspectives of university and school can also serve as a boundary space in which learning can be reinforced (e.g. Gorodetsky & Barak, 2008; Wenger, 2009). Although there is a worldwide adoption of these school-university partnerships, there is not much empirical evidence to underpin this assumption. This article sets out to investigate how teacher educators, mentor teachers and student teachers view learning in PDSs.

THEORETICAL FRAMEWORK AND RESEARCH QUESTION

Professional Development Schools (PDSs)

In the public and scientific debate on the effects of PDSs on (student)teacher learning and development, PDSs are assumed to be effective in the sense that they enhance (student)teachers' learning and continuous development. In their book *Learning teaching from teachers, realizing the potential of school-based teacher education*, Hagger and McIntyre (2006) describe that, according to their vision, "Student teachers should not only learn to do the job competently, they should also

M.A. Flores et al. (eds.), Back to the Future: Legacies, Continuities and Changes in Educational Policy, Practice and Research, 165–187.

learn how to learn to do it better" (p. 7). In order to prepare student teachers for their complex task, they argue that teacher education should give priority to three tasks relating to the classroom expertise of student teachers: developing basic teaching skills, capacity for continuous professional development and a critical and innovative attitude.

PDSs are not only seen as promising for learning and continuous development, they are also assumed to play an important role in another issue in teacher education, namely that of the relationship between theory and practice. Due to their potential integration of theory and practice, PDSs are seen as opportunities to enhance effective teacher education. In "Can teacher education make a difference?," Brouwer and Korthagen (2005) showed, on the basis of a longitudinal study that, in order to successfully integrate theory and practice, teacher education requires close cooperation between school-based and university-based teacher educators. On the basis of this study, they conclude that enhancing effectiveness of teacher education is not only a question of curriculum development, but also one of staff development. Despite their emphasis on teacher education, this conclusion supports the goals of PDSs concerning engaging practising teachers in continuous professional development.

Research has shown that PDSs have a positive impact on the preparation of student teachers. In a comparative study between students educated in a PDS (partnership of a university and 7 schools) and a teacher education programme (the same university and 5 schools), Castle, Fox, and O'Hanlon-Souder (2006) found that PDS students[i] scored significantly higher on aspects of planning, instruction, classroom management and assessment. Qualitative analysis of portfolios also revealed that PDS-trained students showed greater ownership of their school and classroom and more sophistication in applying and integrating INTASC standards.[ii] Advantages of PDSs are acknowledged by both Hagger and McIntyre (2006) and Zanting, Verloop, and Vermunt (2001). Hagger and McIntyre (2006) saw two distinct advantages in the British apprenticeship system that was introduced in 1992. Firstly, they mention the acknowledgement of the expertise of practising teachers. The importance for student teachers of learning from experienced teachers was underestimated in the previous system of teacher education. Secondly, the apprenticeship system proved to be effective for the development of practical skills through daily experience of student teachers both by means of observations in the classroom as by their own teaching experiences. Also, mentor teachers are able to model or demonstrate teacher skills in an authentic situation, instead of having to explain student teachers what to do. Zanting et al. (2001) investigated student teachers' beliefs about learning to teach and the role of mentoring. They found that the complex knowledge that mentor teachers have gathered from their school practice can be a valuable support for student teachers in answering questions that are relevant for their own teaching experience and in understanding and reflecting on their own experience.

In addition to fostering student teacher learning, Hagger and McIntyre (2006) observe the strength of PDSs in perspective to the development of experienced expert teachers. The acknowledgement of the expertise of teachers is of great importance to the commitment of teachers in respect to their own professional development. In his study *Committed for Life? Variations in teachers' work, lives and effectiveness*, Day (2008) describes the importance of lifelong learning for teachers because they are the ones that will help and motivate their student teachers become teachers with the capacity for continuous professional development and a critical and innovative attitude (cf. Hagger & McIntyre, 2006).

Learning in the Community of Practice in the Professional Development School

Learning in PDSs can be theoretically addressed from different perspectives. Wenger (e.g. 2009) sees learning as a socially situated activity, as a deliberate attempt towards shared knowledge production and change, and the creation of a common discourse. Although Wenger's theory does not refer to learning in PDSs specifically, his ideas on social learning can provide interesting insights into learning in the PDS. In this study, PDSs are seen as Communities of Practice (COPs) in which all participants are learning.

Research into seven[iii] partnerships between schools and universities in Australia (Kruger, Davies, Eckersly, Newell, & Cherednichenko, 2009) shows that in effective partnerships there is a focus on learning for all participants in the PDS. In their study Effective and sustainable University-School Partnerships. Beyond determined efforts by inspired individuals, they also found that effective partnerships lead to the participants taking on altered professional relationship-practices that were exemplified by the presence of- and provisions for conversations among the participants (student teachers, mentor teachers and teacher educators). In this way, new enabling structures emerged which crossed the boundaries between school and university, thus initiating new learning relationships.

Boundary crossing, as found in the above mentioned study by Kruger et al, is also an important concept in the theory of Wenger (e.g. 2009) on Communities of Practice (COPs). He argues that learning (of all participants) takes place in the boundaries between the collaborative partners. By seeing boundaries not as sources for problems and misunderstandings, but as opportunities for innovation where new ideas are constructed, Wenger argues that boundaries carry potential for learning.

Gorodetsky and Barak (2008) stress the importance of bringing together the expertise of the different partners in a community. Based on empirical research, they describe how the emergence of a community of student teachers, mentor teachers and teacher educators showed an interesting form of boundary crossing because the participants started to enact new ideas in their own teaching practices. On a theoretical level, they introduce the concept of 'Edge Communities,' a new, in-between culture that bridges the cultural gap between school and university and that leads to profound changes in the practices of the participants. In the edge community, the negotiations of meaning within the community brought to light hidden beliefs and understandings that had been buried deep in the teaching practice. Discussing these beliefs became an inspiration for innovation (cf.

167

Grossman et al., 2009). In a study on individual student teacher learning, Wubbels (1992) showed that beliefs can block change and hinder individual learning. The fact that the study of Gorodetsky and Barak (2008) showed that discussing these very beliefs within the context of a PDS did not hinder learning, but led to inspiration and innovation, makes the concept of an edge community a promising one for fostering learning.

Research Question

This paper reports on an explorative study which focuses on actual experiences of learning in PDSs in the Dutch educational system. In this study, PDSs are seen as communities of practice in which all participants are learning (e.g. Gorodetsky & Barak, 2008; Wenger, 2009). Learning is understood in a broad sense, including new understandings, identity development and change of practices. Organizing PDSs as learning environments, communities of practice for (student)teachers, implies that all participants are learning, resulting potentially in professional development. For PDSs to be effective in reaching the goals mentioned in the introduction, an understanding is needed of the structural and cultural conditions.

This study explores learning in PDSs from the perspectives of various participants: teacher educators, mentor teachers and student teachers. The first two participants seem to be important actors in the supervision of student teachers. Drawing on the theories of Gorodetsky and Barak (2008) and Wenger (e.g. 2009) and) on learning in communities of practice, we describe how learning in Dutch PDSs is experienced by these participants and aim at answering the following research question: *What are the experiences with and opinions of learning in the school-university partnership of a professional development school according to three groups of participants (teacher educators, mentor teachers and student teachers) in the Netherlands and how do these experiences relate to each other?*

METHOD

Context of the Study

This study focuses on school-based teacher education programmes for postgraduate university students, who start one year of teacher education after gaining a masters degree and aim at preparing students for teaching in the upper levels of secondary education.

Teacher education in all universities in the Netherlands has a strong emphasis on linking practical work and coursework, so classes at the university are combined with teaching at schools throughout the year. In the national teacher education curriculum, 50% of the allocated study load consists of school practice. Because learning within the setting of a school has become increasingly important, most students are placed in schools that are part of a PDS that has additional resources for coaching student teachers on the job. In these PDSs, student teachers are supervised by teacher educators from the university and by mentor teachers in the school. The mentor teacher has a number of colleagues (subject matter teachers) in whose classes the student teachers teach. These subject matter teachers provide coaching.

THE STUDY

This paragraph describes the partnerships between two secondary schools and a teacher education institute. Both secondary schools entered separate partnership arrangements with the same teacher education institution. For both partnerships, most arrangements are formulated primarily on the coaching of student teachers. Background information is given about both partnerships.

The Partnership

The education institute that is part of both partnerships is a university-based teacher education institute offering postgraduate programmes for university students. By establishing partnerships with several schools, the institute can provide its students with teaching experience in practice and with good quality supervision in the schools. To guarantee the latter, the institute provides courses that prepare school mentors for coaching student teachers. Also, the institute aims at giving teacher educators the opportunity to cooperate with teachers and students in both educational- and research activities. In their opinion intensive cooperation between institute and school enables partners to get to know each other better and therefore exchange of staff between institute and school becomes more natural.

Partnership A[iv] is between a school for secondary education and the teacher education institute. The school is a comprehensive school that offers all levels of secondary education. Entering the partnership six years ago, the school has several goals in addition to the goals of the teacher education institute. They want to educate their 'own' student teachers; they want to provide settings for professional development of their teaching staff and they aim at becoming an example of a learning community. They also wish to underpin educational innovations with research data ('evidence based').

Partnership B is between an urban school with a long tradition as an experimental secondary school and the teacher education institute. The school only offers the higher levels of secondary education. The partnership was established six years ago. Educating student teachers and retaining them for the school, as well as conducting collaborative educational research are the two pillars of the partnership. By connecting research, teacher education, professional development and innovation, the school hopes to enhance the quality of teaching.

Participants

For each partnership three participants were selected on the basis of their actual participation in the PDS and their current connection with working in the partnership. For partnership A, both teacher educator and mentor teacher have been participating from the start. In partnership B, the teacher educator also participated in the PDS from the beginning whereas the mentor teacher (who was an experienced discipline coach of student teachers) had just started in this specific role. Both student teachers were recently educated in the PDS. They had just graduated and had started working in the school.

Data Collection and Analysis

Data was collected by means of qualitative method and interviews. The interviews were semi-structured and consisted of seven questions, all of them focussing on the interviewees' perception of and experience with the partnership of the PDS. Themes that were questioned were their perception of the goals of the PDS, tasks, roles, cooperation and learning in the PDS, teacher education in the PDS and results and effects of the PDS on the professional development of the participants. For example, participants were asked to describe their understanding of the goals and effects of the PDS on how they assess the competencies of the student teachers and in terms of learning within their own school or institute. They were also asked to reflect on their collaboration with other participants in the PDS, and they discussed their view on the impact the PDS had on their own development. The goal was to gain an in-depth understanding of the experiences and opinions of the participants about learning in the PDS they were involved in.

For all three perspectives separately, the interviews were tried out by the authors and discussed with the interviewees. The interview for teacher educators and school mentors was tried out with two colleague teacher educators who had recent experience in working in PDSs, both as teacher educator and as school mentor. The interview for student teachers was tried out with a student teacher who was just graduated within a PDS context. On the basis of the discussion and feedback, the interviews were fine-tuned by restructuring and rewriting them. The most important aspect that was changed, was that of allowing more general issues to emerge from the protocol questions by means of adding more open questions (e.g. a "grand tour question" to begin with) to the interview (Lichtman, 2006).

The emerging semi-structured interviews (see Appendix 1 for interview protocol) were conducted with six participants individually, two for each perspective (two teacher educators, two mentor teachers and two student teachers) in the partnerships. The first two interviews were conducted by the first two authors; the subsequent interviews were carried out by one of them.

The interviews were recorded on audiotape and transcribed. Analysis and interpretation of the interviews was an ongoing and iterative process.

As illustrated in Table 1, we followed several steps in this process. Firstly, the first two authors read the transcriptions and field notes they made to get on overview of each case. A framework was developed for analysing the interviews in terms of the theories that were drawn upon. The framework consisted of four sensitizing concepts (*Teacher education and student teacher learning, School-*

Table 1. Overview of phases of analysis

Phase	Researchers involved	What data	Focus of analysis
1	Both authors		Develop framework for analysis on basis of theory: *4 sensitizing concepts* (see Table 2)
2	Both authors	Transcribed interviews and field notes	Label interviews according to *4 sensitizing concepts*
	Both authors	Labelled interviews	Comparison and discussion of labelled interviews
	Both authors	Labelled interviews	Agreement on each labelled interview *(within case)*
3	Both authors	Labelled interviews	Analysis of interviews for each role (within role), identification of *recurring themes per role*
	Both authors	Within role analysis	Comparison and discussion of within role analysis, identification of *recurring themes per role*
4	Both authors	Across role analysis	Analysis of *similarities and differences between the three perspectives* (across role)

based teacher education, Communities of practice and *Learning in the PDS*) that were summarized into two categories (*Teacher education in PDSs* and *Learning in the COP of the PDS*). Secondly, we separately labelled the interviews using the categories in the theoretical framework. By comparing and discussing our interpretations, we constantly moved between the data and the literature on PDSs and community learning. We frequently returned to the original data, looking for evidence to strengthen our interpretation. Thus, we came to agree on the analyses of the interviews. Thirdly, after reaching agreement of the analysis for each separate interview (i.e. within case), we moved to analysing the three perspectives (i.e. within role). For each perspective, we identified a number of recurring themes. These themes were categorised on the basis of their focus of attention and were described reflecting the language used by the interviewees. Examples of such categories are "The quality of coaching by teachers" and "Exploring new possibilities together." After this within-role analysis, the fourth step was to look for similarities and differences between the perspectives (i.e. across role). We looked for recurring themes across all three roles and we came to some understandings which were compared to the data across the three perspectives. Table 2 shows the categories and central themes within these categories that were identified.

RESULTS

In our analyses we identified a number of central themes per category. For the category *Teacher education in PDSs*, we found that all participants had strong opinions about the importance of the quality of coaching by teachers. They also saw their main goal as one of helping student teachers learn and develop. Another central issue for both teacher educators and mentor teachers is the need to integrate theory and practice. The student teachers came with similar themes, but as their perspective is a different one, they used different language to describe their experiences. In the category *Learning in the COP of the PDS*, we found it was more difficult to come up with central themes across the participants. Each group of participants clearly described their own perspective, which we have included in Table 2. In the subsequent paragraphs, for each perspective, the themes are illustrated with extracts from the interviews

Within Role Teacher Educators

Both teacher educators see the partnership as a possibility to enhance the quality of the teacher education programme. They describe the importance of the quality of the coaching offered by mentor teachers and subject matter teachers:

> In the partnership, you can cooperate in enhancing the quality of coaching student teachers. This is one of the goals of our partnership.

The way they think this quality improvement can be achieved, is by providing professional training programmes for the (mentor) teachers themselves. That is exactly what they have done and both of them think that the quality of the coaching in the PDS is higher than in traditional schools:

> I would like to keep investing in the quality not only of the mentor teachers, but also of the subject matter teachers.

The teacher educators share the wish to focus on learning and development of the student teachers and they see that in the PDS, this focus has become a shared goal:

> I think it is the core business of the PDS to get the best out of a student, to make him the best teacher possible.

In their vision, the PDS has a better understanding of what makes a rich learning environment in which student teachers can learn and develop:

We notice that students who perform well in schools that don't belong to a partnership, are often asked to accept a paid position with more class hours. In the partnership, this tendency to overload students is less likely. They (PDSs) keep investing in the student by giving him more time and space to learn.

When it comes to assessing the competences of the student teachers in the PDS, the teacher educators have different views. One of them sees a clear difference between student teachers educated in the PDS and those that have been educated in the setting of a traditional school. According to one teacher educator (1), the PDS-students a get a better chance to learn and develop and therefore become better teachers sooner than non-PDS students, whereas the other teacher educator (2) does not see clear differences between PDS- and non PDS-students:

(1) Well, on average students in the PDS perform better, they are educated better and they get better supervision. Because of all those circumstances, they develop more quickly into better teachers.

(2) No, I couldn't say anything about that, I don't see clear differences between PDS- and non-PDS students, and I really can't judge that because there are so many factors involved.

Teacher educator (1) explains these positive effects of learning in the PDS for student teachers because the learning takes place in a COP:

I think that a student in the PDS does not just learn from working in the practice, but because the learning is deepened, enriched. That happens because there is a group of people who are learning together, and they discuss their learning experiences so a mutual language is developed. You get a sort of learning squared.

Another important theme for both teacher educators concerns bridging the gap they experience between theory and practice. Both teacher educators see the PDS as a possibility to integrate theory and practice:

One of the goals of our partnership is to make sure that students are able to learn in such a way that they don't feel torn between two separate worlds, that of the school and the university.

Learning in the COP of the PDS. Teacher educators' view on learning in the COP does not only apply to student teachers' learning, but also applies to themselves:

Working in a PDS makes that I stay on the ball. As a teacher educator there is always the pupils on a weekly basis ensures that you don't lose touch. So for me personally, this means that when I teach classes here at the school, I can actually use real life examples. This enhances my credibility as a teacher educator.

Being a participant in the school sharpened this teacher educator's sensitivity to the daily practice and routines of school life. Furthermore, the teacher educators see the close cooperation between institute and school as a way of exploring new possibilities together:

> My magic word has always been, I want the PDS to be a learning community. I would like to see that a lot of people would have a combined job as teacher and teacher educator. I would also like to change places with a teacher for one day a week, so we could create a win-win situation for both school and institute instead of the institute being in the role of giving while the school is only taking.

Being involved in a schools' daily life again brought several issues to the surface. Confrontation with differences in culture between school and university was one of them:

> When I first started in the PDS, I was confronted with the culture in schools. I had forgotten what it feels like to be a school teacher and now I can incorporate this in my classes at the institute.

Another issue that became apparent to the teacher educators was that of the need to discuss these cultural differences:

> The partners in the PDS have their own culture, their own ideas about priorities in what they want to develop. We have meetings about that. The teacher educators confer about the way they could build bridges between school and institute.

Interestingly, the teacher educators seem to discuss this issue amongst themselves and they do not appear to include the mentor teachers in this discussion.

In the opinion of the teacher educators, investing in building a relationship within the PDS is an important factor for success. Building this relationship does not happen overnight; it takes time and requires frequent contact:

> There are a lot of meetings anyway so we see each other frequently. Because there are regular meetings, you can explain things such as what happens at the institute and why.

Despite the wish to collaborate continuously, both extracts show that the teacher educators' perspective is one of helping the school to improve. By using words like "you can explain," "bring the expertise you gathered to another school," they imply that they will help the school to develop. One of the teacher educators also sees possibilities for the institute to learn from cooperating in the partnership:

> I work in the PDS and that has effects in both the institute and the school. In the institute I can inform everyone what happens in the school, what the issues are, what the needs of the school are. Also, I know about the evaluations and how our students perform. This makes that we can adapt our

policy on the basis of this information, and vice versa. So I am a sort of liaison-officer between both worlds.

Working in a community of practice implies the creation of a shared language. Both teacher educators refer to such a process:

> In the partnership I think we have developed a sort of shared language and that helps when communicating with each other.

Constructing shared knowledge seems to be an important aspect of working in the PDS:

> What it (the PDS) brings is that in the group, the concept of a PDS becomes a shared concept. It provides a context in which everyone can expand their view. I mean, people work from the PDS as a whole, and not just from the perspective of their own part of it, their school or institute.

One of the teacher educators explains why he is so enthusiastic about working in the PDS:

> One can mirror their own practice to that of others. The beauty of it is that we are in a partnership between three schools and two institutes, so there are different perspectives. One has one's own role and the whole becomes 1+1+1 is more than 3.

This enthusiasm clearly reflects the added value for all participants in the PDS as seen by this teacher educator.

Within Role Mentor Teachers

Role Perception of Mentor Teachers in the PDS. Both mentor teachers play a central role in educating the student teachers. They do not only organise teacher education within their own school, they also play a crucial part in connecting school and university. Their central interest is that of the student teachers learning and development as well as the students' well-being:

> I am a sort of liaison-officer between school and university. When a student isn't happy at school, for example, the teacher educator sends me an e-mail so I can take action.

Both mentor teachers not only view the learning and development of student teachers as being dependent on the quality of coaching provided by the subject matter teachers. They also think that student teacher learning in the PDS is enhanced, because in the PDS there is more room for development than in a traditional school:

> The PDS contributes to the quality of the student teachers because a lot of time and effort is invested in terms of supervision and coaching. I really believe that.

175

I have a student teacher who previously worked in a non-PDS. She doesn't stop talking about the warm welcome she experienced here and the amount of time and attention we give her. I can't put my finger on what it is exactly, but I'm sure this contributes to the quality of her development.

In connecting theory and practice, the mentor teachers see an important role for the schools. In their view, theory is offered by the university and student teachers have to connect theory to their practice with the help of their coaches in the school. One of them compares teacher education to medical training:

The hospital is where you get your practical education. There is much more connection between theory and practice in the academic hospital, so that's what we want, too, make sure there is no gap between theory and practice. And also, we want to know exactly what happens at the university so we can connect what they (the ST) learn at university to what we do in the school.

The mentor teachers are aware that they are role models to the student teachers and they see the importance of the adage "teach as you preach." By teaching exemplary classes and workshops they intend to reinforce the connection between theory and practice:

We pretend to give the workshops as we think an ideal teacher should teach. By doing so, we want to stimulate transfer from what happens on those Wednesday afternoons (at university) to what they (the ST) can do with that in their classes on the subsequent Thursdays.

The mentor teachers would like to play a more substantial role in the curriculum of the teacher education programme. In the beginning stages of the PDS, their active participation in the curriculum was encouraged and they had more room to give a personal interpretation of their task, but gradually a stricter division between school-based and university-based curriculum activities has developed:

That's a real pity, five years ago larger parts of the curriculum were taught here at school. We organised classes and workshops on research, on all kinds of themes. All of that has changed, has been crossed off our list by the university.

Learning in the COP of the PDS. Mentor teachers find that having a role in educating student teachers has become a natural task for the school over the years. In the beginning stages of cooperating in the PDS, teachers were hesitant about this role and they were mainly concerned about allocated hours and working load. Now, the mentor teachers see a growing enthusiasm in their school for this task. The presence of young student teachers is appreciated as valuable and this appreciation makes their job of organizing teacher education much easier:

For a long time, this (MT) was a very unpopular job, because you had to wheel and deal to find a subject matter teacher who was prepared to coach student teachers. Because of the PDS there has been a change in culture. In February we have eight student teachers coming, and all subject departments welcome them with open arms. It has helped enormously that in every subject department, we have appointed and educated one coach.

As a part of school development, the mentor teachers see a growing interest in doing research in their school. They are investigating possibilities for expanding practice-oriented research:

> We (MT) have the task to disseminate our expertise. Within our school, and also outside of school. For example publish articles, perform at conferences, etc. According to me the PDS should not just focus on student teachers, but also on experienced teachers, on management, so in my view the PDS should be the driving force of all learning in the school.

The mentor teachers experience more openness in learning. They and their colleague teachers learn because of the presence of others in the sense that it makes them critical and sharp:

> Well, it makes that you start analysing, looking at your own classes critically again.

> Talking to student teachers, they ask about your point of view and vision on education, so you are constantly reformulating your vision and your personal performance. And in the school group (TE & MT) I am starting to learn as well, I try to address different themes and engage in processes.

Participation in the PDS has had a clear effect on broadening the horizons of the mentor teachers. Their work in the PDS has become increasingly varied. They get organisational tasks and those tasks relate to supervising student teachers and coaching subject matter teachers. They cooperate with many different actors in their job as mentor teachers and because of this, their job has got new dimensions which bring new challenges and inspiration to them:

> For me personally being a mentor teacher in the PDS means having a very challenging job, because it requires, well for me it is inspirational to work with many different people, all those people I confer with. At least once a month. We develop workshops, we write things together, we design courses, etc. Well, that makes my job very attractive.

Within Role Student Teachers

When interviewing the student teachers, we found that they had difficulties in reflecting on their education in the PDS from a broader perspective. Their focus was their own personal experience. It seemed that they did not show any insight or interest in learning in the PDS by other participants than themselves. Therefore, the data we collected for this perspective is not as rich as the data we gathered for the other two perspectives.

Teacher Education in PDSs. Recurring themes in the interviews with student teachers were aspects about organization and content of their teacher education programme within the partner school. Both student teachers experience that being educated in the partnership enabled them to learn and develop as student teachers. A shared feeling is that of acceptance into the school as a member of the community:

> What I noticed is that you are accepted as almost a teacher within the school.

Because of this acceptance, they both felt secure in the school. As a result, they experienced the school as a safe learning environment in which they were allowed to make mistakes and experiment within and outside the classroom:

> I was given a lot of opportunities, for example I was allowed to organize a so-called 'night of poetry' and various debating sessions.

The student teachers also felt a lot of room for reflecting on their teaching experience:

> On Thursdays we had collaborative reflection meetings as a group. That was a welcome moment of pause in the week. You could take time and reflect on what had happened and discuss that with your fellow students.

Like the teacher educators, the student teachers are outspoken about the importance of the quality of the daily coaching by the subject matter teachers. The interpersonal relation between those teachers and the student teachers is a crucial factor for them:

> Look, I got on very well with my coach, so that made it OK to stay in one school for a whole year. But I can imagine that if that relationship is not so good, it could be very difficult.

Not all classes and lectures at the university were experienced as being supportive to the student teachers' needs:

> Well, you go back to the big building and you basically sit in the classroom and wait for the one-way traffic that they send to you.

In contrast, the sessions at university about pedagogical content knowledge were experienced as very valuable by the student teachers, because the university teachers were able to link the theoretical notions directly to the daily practice of the student teachers:

> I think classes on pedagogical content knowledge were much more useful to me. They matched with what I was actually doing at school, so what I learned in these classes was really useful. I mean it related to the practice.

178

Although the student teachers did not explicitly mention the aspect of integrating theory and practice, in both interviews it becomes apparent that the student teachers' measurement of the quality of their teacher education depends largely on the applicability of theoretical notions to their school practice. As illustrated in the extract above on pedagogical content knowledge, this knowledge is judged as valuable because of its applicability to their practice. Because the other classes at university do not meet this requirement of applicability, the student teachers do not see them as valuable:

> The classes on educational theory were, especially when we first started the TEP, a world away from the practice in the school and completely separated from our daily experience.

The extract below illustrates that the student teachers experience the school and university as two different worlds:

> I think that the university wants this partnership because it can help them getting closer to the everyday practice of the school. I'm not sure about this, but by cooperating with the school, they can improve their educational quality and philosophy. Because they can see what really happens in the classroom, at a regular, ordinary school and they can incorporate that into their curriculum.

Clearly, according to the student teachers, there seems to be a gap to be bridged between school and university.

Learning in the COP of the PDS.   Learning of the participants in the PDS does not appear to be an issue for the student teachers. Their focus is clearly one of their own personal learning processes. Cooperation between the partners did not emerge in the interviews unless explicitly addressed by the interviewers. By questioning students teachers about issues related to learning in the COP of the PDS, they came up with some surmises. But on the whole they did not question the partnership and took the cooperation in the PDS as a given. They do understand, however, that cooperating in these partnerships can be meaningful for both the schools and the university:

> I can imagine that for teacher educators, when they really get to know the school, it will become easier to understand the student teachers, to know what we are faced with because they know the context of the school.

CONCLUSION AND DISCUSSION

In this concluding paragraph we compare the experiences and opinions of all three groups of participants by describing how their perspectives relate to each other. We focus on similarities and differences between the three perspectives which we subsequently link to the theory we used in our theoretical framework.

In our analyses we identified two overall categories and a number of central themes. To summarize these themes per category and per perspective, we have included them in table 2.

Table 2. Central themes emerging from the interviews

Category Perspective	Teacher education in PDSs	Learning in the COP of the PDS
Teacher Educators	1. Learning and development of student teachers 2. Quality of coaching by teachers 3. Integrating theory and practice	1. Exploring new possibilities together 2. Building a relationship by continuous cooperation 3. Constructing shared knowledge
Mentor Teachers	1. Role perception of mentor teachers in the PDS 2. Quality of coaching by teachers 3. Integrating theory and practice	1. Establishing a new culture 2. Collaborating in research 3. Personal development
Student Teachers	1. Connecting school and university: organisation and content 2. Quality of coaching	1. Understanding the need for collaboration 2. Experiencing hardly any cooperative learning 3. New culture 4. Different goals

Teacher Education in the PDS

From all three perspectives, the value and possibilities of enhancing teacher education in the PDS are acknowledged. On a visionary level, they all agree on that. In this sense, they underpin what Hagger and McIntyre (2006) see as the strength of PDSs in relation to the development of experienced expert teachers. The acknowledgement of the expertise of experienced teachers is seen as being of great importance to their commitment and their professional development. On a more practical level however, we found differences in the way teacher educators perceive teacher education in the PDS. Teacher educators focus on the importance of the quality of coaching by (mentor) teachers. Their main concern is improving that quality by providing training in coaching skills for the teachers in the school. Mentor teachers see their role first and foremost as one of connecting teacher education to professional development of (student) teachers in their school. For them, school development is central theme in the PDS. So, teacher educators provide training for mentor teachers, mentor teachers organise supervision and coaching in their school for both teachers and students. As Day (2008) points out, having a strong feeling of commitment is a prerequisite for effectiveness of teachers. Mentor teachers see new impulses and challenges emerging for teachers in the PDS. Coaching student teachers gives the teachers new inspiration and motivation. In this way, coaching student teachers fosters continuous development of teachers and it also enhances their commitment with school development. Student teachers benefit from all these activities. They stress the importance of the quality of coaches at their school and of the pedagogical content teachers and teacher educators at university. This combination of being a coach and having broad and recent experience as a teacher is also seen as valuable by Hagger and McIntyre (2006) and Zanting et al. (2001). The importance of the quality of coaching becomes evident but is also seen as vulnerable when the interpersonal style of the coach does not fit with the student teacher. Another important issue for student teachers, besides the quality of individual coaches, is the way mentor teachers and teacher educators communicate and the extent to which they are aware of the teacher education programme as a whole.

Modelling (Zanting et al., 2001) is mentioned by both mentor teachers and teacher educators. Both groups notice that cooperating in the PDS helps them improve their own education but it does not become clear how exactly that improvement comes about. Teacher educators find that it helps their credibility, whereas mentor teachers see modelling as a crucial starting point for all their activities, because they feel strongly about effects of the adage of teach as you preach.

Teacher educators and mentor teachers do not agree on the effects of teacher education in the PDS on student teachers' competences. One teacher educator sees differences in terms of the quality of student teachers, but the other teacher educator has reservations about that. In line with the findings of Castle et al. (2006), mentor teachers recognize the value of the PDS in reducing the shock that is often experienced in the transition between being a student teacher and becoming a teacher. They see that student teachers in the PDS become part of the school culture more easily and quickly as they develop from student teacher to teacher. Mentor teachers are positive about the fact that in the PDS student teachers get ample room for development and this fact is also acknowledged by student teachers.

According to all three perspectives, the goal of integrating theory and practice remains problematic. Teacher educators and mentor teachers each feel mainly responsible for their separate components (i.e. classes at university and supervision of the school practice) and little is being developed collaboratively. Because the organization of teacher education within the PDS is well-grounded, we think that the PDS offers opportunities to further integrate theory and practice. This process will require more time and conscious effort and entails getting to know and appreciate each others' expertise. As Brouwer and Korthagen (2005) conclude, this means that universities and schools would have to invest in collaborative staff development.

Learning in the COP of the PDS

Looking at learning in the COP we found many statements that fit with the theories we draw upon. Especially teacher educators focus on the added value of learning in a COP. They frequently refer to 'developing shared knowledge' and use concepts like 'exploring new possibilities together' and 'building a relationship by continuous cooperation' (Wenger, 2009). However, they also notice that the steps they have undertaken to become a COP are complex and the process of becoming a COP is one that requires a lot of effort. Moreover, it is not entirely clear to them, as Wenger also states, how exactly this process can be designed collectively in order to become a COP in which all participants are learning.

As yet, participants invest mostly in constructing a consultative structure that enables them to initiate new forms of learning (Kruger et al., 2009). The mentor teachers also participate in these structures, but they feel a lack of real collectiveness because they experience the teacher educators as being rather prescriptive and directive. On the other hand, the mentor teachers see a new culture emerging in the school (Wenger, 2009) around the supervision- and development of student teachers. The mentor teachers also find a growing openness in discussing the personal experiences of teachers. By welcoming and educating student teachers into the school, new ideas are discussed and developed and teachers develop a learning attitude. Because of this change in attitude, they start discussing educational themes. Therefore, they develop an increasing commitment and sense of ownership for educating student teachers and many teachers have found new challenges and perspectives because of this (Day, 2008).

While at first the PDS focused mainly on teacher education, the focus has gradually shifted to school development and doing research together with the university. So we see a shift from exploring each others' core business to broadening the horizon and investing in building a relationship together (Wenger, 2009).

When looking more closely at learning in the interviews, we found that the participants first and foremost describe their own personal learning, their personal development and how participating in the PDS influences their professional development. Shared knowledge construction by other members of the PDS is not mentioned or seen. Moreover, professional development is seen as a unilateral process that is organised by teacher educators or university researchers for groups of teachers in the school. So, despite the wish to become a COP, we have not found any statements about boundary crossing or mutuality in developing the partnership of the PDS.

Having said this, we found that schools and university do experiment on a regular basis in order to find new possibilities and ideas (Gorodetsky & Barak, 2008; Kruger et al., 2009). In this sense they are exploring new opportunities for innovation. However, these experiments are not always successful and they often fail because of organisational problems.

We looked for experiences with and opinions of learning in the PDS from three perspectives and we wanted to see how these three perspectives related to each other. From the perspective of mentor teachers, we can conclude that working in a PDS enhances the attractiveness of the teaching profession. Collaborating in a PDS could help schools develop and create an attractive working and learning environment for teachers. We did not find evidence for similar conclusions for teacher education institutes in universities. Mostly, teacher educators described working in the PDS as one-way traffic in which they were the ones that brought their knowledge and expertise to the schools. A PDS implies the existence of boundaries between university and school that can be a source of new opportunities (Lave & Wenger, 1991). We found some examples of boundary crossing from school to university, but not vice versa. In that sense, cooperation in the partnership of the PDS is not (yet) based on acknowledgement of mutual expertise of all partners.

The small scale of this study has its limitations. In our opinion it would be interesting to interview not only a larger number of participants for each perspective, but also include other stakeholders such as managers. We also think that conducting group interviews across the three (or more) perspectives could bring about new insights.

As yet, we conclude that developing a COP with participants from school and university is a gradual, time-intensive and complex process. All participants show a high level of ambition and they invest a lot of time and effort in achieving their ambitions. More research into which factors can help or hinder the development of a COP within PDSs is needed.

APPENDIX 1

Interview Protocol Perspectives on Learning in the PDS

Introduction
This interview is conducted for an exploratory study on PDSs in The Netherlands. The study looks into the way PDSs have developed and focuses on effects on the learning of student teachers, of mentor teachers and of teacher educators. This interview focuses on gathering information on the current state-of-the-art with respect to learning in the PDS, on experiences and opinions regarding the PDS and on the effects of creating a learning culture within the school. Apart from this interview with you, we will interview one other mentor teacher, two teacher educators and two student teachers in PDSs.

The interview will take one hour and consists of seven questions and a number of sub questions. The interview will be recorded on audiotape. Analysis of the interviews will be reported in a conference paper. Anonymity is guaranteed and information cannot be retraced to individual interviewees.

Do you have any questions or do wish to make a remark before we start?

Ok, in that case we will start now and I will switch on the recording equipment.

School context
➢ separate list with factual information (such as number of pupils/staff, number of student teachers, who are partners in the PDS)

1. *Grand Tour Question*: What does it mean for you to participate in a PDS?

2. i Why does your school participate in the PDS according to you?
   ii What do you think the *goals* of the PDS are?

3. This question is meant to provide a picture of *how you view the PDS*. To get that picture, I will ask you several questions.

   a. Who *participate* in the PDS? Who decided that? Do all participants function as planned?
   b. What are the *tasks* in the PDS? What do think are core tasks that are specific for a PDS?
   c. What is your *role* in the PDS?
   d. With whom do you *cooperate*? What is the nature of the cooperation? Are you satisfied about the cooperation? What do you get out of it?
   e. Are you

4. This question is meant to provide insight into *learning in the PDS*. Again, I will ask you several questions.

   f. Who are leaning in the PDS? What are they learning? How are they learning?
   g. How does this compare to a non-PDS situation? Is it different? Why do you think this is the case?
   h. Has anything changed in the way you learn since the PDS started?

5. This focuses on the way the *teacher education* in the PDS has been designed.

   i. Is there a *shared vision on teacher education* in the PDS? What is it?
   j. How was this shared vision developed? By Whom? Were you involved?
   k. What does the *workplace curriculum* entail? Which activities take place in the school? Who designed that curriculum? How are the tasks divided?
   l. Have there been any changes in the teacher education programme since your school is part of the PDS?
   m. Student teachers often experience a gap between *theory and practice*. Do you think that that gap has been bridged in the PDS? If so, why has that happened?

    n. Can you describe an event that you think is typical for a PDS?

6.   What is your opinion about *results and effects* of the PDS?

    o. *Quality of student teachers* (compared to pre-PDS period)
        What has improved? What has deteriorated? Ask for explanation.

    p. *Professional development*
        Does working in the PDS influence your own professional development? In what ways? Does it influence your colleagues? How?

    q. *School culture*
        Has your school culture changed since you have become partner in the PDS? In what ways? How do you notice that? Do colleagues who not actively participate in the PDS notice that too?

7.   PDS in the *future*

    r. What would be the first thing you would like to change in the PDS, given the opportunity?

    s. How would you go about that? What would you do? Who would you involve?

Closing off

We have talked about ... (brief summary of topics that were discussed). Is there anything that you would like to add? What do you think about the interview? Do you think you were able to express your opinion?

NOTES

[i]   PDS students n=60; non-PDS students n=31.

[ii]   INTASC standards: Interstate New Teacher Assessment and Support Consortium. These standards describe competences of beginning teachers.

[iii]   From 81 partnerships, 35 provided detailed outlines of the features and practices of their programme. Seven of those 35 were included in the research.

[iv]   For this study, the cooperation between one school and one teacher education institute was investigated. In both partnerships, however, more schools participate.

REFERENCES

Bransford, J., Derry, S., Berliner, D., & Hammerness, K. (2005). Theories of learning and their roles in teaching. In L. Darling-Hammond, J. Bransford, P. LePage, K. Hammerness, & H. Duffy (Eds.), *Preparing teachers for a changing world: What teachers should learn and be able to do* (pp. 358-389). San Francisco, CA: Jossey-Bass.

Brouwer, N., & Korthagen, F. (2005). Can teacher education make a diference? *American Educational Research Journal, 42*(1), 153-224.

Castle, S., Fox, R.K., & O'Hanlon-Souder, K. (2006). Do professional development schools make a difference? A comparative study of PDS and non-PDS teacher candidates. *Journal of Teacher Education, 57,* 65-80.

Darling-Hammond, L., & Hammerness, K. (2005). The design of teacher education programs. In L. Darling-Hammond, J. Bransford, P. LePage, K. Hammerness, & H. Duffy (Eds.), *Preparing teachers for a changing world: What teachers should learn and be able to do* (pp. 390-441). San Francisco, CA: Jossey-Bass.

Day, C. (2008). Committed for life? Variations in teachers' work, lives and effectiveness. *Journal of Educational Change, 9,* 243-260.

Gorodetsky, M., & Barak, J. (2008). The educational-cultural edge: A participative learning environment for co-emergence of personal and institutional growth. *Teaching and Teacher Education, 24,* 1907-1918.

Grossman, P., Hammerness, K., & McDonald, M. (2009). Redefining teaching, re-imagining teacher education. *Teachers and Teaching: theory and practice, 15*(2), 273-289.

Hagger, H., & McIntyre, D. (2006). *Learning teaching from teachers: Realising the potential of school based teacher education.* Buckingham: Open University Press.

Hammerness, K., Darling-Hammond, L., & Bransford, J. (2005). How teachers learn and develop. In L. Darling-Hammond, J. Bransford, P. LePage, K. Hammerness, & H. Duffy (Eds.), *Preparing teachers for a changing world: What teachers should learn and be able to do* (pp. 358-389). San Francisco, CA: Jossey-Bass.

Hawley, W. D., & Valli, L. (1999). The essentials of effective professional development. In L. Darling-Hammond, & G. Sykes (Eds.), *Teaching as the learning profession* (pp.127-150). San Fransisco, CA: Jossey-Bass.

Korthagen, F. A. J., Kessels, J, Koster, B., Lagerwerf, B., & Wubbels, T. (2001), *Linking theory and practice: the pedagogy of realistic teacher education.* Mahwah, NJ: Lawrence Erlbaum.

Kruger, T., Davies, A., Eckersley, B., Newell, F., & Cherednichenko, B. (2009). *Effective and sustainable university-school partnerships. Beyond determined efforts by inspired individuals.* Canberra: Australian Institute for Teaching and School Leadership, Victoria University.

Lave, J., & Wenger, E. (1991). *Situated learning: Legitimate peripheral participation.* Cambridge: Cambridge University press.

Lichtman, M. (2006). *Qualitative research in Education: A user's guide.* Thousand Oaks, CA: Sage Publications.

Little, J. W. (2006) *Professional development and professional community in the learning-centered school.* Arlington, VA: National Education Association.

Wenger, E. (2009). A social theory of learning. In K. Illeris (Ed.), *Contemporary theories of learning. Learning theorists in their own words* (pp. 209-218). New York: Routledge.

Wubbels, T. (1992). Taking account of student teachers' preconceptions. *Teaching and Teacher Education, 8*(2), 137-149.

Zanting, A., Verloop, N., & Vermunt, J. D. (2001). Student teachers' beliefs about mentoring and learning to teach during teaching practice. *British Journal of Educational Psychology, 71*(1), 57.

Zeichner, K. (2008). Where should teachers be taught? Settings and roles in teacher education. In M. Cochran-Smith, S. Feiman-Nemser, & D. J. McIntyre (Eds.), *Handbook of research on teacher education* (pp. 258-393). New York: Routledge.

AFFILIATIONS

Joke Daemen
Freudenthal Institute for Science and Mathematics Education
Utrecht University, The Netherlands

Els Laroes
Department of Education
Utrecht University, The Netherlands

Paulien C. Meijer
Department of Education
Utrecht University, The Netherlands

Jan Vermunt
Faculty of Education
University of Cambridge, United Kingdom

CATHERINE MCLOUGHLIN

TEACHER PROFESSIONAL LEARNING IN DIGITAL AGE ENVIRONMENTS

INTRODUCTION

Although higher education has been taking advantage of Web 2.0 applications to create technologically-enriched learning experiences for students, most of the existing Web 2.0 literature shows that educators do not use those applications to their full potential. That is, the participatory, interactive, collaborative, and social aspects are often missing from learning activities. Furthermore, the impact of social media on teacher education has been rather limited. While expectations have run high about web-based instruction, virtual worlds, social media and the raft of Web 2.0 tools, the impact on teacher professional learning has not been transformative and extensive. Recent research globally indicates that change is constant and that challenges educators need to be fully aware of include the adoption of digital tools to support teaching and assessment in meaningful and authentic ways. The recent emergence of approaches to learning that are based on self-determination and networking such as heutagogy and connectivism help us understand learning as making connections with ideas, facts, people and communities. Learning for the professions has grown beyond mere consumption of knowledge and become a knowledge creation process. The new effective teacher must think more about process than content, enabling learners to operate in the digital world rather than learn a discrete body of facts. The chapter will present the teaching and professional learning possibilities accompanying the social, participatory and collaborative tools that have emerged in the Web 2.0 era.

TEACHER KNOWLEDGE AND LEARNING

With the growth and expansion of the Internet and social computing, digital tools are widely used to mediate social interactions and communication (Lee & McLoughlin, 2011). Social networking sites such as MySpace and Facebook are part of a larger suite of social computing tools that collectively fall under the label of Web 2.0. Extensive research indicates that these technologies are widely embraced and that the majority of students now carry a mobile phone, PDA and/or laptop. These technologies break down barriers at a number of levels, such as private and public space, learning space and social space. Along with the ubiquitous uptake of social networking tools, there has been an increased focus on the importance of students learning social media skills and digital literacies

M.A. Flores et al. (eds.), Back to the Future: Legacies, Continuities and Changes in Educational Policy, Practice and Research, 189–206.

(Ladbrook, 2009; Lankshear & Knobel, 2003). As Johnson, Adams, and Haywood (2011, p. 5) comment:

> Digital media literacy continues its rise in importance as a key skill in every discipline and profession.

In this ever changing context, mediated by digital tools, the expectation is that teachers become experts in the use and application of 21st century approaches and tools (Williams, Foulger, and Wetzel, 2009). As described by ISTE (2012), teachers are now expected to ensure that they can support digital age teaching and learning by developing fluency in the use and application of digital tools and social media in the classroom. The aim of this chapter is to identify collaborative and social processes in the professional learning of teachers, and what part digital tools may have in their development. The chapter argues that there is enormous value in exploring the potential of Web 2.0 tools for professional learning and community building. While several models of teacher professional development have been applied to identify teachers' needs, digital age thinking and networking have changed expectations of what it is to teach and learn in 21st century classrooms (McLoughlin & Lee, 2007). Nevertheless, what constitutes best practice for effective teaching and learning across the lifespan is contested terrain. There exists a varied repertoire of language, concepts, skills, and techniques that purport to make teaching more effective for students' learning (Darling-Hammond, Bransford, LePage, Hammerness, & Duffy, 2007). What is agreed however, is that it is incumbent upon teacher educators to acknowledge that teaching students in increasingly complex and technologically mediated environments requires an understanding of how such technologies can mediate communication, information sharing , pedagogy and community building (Cervetti, Damico, & Pearson, 2008).

To address this gap, the chapter considers pedagogical change and presents a number of theories of learning linked to digital age technologies and the greater connectivity enabled by technology. Next, the chapter investigates what is known about teachers learning, and compares a number of theoretical models that provide insight into the nature of teacher knowledge and learning. Following this review, the core components of these models are distilled and linked with a case study demonstrating that digital tools and their affordances can enable and support teacher learning in a number of productive ways.

PEDAGOGICAL CHANGE AND PROFESSIONAL DEVELOPMENT IN THE INFORMATION AGE

Behind Web 2.0 is a vision that involves using the internet in more creative, social and participatory ways than was previously the case (Lee & McLoughlin, 2011). Web 2.0 can exploit the internet's educational potential for social learning and teaching, as well as informal learning, and brings in an increased emphasis on autonomy, interactivity, creativity and collaboration (Alexander, 2006). One of the ways in which Web 2.0 is making an impact is through the creation of internet-based communities of teachers, through services such as blogs and wikis (Rosen &

Nelson, 2008). While this might be considered an indirect mode of influence on learning, it is nevertheless a significant one. Dissemination websites aimed at practitioners can create a community of discourse for teachers who have a shared interest in the practices and the adoption of innovative pedagogies. To assist teachers in their own professional learning, many websites are beginning to support the exchange of shareable learning objects (see for example TeacherTube). There is a consistent with a trend for teachers to seek professional development activities through a learning community, achieve collaboration and awareness through access to shared ideas and concerns (Cochran-Smith & Lytle, 1992; Paulus & Scherff, 2008). The theme of this chapter is to conceptualise how teacher professional learning might be supported and enhanced through the affordances of Web 2.0 technologies and social media. By applying social-cultural and connectivist learning theories, and by examining innovative views of learning that are gaining currency it is possible to reconceptualise teacher professional learning, as social, experiential, reflective, participatory and constructive, and capable of being supported through distributed networks and digital mediating artefacts.

EMERGING TERMS, THEORIES AND PEDAGOGIES

There are distinct calls for a rethinking of pedagogy to meet the demands of an era in which ubiquitous computing and social connectivity mediated by ICT are reshaping academia (McLoughlin & Lee, 2010). This is evidenced in the emergence of a myriad of buzzwords and terms accompanying ongoing debates on issues depicting changing priorities in pedagogy. For instance, Ashton and Newman (2006) note that we have *pedagogy* (teaching of children) *andragogy* (teaching adults), *ergonogy* (teaching people to work). However, none of these terms captures the imperative of innovative knowledge sharing and creation required in the 21st century. Nevertheless, a number of concepts now in use signal the change from traditional pedagogies to forms of teaching and learning engagement where learners having greater levels of agency, social connectedness and autonomy. For example, some theorists consider *heutagogy,* in which learning is completely determined and directed by the learner, to be the next stage in the evolution of andragogy (Hase & Kenyon, 2000). Heutagogical approaches place the ultimate responsibility for learning on the learner and are aligned with the expectation that individuals must attain learning-to-learn and self-direction in order to succeed in the knowledge society. They are based on the premise that an individual learns continuously through interaction with his/her environment and throughout his/her lifespan, often in the face of ambiguity and need. New Internet technologies, such as Flikr, MySpace, YouTube, Wikis, Blogs, PodCasting, RSS Feeds, and Immersive Environments are creating new networked social environments, opening new possibilities. If one accepts Siemens (2005a, p. 3) statement that "Learning needs and theories that describe learning principles and processes, should be reflective of underlying social environments," then one must accept that new social environments, driven by emerging Internet-based technologies, are reshaping and creating theories of learning. Table 1 summarises a number of theories and paradigms of learning that have emerged in recent education and teacher development literature.

Table 1. Current and emerging learning theories

Author/date	Theory	Principles	Scope for teacher learning
Lave and Wenger (1991); Wenger (1998)	Communities of practice	Members of a community of practice are practitioners who develop a shared repertoire of resources: experiences, stories, tools, ways of addressing recurring problems – in short a shared knowledge base	Engagement in "legitimate peripheral participation" so that through participation , building of social and intellectual capital of the community is enabled
Hase and Kenyon (2000)	Heutagogy	Goes beyond andragogy by advocating self-directed learning, capability and pro-active participation	Focus on knowledge sharing and creation of new knowledge from existing experience
Tangney et al. (2001)	Communal constructivism	Teachers actively create their own knowledge, but are also active in the creation of knowledge for a wider learning community	Create tasks to engage learners in knowledge creation
Laurillard (2002)	Conversation theory	Teacher learning occurs through conversations about a subject matter which serves to make knowledge explicit and to promote reflection	Teacher learning is enabled by conversation, reflective and reciprocal dialogue.
Siemens (2005a)	Connectivism	A theory that combines and integrates principles explored by chaos, complexity theory and networking. Making and sustaining connections is more important than simply knowing	The learning process is characterised by connecting information sets and by making the connections between events and ideas on a global scale
Brown (2005, 2006)	Navigationism	Teachers should be able to find, identify, manipulate and evaluate information and knowledge and be able to share in the knowledge production process.	Navigationism is a broader and more inclusive term than constructivism but includes knowledge creation. Teachers develop skills in navigating digital landscapes

Each of these theories holds some promise and scope for consideration when thinking about the development needs of teachers. Heutagogical approaches place the ultimate responsibility for learning on the learner and are aligned with the expectation that individuals must attain learning-to-learn and self-direction in order to succeed in the knowledge society (McLoughlin & Lee, 2007). Similarly, conversation theory and constructivism indicate that learners learn continuously through interaction with their environment, through dialogue and throughout the lifespan (Laurillard, 2002). A theory that has emerged to describe the social, interconnected and community-based characteristics of learning in contemporary times is connectivism (Siemens, 2005a, 2005b). Connectivism strives to overcome the limitations of behaviourism, cognitivism and constructivism, by synthesising the salient features and elements of several educational, social and technological theories and concepts to create a new and dynamic theoretical construct for learning in the digital age. Furthermore, professional learning for teachers as been recognised as lifelong, networked and implicitly cyclical, according to Siemens (2005a, p. 4):

> Personal knowledge is comprised of a network, which feeds into organisations and institutions, which in turn feed back into the network and then continue to provide learning to individual. This cycle of knowledge development (personal to network to organisation) allows learners to remain current in their field through the connections they have formed.

These conceptualisations of pedagogy and learning challenge us to maximise the potential for teacher professional learning by employing the right blend of metaphors, frameworks and paradigms that capitalise on contemporary social networking tools and ICTs that teachers can use in their everyday lives for understanding, idea sharing, knowledge creation and reflection.

MODELS OF TEACHER KNOWLEDGE AND LEARNING PROCESSES

Teacher knowledge is best seen as dynamic and dialogic, and hence inseparable from the processes of learning (Elbaz, 1990). Teacher learning in turn is an active, experiential process, through which knowledge is enacted, constructed and revised. This does not however mean that teacher knowledge is only to be developed through experience and reflection. Hargreaves (2003, p. 197) comments that teachers are agents of change and that "teachers are having to learn to teach in ways that they have not been taught." The complexity of teacher activity can be seen in the multiplicity of actions that a teacher undergoes during the teaching process including comprehension of subject concepts, transformation of subject knowledge into teaching and instruction, evaluation of learning, reflection and new understanding of the learning process and self-evaluation. Shulman's (1987) model of pedagogical reasoning was originally developed to address this complexity and as a foundation for teaching reform. The most original and significant part of Shulman's classification of teacher knowledge is the category of pedagogical content knowledge (PCK), indicating that teachers do need to possess a specialised knowledge base. However, as teaching continues to evolve, several researchers have revisited Shulman's model with a view to exploring its relevance in the age of Web 2.0. The revised framework of teacher knowledge is *technological pedagogical content knowledge* (TPCK) (Koehler & Mishra, 2009; Mishra & Koehler, 2006). Teachers may have difficulty understanding the complex relationships between technology, pedagogy and content, because these are often taught in isolation in most teacher education programs (Koehler, Mishra, & Yahya, 2007; So & Kim, 2009). Starkey (2010) has also modified Shulman and Shulman's (2004) model in order to reflect the evolution of learning theory since that time, and bring pedagogy to the fore. *Technological pedagogical content knowledge* (TPCK) is grounded on an argument that pedagogically sound applications of technology require teachers to integrate their knowledge on content, pedagogy, and technology, rather than thinking of them as separate domains of knowledge. It also recognises that teachers create knowledge through connections in an open, digitally connected world where they operate in many overlapping communities. Teacher knowledge is complex and multi-faceted, and the nature of teachers' professional learning with ICT tools has been explored in recent studies (e.g. Paulus & Scherff, 2008).

All three models depicted in Table 2 recognise that teacher learning is multifaceted and complex, and that development of teacher skills and knowledge is highly interactive, individualised social and interactive (Darling-Hammond, & Baratz-Snowden, (2005).. Teacher learning involves active, experiential activities and through the processes of engagement and learning, knowledge is created, enacted, considered and revised. Pedagogical thinking is subject to many different influences and factors, and is a constant interplay between formal and informal learning, personal constructs and professional expectations, objective and subjective experiences. Therefore, the development of professional skills and competencies is very much an individual, socio-cognitive learning trajectory, and that it may be enabled by interplay of factors, including practical experience and dialogic participation in communities of practice.

Table 2. Comparison of models of teacher learning

Theorist and model	View of the teacher	Type of knowledge
Banks, Leach, and Moon (1999) [Four categories of teacher knowledge]	Teacher seen as knowledge professional Complex and individual	Subject knowledge School knowledge Pedagogic knowledge Personal constructs
Hoban (2002) [Professional learning System]	Teacher knowledge as constant construction	Transformative and generative
Shulman and Shulman (2004) [Ready, willing and able]	Having vision, reflection, motivation, community, practice, understanding	Ready (having vision) Willing, motivated Able (knowing and begin able to do)

HOW DO TEACHERS LEARN?

The phrase "professional knowledge" is used widely among teacher educators with the assumption that the definition and the processes of acquiring this knowledge are obvious. The language used about teacher learning i.e. "training" and "development" suggest that the process itself is instrumental and unproblematic. Researchers have, on the other hand, shown that the learning process is considerably more complex and that the global, digital age context is bringing about massive changes in how teachers learn (Goodson, 2003; Schlager & Fusco, 2004). As concluded in the previous section on emerging pedagogies and theories, teacher knowledge is dynamic rather than fixed and constructed rather than transmitted. It is also multifaceted, and includes the component processes of experience, reflection and social construction. Schön (1987, 1983) critiqued the ideas that education consisted in the transmission of data. Being able to reproduce codified knowledge was no guarantee of being able to apply it because so many problems existed in "indeterminate zones of practice - uncertainty, uniqueness and value conflict" (Schön, 1987, 1983). He also emphasised that reflection on action was a significant means of learning from experience, and that the knowledge gained from reflective practice can be drawn upon in future situations. This is similar to an aspect of how teachers learn through Vygotsky's (1978) "zone of proximal development" when, for instance, there is a process of mentoring and coaching of new skills knowledge and competencies may be supported by individuals, peers, objects and tools. Somekh (2001) maintains that professional knowledge building flourishes in environments that enable purposeful activity, communication and distributed cognition. In order to understand the role that digital technologies play in the professional learning of beginning teachers, we need to adopt a model that takes into account the elements of learning derived from the above learning theorists (see Table 2). These elements entail purposeful activity, willingness to reflect and the capacity to communicate and share ideas and understandings. With regard to this aspect of learning, the enabling affordances and interactive dimensions of digital technologies play a significant role.

CAN AFFORDANCES OF DIGITAL TOOLS AND SOCIAL MEDIA SUPPORT TEACHER LEARNING?

Web 2.0 applications like blogs, wikis, online social networking sites, photo- and video-sharing sites and virtual worlds have known an exponentially increasing development and popularity over the past few years. Web 2.0 is what we call the democratized Internet or the Internet for everybody, since anyone in the world can easily go online and create and share files. Web 2.0 tools (blogs, wikis, podcasts, social bookmarking, mash-ups) have transformed the Internet into a place for networking, community building and sharing collective experience, some have been led to describe this new phenomenon of massively distributed collective intelligence as "the wisdom of the crowds" (BECTA, 2007; Surowiecki, 2005). Social media and Web 2.0 can be seen as tools which afford learners the potential to engage in meaningful activities for learning. Such activity may be autonomous or collective, and can encourage communication beyond text-based media with easy publication of user-generated artefacts. Stimulating enquiry, supporting collaboration, engaging with new literacies and generating multimodal artefacts are all novels ways of developing knowledge and comprehension. The use of Web2.0 tools can enhance users' abilities and can enable activities and provide structure. Several views of the affordances of these tools prevail. For example, McLoughlin and Lee (2007) identify the following categories of 'affordances' associated with Web 2.0 or social software:

– Connectivity and social rapport;
– Collaborative information discovery and sharing;
– Content creation;
– Knowledge and information aggregation and content modification.

Conole and Dyke (2004) suggest taxonomy of features as follows: speed of change, diversity, communication and collaboration, reflection, multimodality, immediacy, risk, uncertainty. Much of the research investigates how teachers can be better prepared to use these activities in their teaching rather than exploiting these tools as part of their own learning. It is therefore useful to weave together particular types of Web 2.0 affordances with the opportunities for learning that they might offer, and to provide exemplars of tasks. A useful way viewing this is to present a number of purposeful activities with the affordances of Web 2.0 (Fisher, Higgins, & Loveless, 2006). These activities are not discrete, but are rather overlapping and interwoven (see Table 3). In the next section, examples are provided of how teachers can use the affordances of podcasting tools to support a learning community that enables communication, peer-to-peer scaffolding and engagement if reflective dialogue.

Table 3. Linking meaningful/purposeful activity with affordances of digital tools

Affordances	Activities
Distributed cognition	Accessing resources Discovering and inquiring Composing, creating and presenting multimodal texts with digital tools
Engagement	Playing and exploring uncertainty Taking risks Responding to immediacy Learning though multidimensional interactivity
Knowledge creation	Creating and adapting ideas in dynamic ways Modelling Representing ideas in multimodal forms
Community and communication	Sharing ideas and resources Engaging in reflective dialogue Participating in help seeking and peer-to-peer mentoring

CASE STUDY OF TEACHER LEARNING WITH DIGITAL TOOLS AND AFFORDANCES

Given the affordances of digital technologies how might we best apply web 2.0 tools and social media in developing professional knowledge? Similarly, Burden (2010) asks which aspects and affordances of Web 2.0 technologies are capable and suitable for mediating the elements of professional learning? The response is to demonstrate how these digital tools can be integrated into models of professional learning for teachers. In order to exemplify the case that supports how the affordances of digital tools enable teachers to reflect on and develop metaknowledge, or a "metamind" (Fenstenmacher, 1994), a technology supported environment for teacher dialogue was created to support the development of a community of learning (CoL). In the activity, students undertaking practicum placements at geographically dispersed locations were asked to form online peer-to-peer mentoring relationships where they would assist and support one another with the help of web-based social software tools. They undertook scaffolded tasks requiring them to create and share blog entries and voice recordings of critical incidents encountered during each week of the practicum, as well as inviting comment on their responses and reactions from peers. Through their dialogue, they learnt not only about the profession they are entering, but also about themselves as practitioners. By tuning in to one another's experiences and pooling expertise, they became active members of a community and at the same time reflected on and refined their own professional knowledge and skills. This engagement in dialogue connected with their professional development through reflection, and developed their identity as teachers (Kagan, 1992). The way teachers perceive their role defines not only their options, but also the way they construct, interpret and use professional knowledge (Clandinin & Connelly, 1987).

THEORY UNDERPINNING THE CASE

The concept of communities, including both communities of learners (CoLs) and of practice, has been gaining currency in recent years. Since the inaugural work by Lave and Wenger (1991) on situated learning and CoPs, these notions have had a profound influence on both theory and practice in the learning sciences, management, and organizational behaviour. However, the term "community" is still much debated, and there appears to be little consensus on how it should be defined. Whittaker, Isaacs, and O'Day (1997, p. 137) identified the following core characteristics of online communities, which may also be considered valid in a face-to-face (offline) context:

- Members have a shared goal, interest, need, or activity that provides the primary reason for belonging to the community;
- Members engage in repeated, active participation and there are often intense interactions, strong emotional ties, and shared activities occurring between participants;

- Members have access to shared resources and there are policies for determining access to those resources;
- Reciprocity of information, support, and services between members is important;
- There is a shared context of social conventions, language, and protocols.

As with CoPs and CoLs, the original ideas of situated learning and situated cognition theory (Brown, Collins, & Duguid, 1989) represent a major shift in learning theory from traditional psychological views of learning as mechanistic and individualistic, toward perspectives of learning that place greater emphasis on socio-cultural aspects (Greeno, 1998). These theories regard learning as an integral part of generative social practice in the lived-in world (Lave & Wenger, 1991), stressing the importance of acquiring and refining knowledge and skills in situ within real or authentic settings (Collins, 1988). Educators are therefore encouraged to immerse learners in environments that approximate as closely as possible the contexts in which their new ideas and behaviours will be applied. In this project, an eclectic mix of theories was used to provide a strong conceptual framework for the development of social, contextualized, reciprocal relationships among student teachers, in order to develop their professional skills through reflective practice and dialogue.

The rationale for the study was that preservice teacher may experience difficulties in collaborative contexts, especially when colleagues have different backgrounds or when they encounter an unfamiliar school culture. Yet this competence will be of paramount importance in their future profession: not only will they need to collaborate with colleagues who teach different subjects, but they will also need to participate effectively in online professional communities (Butler, Lauscher, Jarvis-Selinger, & Beckingham, 2004). Research has found that the forms of interactions that occur between peers are qualitatively different from those occurring between and an expert and novice, or a teacher and student. More recent studies indicate that peer learning and mentoring relationships in which intellectual capabilities are similar can offer both cognitive challenges and psycho-social support as both parties are more likely to engage in mutual dialogue and shared activities (Paulus & Scherff, 2008; Topping, 2005). For both parties this is a developmental relationship with the purpose of assisting the individuals to achieve a goal, in this case, to learn more about the teaching profession and develop their skills as teachers.

Online Communities of Practice (CoPs) mediated are increasingly believed to be an effective way of coping with professional teacher development and life-long learning (Schlager & Fusco, 2004). The reason why CoPs are so important for professional development is that they are groups of people who share goals and engage in planning, enacting, and reflecting on the work done (Wenger, McDermott, & Snyder, 2002). In CoPs, learning proceeds from dialogue, expertise is distributed and knowledge is socially constructed.

PROCEDURE

During the course of their four-week practicum, each participant was required to reflect and report on several critical incidents that occurred in his/her classroom, in both text and voice formats. Each week, the participants were asked to write a 200 to 300 word journal entry, as well as to produce a 90-second voice recording containing different content to the written report, about a significant critical incident, issue or problem that occurred during practicum. The report was to include a description of the context of the incident, as well as an account of both the actions of the students in the class and the student teacher. In addition, the participants had to identify questions or areas in which he/she required advice or assistance, and invite his/her peers to respond.

On a weekly basis, each participant was also asked to respond to at least one other student teacher, and to provide constructive feedback on his/her postings and helpful comments and support. At the conclusion of the practicum, the participants completed an individual narrative task in which they each created a two-minute podcast recording to be shared with the rest of the student teacher cohort, reflecting on the highlights and challenges of the practicum experience.

WEB-BASED TOOLS USED TO SUPPORT P2P INTERACTION

The research project involved preservice teachers using asynchronous telecommunications (the Wimba Voice Board) for purposeful dialogue during their student teaching experience (the practicum). The study sought to investigate the value of audio-recorded stories of critical incidents on the development of a learning community among the preservice teachers who formed mentoring dyads. The idea of a learning community or community of learning (CoL) is an adaptation of the concept of learning organizations, described by Argyris (1999). Learning organizations are comprised of people who see themselves as connected to each other and the world, where creative thinking is nurtured, and "… where people are continually learning how to learn together" (Senge, 1990, p. 3). The study employed the research framework of Wenger (1998) and Wenger et al. (2002) and employed social networking technologies to support a forum for discussion and interaction. Wenger et al. (2002, pp. 4-5) defined CoL's as, "groups of people who share a concern, a set of problems, or a passion about a topic, and who deepen their knowledge and expertise in this area by interacting on an ongoing basis." According to Wenger (1998), a CoL defines itself along three dimensions: what it is about – *its joint enterprise* as understood and continually renegotiated by its members; how it functions – *mutual engagement* that bind members together into a social entity; what capability it has produced – the *shared repertoire* of communal resources that members have developed over time, which could be in the form of shared understandings, support or idea generation. All three elements apply to social networking environments as well as to face-to-face CoLs. The three structural elements described by Wenger et al. (2002) were used to analyse the interactions that occurred in the online community of preservice teachers. Wenger et al. (2002, p. 29) noted that when these three elements function well together, they make a CoL an ideal "*knowledge structure* – a social structure that can assume responsibility for developing and sharing knowledge."

Participants

The study was conducted within the context of a small cohort of preservice teachers enrolled in a postgraduate program in teacher education. The cohort size was 19 students. The age of the students ranged from 22-43 years, and some had already had teaching experience. The students' expertise and comfort level ranged from those with limited experience and expertise using the Web for communication those who felt very comfortable and used telecommunications on a daily basis. Many students were familiar with how to download podcasts on to an MP3 player and were therefore quite comfortable with the process of creating voice recordings of critical episodes during the practicum.

Data Collection and Analysis Procedures

Using content analysis, the scripts and discourse produced by students were used to explore issues and patterns that were indicators of a learning community. Content analysis, defined as a systematic, replicable technique identifying themes in text into conceptual categories based on explicit rules of coding (Krippendorff, 2004) was used to code and analyse the data. Content analysis enabled the researchers to sift through large volumes of data in a systematic fashion using categories or discourse markers to assign features to data segments. It can be a useful technique for allowing researchers discover and describe the focus of individual, group, institutional, or social attention. Today, content analysis techniques are widely used in the analysis of computer conferencing transcripts, and now combine qualitative and quantitative approaches, which involve not merely counting the occurrences of variables, but also interpreting them through particular theoretical lens. Hara, Bonk, and Angeli (2000) endorse this dual approach, noting its capacity to capture the richness of student interaction.

Using Wenger et al.'s (2002) conceptual framework, the main focus was to identify the discourse elements of *mutual engagement*, *joint enterprise* and *shared repertoire*, which are deemed to be the essential characteristics of a learning community. Evidence was sought for the response to the research questions in the actual content of the transcripts.

RESULTS

Focus Question: Overall, What Elements of a Community of Practice Were Evident in the Peer-to-Peer Mentoring Relationships That Were Planned?

The results of the analysis of the Wimba Voice Board podcasts are depicted in Table 4. A total of 106 messages units were found in the discourse and results are summarised in this table. The categories identified in Wenger et al.'s (2002) conceptual framework were used to code student responses to semi structured focus group discussions. Overall, student comments focussed on the benefits of sharing experiences on their school practicum through the Wimba Voice Board and blog. The majority of comments were related to aspects of established common ground, engagement with others and establishment of rapport. The results showed that students developed sand demonstrated elements of mutual engagement, joint enterprise and shared repertoire.

Table 4. Results showing categories of socio-professional learning

Evidence of community	Explanation	Examples from student discourse	Instances found %
Mutual engagement	Belonging Forming relationships Maintaining identities	On the first posting I feel that if I did have someone who was doing the same thing as me, they would understand more in depth It just sort of helped me when I got home to know that I was not alone	34%
Shared repertoire	Common understandings established Use of shared objects Negotiated experience	Just knowing who is teaching what subjects and what levels so you can share things It was nice to have that community support while we were going through that experience I also see the benefit of having somebody to share ideas	27%
Joint enterprise	Negotiation of ideas Mutual accountability	I agree with Tara in relation to advance planning of units of work, but there is more than one way to plan ahead I found an example of what Joe referred to in his earlier blog entry …	16%
Identity	Awareness of professional skills Learning as doing Sharing expertise and mentoring others	The other thing I realised how many new skills I had to learn Teaching is now something I know about in a real sense. I can finally make the links to theory Knowing that everybody went through the same thing, more than once on some occasions helps, me and I hope it helps them	23%
Total			100%

DISCUSSION OF RESEARCH FINDINGS

Teachers have the onerous and daunting task of enabling students to develop the knowledge and skills necessary to prepare them for further education, employment, and life at large. In the early stages of their professional careers, what teachers desire is a forum for "the voices of teachers themselves, the questions [they] ask, the ways [they] use writing and intentional talk in their work lives" (Cochran-Smith & Lytle, 1992, p. 93). As part of their enculturation into schools, beginning teachers need to communicate and share ideas and to become part of the school learning community. The extracts presented in Table 2 present a snapshot of the interactions that occurred between participants in the online community supported by interactive technologies. During this process, lecturers monitored the blog, but did not intervene directly. During the project, online resources and communication tools were seen a way to meet the variety of beginning teachers' needs, and proved to be both a catalyst and a support for the development of an online community.

The provision of the voice board and blog enabled students to communicate while on practicum, to exchange ideas, reflect on experience and to develop a sense of professional identity. The voice board in combination with the blog enabled reflection on professional growth experiences, as well as providing a solution to the problem of isolation. Results show that the highest number of comments and narratives recorded were related to expressions of mutual engagement and solidarity with others, sharing experiences, establishing common ground and discovering a new professional identity. In addition, participants engaged in roles where they mentored and supported each other and took responsibility for furthering the expertise of the group. This case study provides evidence that Web 2.0 tools can support teacher professional development and provide a platform for connectivity and knowledge sharing.

USING DIGITAL TOOLS TO SUPPORT TEACHER PROFESSIONAL KNOWLEDGE

According to Shulman and Shulman (2004) the accomplished teacher must have vision, a clear sense of classrooms as learning communities and motivation. Fensternacher (1994) also emphasises the value of practical knowledge and practical reasoning in teacher development in teacher education, though he did not explicitly mention ICT. The affordances of digital tools and social media have had a major impact on the social, economic and cultural aspects of society and education. Web 2.0 can support the four features of an accomplished teacher outlined by Shulman and Shulman (2004). Each feature is listed below and an example is provided of how social media can enable these characteristics:

- *Learning in a community*: Digital tools can play a role in gaining access to communities at local and global levels, where they can express shared visions, and review emerging practices. By providing social online spaces for professional communities to communicate and share ideas, digital tools enable teachers to sustain a community orientation to their professional learning. Tools such as shared databases, online conferencing and discussion forums are ideal spaces for knowledge creation and connectivity.
- *Access and networking*: Digital tools give teachers access to a global bank of ideas, views of learning and teaching and alternative strategies for teaching, learning and how schools operate in supporting learning and personal growth.

Teacher vision is developed though informal networking and exploration of the multitude of websites offering professional development and teaching learning resources. Social networking sites allow individuals to connect, develop rapport, share interests, create community, and collaborate with peers. Many of these sites (for example, Facebook started off among small communities of college students in the USA, but have now spilled over into the professional worlds of work (e.g. LinkedIn).

- *Motivation to embrace change*: In the digital age teachers must being willing to expend the energy and persistence to adopt teaching strategies that are aligned with their vision. Teacher capacity to engage with innovation and change is fundamental to the development of professional identity (Hoban, 2002; Starkey, 2010). There are many ways that digital tools can stimulate motivation to learning and grow as a teacher. For example, the web provides access to information and resources and allows participation in global e-communities of practitioners who share ideas and experiences. Through the affordances of distributed cognition, teachers can be motivated to expand their own frameworks for assessment and pedagogy.
- *Reflection*: Critical reflection is regarded as a core component of teacher professional learning and Schön (1983) emphasises the need for teachers to learn from their own practices and from the experiences of colleagues and mentors. Reflective practice can be supportive by a range of digital tools and social media. Digital video and podcasts for example, can enable teachers to capture, observe and review episodes of teaching and to use them as levers for reflection, critical commentary and analysis.

CONCLUSION

This chapter has outlined the various processes that underpin teacher learning within a broad theoretical perspective based on socio-cultural views and theories of learning. Key features or affordances of Web 2.0 technologies are identified as being particularly valuable and harmonious with teacher learning, even though most of these applications were not designed originally for teacher education or even education in the wider sense. Innovative practices supported by social media provide an opportunity for teacher educators to look at wider implementation issues around technical infrastructure, but they must also address pedagogical challenges such as the integration of informal learning experiences, the limitations of existing physical and virtual learning environments and the personalisation of learning experiences. There may be a culture shock or skills crisis when "old world" educators are confronted with the expectation of working with participatory web 2.0 tools, and technologies with which they lack expertise and confidence. For these reasons, there is a need to make time for talking, awareness-raising, and discussion of what pedagogic approaches and tools best support the key competencies identified by Shulman and Shulman (2004). The goal is to facilitate learning, to blend the formal and informal, to support knowledge building and distributed cognition and engagement. The affordances of web 2.0 tools and digital technologies can support the growth of a reflective learning community to enable critical dialogue and communication while nurturing creativity, independent inquiry and communication. This can be achieved by employing the tools, resources and opportunities that can leverage what teacher do naturally – socialise, network and collaborate.

REFERENCES

Alexander, B. (2006). Web 2.0: A new wave of innovation for teaching and learning? *Educause Review*, *41*(2), 32-44.

Argyris, C. (1999). *On organizational learning*. Boston, MA: Blackwell Publishers.

Ashton, J., & Newman, L. (2006). An unfinished symphony: 21st century teacher education using knowledge creating heutagogies. *British Journal of Educational Technology*, *37*(6), 825-884.

Banks, F., Leach, J., & Moon, B. (1999). New understandings of teachers' pedagogic knowledge. In J. Leach & B. Moon (Eds.), *Learners and pedagogy* (pp. 89-110). London: Paul Chapman.

BECTA. (2007). *Emerging technologies for learning*, Volume 2. Coventry, UK: British Educational Communications and Technology Agency. Accesses 30/02/2010. Retrieved from http://www.becta.org.uk/research/emerging_technologies07.pdf.

Brown, J. S., Collins, A., & Duguid, P. (1989). Situated cognition and the culture of learning. *Educational Researcher*, *18*(1), 32-42.

Brown, T. H. (2005). Beyond constructivism: Exploring future learning paradigms. *Education Today*, *2005*(2). Retrieved from http://www.bucks.edu/IDlab/Beyond_constructivism.pdf (accessed 11 January 2006).

Brown, T. H. (2006). Beyond constructivism: Navigationism in the knowledge era. *On the Horizon*, *14*(3), 108-120.

Bruns, A. (2008). *Blogs, Wikipedia, second life and beyond. From production to produsage*. New York: Peter Lang Publishing.

Burden, K. (2010). Conceptualising teachers' professional learning with Web. *Campus-Wide Information Systems*, *27*(3), 141-161.

Butler, D. L., Lauscher, N. H., Jarvis-Selinger, S., & Beckingham, B. (2004). Collaboration and self-regulation in teachers' professional development. *Teaching and Teacher Education*, *20*, 435-455.

Cervetti, G., Damico, J., & Pearson, P. (2008). Multiple literacies, new literacies, and teacher education. *Theory into Practice*, *45*(4), 378-386.

Clandinin, D. J., & Connelly, M. F. (1987). Teachers' personal knowledge: What counts as personal in studies of the personal. *Journal of Curriculum Studies*, *19*(6), 487-500.

Cochran-Smith, M., & Lytle, S. L. (1992). Communities for teacher research: Fringe or forefront? *American Journal of Education*, *100*, 298-325.

Collins, A. (1988). *Cognitive apprenticeship and instructional technology*. Technical Report 6899. Cambridge, MA: BBN Labs.

Conole, G., & Dyke, M. (2004). What are the affordances of information and communication technologies? *ALT-J, Research in Learning Technology*, *12*(2), 113-124.

Darling-Hammond, L., & Baratz-Snowden, J. (2005). *A good teacher in every classroom*. San Francisco, CA: Jossey Bass.

Darling-Hammond, L., Bransford, J., LePage, P., Hammerness, K., & Duffy, H. (Eds.). (2007). *Preparing teachers for a changing world: What teachers should learn and be able to do*. San Francisco, CA: Jossey-Bass.

Elbaz, F. (1990). Knowledge and discourse: The evolution of research on teacher thinking. In C. Day, M. Pope, & P. Denicolo (Eds.), *Insights into teacher thinking and practice* (pp. 15-42). London: Falmer.

Fenstermacher, G. D. (1994). The knower and the known: The nature of knowledge in research on teaching. *Review of Educational Research*, *20*(3), 3-56.

Fisher, T., Higgins, C., & Loveless, A. (2006). *Teachers learning with digital technologies: A review of research and projects.* Bristol: Futurelab.

Goodson, I. F. (2003). *Professional knowledge, professional lives: Studies in education and change.* Maidenhead: Open University Press.

Greeno, J. G. (1998). The situativity of knowing, learning, and research. *American Psychologist, 53*(1), 5-26.

Hara, N., Bonk, C.J., & Angeli, C. (2000). Content analysis of online discussion in an applied educational psychology course. *Instructional Science, 28*, 115-152.

Hargreaves, A. (2003). *Teaching in the knowledge society: Education in the age of insecurity.* Maidenhead: Open University Press.

Hase, S., & Kenyon, C. (2000). From andragogy to heutagogy. *ultiBASE, 5*(3). Retrieved from http://ultibase.rmit.edu.au/Articles/dec00/hase1.pdf [viewed 25 Sep 2010].

Hoban, G. (2002). *Teacher learning for educational change.* Buckingham: Open University Press.

ISTE International Society of Technology in Education. (2012). *Advancing digital age teaching.* Retrieved October 2nd 2012 from http://www.iste.org/standards/nets-for-teachers.

Johnson, L., Adams, S., & Haywood, K. (2011). *The NMC Horizon Report: 2011 K-12 edition.* Austin, TX: The New Media Consortium.

Kagan, D. M. (1992). Professional growth among pre-service and beginning teachers. *Review of Educational Research, 62*, 129-169.

Koehler, M. J., & Mishra, P. (2009). What is technological pedagogical content knowledge? *Contemporary Issues in Technology and Teacher Education, 9*(1). Retrieved from www.citejournal.org/vol9/iss1/general/article1.cfm (accessed 1 April 2011).

Koehler, M. J., Mishra, P., & Yahya, K. (2007). Tracing the development of teacher knowledge in a design seminar: Integrating content, pedagogy and technology. *Computers & Education, 49*, 740-762.

Krippendorff, K. (2004). *Content analysis: An introduction to its methodology,* 2nd edition. Thousand Oaks, CA: Sage.

Ladbrook, J. (2009). Teachers of digikids: Do they navigate the divide? *Australian Journal of Language and Literacy, 32*(1), 68-82. Retrieved from http://alea.edu.au/site-content/publications/Ladbrook.pdf.

Lankshear, C., & Knobel, M. (2003). *New literacies: Changing knowledge and classroom learning.* Buckingham: Open University Press.

Laurillard, D. (2002). *Rethinking university teaching: A conversational framework for the effective use of learning technologies,* 2nd ed. London, UK: Routledge Falmer.

Lave, J., & Wenger, E. (1991). *Situated learning: Legitimate peripheral participation.* Cambridge: Cambridge University Press.

Lee, M. J. W., & McLoughlin, C. (Eds.). (2011). *Web 2.0-based e-learning: Applying social informatics for tertiary teaching.* Hershey, PA: IGI Global.

McLoughlin, C., & Lee, M. J. W. (2007). Social software and participatory learning: Extending pedagogical choices with technology affordances in the Web 2.0 era. In *ICT: Providing choices for learners and learning.* Proceedings ascilite Singapore 2007. Retrieved from http://www.ascilite.org.au/conferences/singapore07/procs/mcloughlin.html.

McLoughlin C., & Lee, M. J. W. (2010). Developing an online community to promote engagement and professional learning for pre-service teachers using social software tools. *Journal of Cases on Information Technology, 12*(1), 17-30.

McLoughlin, C., Lee, M. J. W., & Brady, J. (2008). A learning architecture framework (LAF) for developing community, engagement and professional identity for pre-service teachers. In I. Olney, G. Lefoe, J. Mantei, & J. Herrington (Eds.), *Proceedings of the Emerging Technologies Conference 2008* (pp. 147-157). Wollongong, Australia.

Mishra, P., & Koehler, M. J. (2006). Technological pedagogical content knowledge: A framework for integrating technology in teacher knowledge. *Teachers College Record, 108*(6), 1017-1054.

Paulus, T., & Scherff, L. (2008). Can anyone offer any words of encouragement? Online dialogue as a support mechanism for preservice teachers. *Journal of Technology and Teacher Education, 16*(1), 113-136.

Rosen D., & Nelson, C. (2008). Web 2.0: A new generation of learners and education. *Computers in the Schools, 3*(4), 211-225.

Schlager, M. S., & Fusco, J. (2004). Teacher professional development, technology, and communities of practice: are we putting the cart before the horse? *The Information Society, 19*, 203-220.

Schön, D. (1983). *The reflective practitioner: How professionals think in action.* London: Temple Smith.

Schön, D. (1987). *Educating the reflective practitioner.* San Francisco, CA: Jossey-Bass.

Peter M. Senge (1990). *The fifth discipline: The art and practice of the learning organization.* New York: Doubleday Currency.

Shulman, L. S. (1987). Knowledge and teaching: Foundations of the new reform. *Harvard Educational Review, 57*(1), 1-22.

Shulman, L.S., & Shulman, J.H. (2004). How and what teachers learn: A shifting perspective. *Journal of Curriculum Studies, 36*(2), 257-271.

Siemens, G. (2005a). Connectivism: A learning theory for a digital age. *International Journal of Instructional Technology and Distance Learning, 2*(1), 3-10.

Siemens, G. (2005b). Connectivism: Learning as network-creation. Retrieved September 2012 from http://www.elearnspace.org/Articles/networks.htm.

So, H.-J., & Kim, B. (2009). Learning about problem based learning: Student teachers integrating technology, pedagogy and content knowledge. *Australasian Journal of Educational Technology, 25*(1), 101-116. Retrieved from http://www.ascilite.org.au/ajet/ajet25/so.html.

Somekh, B. (2001). Methodological issues in identifying and describing the way knowledge is constructed with and without information and communications technology. *Journal of Information Technology for Teacher Education, 10*(1 & 2), 157-178.

Starkey, L. (2010). Teachers' pedagogical reasoning and action in the digital age. *Teachers and Teaching, 16*(2), 233-244.

Surowiecki, J. (2005). *The wisdom of crowds.* Anchor Books.

Tangney, B., FitzGibbon, A., Savage, T., Mehan, S., & Holmes, B. (2001). Communal constructivism: Students constructing learning for as well as with others. In C. Crawford et al. (Eds.), *Proceedings of Society for Information Technology and Teacher Education International Conference 2001* (pp. 3114-3119). Chesapeake, VA: AACE.

Topping, K. J. (2005). Trends in peer learning. *Educational Psychology, 25*(6), 631-645.

Wenger, E. (1998). *Communities of practice.* Cambridge, UK: Cambridge University Press.

Wenger, E., McDermott, R. & Snyder, W. (2002). *Cultivating communities of practice: A guide to managing knowledge.* Boston, MA: Harvard Business School Press.

Whittaker, S., Isaacs, E., & O'Day, V. (1997). Widening the Net. *SIGCHI Bulletin, 29*(3), 27-30.

Williams, M. K., Foulger, T. S., & Wetzel, K. (2009). Preparing preservice teachers for 21st century classrooms: Transforming attitudes and behaviours about innovative technology. *Journal of Technology and Teacher Education, 17*(3), 393-418.

Vygotsky, L. S. (1978). *Mind in society: The development of higher psychological processes.* Cambridge, MA: Harvard University Press.

AFFILIATIONS

Catherine McLoughlin
Australian Catholic University
Canberra, Australia

TOM RUSSELL AND SHAWN MICHAEL BULLOCK

DEVELOPING EXPERIENCED-BASED PRINCIPLES OF PRACTICE FOR TEACHING TEACHERS

INTRODUCTION

This chapter constructs six principles of practice for teaching teachers from our shared experiences (2005-2011) engaged in collaborative self-study of our practice of teaching physics curriculum methods to teacher candidates. These collaborative self-studies began with the commencement of Shawn's Ph.D. studies, which Tom supervised. Conscious of Shawn's intention to pursue teacher education in both research and practice, Tom encouraged a collaborative self-study during the doctoral program to enable us both to identify and explore our assumptions about teaching teachers. In 2005-2006, we shared a teaching arrangement where Tom was the teacher of record for the first half of the year and Shawn for the second half of the year, while Tom was on leave. In 2006-2007, we shared responsibility for teaching the physics methods course while Shawn developed his research questions for his thesis. In 2007-2008, Shawn was a participant-observer in Tom's class while also interviewing five teacher candidates from Tom's class about their course and practicum experiences. The final year of Shawn's Ph.D. studies (2008-2009) found us returning to team-teaching and enacting pedagogical approaches based on findings from the research conducted a year earlier.

We now teach in different universities and continue our conversations about teaching teachers in yet another variation on self-study. We find the concept of developing a principled approach (Ambrose, Bridges, DiPietro, Lovett, & Norman, 2010; Kroll et al., 2005) to our practice of teaching future teachers to be a particularly productive way of reviewing and synthesising our years of collaborative self-study. This chapter analyses and interprets those 6 years of self-studies in order to develop principles of practice for teaching future teachers. In doing so, we take seriously the calls by Zeichner (2007) and Loughran (2006, 2010) to both accumulate knowledge across self-studies and to go beyond stories of personal practice to develop principles that have epistemic import. We use the concept of the authority of experience as a central perspective from which to construct principles of practice.

METHODOLOGY

Self-study is not a prescriptive methodology (LaBoskey, 2004; Loughran, 2005; Pinnegar & Hamilton, 2009); self-study researchers draw on a variety of research methods. Self-study provides an important framework for the development of

M.A. Flores et al. (eds.), Back to the Future: Legacies, Continuities and Changes in Educational Policy, Practice and Research, 207–218.

professional knowledge about teaching teachers (Bullock, 2009). Although the term *self-study* might well bring to mind images of solitary researchers thinking deeply about their practice, an important feature of many self-studies is critical friendship with a trusted colleague (e.g., Schuck & Russell, 2005). Costa and Kallick (1993, p. 50) defined a critical friend as "a trusted person who asks provocative questions, provides data to be examined through another lens, and offers critique of another person's work." In our opinion, it is critical friendship that allows self-study methodology to move beyond good-news stories of practice toward deliberate analyses of pedagogy. A recurring emphasis in self-study literature involves the problematic and unexpected features of practice, as self-study methodology "looks for and requires evidence of reframed thinking and transformed practice of the researcher" (LaBoskey, 2004, p. 859). We continue to find LaBoskey's four methodological considerations for conducting self-study to be useful guideposts for our research:

- Self-study is aimed at identifying and reframing problems of practice encountered by the researcher with a view toward improving his or her own pedagogy;
- Self-study challenges the researcher's tacit understanding about teaching and learning by encouraging interaction with colleagues, students, and educational research;
- Self-study generally employs multiple, usually qualitative, methods that are used in the broader education research community as well as qualitative methods that are unique to self-study research;
- Self-study should be made available to the broader education research community for the purpose of consolidating understanding and suggesting new avenues for research (LaBoskey, 2004, pp. 859-860).

This chapter synthesizes and interprets the results of collaborative self-studies that we have conducted since 2005. In response to the challenge issued by Zeichner (2007) to "accumulate knowledge across self-studies," we look critically at our work with a view to suggesting principles of practice for teaching teachers. We accept the view of Kroll et al. (2005) that principles offer a dynamic alternative to the more traditional idea of propositions, because principles are understood to suggest future directions and contextual understanding rather than objective truths. To that end, we offer six principles, supported by warrants developed from relevant literature and from 6 years of collaborative self-study.

SIX PRINCIPLES OF PRACTICE FOR TEACHING TEACHERS

Learning to Think Pedagogically Is at the Core of Learning to Teach

As a teacher educator, it is easy to assume that a methods course should focus on ensuring that those learning to teach understand fully and accurately the content of the curriculum they will teach. It is also easy to assume that recommended practices will be adopted by new teachers once they have been made aware of those practices, typically by reading about them and being told. It took many years of listening to those learning to teach and reviewing our own practices as teacher educators to realise that the central focus of a preservice teacher education program should be on developing the ability to *think pedagogically*. Teachers teach the content of various disciplines to their students; teacher educators must teach their students what it means to think like a teacher. While this always involves working with the subject matter of the curriculum and various disciplined perspectives on education itself, *analysing the relationship between teaching and learning in disciplined ways does not come naturally*. Developing the ability to think pedagogically must begin in preservice teacher education, to initiate a perspective that will continue to develop over a career. Books such as Loughran's (2010) *What Expert Teachers Do* provide excellent support for helping new teachers to think pedagogically.

Learning to think pedagogically is neither obvious nor intuitive for teacher candidates; most have spent a lifetime observing teachers with little incentive to think carefully about why teachers behave as they do. As a result, most teacher candidates come to a Faculty of Education able to do reasonable impressions of how a teacher acts in a classroom. Nevertheless, they tend to be unable to see clear connections between particular teaching strategies they might use and the effects those strategies might have on a students' learning. In short, they are unable to think pedagogically.

Data from a collaborative self-study that we conducted in 2007-2008 uncovered many of the challenges candidates face in thinking pedagogically. That year we decided to enact a pedagogical approach grounded in lesson study (Stepanek, Appel, Leong, Mangan, & Mitchell, 2007) that provided an opportunity for every candidate to plan a lesson in a small group, and for representatives of each group to teach the lesson twice (with the second version of the lesson to be developed according to peers' feedback on the first version). Early in the process it became apparent that candidates were having difficulty providing feedback to peers in ways that were different from suggestions that might be made by associate teachers. Tom called attention to the difficulties they were experiencing shortly after the first lesson study, stating that "a lot of this [peer feedback] reads like 'do X instead of Y.' What I am struggling with is that we haven't named the learning effects .... Can we get better, individually and collectively, at naming the learning effects?" (Russell & Bullock, 2010, p. 26). Although Tom continued to encourage candidates to frame their comments in terms of teaching strategies and learning effects – to think pedagogically – many candidates actively resisted the process. We noted:

> Several teacher candidates argued that there was merely a semantic difference between making a statement such as "do X instead of Y" and making a statement such as "the teaching strategy affected my learning in X ways." (Russell & Bullock, 2010, p. 26)

After continued prompting, we both noticed that the second round of lesson-study presentations prompted candidates to enact slightly riskier pedagogical approaches and to speak more openly about the effects that particular approaches were having

209

on their learning. Overall, though, we concluded that the gains were marginal, largely because requiring a teacher candidate to teach a lesson to peers early in the year requires them to take considerable risk. In hindsight, we realized how much we were asking of teacher candidates. We were asking them to create a whole new language for talking about teaching when they were still struggling to make sense of their deeply-rooted default teaching moves.

Recognise the Significance of the First Meeting of a Course as a Unique Opportunity to Challenge Prior Views of Teaching and Learning by Making Powerful and Unexpected Pedagogical Moves That Engage Teacher Candidates and Stimulate Conversation about Pedagogy

Shawn's first memory of Tom's physics class is the way it began by focusing on a shared classroom experience rather than reading through a course outline and discussing the required assignments. Tom engaged the class both in thinking about physics and in thinking about how to teach physics by using Predict-Observe-Explain (POE) pedagogy (Baird & Northfield, 1992). The procedure is familiar to many science teachers and science teacher educators: A situation is presented to a class and students are asked to make predictions about what will happen, record observations, and suggest explanations. At first the process may seem to be both a metaphor for the scientific method and a way of engaging students in learning to think scientifically.

We have come to believe, however, that POEs transcend an investigation of scientific concepts and go a long way to creating what Sarason (1996, p. 37) has called a "context of productive learning." A context of productive learning emphasizes shared intellectual control between teachers and students and an environment that is conducive to taking risks. Candidates in our physics methods courses typically come from undergraduate degrees such as physics, mathematics, and engineering and they tend to overestimate their conceptual understanding of basic Newtonian physics. POEs help call attention to some of the gaps in their undergraduate learning, with a view to emphasising the importance of exploratory, hypothetical talk rather than stating the correct explanation. POEs are often designed to highlight an unexpected result. We have found that the shared experience of building an incorrect prediction and finding ways to talk productively about how someone might be thinking if they made a particular prediction are early ways to signal our intention of creating a productive classroom environment.

In addition to challenging the cultural tradition of focusing on administration during the first class, beginning the physics methods course with a POE allows Tom to begin developing a relationship of mutual trust. Although candidates may believe initially that the point of a POE is to test their physics knowledge, the way Tom sets up POEs and the subsequent discussions helps to shift candidates' focus toward their learning during the POE process. Candidates are also encouraged to think about how a secondary school student might be thinking during a POE. The following excerpt from data collected at the beginning of our 2006-2007 methods class and first reported in Bullock and Russell (2009) reveals the typical way that Tom begins the academic year:

Tom: If someone thought that the mirror would make the light brighter, how might that person explain that prediction?

[Responses from teacher candidates]

Tom: Notice that every answer you give is a right answer, because I can't argue with how someone might be thinking. Now, if someone thought that the mirror would make the light darker, how might that person explain that prediction?

[Responses from teacher candidates]

Tom: I am going to ask you to do something that will feel strange. Please close your eyes and raises one hand in a fist. When I say that prediction you wish to vote for, please open your hand so that I can count you. [Tom counts the votes for each prediction and then asks people to open their eyes]. That's the wonderful thing about POEs; everyone has taken university courses in physics, yet look at the range of responses.

[Tom moves the mirror in front of the light, revealing that that correct prediction depends on where the candidate's eyes are in relation to the angle of the mirror; for everyone, the area in question appears darker because the direct reflection is on the ceiling.]

Tom: How did that experience make you feel as a student? As you go through the year, remember that school is often a house of right answers. How long does it normally take you to conclude that you gave a wrong answer to a teacher? Most students know in an instant. One of the biggest challenges is how we tell students their answer is wrong. *Conducting a POE means that we don't have to tell students that they are wrong.*

The purpose of doing a POE in the opening minutes of the first class is to send a message: A physics methods classroom can be a safe learning environment in which individuals can offer opinions without fear of being judged as providing a wrong answer. As Holt (1964) observed, the fear of failure dominates many students' experiences of schooling. Post-secondary education is no different, for there is powerful and well-learned desire to give the right answer and please the teacher. Tom was careful to form his questions so that teacher candidates could hypothesize about how someone *might* support a prediction without stating how they personally would explain their own predictions. In this way, Tom indicated that he was interested in exploratory thinking and risk-taking rather than in passing judgement on the candidates' background knowledge in physics. Although we believe that Predict-Observe-Explain is both a powerful pedagogy to use in physics classrooms and a useful touchstone for candidates to begin thinking about the messages we are trying to get across, the broader purpose for beginning with a POE is to initiate a productive relationship with teacher candidates.

Teachers New and Old Are Unlikely to Adopt New Teaching Procedures Unless They Have Experienced Those Procedures Themselves and Analysed the Effects on Their Own Learning

Most teacher educators are aware of Lortie's (1975) concept of the *apprenticeship of observation*. The phrase has a certain initial plausibility, as we have all observed our own teachers through countless hours of schooling. Because preservice teachers have little or no experience of teaching, it is easy to assume that they are empty vessels waiting to be filled with the wisdom of teacher educators' own teaching experiences. Thanks to the growing attention to the importance of working with what children already know, we began to understand how and why telling people new ways to teach has minimal impact on how they teach. Only by experiencing new pedagogical approaches personally and then analysing those experiences systematically can we begin to overcome the tendencies of all teachers and teacher educators to teach as they were taught.

The familiar language of *theory into practice* makes it easy for every teacher educator to assume that words will be sufficient to change practices, yet teaching is one of the most difficult practices to change. What we consider to be normal or appropriate is shaped in powerful ways by our own teachers' practices. Anything different makes us uncomfortable and is also likely to make our students uncomfortable. As Macdonald (1973, as cited in Stenhouse, 1975, p. 170) put it, "Genuine innovation begets incompetence. It de-skills teacher and pupil alike, suppressing acquired competencies and demanding the development of new ones."

Reflective Practice Involves Much More Than Everyday Meanings of the Word Reflection. Teacher Educators Need to Teach People How to Reflect and to Model Explicitly Their Own Reflective Practices

Tom's interest in and understanding of the concept of *reflective practice* (Schön, 1983) was enriched by opportunities to hear Schön lecture at Queen's in 1984 and 1987. Those lectures inspired Tom to build a research agenda on the concept of reflective practice and to focus his research on teacher education generally rather than on teacher education in science. Reflective practice goes well beyond everyday meanings of reflection and focuses on learning from professional experience. Before we can teach others the meaning of reflective practice, it is essential to understand reflection from the perspective of our own professional learning from experience as teacher educators. Analysis of Tom's interviews of his physics methods students in 1992-1993 inspired the concept of the *authority of experience* (Munby & Russell, 1994), which calls attention to the fact that experience can have authority that may compete with and override the authority of reasoned arguments or the authority of position associated with an experienced teacher's advice to a novice.

The Professional Relationship between Teacher Candidate and Teacher Educator Is Crucial to the Teacher Educator's Influence on How a Teacher Candidate Will Teach

In one of the first sociological studies of teaching, Waller (1932/1961) argued that schools play a significant role in the transmission of cultural norms, particularly because school culture is characterized by "complex rituals of personal relationships" (p. 103) between people who engage in a variety of rituals and ceremonies. One of the most familiar ceremonies requires students to sit and listen attentively as a teacher stands at the front of the room and talks about curricular content. Tom disrupts this familiar teacher-student relationship on the first day of the methods course by challenging teacher candidates to take an active role in their learning during predict-observe-explain pedagogy. Bain's (2004) discussion of how the best university teachers treat their students led Tom to renew his attention to the importance of my professional relationship with each person he teaches. This principle is at the core of our professional relationship with each other, a relationship that began in 1997-98 when Shawn was a student in Tom's class and we subsequently published an analysis of that early relationship (Russell & Bullock, 1999).

Our continuing interest in the power of Predict-Observe-Explain pedagogy led us to connect the importance of creating a safe classroom environment with an early and explicit focus on developing a productive relationship with teacher candidates. Another significant way that we build a relationship with teacher candidates is through anonymous feedback that we collect using both index cards and the affordances of course management software. Making "Tickets out of Class" a regular feature of the last few minutes of every class reveals the main messages and questions that candidates are grappling with. As Tom noted, "I have always thought that my teaching required listening to my students and asking them to play back to me the effects of my teaching on their learning" (Russell, 2007, p. 184). Asking candidates to quickly write down a few thoughts about the class has proven to be a simple yet effective way to think about how candidates perceive our teaching. Candidates have also spoken about the efficacy of tickets; one person from our 2008–2009 class offered the comment that "tickets leave us thinking after class." We continue to be fascinated by the diverse range of ideas that candidates take from a given lesson. This reminds us of the significant gap between what the teacher wants from a lesson plan and what the students get out of a lesson. The challenge, for us, is to try to keep that gap as small as possible by ensuring that both teachers and students have open dialogs about shared experiences in the course.

In September, 2009, Tom did something he had never done before, inviting each student (in a class of 16) to meet with him for 20 minutes between the first and second class. His insight into the power of this principle was immediate when he arrived at that second class and realised how different it felt from the first, because he knew each person's name and something about her or him. That early one-on-one meeting paid rich dividends throughout the year. The inspiration for this practice came directly from Shawn's analysis of data he collected for his thesis research. The price in time is high, and the rewards are equally high. Tom has continued and extended the practice by meeting individually with each student (23 in 2010-2011) after the first and second practice teaching experiences. He is struck by the number of students who thank him for the opportunity to meet individually for the purpose of reviewing their professional progress.

Every Teacher Candidate Takes a Uniquely Personal Set of Messages from the Shared Experiences of an Education Course. The Single Most Important Influence on What Candidates Take Away is the Nature of the Relationship That Is Developed with the Teacher Educator

Shawn's study (Bullock, 2011) of the learning experiences of five candidates in the physics methods course in 2007-2008 forced us to abandon the easy assumption that, if all students experienced the same classes, then they all left with roughly the same messages and understandings. Data from 4 focus groups and 20 individual interviews, conducted at intervals during an 8-month preservice program, illustrated how each individual arrives with a unique set of assumptions about teaching and learning; the data forced us to conclude that each individual leaves with a similarly unique set of understandings in response to the learning experiences that are created in the class. In hindsight, we realized that at least part of the difference between the messages that teacher candidates take from their methods courses arises from the different experiences they have had observing teachers over many years as students.

Renewed attention to the many dimensions of the apprenticeship of observation linked with the evidence from Shawn's research focussed our thinking on the uniqueness of what each candidate takes from shared class and program experiences. Data gathered during the 2007-2008 academic year indicated that teaching and learning experiences in the physics methods course stood in sharp contrast to candidates' school experiences prior to the preservice program and also in sharp contrast to what they observed during their practicum placements. The candidates were affected in different ways by the teaching strategies used in their physics course, but they agreed overall that the course was a non-traditional educational experience that differed significantly from their initial expectations. One candidate called attention to the importance of starting off a course by building a strong relationship:

I found that teachers who establish an environment of trust, they're given a break compared to individuals who haven't …. [If] you start down the wrong path you're never going to get off it. It's important to start things the right way, or start out the way that you want the class to go … establish the class environment that you want for the semester and model it. (Bullock, 2011, p. 72)

Another candidate highlighted the foundational importance of relationships in teaching:

Working towards the relationship is pretty integral. It's not just sort of like a helpful thing, like "This will go better if you like me" or "You'll listen to my lectures more if you think I'm a fun person." But more that that relationship is actually a specific part of the teaching, and that if that relationship's not working, then there's some kind of failure there on someone's part. (Bullock, 2011, p. 72)

These two candidates viewed the relationship that Tom cultivated with his students as more than a nicety that made coming to class pleasant; it was a specific, foundational part of his teaching. Significantly, when asked what they learned from the physics methods course that was unique compared to the rest of their teacher education program, these same two teacher candidates bluntly replied: "How to teach" (Bullock, 2011, p. 126). Although he did not want to come across as a "Tom cheerleader," one of the candidates explained: "What I mostly learned from physics class was just the way Tom taught" (Bullock, 2011, p. 129). The other four candidates echoed his statement, albeit in different ways. Some candidates were impressed by the range of active-learning pedagogies, such as POEs, used in the methods course, particularly when those pedagogies caused them to rethink how they learned. Other candidates took an early interest in how Tom cultivated his relationship with the class. By the end of the course, each of the five candidates agreed that *how* Tom taught was in fact the content of the methods course, and that the way he taught was predicated on a strong relationship with the class founded on mutual trust.

The 2008-2009 methods course was markedly different from the previous 4 years due to a cluster of candidates whose initial school experiences were in countries from which they later moved to Canada. These candidates compelled us to recognize yet another layer of significance in the apprenticeship of observation, namely, that our own apprenticeships of observation made it easier to predict the assumptions that candidates would have about teaching and learning from their apprenticeships, *provided that they also went to school in Canada.* This extra layer of complexity seems particularly relevant to future research into the effects of the apprenticeship of observation on teacher candidates' prior assumptions about teaching.

CONCLUSIONS

As we work to help teacher candidates learn to study their own development as learners and as teachers, studying our own practices has become an increasingly important part of giving genuine meaning to reflective practice and constructivist teaching approaches. We believe that characteristics of self-study such as critical friendship and reflection-in-action make sustained collaborative self-studies an important tool to help teacher educators to examine the assumptions underlying their practices and critical features of their pedagogy. Studying our own practice is not an end in itself but a driving force for reframing how we think about our practice in order to develop new, more engaging and productive practices.

By creating a context of productive learning with teacher candidates in their preservice year, we conclude that we can also create a strong potential for meaningful dialogue as the candidates enter the teaching profession. One of the inevitable challenges is that each new group of candidates has not shared with us the events that led to the new practices we develop. This reminds us of the importance of being explicit with candidates about why we believe that specific practices with which they may be unfamiliar or uncomfortable are relevant to their professional learning as they experience the transition from student to teacher.

In closing, we repeat the six principles of practice, this time without discussion so that they may be viewed as a set of principles rather than as individual ones.

- Learning to think pedagogically is at the core of learning to teach;
- Recognise the significance of the first class as a unique opportunity to challenge prior views of teaching and learning by making powerful and unexpected pedagogical moves that engage teacher candidates and stimulate conversation about pedagogy;
- Teachers new and old are unlikely to adopt new teaching procedures unless they have experienced those procedures themselves and analysed the effects on their own learning;
- Reflective practice involves much more than everyday meanings of the word *reflection*. Teacher educators need to teach people how to reflect and to model explicitly their own reflective practices;
- The professional relationship between teacher candidate and teacher educator is crucial to the teacher educator's influence on how a teacher candidate will teach;
- Every teacher candidate takes a uniquely personal set of messages from the shared experiences of an education course. The single most important influence on what candidates take away is the nature of the relationship that is developed with the teacher educator.

We see these as a set of principles grounded in our practice and subject to rigorous, on-going, critical analysis through collaborative self-study. To further highlight the fact that these principles are dynamic works-in-progress, we state some of the tensions that continue to challenge us as we develop, critique, and reframe our pedagogies of teacher education:

- Each year we work with new groups of teacher candidates who are unique both as individuals and as a group. How do we adapt what we have learned from working with groups of candidates over a number of years while acknowledging that new classes only experience the methods course once?
- How do we continue to find ways to help candidates quickly and continuously identify their prior views about teaching and learning acquired in their apprenticeships of observation?

- How can we improve our ability to listen actively to our teacher candidates' individual concerns and work with them to track their progress through the year?
- Teacher educators and teacher candidates often find it difficult to enact new and unfamiliar pedagogies that are consistent with their vision of the kind of teacher they want to become. How do we turn this challenge to our advantage in a methods course?

Both the culture of school and the related culture of a Faculty of Education can easily mask the big-picture issues of teaching and learning. How can we call attention to these big-picture issues when the pragmatic needs and concerns of teacher candidates often feel so visceral and immediate?

REFERENCES

Ambrose, S. A., Bridges, M. W., DiPietro, M., Lovett, M. C., & Norman, M. K. (2010). *How learning works: Seven research-based principles for smart teaching.* San Francisco, CA: Jossey-Bass.

Bain, K. (2004). *What the best college teachers do.* Cambridge, MA: Harvard University Press.

Baird, J. R., & Northfield, J. R. (1992). *Learning from the PEEL experience.* Melbourne, Australia: Monash University Printery.

Bullock, S. M. (2009). Learning to think like a teacher educator: Making the substantive and syntactic structures of teaching explicit through self-study. *Teachers and Teaching: Theory and Practice, 15,* 291-304.

Bullock, S. M. (2011). *Inside teacher education: Challenging prior views of teaching and learning.* Rotterdam, The Netherlands: Sense Publishers.

Bullock, S. M., & Russell, T. (2009, May). *Creating a context of productive learning in a physics methods course: A retrospective analysis of four years of self-study of teaching and learning together.* Paper presented at the meeting of the Canadian Society for the Study of Education, Ottawa, ON.

Costa, A. L., & Kallick, B. (1993). Through the lens of a critical friend. *Educational Leadership, 51*(2), 49-51.

Holt, J. (1964). *How children fail.* New York: Pitman Publishing Company.

Kroll, L. R., Cossey, R., Donahue, D. M., Galguera, T., LaBoskey, V. K., Richert, A. E., & Tucher, P. (2005). *Teaching as principled practice: Managing complexity for social justice.* Thousand Oaks, CA: Sage.

LaBoskey, V. K. (2004). The methodology of self-study and its theoretical underpinnings. In J. J. Loughran, M. L. Hamilton, V. K. LaBoskey, & T. Russell (Eds.), *International handbook of self-study of teaching and teacher education practices* (pp. 817-870). Dordrecht: Kluwer Academic Publishers.

Lortie, D. C. (1975). *Schoolteacher: A sociological study.* Chicago: University of Chicago Press.

Loughran, J. (2005). Researching teaching about teaching: Self-study of teacher education practices. *Studying Teacher Education, 1*(1), 5-16.

Loughran, J. (2006). *Developing a pedagogy of teacher education: Understanding teaching and learning about teaching.* London: Routledge.

Loughran, J. (2010). *What expert teachers do: Enhancing professional knowledge for classroom practice.* London: Routledge.

Munby, H., & Russell, T. (1994). The authority of experience in learning to teach: Messages from a physics methods class. *Journal of Teacher Education, 45,* 86-95.

Pinnegar, S. E., & Hamilton, M. L. (2009). *Self-study of practice as a genre of qualitative research: Theory, methodology, and practice.* Dordrecht, the Netherlands: Springer.

Russell, T. (2007). How experience changed my values as a teacher educator. In T. Russell & J. Loughran (Eds.), *Enacting a pedagogy of teacher education: Values, relationships, and practices* (pp. 183-191). London: Routledge.

Russell, T., & Bullock, S. (1999). Discovering our professional knowledge as teachers: Critical dialogues about learning from experience. In J. Loughran (Ed.), *Researching teaching* (pp. 132-151). London: Falmer Press.

Russell, T., & Bullock, S. M. (2010). From talk to experience: Transforming the physics methods course. *Brock Education Journal, 20*(1), 19-33.

Sarason, S. B. (1996). *Revisiting "The culture of the school and the problem of change."* New York: Teachers College Press.

Schön, D. A. (1983). *The reflective practitioner: How professionals think in action.* New York: Basic Books.

Schuck, S., & Russell, T. (2005). Self-study, critical friendship, and the complexities of teacher education. *Studying Teacher Education, 1*(2), 107-121.

Stenhouse, L. (1975). *An introduction to curriculum research and development.* London: Heinemann.

Stepanek, J., Appel, G., Leong, M., Mangan, M. T., & Mitchell, M. (2007). *Leading lesson study.* Thousand Oaks, CA: Corwin Press.

Waller, W. (1932/1961). *The sociology of teaching.* New York: Russell & Russell.

Zeichner, K. (2007). Accumulating knowledge across self-studies in teacher education. *Journal of Teacher Education, 58*(1), 36.

AFFILIATIONS

Tom Russell
Faculty of Education
Queen's University, Kingston, Ontario, Canada

Shawn Michael Bullock
Faculty of Education
Simon Fraser University, Burnaby, British Columbia, Canada

TOM RUSSELL AND ANDREA K. MARTIN

CHALLENGES TO PROMOTING QUALITY IN PRESERVICE PRACTICUM EXPERIENCES

INTRODUCTION

This chapter arises from our concerns, developed over 10 years of practicum supervision experiences, that while the practicum continues to be perceived as the single most important and valuable element of our preservice program, the practicum still falls far short of its full and necessary potential in preparing new teachers for their full-time teaching responsibilities. We draw on relevant literature, on personal experiences in schools, and on perceptions of associate (cooperating) teachers expressed in a focus-group discussion. The data and previously reported findings indicate that promoting quality in practicum experiences is a complex challenge. Until teacher education programs begin to come to terms with the fundamental authority of experience for all types of learning, their structures are likely to contradict their research-based premises and rhetoric, leaving candidates discounting the significance of their formal courses in education. Our efforts to inquire into our own teaching and to listen to teacher candidates and associate teachers on the topic of improving the quality of practicum learning experiences have generated a robust agenda for further exploration. The chapter concludes with that agenda comprised of six recommendations for improving the quality of practicum learning.

The ultimate folly of teacher education institutions involves trying to improve schools by filling new teachers with dreams of new research-based practices without first attending to and improving the teacher educators' own teaching. Darling-Hammond (2006, pp. 279-280) cites the only-too-plausible criticism that "one reason professors spend so much time trying to change K-12 schools is that they know they cannot change their own organizations." The reality that preservice programs can never fully prepare a new teacher for school realities has been recognized by the creation of induction programs. Connecting messages from education classrooms to in-school contexts is one rationale for promoting the quality of learning from practicum experiences. Promoting such quality requires teaching candidates how to learn from their practicum experiences in ways that make explicit the perspective of school as a culture (Sarason, 1996) and the inherent complexity of creating classroom contexts of productive learning (Sarason, 1998).

M.A. Flores et al. (eds.), Back to the Future: Legacies, Continuities and Changes in Educational Policy, Practice and Research, 219–230.

OBJECTIVE AND CONTEXT

This chapter reports the authors' personal understandings and interpretations of challenges to promoting quality in the practicum element of initial teacher education programs. It arises from our concerns developed over 10 years of practicum supervision that, while the practicum continues to be perceived as the single most important and valuable element of our preservice program, the practicum still falls far short of its full and necessary potential in preparing new teachers for their full-time teaching responsibilities. In constructing our argument, we draw on relevant literature, on personal experiences in schools, and on perceptions of associate (cooperating) teachers expressed in a focus-group discussion.

We offer recommendations for promoting quality in preservice practicum experiences by interpreting teacher candidates' and associate teachers' perspectives. Darling-Hammond (2006, p. 279) cites the longstanding concern that "candidates do not learn deeply about how to understand and handle real problems of practice." Nuthall reviewed his own extensive career in educational research and drew these insights:

> It is important to search out independent evidence that the widely accepted routines of teaching are in fact serving the purposes for which they are enacted. We need to find a critical vantage point from outside the routines and their supporting myths .... The approach I have learned to take is to look at teaching through the eyes of students and to gather detailed data about the experiences of individual students. (Nuthall, 2005, p. 925)

Through conversations with teacher candidates and associate teachers, we are trying to create critical vantage points for ourselves and others to challenge familiar myths associated with practicum learning. We take Nuthall to be seeking a critical vantage point that recognizes that the cultural features of schooling tend to be invisibly embedded in the daily routines of the teacher-student relationship. Routines are both necessary and inevitable, but any efforts to create more productive contexts for learning will necessarily fail if the cultural features of schooling are not identified explicitly and addressed directly. This chapter documents our initial efforts to help teacher candidates interpret their professional learning experiences in terms of the cultural features of practicum settings and our attempts to understand more fully the complex challenges of learning from practicum experiences.

THEORETICAL PERSPECTIVES AND MODE OF INQUIRY

We begin with literature on conceptual change and development (see also Duschl & Hamilton, 1998) that is linked to literature on reflective practice, because changes in thinking and changes in practice go hand-in-hand with the development of new understandings. Kagan (1992) summarizes the recommendations of Posner, Strike, Hewson, and Gertzog (1982) for how teachers can promote students' conceptual change. Teachers must (a) help students make their implicit beliefs explicit, (b) confront students with the inadequacies of their beliefs, and (c) provide extended opportunities for integrating and differentiating old and new knowledge, eliminating brittle preconceptions that impede learning and elaborating anchors that facilitate learning.

Hodson (1998) makes the case that, in science teaching, creating conditions for cognitive conflict where teachers challenge students to look for limitations in their views or deliberately provide examples of discrepant or surprising events, often through hands-on demonstrations or activities, can spur reconceptualisation. However, we question the extent to which preservice teacher education anchors the practicum within a conceptual change framework, explores conceptual change theory, probes the concepts that teacher candidates hold about teaching and learning, provokes cognitive conflict, and supports candidates with approaches and strategies to encourage and sustain conceptual change. Unless prospective teachers are *directly* challenged to confront their own alternative conceptions and work through the process of conceptual change, it is highly unlikely that they will be able to support their own students in doing so. Unless learning from practicum experiences is *explicitly* supported and interpreted, those learning to teach are not likely to move beyond what they have already learned from a long "apprenticeship of observation" (Lortie, 1975). Lortie named some of the reasons why practice teaching cannot be allowed to just happen:

> Because of its casualness and narrow scope, ..., the usual practice teaching arrangement does not offset the unreflective nature of prior socialization; the student teacher is not forced to compare, analyze, and select from diverse possibilities. The risk is, of course, that practice teaching may simply expose the student to one more teacher's style of work. The value of practice teaching is attested to by many who have participated in it, but there is little indication that it is a powerful force away from traditionalism and individualism. It may be earthy and realistic when compared with education courses; but it is also short and parochial. (Lortie, 1975, p. 71)

Clift and Brady (2005, p. 311) offered the following conclusion that we find essential in recognizing the importance of attending systematically and explicitly to the individual teacher candidates' beliefs about teaching and learning as they attend education courses and participate in practicum experiences:

> Although it is well documented that prospective teachers often feel conflict among the messages they receive from different university instructors, field-based teacher educators, and school settings, it is also the case the prospective teachers resist coherent messages when they find it difficult to engage in recommended practices. When field placements reinforce and support the practices advocated by the teacher education program, individuals may still resist changing beliefs or practices because they are personally uncomfortable with the competing beliefs and practices. Practice and beliefs

are mediated by their prior beliefs and experiences, course work, and current perceptions of curriculum, students, pedagogy, and other factors.

We believe that the degree of resistance to new practices is widely underestimated by teacher educators. Quite simply, teaching practices are hard to change, in part because they generate uncertainty for both the prospective teacher and for the students being taught.

We draw on Sarason's (1998) discussion of "contexts of productive learning" as a powerful way to think about educational experiences. Finally, from Nuthall's (2005) account of his journey as a researcher, we construct an image of teachers, teacher educators and researchers as potentially "lost in school," unable to see the critical features of the culture in which they carry out their work. One element of this perspective involves the traditional view that theory is first taught and then practiced (Russell, 2005). The possibility that many prospective teachers are in some sense lost in school has helped us to see more clearly what we want to avoid and what we want to achieve in our teaching and in a teacher education program. Korthagen and Kessels (1999) have highlighted the risk of emphasizing procedural knowledge over the perceptual knowledge they refer to as *phronesis*:

> The danger of an overemphasis on procedural knowledge in teacher education is that student teachers learn a lot of methods and strategies for many types of situations but do not learn how to discover, in the specific situations occurring in everyday teaching, which methods and strategies to use. (p. 7)

We see further elaboration of the idea of being lost in school in the following conclusions drawn by Segall (2002) in a discussion of what is typically missing from teacher education classroom experiences:

> Because prospective teachers are not invited to critically examine the underlying assumptions in educational conventions and practices (Kincheloe, 1993), they tend to ignore not only how those aspects impact their own education as students but also how they will structure their own classrooms in the future. As a result, ..., student teachers become more interested in learning how to perform expected actions than in analyzing those actions or the expectations that generate such actions. (Segall, 2002, p. 159)

Similarly, Bullough, Knowles, and Crow (1991, pp. 189-190) have described a need for preservice teachers

> to be helped to become simultaneously students and architects of their own professional development. They need assistance to develop frameworks for thinking contextually and reflectively about their development; they need to become students of schooling and those aspects of institutional life, school practice, and interpersonal relations that are likely to enable or inhibit their development as professionals.

Working against teacher candidates becoming architects of their own professional development are the assumptions that may be held by a teacher educator:

> As teacher educators we must resist the tendency … to view ourselves primarily as theorists in specialist areas, leaving practice to be addressed by others or figured out by student teachers on their own. Theory and practice are inextricably connected: if we are not familiar with practical realities, we are ill-equipped to develop sound theories or teach it to others. (Kosnik & Beck, 2009, p. 9)

When Munby and Russell (1994, p. 94) analyzed the views of a group of teacher candidates, they arrived at the following insights about the authority that derives from experience:

> The basic tension in teacher education derives for us from preservice students wanting to move from being under authority to being in authority, without appreciating the potential that the authority of experience can give to their learning to teach. The challenge for teacher education is to help new teachers recognize and identify the place and function of the authority of experience. If this is not done, the authority of experience can fall victim to the danger that accompanies all versions of authority: mere possession is not enough because authority can be abused.

Becoming aware of the implications of one's teaching of children is virtually impossible without first becoming aware of the implications of how we ourselves were taught. Awareness is only the first stage in the process of making teaching explicit, because awareness immediately begs analysis, interpretation, re-thinking and action. Without awareness, one is likely to remain lost in school, oblivious to assumptions about student learning implicit in one's teaching actions. Making explicit our assumptions about teaching and learning experiences in education classrooms is an essential prelude to enacting similar analyses of practicum experiences. Once personal assumptions become more explicit, one can move on to confront more productively the dilemmas of practice and to develop the ability to see the classroom links between teaching and learning (Hiebert, Morris, Berk, & Jansen, 2007).

Following arguments offered by Loughran (2006), we used these perspectives to establish principles for a productive teaching-learning relationship. These principles would then guide our day-to-day support and supervision of candidates during their practicum placements:

– Teaching and learning must be seen as a relationship, and our relationship with each teacher candidate must be a focal point of our work;
– The tyranny of talk must be challenged by using a range of structured procedures for listening to candidates during their practicum experiences;
– We must go beyond the technical by showing teacher candidates how to situate their practicum experiences in relation to their formal education courses;
– We must see learning to teach through teacher candidates' eyes and encourage an inquiry stance toward professional practice;

– We must make the tacit explicit by acknowledging the complexities of incorporating new strategies into one's teaching and by identifying features of the school culture that make change difficult.

RESEARCH METHODOLOGY

Our modes of inquiry are qualitative, seeking emergent themes and patterns in interview and self-study data. In this chapter we report two types of data. Data of the first type are drawn from a focus-group discussion with associate teachers; data of the second type are drawn from a self-study of the work of a faculty practicum supervisor. The focus-group included six elementary teachers who were invited to share their perspectives on practicum learning in a 2-hour discussion structured by a set of open-ended questions. A verbatim transcript of the focus-group discussion was prepared and subjected to reading and re-reading by several individuals to identify points of convergence and divergence. Data were coded to establish categories and methods of constant comparison were used to identify themes and patterns in the focus-group data. The self-study portion of our study attended to guidelines for quality in self-study research outlined in the seminal work of Bullough and Pinnegar (2001). We took particular note of the following point:

> Quality self-study research requires that the researcher negotiate a particularly sensitive balance between biography and history. While self-study researchers acknowledge the role of the self in the research project …, such study does not focus on the self per se but on the space between self and the practice engaged in. There is always a tension between those two elements, self and the arena of practice, between self in relation to practice and the others who share the practice setting. (p. 15)

We believe that two quite different types of data related to quality of practicum learning experiences provide complementary perspectives on a complex and challenging issue. In reporting on small data sets, we are, however, guided by a decade of efforts to understand the effects of the initial teacher education program in which we teach (see Martin & Russell, 2005, 2010, 2012; Russell, 2005).

DATA

Insights from a Focus Group with Associate Teachers

The associate teachers offered four specific suggestions for improving the quality of practicum experiences.
1. The teacher candidate's teaching persona is crucial.
   – Leave your ego at the classroom door. The practicum is a humbling experience;
   – Be collegial – teaching is a political business;
   – Learn as much as you can, then share it with others in classes.
2. Early and energetic engagement in the practicum setting is imperative.

- Show initiative. Be willing to engage, and be willing to rise from the ashes when you crash and burn;
- Connect with kids, even the ones you don't like or understand; work hard to challenge and engage the students.

3. The contexts of classroom, school, curriculum, and parents are just as significant as the context of the university program itself.
   - "School-university partnership" is so much more than the countless details of what the university expects when it sends teacher candidates to schools that agree to receive them;
   - Teachers and teacher educators must share the "big picture" of helping candidates learn to teach by learning from experience;
   - The theory-practice gap is more complex than we thought. So many daily responsibilities of teachers and faculty are invisible unless one is personally present and enacting them. Yet practical responsibilities can become all-consuming in an environment that offers few opportunities to focus on the big picture, as well.

4. The teacher candidate's relationships with students, associate teachers, and university supervisor are central to productive practicum learning.
   - Collegiality is essential at every level and must be practiced;
   - Be open and willing to share with everyone and learn from everyone;
   - The practicum is not about associate teachers transmitting a set of directives from the university. Productive practicum learning requires constructive relationships among candidates, associate teachers, and faculty supervisors. Productive practicum learning also requires a dynamic process in which associate teachers and faculty supervisors meet, optimally on a regular basis, as colleagues with the shared purpose of assisting and guiding the teacher candidate.

Each teacher candidate, associate teacher, and faculty supervisor is unique and speaks from both beliefs and experiences. Learning to do well in the practicum setting has little in common with learning in a university classroom, if that classroom focuses narrowly on transmitting elements of a professional knowledge base for teaching. In the practicum there are no right answers, only complexities and puzzles that have the potential to provoke conceptual change if those learning to teach are open to learning from students, teachers, and teacher educators.

Feiman-Nemser and Remillard (1996, p. 78) framed the challenge thoughtfully in the following words:

We have separated the "what" from the "how" of learning to teach in order to focus on the question of what teachers need to learn. Ultimately, content and processes of learning to teach must be brought together, since how teachers learn shapes what they learn and is often part of what they need to know. Unfortunately, we know even less about the processes of learning to teach than we do about the content.

Our particular interest is in better understanding those learning processes as well as improving their quality. By listening to six highly experienced associate teachers, we were reminded of the importance of humility on the part of everyone involved in learning from practicum experiences. Helping people learn to teach is *not* about demonstrating how much we know about teaching; helping people learn to teach *is* about putting our own on-going professional learning at the service of those just beginning the required unlearning, learning and relearning. Similar conclusions emerged from the self-study of the activities of a faculty supervisor interacting with teacher candidates and associate teachers.

Insights from a Faculty Supervisor's Self-Study

In a self-study of his own work as a supervisor of teacher candidates' practicum experiences, Russell (2002) attempted to understand the consequences of a new program structure that made significant changes to the traditional expectations for the role of faculty supervisor.

> The central question that emerged for me was: *"How can I help each candidate improve the quality of professional learning during the early extended practicum?"* Although this central question focuses on candidates, a second question was always prominent: ... *"How can I help to improve the quality of the professional relationship between this school and the Faculty of Education at Queen's University?"* My self-study, then, is based on an action research design with a view to documenting and understanding each individual's experiences of learning to teach. (p. 77, emphasis in original)

The process of studying his own behaviour in a role that involved at least 30 individuals (associate teachers and teacher candidates) in one school helped Russell realize how easy it is to take events for granted. Self-study opened his eyes to the complexity of the new program structure and the many dimensions of improving the quality of practicum learning.

> With the clarity of hindsight, I realize that there were many moments when I tended to assume that simply *being in the school* was the basic requirement for success in the new role, in the eyes of those learning to teach and in the eyes of the experienced teachers to whom the teacher candidates were assigned. Personal experience and self-study of that experience have taught me how much more complex the matter is ... We continue to tinker with the structure as we also attempt to re-examine and re-define its underlying assumptions and our collective beliefs about learning to teach. Predictably, teacher educators are no better at changing their practices than are teachers anywhere else. (p. 74)

The gathering of data from those he was supervising led to the following challenges to familiar assumptions:

> This self-study has forced me to reconsider my early premise that visits to schools to observe preservice candidates are, in and of themselves, valuable to all concerned. School visits are made with the best of intentions, yet we

have little evidence of the impact of a faculty member's school visits on candidates' professional learning or on the school-university relationship. We would be foolish to assume that visits are good, in and of themselves. Spending more time in schools does not automatically contribute to candidates' professional learning, but *time spent in schools is a fundamental base on which broader goals and relationships can be constructed.* (Russell, 2002, p. 84)

While experience is powerful, learning from experience is far from automatic, perhaps because all levels of formal schooling pay little attention to learning from experience. Candidates' initial mindsets now seem even stronger than I realized. (p. 84)

Richardson-Koehler (1988) captured several familiar features of the supervisor's role in words that continued to resonate and ring true in this self-study:

The role of the university supervisor is ambiguous at best, and that role in relationship to the expectations for the cooperating [associate or mentor] teacher is even more confused ... The degree to which the university supervisor can affect the classroom practices of student teachers, given the structure of the experience, is questioned by supervisors themselves ... Like the supervisors in an earlier study that I conducted, ... I felt that as a supervisor I was not affecting the student teachers' classroom practices very much, at least in comparison with the cooperating teachers. Short observation and feedback sessions once every two weeks do not constitute adequate supervision... I therefore began to describe my role as that of supervising a process, rather than the student teachers ... A discussion of routines constituted a potential criticism of the cooperating teacher's performance. (Richardson-Koehler, 1988, p. 32)

Russell's self-study of his supervision of practicum experiences concluded as follows:

My most compelling insight is that teacher candidates, experienced teachers, and faculty liaisons can be expected to approach supervisory interactions with "default" assumptions driven by unexamined personal experiences. At the outset, self-study is a way to bring such assumptions to the surface; over time, self-study is a way to keep one's focus on the goal of extending our professional understanding of what it means to learn from experience in the classroom and school settings. With that long-term end in view, genuine partnerships may emerge from a base of significant time spent with candidates and experienced teachers, unpacking not only observations of candidates' teaching but also our fundamental premises about teachers' professional learning. (Russell, 2002, p. 86)

Clearly, the familiar practice of short bursts of observation and discussion is inadequate. Familiar school routines are not about exploring the big picture.

Initiating and supporting productive learning from practicum experiences requires us to unlearn familiar practices in order to invent new supervisory practices that centre on the process of learning from experience.

CONCLUSIONS

Data from the perspectives of associate teachers and a faculty supervisor as well as focus-group conversations with teacher candidates (Martin & Russell, 2005) lead us to suggest that promoting quality in practicum experiences is far more complex than our everyday assumptions would suggest. We all approach the practicum experience with traditional assumptions of which we are typically unaware until dissonant experiences compel us to notice and examine our assumptions. Without doubt, continual inquiry into practice requires extended cycles of ongoing dialogue and co-learning, with multiple opportunities for critical reflection (Beck & Kosnick, 2006).

In our Faculty, program re-structuring generated many new expectations as well as new challenges. As expectations failed to materialize and as challenges proved to be more complex than anticipated, we were forced to re-examine our own practices and to move beyond the default perspectives of teaching as telling and learning as listening. We have no simple recipes, but we have far greater understanding of the reasons why promoting quality in practicum experiences continues to be an elusive yet profoundly important goal.

A conceptual change approach that supports many new pedagogical strategies often recommended to new teachers raises major challenges, given that a basic structural premise of many teacher education programs is that new strategies are first learned in university classes and then practiced in school placements. *Until teacher education programs come to terms with the fundamental importance and authority of experience for all types of learning, their structures are likely to contradict their research-based premises and rhetoric, leaving candidates continuing to overlook or discount what they could, with teacher educators' support, be learning from practicum experiences.*

We conclude with a robust agenda for an action plan based on our efforts to inquire into our own practices and experiences and to listen to teacher candidates and associate teachers on the topic of improving the quality of practicum learning:
- Challenge directly and powerfully the implicit, unexamined assumptions of teacher candidates about how they learn from experience and about how they make sense of their previous school history (Lortie's "apprenticeship of observation");
- Expose the cultural myths that prevent new teachers from making sense of classroom routines and interactions (Nuthall, 2005, p. 918);
- Acknowledge the inherent and necessary complexity of becoming a teacher (Darling-Hammond, 2006, pp. 38-40);
- Recognize that a candidate in a preservice program necessarily follows a trajectory that requires a long-term perspective on practicum learning (Clift & Brady, 2006, p. 331);

- Challenge our implicit assumptions about the nature of school-university partnerships, assumptions that can compromise efforts to support productive practicum learning;
- Create opportunities for on-going dialogue among associate teachers and faculty supervisors about the nature of professional learning and the process of learning to teach.

ACKNOWLEDGEMENTS

We acknowledge two sources of support: A series of TEACH grants from the Research Office of the Faculty of Education at Queen's University, and Tom Russell's 2004-2008 grant from the Social Sciences and Humanities Research Council of Canada.

REFERENCES

Beck, C., & Kosnik, C. (2006). *Innovations in preservice teacher education: A social constructivist approach*. Albany: State University of New York Press.

Bullough, R. V., Jr., Knowles, J. G., & Crow, N. (1991). *Emerging as a teacher*. London: Routledge.

Bullough, R. V., Jr., & Pinnegar, S. (2001). Guidelines for quality in autobiographical forms of self-study research. *Educational Research, 30*(3), 13-21.

Clift, R. T., & Brady, P. (2005). Research on methods courses and field experiences. In M. Cochran-Smith, & K. Zeichner (Eds.), *Studying teacher education: The report of the AERA panel on research and teacher education* (pp. 309-424). Mahwah, NJ: Lawrence Erlbaum Associates.

Darling-Hammond, L. (2006). *Powerful teacher education: Lessons from exemplary programs*. San Francisco: Jossey-Bass.

Duschl, R. A., & Hamilton, R. J. (1998). Conceptual change in science and in the learning of science. In B. J. Fraser, & K. G. Tobin (Eds.), *International handbook of science education* (pp. 1047-1065). Dordrecht, the Netherlands: Kluwer Academic Publishers.

Feiman-Nemser, S., & Remillard, J. (1996). Perspectives on learning to teach. In F. B. Murray (Ed.), *Teacher educator's handbook: Building a knowledge base for the preparation of teachers* (pp. 63-91). San Francisco: Jossey-Bass.

Hiebert, J., Morris, A. K., Berk, D., & Jansen, A. (2007). Preparing teachers to learn from teaching. *Journal of Teacher Education, 58*, 47-61.

Hodson, D. (1998). *Teaching and learning science: Towards a personalized approach*. Buckingham, UK: Open University Press.

Kagan, D. M. (1992). Implications of research on teacher belief. *Educational Psychologist, 27*, 65-90.

Kincheloe, J. L. (1993). *Toward a critical politics of teacher thinking: Mapping the postmodern*. Westport, CT: Bergin & Garvey.

Korthagen, F. A. J., & Kessels, J. P. A. M. (1999). Linking theory and practice: Changing the pedagogy of teacher education. *Educational Researcher, 28*(4), 4-17.

Kosnik, C., & Beck, C. (2009). *Priorities in teacher education: The 7 key elements of pre-service preparation*. London: Routledge.

Lortie, D. C. (1975). *Schoolteacher: A sociological study*. Chicago: University of Chicago Press.

Loughran, J. (2006). *Enacting a pedagogy of teacher education: Values, relationships and practices*. London: Routledge.

Martin, A. K., & Russell, T. (2005). Listening to preservice teachers' perceptions and representations of teacher education programs. In J. Brophy, & S. Pinnegar (Eds.), *Learning from research on teaching: Perspective, methodology, and representation* (pp. 3-39). Amsterdam: Elsevier.

Martin, A. K., & Russell, T. (2010). The potential role of field experiences in teacher education programs. In T. Falkenberg, & H. Smits (Eds.), *Field experiences in the context of reform of Canadian teacher education programs* (pp. 275-283). Winnipeg, MB: Faculty of Education of The University of Manitoba. Available online: http://home.cc.umanitoba.ca/~falkenbe/Publications/Falkenberg_&_Smits_(2010)_(vol.2).pdf

Martin, A. K., & Russell, T. (2012, April). *Is a teacher education program a context for productive learning?* Paper presented at the meeting of the American Educational Research Association, Vancouver.

Munby, H., & Russell, T. (1994). The authority of experience in learning to teach: Messages from a physics methods class. *Journal of Teacher Education, 45*, 86-95.

Nuthall, G. (2005). The cultural myths and realities of classroom teaching and learning: A personal journey. *Teachers College Record, 107*, 895-934.

Posner, G. J., Strike, K. A., Hewson, P. W., & Gertzog, W. A. (1982). Accommodation of a scientific conception: Toward a theory of conceptual change. *Science Education, 66*, 211-227.

Richardson-Koehler, V. (1988). Barriers to the effective supervision of student teaching: A field study. *Journal of Teacher Education, 39*(2), 28-34.

Russell, T. (2002). Guiding new teachers' learning from classroom experience: Self-study of the faculty liaison role. In J. Loughran, & T. Russell (Eds.), *Improving teacher education practices through self-study* (pp. 73-87). London: RoutledgeFalmer.

Russell, T. (2005). Using the practicum in preservice teacher education programs: Strengths and weaknesses of alternative assumptions about the experiences of learning to teach. In G. F. Hoban (Ed.), *The missing links in teacher education design: Developing a multi-linked conceptual framework* (pp 135-152). Dordrecht, the Netherlands: Springer.

Sarason, S. B. (1996). *Revisiting "The culture of the school and the problem of change."* New York: Teachers College Press.

Sarason, S. B. (1998). *Political leadership and educational failure.* San Francisco, CA: Jossey-Bass.

Segall, A. (2002). *Disturbing practice: Reading teacher education as text.* New York: Peter Lang.

AFFILIATIONS

Tom Russell
Faculty of Education,
Queen's University, Kingston, Ontario, Canada

Andrea K. Martin
Faculty of Education
Queen's University, Kingston, Ontario, Canada

SONJA VAN PUTTEN, GERRIT STOLS AND SARAH HOWIE

PROFESSIONAL IDENTITY: A CASE STUDY OF PRESERVICE MATHEMATICS TEACHERS IN SOUTH AFRICA

INTRODUCTION

"Who is the self that teaches?" is the question at the heart of my own vocation. I believe it is the most fundamental question we can ask about teaching and those who teach – for the sake of learning and those who learn. By addressing it openly and honestly, alone and together, we can serve our students more faithfully, enhance our own wellbeing, make common cause with colleagues, and help education bring more light and life to the world. (Palmer, 2007, p. 8)

The question posed above about "the self that teaches" which is at the heart of Palmer's vocation also shapes the very core of this investigation. The young South African education student who decides to teach mathematics is a person with the potential to make a difference to the mathematics classrooms in this country. So this research purports to gain insight into the professional identity of the preservice mathematics teacher for "the sake of learning and those who learn."

The term "identity" comes from the Latin, *identitas*, literally meaning "sameness," which seems ironic given the uniqueness of identity as an individual construct. However, to the casual observer on any ordinary weekday on the campus of the University of Pretoria's (UP) Faculty of Education, there is a certain "sameness" to be seen: the students are all young, apparently focused as they file into the lecture halls, all apparently unified in their intention to become teachers, all interacting in the context of their tertiary training. There is thus a sociologically constructed 'group identity,' such as is described by Wenger (2000) as a community of practice, of which a casual observer might become conscious. According to Gee (2000), there are several terms in circulation which also refer to identity, such as 'subjectivity' for example. However, to him the concept is best encapsulated as follows: "Being recognized as a certain 'kind of person,' in a given context, is what I mean here by 'identity.' In this sense of the term, all people have multiple identities connected not to their 'internal states' but to their performances in society" (p. 99). He continues to say:

In today's fast changing and interconnected global world, researchers in a variety of areas have come to see identity as an important analytic tool for understanding schools and society. A focus on the contextually specific ways

M.A. Flores et al. (eds.), Back to the Future: Legacies, Continuities and Changes in Educational Policy, Practice and Research, 231–253.

in which people act out and recognize identities allows a more dynamic approach than the sometimes overly general and static trio of "race, class, and gender." (p. 99)

While there is a generally observable "community of practice" (Wenger, 2000) type of identity amongst the education students at UP, when the observer is not 'casual' and the focus of research narrows down beyond what can be noticed by just walking along the faculty's corridors, the question of professional identity arises – who are these students as professionals in their field? In Gee's words, what kind of person is this in this given context? Now the "clarity of identity as a variable" in terms of their *professional* identity as *preservice* teachers of a specific subject (mathematics, in this case) is not evident and requires investigation. What does it look like? How is it acted out in the classroom?

According to Borko and Putnam (1996), students come into tertiary training with "entering perspectives [that act] as a filter that determines how experiences within the teacher education program are interpreted" (p. 679). These filtering "perspectives" are recognised in this study as part of the professional mathematics teacher identity (PMTI) of such students, which is already in existence before they attend a single university module. These students are eventually, after three years of training at UP, sent out to schools for a practical teaching period. Palmer (2007) declares that "we teach who we are" (p. 2). By implication then, that "who we are" only becomes visible when "we teach." So, the professional identity of these preservice mathematics teachers needs to be observed in action in the classroom, so that we can gain insight into the "kind of person" (Gee, 2000, p.99) that is to be released to teach in the South African mathematics classroom.

CONTEXT OF THE STUDY

In South Africa, despite internationally recognised changes that have taken place in the country since 1994, there remains a deep and serious concern about the state of mathematics education in this country. The word "crisis" has been bandied about in the media and a large portion of blame has been placed upon the teachers and what happens or does not happen in the classroom. Ensor and Galant (2005) analyse the situation as follows: "While the pathology is widespread ... we are concerned that research has this far failed to ascribe to teachers and learners a positive subjectivity [identity]. We know what they don't do, but we have not adequately grasped *why* they do what they do" (p. 301) (emphasis added). This 'why?' may well be answered by an investigation into the professional identity in the early stages of its development. Bullough (1997) confirms this:

Teacher identity – what beginning teachers believe about teaching and learning as self-as-teacher – is of vital concern to teacher education; it is the basis for meaning making and decision making. ... Teacher education must begin then by exploring the teaching self. (p. 21)

At UP, all students in the Faculty of Education who choose to train as teachers of mathematics have taken *mathematics* as a Grade 12 subject. In South Africa, all learners take mathematics as a subject to the end of the ninth grade of their school career. After that, they may choose to do either *mathematical literacy* or *mathematics* to Grade 12 level. Therefore these students have each been in a mathematics class for twelve years before commencing their tertiary studies. As students in the Department of Science, Mathematics and Technology Education, they are required to complete, amongst others, modules about mathematical content, the methodology of teaching mathematics, and teaching practicum, and after four years they are released into the professional world of teaching.

PROFESSIONAL TEACHER IDENTITY

In this study professional identity is seen as a narrower version of the concept of identity. It is not the same as the "core identity" which "holds more uniformly, for ourselves and others, across contexts" (Gee, 2000, p. 99); and "is experienced by individuals as 'core' or 'unique' to themselves in ways that group and role identities are not" (Hitlin, 2003, p. 118). Professional teacher identity can simply be defined as 'who I am at this moment in this context' (Beijaard, Meijer, & Verloop, 2004).

PMTI is a further narrowing of professional teacher identity in that it relates 'who I am' specifically to the mathematics classroom and the subject itself. PMTI is also narrower than Mathematics Teacher Identity, described by Bohl and van Zoest (2002) as a unit of analysis, which may include those who, although they teach mathematics from time to time or for a period, are in fact not professional mathematics teachers – they may have been co-opted into teaching the subject because there is no one else to do so in a particular school, or some such circumstance. In South Africa this happens frequently. Graven (2004), for example, tells the story of some teachers she worked with:

> For example, Moses explained that it was not considered politically acceptable as a black student to study mathematics when he was at school and college. Rather, one had to study history and other subjects considered important for the struggle against apartheid ... Moses had therefore studied to become a history teacher but became a teacher of mathematics due to the shortage of mathematics teachers. Another teacher, Barry, despite having taught mathematics and headed a mathematics department for many years, explained that he was not a mathematics teacher since he did not 'even' study mathematics at high school. He called himself an art teacher since this is what he had studied ... Similarly ... Beatrice used to introduce herself as 'the music teacher' despite teaching predominantly mathematics classes. These examples illustrate an effect of South Africa's apartheid history. (p. 189)

The term Professional Mathematics Teacher Identity is posited in this research as involving an individual who has studied the subject for the specific purpose of teaching it.

According to Beijaard, Verloop, and Vermunt (2000), this identity can best be studied through investigation of the teacher's perception of self as Subject Specialist, Teaching-and-learning Specialist and Nurturer (referred to in their study as pedagogics expert). In their research they assumed that "teachers' perceptions of their professional identity reflect their personal knowledge of this identity" (p. 750). According to Fearon (1999), identities should be seen "both as things to be explained and things that have explanatory force" (p. 2). Thus, while the student can be asked to explain the nature of her PMTI, the nature of her PMTI also explains what she does in the classroom. Only in seeing the identity in action can analysis take place of the perceptions which constitute it.

CONCEPTUALISATION OF THE RESEARCH

In the interests of an in-depth investigation into preservice PMTI, this identity is examined in terms of how it develops and what it looks like. The literature (van Zoest & Bohl, 2005; Varghese, Morgan, Johnston, & Johnson, 2005; Boaler, Wiliam, & Zevenbergen, 2000; Beijaard, 1995; Kagan, 1992) indicates that teacher identity is not a simple, unitary construct, but has both social (in-the-community) and personal (in-the-mind) roots, and that its nature is complex (Cooper & Olson, 1996; Stronach, Corbin, McNamara, Stark, & Warne, 2002; Zembylas, 2003; Beijaard et al., 2004).

In trying to address this complexity, several questions can be posed which will allow the concept to be unpacked. In what way do the influencers of PMTI shape its development? What are these students' perceptions of their PMTI? How is this identity actualised in the classroom? This study looks at sociological and personal influencers which lie within the various contexts through which the student moves or has moved, like their schooling, cultural and family history, and the university experience itself. Researchers like Thompson (1984), Ernest (1988), Cooney (2003) and Cross (2009) have also found that the teacher's view of the subject mathematics has an effect on their professional identity. The preservice teachers' view of mathematics is important because it has an impact on the way they teach.

Adler and Davis (2006) call this a "specificity to the way that teachers need to hold and use mathematics in order to teach mathematics – and [that] this way of knowing and using mathematics differs from the way mathematicians hold and use mathematics" (p. 272). The actual nature of PMTI is best accessed through the perceptions of the person whose PMTI is being investigated, because, as Beijaard et al. (2004) explain, "[t]he world of the self may appear to the outsider to be subjective and hypothetical, but to the individual experiencing it, it has the feeling of absolute reality" (p. 108). If Palmer (2007) is to be believed and "we teach who we are" (p. 2), then "who we are" as opposed to "who we think we should be" is what can be observed in the classroom. In observing the students at work in their classrooms, it is the intention to see how they carry out the various roles that teaching mathematics requires of a teacher. By observing the person's classroom practice in terms of their mathematical expertise, their teaching-and-learning skills and the way they interact with the learners in a nurturing role, the actualisation of their PMTI can be studied in terms of Beijaard et al. (2000) categories. A more detailed breakdown of these categories is provided by Thompson (1984), who found that teaching-and-learning skills can be investigated through observing what the person sees as evidence that the learners understand, where the locus of control in the classroom lies i.e. whether the person's practice is teacher/learner centred, and how flexible their planning allows them to be. This three-pronged conceptual framework for the investigation of PMTI can be visualised as in Figure 1.

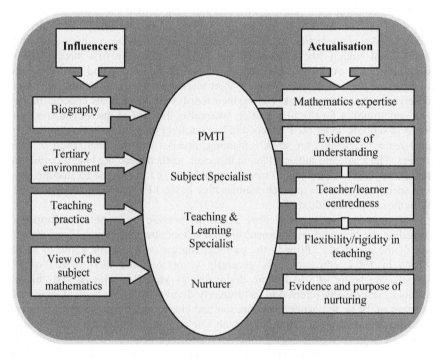

Figure 1. PMTI conceptual framework

METHOD

After an extensive literature study was completed, in which the development and nature of professional identity was investigated, it was decided that qualitative methodology was appropriate and that a case study would best facilitate the in-depth investigation of the PMTI of students at UP.

Sample and Participants

The target population for this case study was the mathematics education students of 2010 in the Department of Science, Mathematics and Technology Education of the Faculty of Education at UP. UP accommodates a large demographic diversity and a range of backgrounds in terms of the schools from which the students have matriculated. According to Paterson and Arends (2009), UP is the second most popular tertiary institution in South Africa for prospective educators, and thus is particularly characterised by the diversity of its students.

At the University of Pretoria, the BEd (Bachelor of Education), a four-year degree, is constructed in such a way that the subject methodologies constitute a year-long module which is offered in their third year of study. The elective subjects, like mathematics, are taken alongside of education modules and other professional studies like educational psychology across the first three years of study. For three weeks at the beginning of each of the second and third years the students are sent out to schools on a short teaching practicum exercise, in which observation is their main task. During their fourth year the students undergo further academic training for the first quarter, whereafter they spend the second and third terms at schools doing their "internship" or teaching practicum. In the fourth term they return to campus for small remaining modules and the finalisation of their studies. The academic subjects like, in this case, mathematics, are taught during the first three years of study only. From this population (65 in all), the 25 students who had specifically chosen to teach mathematics in the FET phase (grades 10 to 12) form the sample for this study.

The participating students were asked to provide biographical information regarding the type and environment of high school attended Grade 12 results and sex of the participant. Prior to the political changes which came about in South Africa in 1994, education was generally segregated and there were "white" schools, the better of which were designated as Model C schools, and "black" schools, later usually referred to as "formerly disadvantaged" schools. Despite the changes of 1994, the general constitution and character of many of these schools have remained constant. Three men (one English, one isiZulu and one Ndebele) and three women were selected (one Afrikaans, one Sesotho, and one Indian) in order to provide a spread representing teachers of various races, cultures and backgrounds. Table 1 demonstrates the selection process and constitution of the subsample.

Data Collection: Strategies and Instruments

Two sets of individual interviews were held with these six students, one before and one after the teaching practicum. Classroom observation was done with them during their teaching practicum in the second term of the school year to strengthen the data collected verbally in the interviews. The questions were thus based on their observation of the student's subject knowledge, teaching-and-learning skills, and nurturing propensities.

Table 1. *Distribution according to sex, race, and high school of students in subsample*

Code name	School environment: city/ rural	Type of school: formerly model c/ formerly disadvantaged/ private	Matric mathematics symbol
Female-white			
Martie	CITY	C	
Female-black			
Thandi	CITY	PVT	E
Female- Indian			
Ayesha	CITY	DISAD	
Male-white			
John	CITY	PVT	D
Male-black			
Thabo	RURAL	DISAD	C
Sipho	CITY	C	B

Interviews

We cannot observe feelings, thoughts, and intentions … [nor] how people have organised the world and the meanings they attach to what goes on in the world. We have to ask people questions about those things. (Patton, 2002, p. 341)

Prior to the commencement of the practicum, individual interviews were conducted with each of the sub-sample members. These interviews were semi-structured, and the questions were designed to further clarify and provide depth and insight into the beliefs expressed and explanations given in the inquiry sheet. At the end of the third school term, which brings to an end the long practicum in which the Fourth Year students participate, the sub-sample was again interviewed individually. The semi-structured interviews held at this point yielded data regarding the overall practicum experience, as well as insights into tendencies and behaviours observed in the videoed lessons. The coded videos of the classroom observations were watched and discussed during the interviews.

Classroom observation. Although the students had quite clearly expressed their ideas about how they teach and who they are as mathematics teachers in the initial interviews, the classroom observations were designed to give insight into theory-in-use as differentiated from espoused theory (Argyris & Schön, 1974; Maxwell, 1996). According to Patton (2002),

Interviews present the understanding of the people being interviewed ... interviewees are always reporting perceptions – selective perceptions ... By making their being own perceptions part of the data – a matter of training, discipline, and self-awareness – observers can arrive at a more comprehensive view of the setting being studied ... (p. 264)

Two lessons taught by each student were "non-participatively" (Creswell, 2002, p. 200) observed and digitally recorded. The students were not warned in advance of the specific lessons to be recorded, so that their classroom practice would be as natural as possible in what were, by the very nature of observed behaviour, unnatural circumstances. The recordings were also transcribed, coded and analysed.

Analysis

According to Patton (2002), "Qualitative analysis transforms data into findings. No formula exists for that transformation. Guidance, yes. But no direction" (p. 432). The process, he says, "involves reducing the volume of raw information, sifting trivia from significance, identifying significant patterns, and constructing a framework for communicating the essence of what the data reveal" (p. 432). The sifting and pattern-identifying procedures to which Patton refers were carried out in this study by using the data analysis programme, Atlas.ti.

The interviews were digitally recorded and the observations were videoed. These recordings were professionally transcribed, without grammatical corrections or exclusion of ums and other verbal eccentricities. Both deductive and inductive coding was used initially as Open Coding, and then as Code by List: the elements in the conceptual framework were used as broad code subjects, like "Evidence of Understanding" – hence the deductive aspect of the coding; then a variety of sub-codes were created, drawn from what was said – hence the inductive aspect. For the initial interviews (prior to the teaching practica) fifty six codes were generated, for the second interview set, seventy seven, and for the videos as for the inquiry sheet data, twenty three. The number of codes created was a function of the desire to code even nuances of meaning. According to Denzin and Lincoln (2003), coding serves two purposes: "First, codes act as *tags* to mark off text in a corpus for later retrieval or indexing ... Second, codes act as *values* assigned to fixed units" (p. 277). Both purposes were used in this study, which is why the data was 'code-saturated.'

PRESENTATION OF THE CASES

Two of the six cases are presented here in order to allow a detailed focus on the interview and observation data.

Ayesha

Ayesha, an Indian student, was educated in a private school in the rural area where she grew up. In the questionnaire she described this school as disadvantaged. Her home language is mostly English. Her performance as a student at university represents steady effort, producing sound results. Her overall average is 58%, with a mathematics average of 59.3%.

Interview Data. Ayesha felt very strongly about the influence of her high school teachers and her family. Her teachers, in her opinion, were very traditional and did not do justice to the subject and the learners in front of them. The thought occurred to her that she could possibly teach it better; she could make a difference. In fact, when asked about her high schooling she did not discuss it from the point of view of a learner in the school, but rather as a clinical observer ticking off its inadequacies: "I think that school, it needs a lot of development because they don't have any extra murals whatsoever and they have like one or two sports probably. They don't even have the equipment, nothing whatsoever." Her description of a good mathematics teacher was not related in any way to her high school experiences. Rather, she discussed the concepts of learner-centredness and teacher-centredness as taught in her tertiary training. She did however compare what she learned to be good practice, with her high school experience:

AYESHA: In ... let me say, right now I would teach in a better way ... so.

INTERVIEWER: How were you taught at school?

AYESHA: Which subject? Are you talking about mathematics?

INTERVIEWER: Mathematics.

AYESHA: Mathematics, it was just drilled into us. Yes, we had an extremely strict teacher; I think she took us outside the classroom like once. Ok, that's still fine that she at least took us out, but it was just once. There used to be charts in her room but there was no learner-centredness, there was no interaction – there was some kind of interaction but we used to be more scared of her than liking the subject.

INTERVIEWER: So it was very traditional?

AYESHA: Ja, very traditional.

From this it seems Ayesha's belief regarding good mathematics teaching generally revolves around involvement of the learners in what she describes as an interactive style of teaching.

While her schooling experiences acted as a negative motivator, her family provided positive motivation for teaching mathematics. In particular, when asked what the greatest influence on her was to choose teaching as a career, her answer was: "It was my father, not the mathematics teacher but the teacher part. Because all my life I did want to become a vet." However, her veterinarian dream did not prepare her for the realities of animal surgery, so she found herself in a quandary with regard to career choice:

Because I have a passion for animals, so I wanted to become a vet, but I think the whole operating and the dissections and all that freaked me out and then my father said, "Become a teacher." And I thought, yes, children are my second passion.

Her father, who had been a teacher in India, was able to assist her in identifying her love for children as a reason to teach and it would seem that this deciding moment in her life was based on her father's input. She then remembered that she was also passionate about children. Her cultural background, of which her father reminded her, played the deciding role. Her father, clearly a strong influence in her life, pointed out to her the cultural requirement of an Indian wife looking after her own children at home.

So he thinks that ... because for us Indians it's better if the woman has a job where she can even be attendant to her children. So he feels that, even during my holidays, they would have holidays also and then I can be attentive to the children. He thought ahead for married life, but I thought about it and then I said that I do like children, I do want to educate the future and I see that there are many teachers who are not qualified but because the schools are desperate they are appointing those. So I said let's do it.

While recognising the legitimacy of his motivation and the fact that he had thought ahead of her life as a married woman, she also identified within herself the desire to make a difference to future generations. When asked whether she thought she really could make a significant difference as a mathematics teacher, her reply was emphatic: "Yes, yes!"

It would seem, therefore, Ayesha's cultural predisposition to parental guidance is so embedded that her own desires are easily dislocated. In point of fact, her decision to become a mathematics teacher seems to have been based on a process of reasoning rather than an inherent compulsion. She loved children; she wanted to make a difference to them by being a good mathematics teacher, therefore, "Let's do it." Nevertheless, her reasoned approach was not devoid of passion, as demonstrated in her response to the question of whether she really could make a difference. Upon being questioned a little more deeply, she confirmed that in fact she believed that she was born to teach.

This did not preclude doubts about the wisdom of her career choice when it was met with disparagement from people for whose opinion she cared.

I just want to add on to that, when I did come to university and people would ask me things like, 'What are you studying?' and then I would say, 'Teaching' and they would be like 'Teaching?!' I got that a lot, I even went into some ... ok, it wasn't depression, but I was a little sad and I was thinking whether I should change my course and ... because people around me, they do influence my decisions and stuff because, ja, they're the people around me. I was thinking whether I should change my course but no, I'm fourth year now, I'm almost finished and I'm going to be a good teacher and educate the future.

There is a strong sense of resignation and making-the-best-of-one's-lot in these words. It would appear that the negative views of others regarding teaching as a career very nearly outweighed her father's positive view. However, having embarked on a course and, in her opinion, being past the point of no return, she settled into an acceptance of her vision of herself as a mathematics teacher since this was in accordance with her desire to make a difference to future generations and to comply with her culture's requirements.

She believes there is a discord between what she was taught at university and what she actually experienced as a student teacher, and between *the way* she was taught at school and the way *she* taught at school. This may well be ascribed to what Feiman-Nemser and Buchmann (1985) identified as the "two-worlds" pitfall in which the more theoretical aspects of teacher training appear to be in conflict with "real world" of the classroom. Her perception is that her tertiary training within the confines of the university lecture halls was not adequately connected to the real-world classroom. She believes the school to have been a better mentor than the university.

While in the lecture hall the study of mathematics allowed for a certain level of creativity, at school she believes that there is no question of creativity, other than in the lower grades, she said, where one may use boxes and colours and so on. In fact, in the video she was seen to be demonstrating congruency to a Grade 8 class using pink cardboard triangles. Asked why she did this, she said she was afraid the learners might otherwise find the lesson "boring and dreary." In Grade 12, according to her understanding, there is no time for creativity in mathematics classes. She nevertheless believed that creativity was essential since this is what she was taught at university:

I can't remember the name of the module but it was something about the right brain and the left brain and they inter-correlate. I found that very striking because if both your sides, well, the sides of your brain are working, it will be more effective and you would understand better. So in mathematics, when you do something creative, it would awaken both sides of your brain and that's why I think it's important.

She described her attitude toward the subject as "passionate." The reason for this was, "because I understand it and want to share it with other people and I want them to understand it too." In terms of Ernest's (1988) model, it would seem as if Ayesha's view of mathematics is an amalgam of the instrumentalist and Platonist views: she believes it to be about numbers, which though infinite, are rule-bound. As a subject, it can be understood through the learning of steps and procedures.

241

However, she believes that didactical expertise is not something one can be taught: "… one can't really teach someone how to teach, I think it comes to you naturally …." However, this instinct seems to have been at least partially influenced by what she experienced during her own schooling: she teaches while the learners listen. Ayesha believes that, as a mathematics teacher, she should explain repeatedly until she feels understanding has been reached. In order to facilitate this, she breaks down procedures into recognisable steps. At the same time, she sees herself as a moral preceptor:

> Learners tend to look up to their teachers as role models. In order for the learners to be morally well developed, we as teachers need to be an ideal icon. Learners do not do as they are told to; but they follow what they see, therefore we have to practise what we preach.

Being an example and a leader in rectitude does not necessarily involve personal interaction with the learners. In the video footage of Ayesha's teaching, it is noticeable that Ayesha maintains a dispassionate distance from the learners and does not enter into personal interaction with any learner either during the actual teaching part of the lesson, or during the part where she walks amongst the learners as they complete the examples she gave them.

Observation Data. This student demonstrates a determination for the learners to be fully occupied throughout the lesson, so that there is no time for discipline problems to arise. Her lessons were well-structured and organised, and the learners behaved circumspectly. Her approach toward the content in her lessons tends to be formal, demonstrating her confidence in the subject's reliability in terms of consistency, logic and precision. She was able to teach the mathematical content confidently and she certainly knew the procedures off by heart.

She, like a case described by Thompson, expects her learners to "assimilate the content. Assimilate means 'see' the relationships between the new topic and those already studied, as explained by the teacher" (Thompson, 1984, p. 63). In order to make sure that this "seeing" happens, she is willing to explain the same thing several times and will repeat instructions if necessary. She interspersed her teaching with chorus-answer type questions which may be interpreted as symptomatic of a desire to make sure that everyone understood all of the time. She appeared to believe that such answers were true reflections of the learners' understanding.

INTERVIEWER: And your own style? Do you involve the children?

AYESHA: Yes, I do. Every time, almost after every sum I want to make sure they are following, I always ask them if they're following, if they understand and if they have any questions. I try to be as approachable as I can.

Ayesha favours chorus-answer questions like:
– Do you all understand?
– Angle A is equal to …?

– Angle B is opposite Angle E, isn't it?
– Side AB is equal to side BC, yes, no?

No participation from the learners beyond answers to questions such as those above, or posing their own questions when they do not understand, is invited or encouraged. The learners are not prompted to suggest their own explanations or theories to explain the geometric procedures with which they were busy.

While the learners were given the opportunity to complete individual exercises in their books, she walked around the class repeatedly, checking their work, but not pausing to interact on a personal basis. Again like the case described by Thompson's (1984), Ayesha believes that "the teacher must establish and maintain an atmosphere of order, respect and courtesy in the classroom" (p. 63). She believes that questions must be dealt with immediately, as they arise, and while the learner still remembers her concern and has the courage to enquire. She also believes that posing questions to the class as a whole is more effective than posing a question to an individual. Asked why she favours this technique, she explained that individuals might be uncertain and would slow the whole lesson down while they wonder about the answer. If however the answer to the question is obvious, she sees the question as rhetorical, simply a mechanism to keep the class moving along through the work. In the video it can be seen that she believes in continuing to talk while she is writing on the board, with her back turned to the class. She explained that she does not think it wise to stop talking in order to write because that would give learners the opportunity to start chatting amongst themselves.

In her style of teaching, Ayesha combines two of Ernest's models: she is at times an Instructor, presenting procedural information accurately and intelligibly, and at other times an Explainer, willing and able to explain a concept or procedure repeatedly and from different perspectives. Her lessons are thoroughly planned since she believes lesson plans should be quite rigid for the maintenance of sound discipline. Despite what she says about caring for the learners on a personal level, this "care" has an ulterior motive – its purpose is to eliminate blockages to understanding, which, as an "explainer," is her main mission.

In summary, while Ayesha espouses learner-centredness and learner participation, in observing Ayesha teaching, the influence of her high school mathematics classes can be seen – she teaches procedure which the learners have to memorise. Interaction between her and the learners is very limited. Ayesha's PMTI was certainly developed through the tertiary training she underwent, but her "sense-making" of what she was taught during this time was filtered through existing beliefs of what mathematics teaching is in practice: the teacher teaches and the learners respond according, usually, to specific prompts. Ayesha sees herself primarily as a mathematics specialist. In terms of Ernest's model, Ayesha would seem to be both an instructor and an explainer whose mission it is to transfer information as accurately and intelligibly as possible to her learners. Questions outside of the 'perimeter' of the lesson plan are not encouraged. She believes that a good lesson is an interactive one – yet her lessons are not designed to encourage learner participation. This apparent conflict is resolved when she explains that she makes a point of asking the class continually whether they understand. They answer in chorus. She describes this as interactive teaching. Ayesha is particularly concerned with discipline, and believes that if she stops talking or allows the learners a freer participation, discipline will be lost. She believes a good teacher is a moral preceptor who cares about a learner's problem inasmuch as they inhibit learning. She is friendly, without being particularly warm or caring in her attitude.

Sipho

This student received his high school education in a school which fitted into the erstwhile 'Model C' category in a large town situated in an otherwise rural area. As a young black learner he experienced the mathematics classroom as a place where he had to prove himself. He achieved an E (40-49%) at the end of Grade 12. At university he worked consistently and well, achieving an overall mark of 61%, with an average of 62.5% for mathematics.

Interview Data. Sipho's high school experiences are hugely influential in his PMTI. His teacher appeared to be prejudiced against the non-white learners:

> Where I was taught, the school I went to was...we had white people and black people and we had a white mathematics teacher. Now, the treatment towards us, towards all of the black learners in the classroom was very bad and she was racist, you know, and every time she would demoralise us. She would make comments, like really seriously bad comments ... Like "You wouldn't pass," "You won't make it," "This subject is not for you," "Consider choosing another subject" and at that time there was no [subject called mathematical] literacy so you had to change [to standard grade]. I experienced in the classroom where we were mostly half-half, half black, half white – the Indians and the coloureds fell into the black category. Most of them dropped out, left mathematics, moved from higher grade to standard grade ... Things like that, to me, were an eye opener so I just decided that I wanted to make a change, make a difference and to prove that particular teacher wrong that we can, and we will.

It would seem, therefore, that this student was driven by a need not only to prove himself, but to help others prove themselves as capable students and educators of mathematics, flying in the face of racial prejudice. He felt then already that he could do better: he could not only become a teacher of mathematics, contrary to his teacher's pronouncements, but he could show that it is possible to treat everyone in a classroom with equal respect.

Sipho entered university directly upon leaving school, determined to learn to teach mathematics. In his initial interview Sipho indicated that the greatest positive influence of his tertiary training on his identity as a teacher lay in a psychology module, in which the students were taught about the way learners think and learn:

> Ma'am, it has to do with the psychology. I am very lucky that I came to TUKS [University of Pretoria] and here they presented a psychology module

throughout the whole three years and that helped me a lot in understanding the other person, learner- the person that's in front of you. Well, obviously I will be a teacher so I see things differently now, I'll view everything differently as I will be standing in front and looking at the learners, looking into their eyes.

Sipho realised the need to compartmentalise his experiences and beliefs. He identified three areas as his sources of beliefs and development: his experiences and convictions carried over from his own schooling; what he was learning at university in terms of subject knowledge and methodology, as well as the "psychology" he referred to earlier; and then what he was learning from his peers and their ideas of how the subject should be taught. Eventually he was able to integrate knowledge and beliefs from these three areas into what he describes as his own style, who he is in the classroom. He did however find that there was a difference between what he was taught at university and what he experienced first-hand at school. He was not quite prepared for the dynamic of the classroom, since nothing at university resembled the classroom, and no theory can explain how it "actually is."

Above all, he would never teach the way he was taught as a learner. His teacher at the high school he attended as a learner he believed to be racist in that she frequently pronounced derogatory or demoralising statements over the black learners in her class. She did not believe in their potential, and was not reticent in saying so. He determined at that time to be different in his own classroom, and remained true to that conviction. All the same, issues of race remained part of his teaching experience while on practicum:

Well, I've experienced this thing at [a high school], Ma'am when we were teaching mathematics. Those learners, they are white learners, most of them. You know, just because you're a black teacher and I'm still young they didn't really take me seriously so I had to go the extra mile to prove it to them that I can teach this and I have the skill to help you to understand. Well, I've developed that skill through the years.

In his initial interview, Sipho described his idea of a good mathematics teacher in terms which touched on all three of the categories: someone who knows the subject, who is an expert in didactical strategies to make the subject accessible, and someone who is concerned with the feelings of the learners:

A good mathematics teacher would be a teacher that's very professional and understands the subject, understands the psychology … the mentality that goes with mathematics. In order for you to teach it you have to understand it, you have to understand the whole idea, the feeling people have with this subject.

His emphasised the importance of understanding the way the learners think and feel. "Teaching is a two way process of communicating, the learners' views and opinions should be regarded as equally important because it brings about some sort of uniqueness in the learners," declares Sipho. Because of his personal experiences with a teacher who had a derogatory attitude towards certain learners, Sipho is particularly aware of the way in which a teacher speaks to a learner or responds to learner error. He believes that discouragement and demoralisation are inevitable results of a teaching style in which the diversity amongst learners is not understood and accommodated.

Sipho attaches great value to relationships with the learners. For this reason he found that the limited timespan of the practica was inhibiting: "Well, with the time that we were given it was very hard. By the second week you can bond, you start bonding and then the third week you have to go." Were he to prioritise the dynamics of the classroom, Sipho declares, "Learners first, content second." Nevertheless, he describes himself as primarily a subject specialist who is "covered in that area."

Observation Data. In the video footage Sipho presents the mathematical content with confidence, despite making mistakes in his explanations and calculations on the blackboard, and is not at a loss to answer any questions the learners might have. He is unhesitant in his presentation and does not refer to notes or the textbook as he teaches. He is seen to use objects to hand, even the learners themselves, to illustrate the concept (ratios) that he was explaining.

He finds that asking questions of the whole group, eliciting choir-type responses provides sound evidence of understanding or the lack thereof. Firstly, he feels that the individual learner remains safe in this type of questioning – he wants to "save their embarrassment" – and secondly, he is able to gauge the reactions of individuals in the group response: "I want to hear those guys active and from there I notice, why is he quiet? There's that, it's sort of like a little study for me, getting to know the learners."

In his determination to keep the learners involved in the lesson, Sipho adopts what he calls a "dramatic" style. This involves walking up and down the class, rubbing his hands together and generally just "talking to them, make them free, set them at ease." This particular style, Sipho explains, does not work for all the learners in the class – some will find it silly.

Involvement of learners, to Sipho's way of thinking, includes allowing them to teach and to be given the opportunity to demonstrate their understanding of a concept. In the video footage, he is seen to invite a learner to explain her answer on the board. He explained why:

That girl that came up there, I remember, she was the one that was busy. She was all of the time asking, asking so then I wanted to see what she knows, I wanted to find out more, give her the chance because she was … she was jumping up and down, jump … jumping for attention, so I gave it to her, satisfy all their needs, try at least to satisfy all their needs. She wanted to be seen, she wanted to present something to all of us, so give her the opportunity why not and see where it goes.

In the video footage, Sipho invites learners to participate freely in the lesson, often at the cost of discipline in the classroom. His approach is visibly friendly and jocular: it would seem that his primary strategy is to make the learners enjoy being with him in the class. Part of this strategy implies a negotiation of meaning in the actual content of the lesson: he strives to draw information from the learners by asking questions and prompting them to access the prior knowledge they might have to be able to do the work at hand. He also tried to make the work relevant to the everyday lives of the learners: for example, in teaching about ratio, he used the demographics of the classroom to illustrate comparisons.

The purpose for planning a lesson, according to Sipho, is to "organise yourself." While the lesson plan provides the basic structure of the lesson, it does not necessarily determine how the lesson is presented: "a different audience and you present it differently. It … it all boils down to … to the … to the audience, how they respond." Sipho believes that caring implies encouraging the learners and not "crushing" them in any way. Therefore, when an incorrect response is offered by a learner in the video and the class is seen to laugh, he stops the laughter immediately.

Perhaps because of his experiences as a learner, Sipho is tremendously culturally aware. He therefore dedicates time and thought to dealing with cultural diversity in the classroom, despite the difficulties involved. His belief that skin colour is a barrier to be overcome in the classroom seems to carry the same weight that language does. His home language is not the same as that of most of the learners in Pretoria. He therefore has made a huge conscious effort to become familiar with the more common local languages so that language differences do not constitute an obstacle in his practice. This is important to him, despite the fact that all tuition in the classroom takes place in English.

SIPHO: Yes, I use multiple methods, Ma'am, because the learners are very different. First of all: the culture, our cultures are very different and the language that we speak.

INTERVIEWER: What do you mean by cultures are different?

SIPHO: I'm from mostly rural background and …

INTERVIEWER: What is your home language?

SIPHO: Seswati and here it's mixed, it's mostly Tswana and Sepedi and Sotho.

INTERVIEWER: Can you speak their language?

SIPHO: I can hear [understand] it and I try, but I'm not that fluent yet. So with the language, taking just the language into account, I try to accommodate them. But in most cases you find that they will use their language most of the time and they will try to express themselves in their language - I do not discourage that, instead I use that, I give them the stage. One of the learners in the classroom might know English, might know how to translate it. Instead of showing them that maybe I do not understand in this particular sentence that you mentioned and how you express yourself, I would use that learner to explain to the class as if one of the learners didn't understand, because you'll find in the classroom that one of the learners *don't* understand. So I'll use methods like that just to come around, work around that.

Sipho's main concern, it would seem, is that all his learners recognise that he treats them equally and respects their cultural and language differences. It would appear that the actual mathematical content of the lesson takes second place to this concern.

In summary, Sipho was driven to prove to himself and his erstwhile teacher that he could not only *do* mathematics, but that he could *teach* it; and that he would demonstrate that racial prejudice is taboo in any classroom. His tertiary training changed and shaped him: in particular, he found that Educational Psychology opened his understanding as to how learners actually learn and how teaching should be adapted to accommodate learning styles. However, he found that there was a discrepancy between what he was taught at university and what he experienced in the reality of the school. The theory had not quite prepared him for the practice. He did his teaching practica in former Model C schools in Pretoria, where his classes were racially mixed. He found that he had to prove to the white learners that his knowledge of mathematics and his ability to communicate that knowledge were more relevant to the classroom than his skin colour. His view of mathematics seems to fit into Ernest's (1988) Problem-solving category. He sees the subject as involving logic and reasoning with a view to deciphering the links between mathematics and the real world.

Sipho *believes* that being a subject specialist carries the greatest significance in his PMTI, but evidence of this practically being the case is absent: the video footage indicates that he is more concerned with making his learners feel comfortable in his class so that they can be free to participate in the lesson. He also believes that learners have a negative attitude towards mathematics which needs to be addressed. In describing a good mathematics teacher, he said that, "In order for you to teach it you have to understand it, you have to understand the whole idea, the feeling people have with this subject."

He sets great store by his knowledge of educational psychology which allows him to understand what the learners think and feel ... He also wants his classes to be fun, a strategy he believes makes learners *want* to be attentive in his class. He is concerned about shy or reticent learners and this is one of the reasons for which he uses choir-response questions- it allows the shy learner to remain hidden. The teaching strategies he employs he describes as "dramatic," and include walking up and down the class making large gestures with his hands. He believes this sets the learners at ease – making the atmosphere more social, if a learner seems to disapprove, he is able to become more serious – thus keeping all the learners engaged. He believes it is useful to allow the learners to teach from time to time: for this task he selects learners who seek attention or approval. In this way he is able to satisfy the need of the learner, while at the same time finding out what such a learner knows. Sometimes class discipline is sacrificed in his application of these strategies. He does not perceive this as a problem, as long as he is able to draw the learners out to reveal their prior knowledge and to lead them in constructing their own understanding. He plans his lessons in order to be organised, but believes in being responsive to the "audience" – if deviation from the plan is necessary, he will do so. In terms of Ernest's (1988) categories, he is a facilitator. He is driven to facilitate relationships and cultural respect. He wants to please, and to be liked and accepted by his learners.

FINDINGS

The strongest influence for these students lay in their personal background. Ayesha wanted to be a veterinary surgeon, but was dissuaded by her father who reminded her of the duties of a wife and mother of her culture. In Ayesha's classroom practice she is seen to be a traditionalist teacher who teaches for learner achievement by emphasising procedure, very much like her description of her own high school mathematics teacher. Sipho walks around the class, pausing to talk and laugh with individuals everywhere. He goes out of his way to show the learners that he values each one as an individual. It is thus a finding of this research, in corroboration of the literature studied, that PMTI is influenced by elements related to specific contexts, and particularly by schooling experiences. In fact, Liljedahl (2002) states that "... the formation of teachers' beliefs about mathematics teaching and learning come from their own experiences as a learner of mathematics" (p. 2).

Of secondary importance in their PMTI's were their experiences both at university and during the teaching practica. While each of them developed a deeper understanding of the psychology of learning and teaching, this did not dominate their classroom practice and was mainly evident in what they *said* in the interviews. In this regard, Ball (1988) calls teacher education "a weak intervention" (p. 40), not changing the fact that "are most likely to teach math just as they were taught" (Ball, 1988, p. 40). To some extent, the teaching practica allowed them to weigh up what they had learnt in the university lecture hall (i.e. the theory) with what they saw and experienced in the school classroom (i.e. the practice). This is exactly what Feiman-Nemser and Buchmann (1985) called the two-worlds pitfall.

The single factor which these students claimed to recognise within themselves was the desire to "make a difference." They felt that there was that within their PMTI which made them inherently teachers and which received satisfaction from the "aha" moments when learners understood what was being taught. Their perceptions of themselves in terms of the three aspects of PMTI which are studied in this research are not necessarily directly in line with what is observed of their classroom practice. These perceptions are held in such a way as to be an intrinsic part of who they think they *are* as teachers, but, paradoxically, not necessarily of what they *do* as teachers.

While these students recognise the importance of being a subject specialist and what its position should be in their PMTI, they have doubts about their ability to live up to the level of mathematical expertise that the term implies. Ayesha explained as follows: "... I *want* to be a subject specialist; I *want* to know my work." Yet she believes that, because she is able to field learner questions successfully, she in fact *is* a subject specialist. Sipho is driven to teach in such a way that the learners are continually encouraged, and so he has adopted a teaching style which can best be described as entertaining. He sees himself as someone who knows and loves his subject and who knows and loves the learners, particularly in view of their cultural diversity, so his PMTI is characterised by these two beliefs and his determination to integrate them. Denigrated at school because of his colour and despite his mathematical prowess, Sipho is determined to 'make right,' to treat the learners with respect, to the point of trying to speak their various languages even if they are far removed from his own. Ayesha, while believing that "children are my second passion" and expressing her willingness to be available to them and to help them overcome the learning impedimenta resulting from the fact that "some people are depressed, some people have ADHD and ja ...," holds herself aloof from her learners. This may be attributable to the belief that teachers should be moral preceptors and role models for their learners.

Ayesha has a formal approach to both the subject mathematics and the way it is to be taught, and even tends to be traditional in her presentation of the concepts she is teaching. She instils rules and procedures. Sipho, by contrast, teaches by leading the learners to the discovery of the truth that they were intended to find as an outcome of the lesson.

From a purely visual point of view, these two students present completely differently in the classroom. Ayesha maintains a formal distance: she teaches from the front of the class, rarely leaving the space between the teacher's desk and the board. Even the cardboard triangles she was using to illustrate a point were shown to the class from there. Her expression is friendly and her delivery calm and formal. Sipho moves all around the class, talking in an animated way and gesturing with his hands. He frequently bends over a learner's desk talking briefly to individuals here and there as he is teaching, not just when the learners are writing.

While these students have a strong sense of the 'rightness' of a learner-centred classroom, their interpretation of the concept varies dramatically. For Ayesha, allowing the learners more scope in the class for participation means discipline problems – for Sipho that is no concern at all. Ayesha does not readily deviate in any way from her lesson plan: she needs to keep all the learners busy all the time for discipline reasons. Sipho plans for deviation from the lesson plan: he believes that a lesson plan provides structure, but not rigidity and he leaves space to manoeuvre both for himself and his learners in terms of the lesson plan.

The pastoral role which the South African education department requires that teachers fulfil is subject to interpretation as to what its practical outworking may be. To Ayesha it means simply being approachable as she stands next to the learner's desk and looks at his mathematics exercise book. Sipho strives to overcome barriers based on language and colour differences and to show that he values all learners equally.

CONCLUSION

What has become particularly evident in this cross-case analysis is how very closely linked the students' PMTI's are with their own personalities Ayesha is somewhat reserved and teaches in a formal way; Sipho has an enthusiastic and effervescent personality and his classroom is a stage for him and his learners to engage actively in the work at hand. However, the most striking finding is the discrepancy between these students' perceptions of their PMTI and its realisation in the classroom. While they students say they *are* something which in fact they are *not*; they also say they are definitely *not* something, which in fact they *are*. This mismatch within their own PMTI's is not evidenced by any apparent internal conflict. Where Beijaard et al. (2000) assumed that "teachers' perceptions of their professional identity reflect their personal knowledge of this identity" (p. 750), it is possible that the incongruence of these students' PMTI perceptions and the reality of their actualisation may be attributed to their *not* having "personal knowledge of this identity." Possible explanations for this lie within their inexperience: they have had very little opportunity to test the robustness of who they think they are against who they *actually* are in the classroom; they have acquired neither the habit nor the skills of true reflection. These students thus demonstrate that while they may certainly be teaching who they are, this is not necessarily who they *think* they are. They may believe that they are subject specialists, teaching-and-learning specialists and nurturers, but when they are observed at work in the classroom these specialisations are not necessarily, or at least not consistently evident.

It was never the aim of this study to generalise its findings. The objective was to describe the PMTI of students in their final year of mathematics teacher training at UP. No single, common PMTI could be identified. However, PMTI *does* exist in these young students. Each student, unique in background, way of thinking and ambitions, evinced a distinctive PMTI. The principal finding is that the actualisation in the classroom of this PMTI is not necessarily congruent with what the person believes to be their PMTI.

REFERENCES

Adler, J., & Davis, Z. (2006). Opening another black box: Researching mathematics for teaching in mathematics teacher education. *Journal for Research in Mathematics Teacher Education, 4*, 270-296.

Argyris, C., & Schon, D. (1974). *Theory in practice: Increasing professional effectiveness.* San Francisco, CA: Jossey Bass.

Ball, D. L. (1988). Unlearning to teach mathematics. *For the Learning of Mathematics, 8*(1), 40-48.

Beijaard, D. (1995). Teachers' prior experiences and actual perceptions of professional identity. *Teachers and Teaching, 1*(2), 281-294.

Beijaard, D., Meijer, P.C., & Verloop, N. (2004). Reconsidering research on teachers' professional identity. *Teaching and Teacher Education, 20*, 107-128.

Beijaard, D., Verloop, N., & Vermunt, J. D. (2000). Teachers' perceptions of professional identity: An exploratory study from a personal knowledge perspective. *Teacher and Teacher Education, 16*(2000), 749-764.

Boaler, J., Wiliam, D., & Zevenbergen, R. (2000). *The construction of identity in secondary mathematics education.* Retrieved July 28, 2008, from http://nonio.fc.ul.pt/mes2/dylanboro.doc.

Bohl, J. V., & Van Zoest, L. R. (2002). Learning through identity: A new unit of analysis for studying teacher development. In A. D. Cockburn, & E. Nardi (Eds.), *Proceedings of the International Group for the Psychology of Mathematics Education Annual Meeting* (pp. 137-144). Norwich: University of East Anglia.

Borko, H., & Putnam, R. T. (1996). Learning to teach. In H. Borko, & R. T. Putnam, *Handbook of educational psychology* (pp. 673-708). New York: Macmillan.

Bullough, R. V. (1997). Practicing theory and theorizing practice. In J. Loughran, & T. Russell (Eds.), *Purpose, passion and pedagogy in teacher education* (pp. 13-31), London: Falmer Press.

Cooney, T. (2003). *Mathematics teacher education in rural communities: Developing a foundation for action.* Paper presented at the ACCLAIM Research Symposium, McArthur, OH.

Cooper, K., & Olson, M. (1996). The Multiple 'I's' of teacher identity. In M. Kompf, T. Boak, W. R. Bond, & Dworet (Eds.), *Changing research and practice: Teachers' professionalism, identities and knowledge.* London: Falmer Press.

Creswell, J. W. (2002). *Educational research: Planning, conducting, and evaluating quantitative and qualitative research.* Upper Saddle Creek, NJ: Pearson Education.

Cross, D. I. (2009). Alignment, cohesion and change: examining mathematics teachers' belief structures and their influence on instructional practices. *Journal of Mathematics Teacher Education, 12*, 325-346.

Denzin, N. K, & Lincoln, Y. S. (2003). *Collecting and interpreting qualitative materials.* Thousand Oaks, CA: Sage Publications.

Ensor, P., & Galant, J. (2005). Knowledge and pedagogy: sociological research in mathematics education in South Africa. In R. Vithal, J. Adler, & C. Keitel (Eds.), *Researching mathematics education in South Africa: Perspectives, practices and possibilities* (pp. 281-306). Cape Town: HSRC Press.

Ernest, P. (1988). *The impact of beliefs on the teaching of mathematics.* Paper presented at the ICME IV, Budapest, Hungary.

Fearon, J. D. (1999). *What is identity (as we now use the word)?* Retrieved March 3, 2011 from http://www.stanford.edu/~jfearon/papers/iden1v2.pdf.

Feiman-Nemser, S., & Buchmann, M. (1985). Pitfalls of experience in teacher preparation. *Teachers College Record, 87*(1), 53-65.

Gee, J. P. (2000). Identity as an analytic lens for research in education. *Review of Research in Education, 25*, 99-125.

Graven, M. (2004). Investigating mathematics teacher learning within an in-service community of practice: the centrality of confidence. *Educational Studies in Mathematics, 57*, 177-211.

Hitlin, S. (2003). Values as the core of personal identity: drawing links between two theories of self. *Social Psychology Quarterly, 66*(2), 118-137.

Kagan, D. (1992). Professional growth among pre-service and beginning teachers. *Review of educational Research, 62*(2), 129-160.

Liljedahl, P. (2002). *Changing beliefs, changing intentions of practices: The re-education of pre-service teachers of mathematics.* Retrieved April 27, 2009, from http://stwww.weizmann.ac.il/G-math/ICMI/liljedahl_Peter_ICMI15_propShorten1.doc.

Maxwell, J. A. (1996). *Qualitative Research Design.* Thousand Oaks, CA: Sage Publications.

Palmer, P. J. (2007). *The courage to teach: Exploring the inner landscape of a teacher's life.* San Francisco, CA: Jossey-Bass.

Paterson, A., & Arends, F. (2009). *Teacher graduate production in South Africa.* Cape Town: HSRC Press.

Patton, M. Q. (2002). *Qualitative research and evaluation methods* (3rd ed.). Thousand Oaks, CA: Sage Publications.

Stronach, I., Corbin, B., McNamara, O., Stark, S., & Warne, T. (2002). Towards an uncertain politics if professionalism: teacher and nurse identities in flux. *Journal of Educational Policy, 17*(1), 109-138.

Thompson, A.G. (1984). In A. J. Bishop (Ed.), *Mathematics education – Major themes in education* (pp. 58-76). New York: Routledge.

Van Zoest, L. R., & Bohl, J. V. (2005). Mathematics teacher identity: A framework for understanding secondary school mathematics teachers' learning through practice. *Teacher Development, 9*(3), 315-345.

Varghese, M., Morgan, B., Johnston, B, & Johnson, K.A. (2005). Theorizing language teacher identity: Three perspectives and beyond. *Journal of Language, Identity & Education, 4*(1), 21-44.

Wenger, E. (2000). Communities of practice and social learning systems. *Organization, 7*(2), 225

Zembylas, M. (2003). Interrogating "teacher identity": Emotion, resistance and self-formation. *Educational Theory, 53*(1), 107-127.

AFFILIATIONS

Sonja van Putten
Department of Science, Mathematics and Technology Education
Faculty of Education
University of Pretoria, South Africa

Gerrit Stols
Department of Science, Mathematics and Technology Education
Faculty of Education
University of Pretoria, South Africa

Sarah Howie
Department of Science, Mathematics and Technology Education
Faculty of Education
University of Pretoria, South Africa

SECTION 4

PEDAGOGY AND TUTORING IN HIGHER EDUCATION

FLÁVIA VIEIRA

THE SCHOLARSHIP OF PEDAGOGY IN ADVERSE SETTINGS

Lessons from Experience

INTRODUCTION

Give me the easy life, give me research; let me not be troubled by teaching. Such an attitude is understandable, even if it is not easily forgivable. (Barnett, 1997, p. 21)

Inquiring into pedagogy in higher education is an imperative of any educator seeking to improve teaching and learning, and also a requisite for enhancing the profession. However, not all settings are favourable to the scholarship of pedagogy (SoP),[1] even though current quality policies encourage an increased investment in teaching. Historical and structural constraints often hamper efforts to turn teaching into a field of inquiry and make it "community property" (Shulman, 2004a).

Drawing on lessons from my experience with other colleagues within local, multidisciplinary SoP projects developed from 2000 to 2010, I will present it as a multifaceted practice that involves a reconfiguration of professional identities and whose ultimate goal is the collective transformation of institutional cultures. In adverse settings like ours, it is a transitional and risky practice that challenges prevalent cultures as regards teaching and research, raising issues about professionalism and merit in higher education. Nevertheless, our experience shows that SoP can become a transformative learning experience that promotes not only the status and role of pedagogy, but also our struggle for ideals and empowerment in higher education institutions (Cranton, 2011). Sustainability issues are discussed, with a focus on how situational constraints can stifle unconventional forms of inquiry.

LESSON 1: SoP IS MORE THAN JUST ANOTHER FORM OF RESEARCH

Engaging in SoP

Teaching is a moral imperative. The responsibility to educate others carries with it the responsibility to educate ourselves. Therefore, the first reason to engage in SoP is of a moral kind: we want to become better educators. This is the basis for other reasons that justify investment in SoP and turn it into a political endeavour: to understand and transform teaching and learning processes so as to meet the

M.A. Flores et al. (eds.), Back to the Future: Legacies, Continuities and Changes in Educational Policy, Practice and Research, 257–276.

challenges of an "age of supercomplexity" (Barnett, 2000); to make teaching "community property," thus counteracting "pedagogical solitude" (Shulman, 2004a); to increase collegiality and interdisciplinary dialogue through communities of practice (Brew, 2003, 2010); to promote teacher professionalism and empowerment through challenging and transforming prevalent academic regimes (Cranton, 2011; Mårtensson, Roxå, & Olsson, 2011; Socket, 2000).

Back in 2008, I was preparing a paper with two colleagues about "what being a teacher at university means" (Vieira, Almeida, & Silva, 2008), and we decided to base it on our personal understandings and experience of SoP. Before composing the text, we agreed to write personal narratives around the four topics we wanted to explore:

– *Why we became involved in SoP;*
– *Improving the education of students, improving our own education;*
– *Collaborative practices: value and constraints;*
– *The feasibility of SoP in adverse settings.*

I present my narrative below in order to illustrate the many reasons why I believe that SoP is both defensible and difficult in contexts like ours, where it is a marginal practice. The narrative relates to my experience as a teacher educator and a member of multidisciplinary SoP projects which I will refer to in more detail later in the chapter.

As an educational researcher and a teacher educator for more than 25 years at my university, I have always advocated reflective teaching towards learner autonomy in schools. In my work with preservice and in-service teachers, I have strived to put my energy, knowledge and experience in the service of that purpose, making the most of whatever reflective strategies I found useful. The results have never been disappointing: seeing schoolteachers use and value professional inquiry as a basis for innovation has made my faith in teacher research grow stronger and stronger.

However, it was not until 2003, when I first conducted a self-study project to explore more in depth the value of an experience-based approach to teacher education, that I realised *my own lack of expertise as a teacher-researcher*. Until then I had never investigated my practice in a systematic way, that is, I had not been practising an important part of what I had been 'preaching' – pedagogical inquiry. Since then, though, I became involved in SoP and I believe I will never go back to my previous teaching mode. What changed?

First of all, I have become more aware that the education of others depends strongly on my own education as a teacher – my willingness and ability to inquire into the possibilities and shortcomings of my professional theories and action; I have been more attentive to the impact of my teaching, trying to develop and interpret it on the basis pedagogical data (my own teaching reflections, teachers' assignments and reflective records, their action research experiments in schools …), thus also developing my pedagogical research skills; I have engaged more often in pedagogical conversations with colleagues (and with students as well), in the dissemination of pedagogical experiments, and also in academic discussions regarding pedagogical issues at the university; through my involvement in multidisciplinary SoP projects, I have become more in touch with the diversity of pedagogical approaches on campus, and more curious to learn about them; as I enhanced what I might call my "pedagogical sensitivity," I also started to read higher education literature, attend and organise specialised seminars, and get in contact with experts in the field; last but not least, I think I have developed a professional identity that is more in tune with what I believe being a teacher in higher education means.

A further gain of this experience is that I am now more aware and critical of the negative effects of pedagogical solitude, the "publish or perish" norm, the over-emphasis on disciplinary research at the expense of teaching-based inquiry, the isolation of disciplinary fields, and the corresponding lack of interdisciplinary dialogue and cooperation. But I also feel more motivated and self-confident to struggle against these cultural constraints and find spaces for manoeuvre, even though that struggle is rather slow and invisible, and not necessarily translated into academic merit, at least not in the conventional way, and certainly not in the short run.

Fortunately, I have not been alone in this struggle. Since 2000/2001, when I first coordinated a project on pedagogy at university, I have worked with colleagues from various disciplinary fields and this has encouraged me greatly. I have been involved in various forms of peer collaboration: dialogue about pedagogical issues and experience (reflective seminars, feedback on the design of didactic and research strategies, reflection on achievements ...); peer observation (involving dialogue writing on observed practices); group analysis of data from descriptive research studies; feedback on and co-writing of reports of experience; joint presentation and co-authoring of papers; co-organisation of seminars and conferences. All these facets of peer collaboration represent an invaluable gain from being engaged in SoP projects.

The dynamics of peer support in these projects seems to vary according to the participants' educational experience and knowledge, self-confidence to undertake pedagogical inquiry, and interpersonal relationships. Collaboration in not easy though, especially as it goes against the grain as regards pedagogical work at university. Busy agendas and time constraints reduce it greatly, but the main difficulty seems to be keeping committed to collaborative SoP in an institutional scenario where disciplinary research is worshiped as the core activity of the "excellent scholar" (even though scholars spend a great deal of their time, effort and ingenuity in teaching).

Although the feasibility of SoP in adverse settings is not very high, it surely allows us to better understand ourselves as educators, and to better educate our students, and this should be reason enough to keep on trying to vulgarise it in our universities. In my case, it has allowed me to expand and validate my pedagogy as a teacher educator. It has allowed me to excavate my *self* – who I am and why, what I want for my students and what for, what external and internal forces constrain my theories and practices and what I can do to counteract them … For me, and certainly for other colleagues too, being involved in SoP has become a *moral and political imperative*. If I had to sum up my experience, I would say that it has been an exciting journey of self-discovery, an emotional and intellectual challenge to become a better educator, within a more collective struggle to build re(ide)alistic practices that transform the role of pedagogy in the academic milieu.

I fear that the kind of projects we have developed are not sustainable in the long run – their management is difficult and slow, their productivity barely meets conventional standards, and the cultural changes they require are not compatible with the growing concern for accountability and the so called "research excellence." Nevertheless, I truly believe that SoP is *socially significant* in terms of teachers' professional development and satisfaction, and the enhancement of pedagogy in higher education. Furthermore, and perhaps more importantly, it represents an active form of resistance to an academic regime that has systematically failed to assign a prominent status to teaching or empower teachers to become critical pedagogues, as if the relevance of universities did not lie partly, if not mostly, in their ability to *educate*. (Flávia Vieira, 2008, narrative of experience)

This personal account highlights the fact that SoP is much more than just another form of research. I would define it broadly as *the integration of teaching, research and professional development, mainly through teacher inquiry into pedagogy, peer collaboration and the dissemination of pedagogical knowledge and practice.* Although it is primarily aimed at a critical understanding and transformation of pedagogical practices towards quality learning, it also reshapes professional identities, challenges dominant ideologies, and seeks to reconfigure pedagogical cultures. In the following section I describe briefly what SoP may entail, based on multidisciplinary projects developed at the Institute of Education at my university.

An Example of SoP

Back in 2000, the directive board of the research unit where I belong decided to launch a contest for projects on pedagogy at university, based on a recommendation from the external advisory board. This was an innovative initiative, since pedagogy was not even a topic of debate in our country. Together with six other colleagues, we submitted a project that consisted of an extensive survey to teachers and students on campus about representations of pedagogy (ideal vs. perceived practices; factors that facilitate/ constrain practice). It was the only project submitted to the unit and it was approved. This was the starting point for the development of four multidisciplinary sequential projects (see Table 1) where I was always involved as coordinator and co-researcher. They were carried out from 2000 to 2010, involving scholars from various disciplines within the fields of education, psychology, science, nursing, languages, engineering, and economics. These projects came to be known as "the TPU projects," TPU standing for *Transforming Pedagogy at University* (see Vieira, 2009a, b, c).[ii] Our goals as regards the transformation of pedagogy were:

– to enhance an inquiry-oriented approach to pedagogy, based on a notion of "quality as transformation," where student enhancement and empowerment are valued (Harvey & Knight, 1996; Kreber, 2006);
– to develop case studies whereby innovative educational methodologies and resources might be explored, evaluated and disseminated;
– to encourage the constitution of multidisciplinary teams of educational and non-educational faculty for the construction of educational knowledge and the renewal of educational practices.

Taken together, these projects illustrate various facets of SoP work: *defining and validating a conceptual framework; understanding the institutional context; exploring pedagogy; making pedagogy visible; questioning and theorising SoP*.

Table 1. The TPU projects (2000-2010)

TPU PROJECTS	Project 1 [2000/01]	Project 2 [2002/04]	Project 3 [2004/06]	Project 4 [2007/10]
Defining and validating a conceptual framework	Defining pedagogic principles	Putting pedagogic principles into practice and assessing their value Expanding pedagogical knowledge		
Understanding the context	Survey on pedagogic principles; factors that affect practice		Survey on innovative practices on campus	
Exploring pedagogy		Case studies of innovation conducted by teachers-as-researchers in diverse disciplinary settings Peer collaboration and observation Seminars for pedagogical reflection		
Making pedagogy visible	Pedagogical conversations within communities of practice Sharing, dissemination and publication			
Questioning and theorising SoP	Retrospective and prospective analysis of projects: rationale, nature, direction, impact, constraints, possibilities			

Defining and Validating a Conceptual Framework.   Pedagogy is not a value-free activity and must be guided by some conceptual framework. We started our work by defining eight pedagogical principles with transformative potential: Intentionality, Transparency, Coherence, Relevance, Reflectivity, Democratisation, Self-direction, and Creativity/Innovation (see Table 2). These principles guided our subsequent explorations of pedagogy.

Table 2. The TPU pedagogical principles

Intention	Pedagogical action is based upon educational assumptions and aims regarding formal education and how it relates to society; it promotes scientific, technical/professional, cultural, social and personal development.
Transparency	Pedagogical action involves explicitness of the educational assumptions and aims that orient it, of the nature of the methods used, of the learning processes themselves and of the assessment criteria and procedures adopted.
Coherence	Pedagogical action is consistent with its educational assumptions and aims, with the nature of the disciplines and with the assessment criteria and procedures.
Relevance	Pedagogical action accommodates diverse expectations, needs, learning paces and interests; it integrates and promotes knowledge, languages and experiences that are relevant to the future profession, as well as contacts with the professional contexts and an articulated view of the curriculum.
Reflectivity	Pedagogical action promotes critical thinking, by integrating a critical reflective approach towards its assumptions and aims, contents and methodology, assessment, learning processes, the role of the various disciplines of the curriculum and the relation between the curriculum and the professional world.
Democratisation	Pedagogical action is based upon values of democratic citizenship: justice, respect for differences, freedom of thought and expression, communication and debate, negotiation of decisions, collaboration and co-operation.
Self-direction	Pedagogical action promotes the development of self-management attitudes and skills: self-directed working plans, self-evaluation, independent study skills, intellectual curiosity, willingness to learn, self-esteem and self-confidence.
Creativity/ Innovation	Pedagogical action stimulates processes of understanding and intervention with social and professional implications; it promotes personal interpretation and multi/ inter/ transdisciplinary views of knowledge and reality, as well as research and problem solving abilities, abilities to develop personal projects and to intervene in professional contexts, and also openness towards innovation.

Understanding the Institutional Context.   We need to understand the "ideological map" of our institution in order to understand our position within it (Freire & Shor,

1986). With this purpose in mind, we conducted two survey studies focussing on representations of pedagogy and the nature of innovative practices on campus.

The first study (Vieira, 2002; Vieira et al., 2002) revealed a significant gap between teachers' and students' idealised views of pedagogy, which were in tune with the eight principles we had defined, and their perceptions of pedagogical practices, where reflectivity, democratisation, self-direction and creativity/ innovation were seen to be lacking. Although various factors were perceived to limit the transformative potential of pedagogical practices, the most influential ones were related with the institutional culture (e.g. no support or rewards for innovation) and working conditions that inhibit learner-centredness (e.g number of students). This study also involved a critical analysis of the institutional student feedback questionnaire used to evaluate teaching on campus at that time, showing that this instrument was value-free and did not imply any direction as regards the purposes of teaching and learning, that is, it did not reflect any vision of pedagogy (Melo, Silva, Gomes, & Vieira, 2000).

The second survey (Alves, Vieira, & van-Hattum, 2005) allowed us to understand the nature and impact of about 40 innovative practices that were being carried out on campus at a time when pedagogy was becoming an institutional concern, mainly as a result of the Bologna Process. Those practices were quite varied in context, focus, scope, and duration. They all represented dispersed efforts to focus teaching on learning and enhance student achievement, but there was not a clear link between teaching, research and professional development. The idea of SoP was not a guiding principle, and most initiatives were not disseminated. A large number were developed on an individual basis, with no institutional support.

There was a third survey conducted in 2009/10 which was not integrated directly in the TPU projects but was developed within the same research group, which focused on faculty representations of various aspects of academic life on campus, including teaching and research (Sá, Vieira, Morgado, Almeida, & Silva, 2010; Vieira, Morgado, Almeida, & Silva, 2011). This study allowed us to understand that although faculty value and invest greatly in teaching, they also perceive teaching to be undervalued in their working context and affected by competing values and practices, particularly as regards the teaching-research nexus. Investment in teaching is not valued for promotion and is inhibited by increasing disciplinary research demands, which generates dilemmas as to what should be prioritised. Furthermore, institutional assessments of teaching do not take into account central aspects for the development of SoP: pedagogic updating, innovation, inquiry, and peer collaboration.

These descriptive studies were important to realise that the pedagogical culture of the institution was both *in need of change* and *a constraint to change*. Our own work was in tune with this idea. It challenged established values and practices, and it was potentially threatened by them.

Exploring Pedagogy. SoP involves developing the profession *from the inside*, through teacher-led inquiry and peer collaboration. In our projects we took the role of teacher researchers and explored our teaching practices so as to understand and transform them. Our case studies were guided by the pedagogical principles referred to before and entailed the experimentation of various learner-centred strategies, such as journals and portfolios, project work, case-based pedagogy, and self- and co-assessment. We carried out peer observations and conducted joint seminars on pedagogical issues, with a focus on learner-centredness and action research. These seminars allowed us to discuss possibilities for action and share experiences within a supportive environment.

The case studies were conducted in various disciplinary fields. Each teacher chose a focus for action according to his/ her own interests and development needs, trying to implement strategies to improve teaching and learning. Various procedures were used to assess practice, such as informal observations and conversations with students, questionnaires and interviews, reflective records of teaching and learning, and also the analysis of students' assignments.

The pedagogical experiments were varied not only in terms of context, goals and strategies, but also as regards the complexity of inquiry. In general, educational scholars were more prepared to undertake pedagogical research based on educational theories, and some of them played an important role in supporting colleagues working in other fields. Collegial support and collaboration were also crucial to build common ground on pedagogical assumptions and principles for action.

Making Pedagogy Visible. Through engaging in pedagogical conversations, narrating experience and disseminating knowledge and practices, pedagogy can become "community property" (Shulman, 2004a), which allows others to scrutinise and build upon one's work. We published accounts of pedagogical case studies, as well as results from survey studies and theoretical explorations of SoP. We also organised seminars and conferences on higher education, which were (and still are) rare in our country.

In adverse settings, making pedagogy visible is primarily a strategy for developing SoP, more than just another way of publishing and getting credits for ones' work. When SoP is a marginal practice and "a hard sell" (Boshier, 2009), dissemination can play a major role in sensitising others to its potential value and opening up avenues for cultural change.

Questioning and theorizing SoP. Through talking, reflecting and writing about experience, and also through reading about higher education and SoP, we were able to deepen our understanding of the rationale, nature, direction, impact, constraints and possibilities of SoP in our setting. Actually, this chapter is both a result from and an example of questioning and theorising SoP.

We learned that SoP can be developed as a distinct, multifaceted mode of inquiry that integrates different forms of scholarship as defined by Boyer (1990). We were involved in conceptualisations of pedagogy as a transformative practice; studies of the institutional culture; explorations of teaching approaches – some of which, like my own, entail applications in professional contexts; dissemination of pedagogical knowledge and practice; organisation of forums for debate on pedagogy in higher education; collaborative development of multidisciplinary communities of practice. From this perspective, SoP can become a holist approach as Boshier (2009) suggests in his interpretation of Boyer. Claiming that "teaching is the frame factor" (p. 5), he contends that "There is no such thing as a separate scholarship of discovery, scholarship of integration or scholarship of application. Discovery, integration and application are interacting elements of SoTL. Disaggregating them creates enormous challenges for promotion candidates and ruptures the ecology of what Boyer was thinking" (p. 6).

We also learned that SoP promotes transformative learning, whereby the various contexts of teaching are critiqued, challenged and eventually transformed (Cranton, 2011). We became more aware of the institutional ideologies and how they affect academic life; we became more critical towards what makes that life meaningless and even irrational, and also more apt to resist constraints by finding spaces for manoeuvre; we became more demanding towards ourselves and others, but also more willing to engage in critical dialogue; we reinforced our beliefs and aspirations as professionals, and became more able to defend them in public. Even though none of these aspects can be measured, they are relevant features and outcomes of SoP, preparing us to strive for ideals and contest disempowering discourses and practices.

Finally, we learned that when pedagogy is not a priority of the professoriate or the policies that govern academic life, SoP raises issues of professionalism and merit. The following sections focus on constraining factors and limitations of our work, illustrating SoP as a transitional, risky practice that challenges and is challenged by established regimes.

LESSON 2: SoP IN ADVERSE SETTINGS IS A CONSTRAINED PRACTICE

Swimming against the Tide

As I have pointed out elsewhere (Vieira, 2009a, b), the idea of SoP is quite unfamiliar to the Portuguese academic community in general. To a large extent, pedagogy is not yet seen as a worthwhile field of inquiry. Even though the Bologna Process led institutional managers to become more committed to innovation, staff development and the assessment of teaching quality, research is mostly discipline-based and only one aspect of scholarship, the "scholarship of discovery" (Boyer, 1990), tends to be given institutional and professional credit.

Scattered research groups across the country have worked on higher education, very seldom with a focus on pedagogy. As in many other parts of the world, higher education research in Portugal is becoming a specialised territory owned by a few experts, which may explain why its local impact on teaching practices and policies is often reduced or null (cf. Teichler, 2000). Furthermore, we have no specialised journals on higher education, no established academic development centres and staff development programmes, and very few institutional reward systems to enhance classroom innovation and research.

Who we are and what we do *as teachers* gets little attention in our academic career. This can seen in Table 3, where I present some results from a survey questionnaire on faculty representations of academic life in my university, showing that teaching is perceived to be less valued for promotion than all the other factors listed (including non-academic factors), although most respondents believe it should be as important as research and service (Sá et al., 2010; Vieira et al., 2011).

We might argue that SoP development might usefully contribute to changing the current state of affairs. Paradoxically though, it is precisely this state of affairs that hampers SoP development. Academic work is fraught with conflicting rationalities that make one's choices problematic. Merit and promotion are at stake.

Table 3. Faculty representations of career promotion factors

(n=290)	Importance in working context (% VI+I)	Importance from personal perspective (% VI+I)
Research	89.4	99.3
Belonging to groups of influence	73.0	5.0
Management	63.7	60.6
Nr or years in a post/the institution	61.7	33.8
Family/ friendship relationships	51.6	1.9
Service	45.7	81.4
Teaching	*37.4*	*98.3*

VI: Very Important I: Important

Shulman (2004b, p. viii) uses a four-fold table to represent (lack of) academic success in terms of "disciplinary and pedagogical virtue," identifying four kinds of scholars (see Table 4). He uses the metaphors of *pathfollowers* and *pathfinders* to refer respectively to "those who behave as most of their disciplinary colleagues expect them to, and those who elect to go against the grain" (p. vii). Engaging in SoP often means going against the grain and becoming a pathfinder, which is not compatible with academic cultures where disciplines are like "barricades" (Poole, 2009) and border crossing among disciplines, peer collaboration and non-disciplinary research tend to be dismissed.

Table 4. Academic work as pathfollowing and pathfinding (Shulman, 2004a)

		Conforms to disciplinary convention?	
		Yes	No
Leads to academic advancement?	Yes	Successful Pathfollowers	Successful Pathfinders
	No	Unsuccessful Pathfollowers	Unsuccessful Pathfinders

Shulman (op. cit.) warns us about the risks and extra demands of becoming successful pathfinders in a world where pathfollowing represents the mainstream culture. He challenges us to build a more balanced conception of the scholarly career, which is very remote from reality in many contexts of practice, where "teaching and research are frequently, even habitually, regarded as rivals: time and status pitting for the 'learning' of one against the 'learning' of the other" (Light, 2003, p. 157).

Boshier (2009, p. 13) suggests that given the problems encountered in SoP development, faculty might be better off using the traditional research/ teaching/ service framework for promotion, and he adds that if they choose to opt for SoP they should understand that the model proposed by Boyer (1990) "was built on shaky foundations and has not improved with age." In building his arguments about the risks of SoP, he talks about the conceptual confusion surrounding it, the inoperativeness of quality evaluation systems that rest in a disaggregated approach to the forms of scholarship proposed by Boyer, and the over-reliance of SoP promoters on the value of peer review to assess scholarship, given that peer review tends to be a competitive and conservative practice. His points of view are certainly worth considering, but we can take them both as warnings about the risks of SoP *and* as warnings about the flaws of established procedures for promotion and peer review.

SoP is often a counter-hegemonic practice. As we developed our projects, we knew that we were clearly swimming against the tide.

Shortcomings and Achievements of SoP as a Transitional Process

The most common way used to assess the value of SoP is the application of universal quality research standards. Table 5 (Vieira, 2009a) summarises a possible evaluation of our work as a pathfinding, transitional process, based on the research-oriented scholarship criteria set up by JoSoTL (*The Journal of Scholarship of Teaching and Learning*):[iii] clear goals, adequate preparation, appropriate methods, and significant results. For each criterion, I point out potential shortcomings resulting from perceived constraints (left-hand column) and the strategies we used to counteract them, which are also achievements of our work (right-hand column).

Overall, we can say that our work has limitations as regards the JoSoTL standards, and also that it entailed significant progress. Nevertheless, I would argue that we should not assess the value of SoP regardless of its relevance *in context*. Moving from universal standards to *situational relevance* may help us better understand its value in adverse settings, allowing other colleagues in similar circumstances to appreciate its challenges and gains. Furthermore, when we overvalue a research-based notion of SoP, we are dismissing its other facets and casting it into just another measure of research activity (Bowden, 2007; Kreber, 2006; Silva, 1999).

The feasibility of SoP – as regards its scope, impact and sustainability – is affected by cultural circumstances. From a situational perspective, its value depends on whether it promotes change as regards:

– the dominant academic culture(s): *value as cultural subversion/ innovation,*
– the teacher's background history: *value as professional transformation,* and
– SoP itself as a field of inquiry: *value as the enhancement of the teaching profession,* both theoretically and in practice.

In settings like ours, where SoP is a pathfinding, transitional process that goes against the grain, one should not expect high academic success from pathfinders as regards cultural change and the enhancement of the teaching profession. The constraints and shortcomings presented in Table 5 help us understand why this is so, and the following section will highlight other problems related to local research cultures that may hamper SoP development.

Nevertheless, our experience clearly shows that engagement in SoP in these settings brings about small-scale cultural subversion, pedagogical innovation, and professional transformation (see Vieira, 2009c). It also raises awareness of the potential benefits of the vulgarisation of SoP. In our last project, 16 participants expressed their views about why SoP should be expanded in institutional settings. According to them, the following aspects would be promoted (Vieira, Silva, & Almeida, 2009):

– Communities of practice (research-teaching-professional development);
– Inquiry-based innovation, professional transformation and empowerment;
– Learner-centred pedagogy (paradigm change);
– Individual coherence with methodological diversity;
– Sharing, disseminating, building on good practices;
– Collective investment in pedagogy & SoP;
– Collaborative culture, cross-disciplinary dialogue, institutional cohesion;
– Institutional acknowledgment of pedagogy, professional development & SoP;
– The university as an inclusive, transformative environment.

This was our vision of the possible, although we were quite aware that reality fell short of our ideals. Too short, in fact.

LESSON 3: RESEARCH CULTURES MAY STIFLE CHANGE

Swimming against the tide means taking risks and assuming risks. It also means constantly waiting for punishment. I always say that those who swim against the tide are the first to be punished by the tide, and cannot expect to be offered weekends on tropical beaches! (Freire & Shor, 1986, translated)

Table 5. Our work: SoP as a pathfinding, transitional process

Constraints and shortcomings [Circumstances → Effects]	Achievements [Development Strategies]
Clear goals: All scholars must be clear about the goals of their scholarship. What is the purpose of the scholarship and are the goals clearly stated?	
Lack of tradition in SoP → low sense of direction, fuzziness of SoP goals Diverse pedagogic & research traditions → problems in cross-disciplinary dialogue, low coherence among studies	Collaboration to find common ground (dialogue, support, feedback, joint paper presentation/ writing...) Discussion of assumptions and choices as regards pedagogic quality
Adequate preparation: All scholars have the background knowledge and skills to successfully investigate the problem. Does the scholar have the prerequisite skills to thoroughly investigate the problem?	
Reduced educational knowledge & SoP skills → difficulties in problem-framing, technical view of education, low self-confidence/ ability to undertake inquiry (mainly from non-educational scholars)	Joint reflective sessions/ seminars on pedagogical & research issues, led by educational scholars Supportive environment & opportunities to share experiences Readings on higher education & SoP
Appropriate methods: Scholarship must be carried out in a competent manner for results to have credibility. Did the scholar use the appropriate procedures to investigate the problem?	
Reduced educational knowledge & SoP skills → over-reliance on well-established teaching/research practice within disciplines, difficulties in designing teaching/research methodologies that are responsive to the complexity of educational problems (mainly from non-educational scholars)	Joint reflective sessions/ seminars on pedagogical & research issues, led by educational scholars Inquiry that is context-sensitive and responsive to relevant concerns Development of pedagogic & research competence as an outcome of inquiry Openness to diverse, more and less sophisticated forms of inquiry
Significant results: One of the most critical criteria in judging the quality of scholarship is whether scholarship can be used as the building blocks of knowledge in the field. Scholarship may not always result in "significant" results but to have quality the results must inform scholars in the field. Does the scholarship help build the knowledge base in the field?	
Conflict between SoP, other research agendas and workload → research/ writing delays, insufficient exploration of data, limited conclusions Lack of time/ opportunities to share SoP results and undertake comparative analyses of case studies → limited understanding of the nature and impact of SoP	Analysis of experience in terms of value for teachers and students Focus on implications of SoP for future practice Supportive environments to share experiences and results Dissemination and supportive peer review/critique

The passage above is always in my mind when I think about the TPU projects and the way they came to an end in 2011. Along with the difficulties pointed out in Table 5, there were other important threats to the sustainability of our work, not only as regards those projects, but in fact all the work carried out by the research group that conducted them.

The TPU projects, together with other projects, were developed by the research group *Higher Education: Images and Practices,* formally created in our Education research unit in mid-2004 on the basis of previous research, and coordinated by me since then. The group's overall purposes were:

– To value, promote and support multidisciplinary research into higher education;
– To question and transform dominant forms of academic work: the disciplinarisation of knowledge and research; the divorce between teaching, research and professional development; the divorce between the university and working contexts;
– To understand higher education institutional contexts, promote SoP and communities of practice, and enhance the relation between the university and working contexts in the production of educational knowledge and change;
– To produce and disseminate knowledge on higher education images (perceptions, representations, values) and practices.

The group was set up as a small multidisciplinary, interdepartmental team in the Institute of Education. Since most research was departmentalised, it was difficult to create it and most of its members also belonged to other groups in their own departments. For the same reason, it was difficult to expand the group internally, although we had a high number of external collaborators. In 2011 it integrated nine Phd faculty working in the fields of didactics, teacher education, supervision, curriculum studies, educational technology and educational philosophy. Four of the members were in the group on a full-time basis and five also belonged to other groups. The external collaborators were colleagues from other colleges and universities, and also from other professional contexts (mainly schoolteachers who worked on projects aimed at promoting school-university networks).

The sustainability of this group was always in danger due to a number of historical and structural factors related to the local research culture, which was strongly influenced by external assessment and funding policies. Table 6 summarises relevant differences between that culture and the group.

In the last external research assessment conducted across the country in 2007 by the Foundation for Science and Technology (the governmental organism responsible for assessing and funding research units), referring to the period between 2004-2006, our research unit, like other Education units in the country, was rated lower than in previous assessments, which resulted mainly from the use of more restrictive criteria to assess productivity. Funding was reduced, and the unit was advised to use group merging as a strategy to increase productivity levels, which did not happen until 2011. Several reasons may account for this, the main one being that the merging recommendations were seen to disregard group differences. For example, the 2007 report recommended that we merged with the

Table 6. Why sustainability was in danger

The Local Research Culture	Our Research Group
High disciplinarisation of educational research	Multidisciplinary teams Cross-disciplinary dialogue
Departmentalisation of research groups within a competitive framework	Interdepartmental teams within a collegial framework Collaboration with colleagues from other colleges and with professionals
No tradition in higher education research and SoP	Focus on higher education issues with a growing emphasis on SoP
Low value of pedagogical research in general, including SoP	High value of pedagogical research (along with other forms of research)
Low value of local/social relevance of research (growing focus on external funding and quantity of publications)	Primary focus on local/ social relevance of research
Decreasing status of external collaborators, and no account of their publications unless produced with research unit members (since 2010)	Significant role of collaborators in multidisciplinary teams and respect for their autonomy as paper producers

group of researchers affiliated in the department of educational sociology and management, in order to start investigating policy issues in higher education. This might be a good strategy, but it was not viable for two main reasons: the other group did not focus on higher education research and was totally departmentalised, resisting the idea of interdepartmental collaboration. Divergent research interests and ideological positions impeded any attempt to merge.

In the 2007 assessment report our group was also recommended to increase internationalisation, and we improved in this and other aspects. Our productivity ratio in 2010 was above four and below three of the other seven groups. However, the sustainability problems pointed out in Table 6 above did persist, and were increasingly evident as the internal research policies changed to comply with external demands. Therefore, in 2010 and again in early 2011, we proposed to merge with the curriculum group, since it integrated some of our past and current group members and shared some of our interests. However, that proposal was not consensual in the other group, the main reason pointed out being that merging might affect their identity as a group.

In March 2011, the unit was visited for the first time by a newly appointed external advisory board composed by national and foreign educational experts. A major purpose of the visit was to appreciate our research activity and issue recommendations that might help us get a better assessment in the following external assessment[iv]. The advisory board had a long meeting with the groups' coordinators, where they listened to our presentation of research, asked questions and offered suggestions; they also had access to the 2007 external assessment report and to quantitative records of productivity since then, although they did not read any of the publications.

In the presentation of our group I summarised its history, projects, achievements, constraints, and recent publications. We had developed 10 projects (including 4 on SoP) and had organised 6 national conferences and 1 Iberian conference. In the two previous years (2009/2010) we had published 3 books (1 abroad), 27 book chapters (11 abroad), 17 journal articles (14 in peer reviewed journals), 2 books of proceedings and 48 papers in proceedings (43 presented in international conferences).

At the end of the meeting, a short evaluative statement was made about each group. Two groups were pointed out as being particularly problematic, one for not being productive and the other – ours – for being a professional development group rather than a research group. I have to say I was surprised (to say the least) with this statement, because it was neither true nor fair. I asked for clarification and tried to argue against it, but no further explanation whatsoever was provided by the advisory board members.

On the basis of the visit, the advisory board produced a brief report with a set of general recommendations, among which was the following:

> The research group Higher Education: Images and Practices should be seen as a professional development group, not a research group, and its members should be invited to apply to join other research groups. (Advisory Board Recommendations, March 25, 2011)

What is perhaps most striking about this statement is that educational experts continue to separate research from professional development within *Research & Development Units*. It is true that part of our work involved professional development, not only at university but also with secondary schoolteachers and other professionals, but it is also true that professional development had always been associated with research purposes and outcomes. We were being formally declared as non-researchers, and this was a serious insult to our work.

The external recommendation was subsequently used for extinguishing the group and dispersing its members, with no further arguments, despite the formal statements presented by me on behalf of the group in internal meetings where this problem was discussed. We contested the reason why the group was being extinguished, clarified the situation of the group and why its sustainability was at risk, and reclaimed more transparency and justice in the decision process. The final voting at the scientific board of the Institute showed that the decision to extinguish the group was far from being consensual, but the real reasons behind this decision, namely the mismatch between research cultures pointed out above in Table 6, were never acknowledged and assumed formally, even though they were clear for our group and made clear to our peers. In fact, we had published about them! This clearly shows how higher education institutions often refuse to be self-critical and prefer to function on the basis of a corporate culture that sweeps the truth under the carpet.

Our story shows that a lot is at stake when research practices (including SoP) are not mainstream. Our group did not conform entirely to local patterns of academic work. Actually, one of our purposes was *to question and transform dominant forms of academic work,* and this was both our incentive and the reason why we encountered problems, not only related to the development of the work itself, but also related to how that work was perceived by others. By assuming both the *need for change* and the *risks of change,* we had accepted the paradox that the threats to sustainability were also reasons for persisting, and from my point of view, our failure to make the group sustainable is also a sign of the institutional failure to value and support emerging, innovative approaches that go against the grain. Our story further reveals the pervasive effect of narrow quality assessment rationales and practices, which leave little or no room for unconventional modes of inquiry, create "survival anxiety" (Schein, 2010), and block contestation (Morley, 2003).

FINAL CONSIDERATIONS

After highlighting problems impeding SoP development, particularly in research-intensive universities, Boshier concludes that attempts to build it "are linked to big, difficult and contested discussions about the purposes of the twenty first-century university" (2009, p. 13). Our experience reflects this view. Higher education institutions are sites where competing rationalities create a "struggle of opposites," reflecting the fact that "any system development always contains elements of counterdevelopment" (Morgan, 2006, p. 282). The question is: to what extent are higher education institutions capable of catering for diverse rationalities, investing in their intellectual capital, and cultivating a culture of respect (Gapa, Austin, & Trice, 2007)?

SoP raises issues about priorities and rationales regarding what counts as teaching, research, professionalism, and merit. Its development may run counter to hegemonic cultures and its situational relevance may be intrinsically related to its lack of feasibility. It demands willingness and ability to pursue ideals in spite of the risks involved, but institutional support is crucial. In fact, our work on higher education and SoP started from an incentive of the research unit directive board back in 2000, based on a recommendation from an external advisory board; 10 years later, another directive board, also based on a recommendation from an external advisory board, proposed to extinguish our research group. The irony is even greater given the fact that we would now expect to have better conditions and more freedom for developing pedagogical inquiry than we had 10 years ago, particularly with the Bologna Process in the case of Europe. However, this is not necessarily the case. Although pedagogy in higher education has become a focus of attention, institutions continue to be at odds with it. Furthermore, due to increasing external pressures and quality demands, academic freedom has been progressively reduced by measures that increase internal control towards collective action and institutional autonomy (Henkel, 2007; Winter, 2009). Actually, one of the arguments pointed out to accept the advisory board recommendation was that the extinction of the group, along with other measures, would help the unit get a better external assessment and thus avoid the risk of not being recognised as a high quality research unit. In short, the distinction should be seen as a kind of "solidarity measure." Even if we accept this argument, which is refutable on many grounds, we also need to understand that one of the consequences of suppressing the group was that the development of higher education research at our unit became even more difficult and less visible than before. In fact, the measure taken is not just about the group or the unit: it is about the low value assigned to research into higher education, the resistance to new forms of academic work, and the marginalisation of emergent fields of inquiry like SoP. Paradoxically, in the beginning of January 2012 the unit divulged a report issued in July 2011 by the Scientific Council for Social Sciences and the Humanities, an advisory board of the Foundation for Science and Technology, which recommends, based on a consultation made to 85 research units across the country, that multidisciplinary research and emergent fields of inquiry should be promoted and supported in order to ensure a more appropriate response to complex issues and a more pluralistic approach to research development (Mattoso et al., 2011). The same report recommends the revision of research assessment criteria along these lines. Well ... what can we say? This is not a rhetorical question. At this point, I really do not know the answer.

We need to learn to manage and find our way through the conflicting rationalities and rival aspirations that make the modern university "utterly incoherent" (Barnett, 1997, p. 8). We may decide to discard SoP on the basis of existing constraints and embrace pathfollowing, but we may also decide to struggle for SoP so as to enhance pedagogy and make academic inquiry more holistic. Both decisions bring about advantages and risks. However, the positive achievements documented in reports of SoP in action, even in research-intensive universities (e.g. Brew, 2010; Mårtensson, Roxå, & Olsson, 2011), suggest that perhaps we should keep promoting it despite difficulties. Ultimately, what is in question is both our *duty* and our *right* to become better educators.

NOTES

[i] The expression "scholarship of pedagogy," although equivalent to the common expression "scholarship of teaching and learning" (SoTL), is used because the notion of "pedagogy" highlights the interconnectedness of teaching and learning.

[ii] These projects were funded by the Centre for Research in Education at the Institute of Education, University of Minho. They were developed within the research group *Higher Education: Images and Practices* (coord. F. Vieira) and involved around 35 faculty members from various departments and disciplinary fields, some of whom participated in all the projects.

[iii] The editorial board of JoSoTL (*The Journal of Scholarship of Teaching and Learning*) present these standards in the Guidelines for Reviewers (http://www.iupui.edu/~josotl/review_guide.htm). The standards are taken from the book *Scholarship Assessed: Evaluation of the Professoriate*, by Charles Glassick, Mary Huber, and Gene Maeroff (1997, San Francisco: Jossey-Bass).

[iv] This assessment, to be carried out by the Foundation for Science and Technology, has been postponed since 2010 and has not taken place until the time when this chapter was prepared.

REFERENCES

Alves, P., Vieira, F., & Van Hattum, N. (2005). Experiências de inovação pedagógica na Universidade do Minho: Direcções emergentes. In B. Silva & L. Almeida (Orgs.), *Actas do VIII Congresso Galaico-Português de Psicopedagogia* (pp. 2009-2021). Braga: Universidade do Minho.

Barnett, R. (1997). *Realizing the university.* London: Institute of Education, University of London.
Barnett, R. (2000). University knowledge in an age of supercomplexity. *Higher Education, 40*(4), 409-422.
Boshier, R. (2009). Why is the scholarship of teaching and learning such a hard sell? *Higher Education Research & Development, 28*(1), 1-15.
Bowden, R. (2007). Scholarship reconsidered: Reconsidered. *Journal of the Scholarship of Teaching and Learning, 7*(2), 1-21.
Boyer, E. (1990). *Scholarship reconsidered: Priorities of the professoriate.* Princeton: The Carnegie Foundation for the Advancement of Teaching.
Brew, A. (2003). Teaching and research: New relationships and their implications for inquiry-based teaching and learning in higher education. *Higher Education Research & Development, 22*(1), 3-18.
Brew, A. (2010). Imperatives and challenges in integrating teaching and research. *Higher Education Research & Development, 29*(2), 139-150.
Cranton, P. (2011). A transformative perspective on the scholarship of teaching and learning. *Higher Education Research & Development, 30*(1), 75-86.
Freire, P., & Shor, I. (1986). *Medo e ousadia – O cotidiano do professor.* S. Paulo: Editora Paz e Terra. Available at http://www.bibliotecadafloresta.ac.gov.br.
Gapa, J. M., Austin, A. E., & Trice, A. G. (2007). *Rethinking faculty work: Higher educations' strategic imperative.* San Francisco, CA: Jossey-Bass Publishers.
Harvey, L., & Knight, P. (1996). *Transforming higher education.* Buckingham: The Society for Research into Higher Education & Open University Press.
Henkel, M. (2007). Can academic autonomy survive in the knowledge society? A perspective from Britain. *Higher Education Research & Development, 26*(1), 87-99.
Kreber, C. (2006). Developing the scholarship of teaching through transformative learning. *Journal of the Scholarship of Teaching and Learning, 6*(1), 88-109.
Light, G. (2003). Realizing academic development: A model for embedding research practice in the practice of teaching. In H. Eggins & R. Macdonald (Eds.), *The scholarship of academic development* (pp. 152-162). Buckingham: The Society for Research into Higher Education & Open University Press.
Mårtensson, K., Roxå, T., & Olsson, T. (2011). Developing a quality culture through the scholarship of teaching and learning. *Higher Education Research & Development, 30*(1), 51-62.
Mattoso, J., Alvelos, H., Duarte, I., Ferrão, J., Amaral, J. F., Lima, L. P., Mesquita, P. E., Perez, R. M., & Koulaidis, V. (2011). *Ciências Sociais e Humanidades: Mais excelência, maior impacte – Internacionalização, pluralismo, pluridisciplinaridade, avaliação, disseminação e relação entre as políticas científicas nacional e comunitária.* Report by the Scientific Council for Social Sciences and the Humanities, Foundation for Science and Technology, Portugal, July.
Melo, M. C., Silva, J. L., Gomes, A., & Vieira, F. (2000). Concepções de pedagogia universitária – Uma análise do questionário de avaliação do ensino ministrado na Universidade do Minho. *Revista Portuguesa de Educação, 13*(2), 125-156.
Morgan, G. (2006). *Images of organization.* Thousand Oaks, CA: Sage.
Morley, L. (2003). *Quality and power in higher education.* Maidenhead: SRHE & OUP.
Poole, G. (2009). Academic disciplines: homes or barricades?. In C. Krebber (Ed.), *The university and its disciplines – Teaching and learning within and beyond disciplinary boundaries* (pp. 50-57). New York: Routledge.
Sá, J., Vieira, F., Morgado, J. C., Almeida, J., & Silva, M. (2010). Representações da vida académica: tensões e paradoxos. In J. L. Silva et al. (Orgs), *Actas do Congresso Ibérico Ensino Superior em Mudança: Tensões e Possibilidades* (pp. 583-593). Braga: Universidade do Minho.
Schein, E. H. (2010). *Organizational culture and leadership*, 4th ed. San Francisco: Jossey-Bass.
Shulman, L. (2004a). Teaching as community property: Putting an end to pedagogical solitude. In L. Shulman (paper collection ed. by P. Hutchings), *Teaching as community property – Essays on higher education* (pp. 139-144). San Francisco, CA: Jossey-Bass. (First published in 1993.)
Shulman, L. (2004b). Four-word: Against the grain. In M. T. Huber (Ed.), *Balancing acts: The scholarship of teaching and learning in academic carreers.* Retrieved November 25, 2004, from http://www.carnegiefoundation.org.
Silva, M. C. (1999). The scholarship of teaching as science and art. *Inventio, 1*(1). Retrieved December 4, 2003, from http://www.doit.gmu.edu/Archives/feb98/msilva.htm.

Socket, H. (2000). Creating a culture for a scholarship of teaching. *Inventio, 2*(1). Retrieved December 4, 2003, from http://www.doit.gmu.edu/inventio/past/display_past.asp?pID= spring00&sID=socket.

Teichler, U. (2000). The relationship between higher education research and higher education policy and practice: The researchers' perspective. In U. Teichler & J. Sadlak (Eds.), *Higher education research – Its relationship to policy and practice* (pp. 3-34). Oxford: Pergamon.

Vieira, F. (2002). Pedagogic quality at university: What teachers and students think. *Quality in Higher Education, 8*(3), 255-272.

Vieira, F. (2009a). Developing the scholarship of pedagogy – Pathfinding in adverse settings. *Journal of the Scholarship of Teaching and Learning* (JoSoTL), *9*(2), 10-21.

Vieira, F. (2009b). Em contra-corrente: O valor da indagação da pedagogia na universidade. *Educação, Sociedade e Culturas, 28*, 107-126.

Vieira, F. (Org.). (2009c). *Transformar a pedagogia na universidade: Narrativas da prática.* Santo Tirso: De Facto Editores.

Vieira, F., Almeida, J., & Silva, J. L. (2008). What does *being a teacher at university* mean? Professional development through the scholarship of pedagogy. In *Proceedings of the 53rd World Assembly of the International Council on Education for Teaching. International Yearbook on Teacher Education* (pp. 629-638). II, Wheeling: ICET.

Vieira, F., Gomes, A., Gomes, C., Silva, J. L., Moreira, M. A., Melo, M. C., & Albuquerque, P. B. (2002). *Concepções de pedagogia universitária – Um estudo na Universidade do Minho.* Braga: Universidade do Minho, CIEd.

Vieira, F., Morgado, J. C., Almeida, J., & Silva, M. (2011). *Faculty views of academic life – Perceived culture vs. ideal perspectives.* Paper presented at the ECER (European Educational Research Association) Conference, Freie Universitat Berlin (Germany), September.

Vieira, F., Silva, J. L., & Almeida, J. (2009). Transformar a pedagogia na universidade: Possibilidades e constrangimentos. In F. Vieira (Org.), *Transformar a pedagogia na universidade: Narrativas da prática* (pp. 17-38). Santo Tirso: De Facto Editores.

Winter, R. (2009). Academic manager or managed academic? Academic identity schisms in higher education. *Journal of Higher Education Policy and Management, 31*(2), 121-131.

AFFILIATIONS

Flávia Vieira
Institute of Education
University of Minho, Portugal

SANDRA FERNANDES AND MARIA ASSUNÇÃO FLORES

TUTORS' AND STUDENTS' VIEWS OF TUTORING: A STUDY IN HIGHER EDUCATION

INTRODUCTION

As a result of the demands of the Bologna process, teaching and learning in higher education have been challenged and changed from a traditional transmission-oriented perspective to an interaction oriented perspective, one in which the students are at the center of the learning process (Murray & McDonald, 1997). Within this context, mentoring and tutoring have shown a growing interest in the past few years, as several initiatives have been developed to enhance a culture of guidance and support to university students (Barnett, 2008; Bordes & Arredondo, 2005; Campbell & Campbell, 1997; Mangold, Bean, Adams, Schwab, & Lynch, 2003; Murray, 2001; Salinitri, 2005).

Mentoring, in its diverse forms, is seen as a way to help and guide students both at academic and professional level. According to Brown, Davis, and McClendon (1999) and Murray (2001), mentoring can be broadly defined as a one-to-one relationship between an experienced and less experienced person for the purpose of learning or developing specific competencies. Other researchers present a more specific view of this type of support. Blackwell (1989), for instance, argues that it "is a process by which persons of a superior rank, special achievements, and prestige instruct, counsel, guide and facilitate the intellectual and/or career development of persons identified as protégés" (p. 9).

Within the context of higher education, existing literature suggests the lack of consistency in the definition of mentoring along with the ambiguity in regard to its scope (e.g. Dickey, 1996; Johnson, 1989; Miller, 2002; Rodriguez, 1995). A careful look at the mentoring literature points to the lack of consensus of a generally accepted definition of mentoring (Jacobi, 1991). It also reveals an array of studies loosely aligned with the concept of mentoring.

According to Jacobi's review (1991), a number of issues need to be addressed in this research field, namely, the lack of understanding of: "a common definition and conceptualization of mentoring; the prevalence of both informal and formal mentoring relationships; the extent, and the ways in which mentoring contributes to academic success; and the mentoring functions that are most important to academic success of college students" (p. 525). Furthermore, research on evaluation of mentoring programs in education show weak designs, based on subjective data, reported without adequate evidence of reliability and validity. In fact, apart from Campbell and Campbell's (1997) study, it is difficult to identify research on the

M.A. Flores et al. (eds.), Back to the Future: Legacies, Continuities and Changes in Educational Policy, Practice and Research, 277–295.

effects of a university mentoring program on undergraduate retention and performance.

A critical analysis and synthesis of empirical studies centered on mentoring college students, between 1990 and 2007, was carried out by Crisp and Cruz (2009). Their goal was to make an attempt to update the review article developed by Jacobi, in 1991. The authors concluded that a solid theoretical understanding of how mentoring is perceived by different groups of students and the major components and characteristics involved in a mentoring experience is needed. Also, the impact of mentoring experiences on student outcomes needs to be explored further through rigorous methodological studies. Overall, findings have been positive and have indicated a positive relationship or impact of mentoring on student persistence and/or grade point average of undergraduate students (Campbell & Campbell, 1997; Kahveci, Southerland, & Gilmer, 2006; Mangold et al., 2003; Pagan & Edwards-Wilson, 2003; Salinitri, 2005; Wallace, Abel, & Ropers-Huilman, 2000). Additionally, Bordes and Arredondo (2005) found a positive relationship between first year students' perceptions of mentoring and their comfort with the university environment. However, future research must focus on longitudinal studies (Paglis, Green, & Bauer, 2006) and explore the role of various individuals in a students' mentoring experience (Wallace et al., 2000).

It is important to note, however, that besides the disagreement in regard to what mentoring is and the characteristics which it entails, Jacobi's (1991) review identified three aspects in which researchers are in accordance about mentoring. These continue to be largely reinforced in the literature: first, mentoring relationships are focused on the growth and accomplishment of an individual and include several forms of assistance (Chaos, Walz, & Gardner,1992; Ehrich, Hansford, & Tennent, 2004); second, a mentoring experience may include broad forms of support including assistance with professional and career development, role modeling and psychological support (Brown et al., 1999; Campbell & Campbell, 1997; Chao et al., 1992); and third, mentoring relationships are personal and reciprocal (Davidson & Foster-Johnson, 2001; Green & Bauer, 1995; Johnson, 1996).

Another concern that has also been discussed in the mentoring literature is the role of the mentor. An analysis of the core functions of mentoring shows that the role of the mentor has not always been limited to faculty and this support has been also provided by college and university staff, senior or graduate students, peers, friends (Zalaquett & Lopez, 2006). According to Philip and Hendry (2000), for instance, there are five types of mentoring relationships that adolescents and young adults may experience. These include, as stated in the review by Crisp and Cruz (2009): "classic mentoring (one-on-one relationship between experienced adult and a younger person, similar to an apprentice), individual-team (young group of people look to an individual or a few individuals for advice), friend-to-friend (provides a safety net, common among women friends), peer-group (among a group of friends, often when exploring an issue), and long-term relationships with "risk taking adults (similar to classic mentoring, but the person being mentored has a history of rebellion)" (pp. 528-529).

Mentoring and tutoring are sometimes used interchangeably. Miller (2002) explored the concept of mentoring and the objectives of mentoring programs in a review of the education literature and he sees tutoring as one of the several themes included in mentoring. The author states that tutoring is different from mentoring as the focus of tutoring is on subject learning whereas the focus of mentoring is on life learning. Crisp and Cruz (2009) corroborate this perspective, arguing that tutoring can be included in one of the four major domains included in the mentoring concept, which is seen as an "academic subject knowledge support aimed at advancing a student's knowledge relevant to their chosen field" (p. 539). In this view, mentoring involves providing students with support to their academic success inside the classroom, fostering the acquisition of necessary skills and knowledge. In contrast to mentoring which focuses on life learning (Miller, 2002), this type of process deals with employing tutorial skills and focusing on subject learning (Roberts, 2000).

Similar to mentoring, tutoring can be defined in different ways in different institutions. Thus the tutoring process embodies a wide range of characteristics and features (see Flores, Veiga Simão, & Carrasco, 2012). According to Thomas and Hixenbaugh (2006), tutoring may be designed for all students, or just for those in need; it may be proactive or reactive; integrated into the curriculum or an additional support activity; based on interpersonal relations or service-oriented. Also, Carrasco Embuena and Lapeña Pérez (2005) identified a set of common characteristics featured in several tutoring models in Higher Education (Boronat, Castaño, & Ruiz, 2007). These include different perspectives on tutoring such as:
- a form of guidance which is intended to promote and facilitate the development of students, in the intellectual, emotional, personal and social dimensions;
- a teaching task which personalizes university education through supervision at an individual level, which enables students to build their knowledge and attitudes and bring them to maturity, helping them plan and develop their academic progress;
- an action which enables active integration and preparation of students in the university institution, channeling and connecting with the different university services (administrative, teaching, organizational, etc.), ensuring the adequate and cost-effective use of the different resources which the institution makes available.

In this chapter, a tutoring process carried out within the context of an engineering program at the University of Minho, Portugal, will be analyzed. The purpose of this paper is to discuss the role of the tutor in higher education, focusing upon tutors and students' views and experiences of the tutoring process.

Tutoring in Project-Led Education

Tutoring is an important part of supporting student learning in Project-Led Education (PLE) and Problem-Based Learning (PBL), in so far as in these learning environments students become actively engaged in their learning process and

279

faculty move from the role of transmitters of knowledge to the role of facilitators (Albanese & Mitchell, 1993; Powell & Weenk, 2003).

Although both PLE and PBL aim at fostering student-centeredness, teamwork, interdisciplinarity, development of critical thinking and other competencies (de Graaff & Kolmos, 2003, 2007), they present, however, some differences. Problem-Based Learning focuses on small-scale problems related to a small number of issues within a given theme (Albanese & Mitchell, 1993; Boud & Feletti, 1997). A group of students meet for a small period of time and collectively reach a good understanding of the problem. In PBL, the emphasis is placed on making a diagnosis, providing an explanation, or interpreting a situation. In Project-Led Education, in turn, students work together in teams to solve large-scale open-ended projects (Helle, Tynjälä, & Olkinuora, 2006). Powell and Weenk (2003) described PLE as a:

> ... team-based student activity related to learning and to solving large-scale open-ended projects. (...) A team of students tackles the project, provides a solution, and delivers a 'team product', such as a prototype or a team report at an agreed delivery time (a deadline). Students show what they have learnt by discussing the 'team product' with each other and reflecting on how they have achieved it. (p. 28)

Several authors involved in research on project-led education and problem based learning have discussed the different roles that the tutor may play when participating in these kinds of approaches (Albanese & Mitchell, 1993; de Grave, Dolmans, & van der Vleuten, 1999; Dolmans et al., 2002; Neville, 1999; Powell & Weenk, 2003; Silver & Wilkerson, 1991).

Powell and Weenk (2003), for instance, suggest a number of possible roles of the tutor. They include the tutor as settler of the exercise (determining the form and content of the project), as the stimulator of the students (by showing interest and encouraging students to overcome difficulties), as monitoring the learning process (supporting students and providing feedback throughout the project) and finally, the tutor can act as a technical expert and as an evaluator. The authors state that the tutor may perform several roles and that these should not be viewed in a prescribed matter. Based on the characteristics of the project (Helle, Tynjälä, & Olkinuora, 2006), certain roles are more or less appropriate. Being the settler of the exercise, a technical expert or an evaluator of a project implies content specific knowledge of the tutor which cannot be expected in the case of a tutor who is especially appointed to take the role of supporting teamwork and project management. This is usually the case of tutors involved in extensive interdisciplinary projects, as is the case of the study reported in this chapter to which we now turn.

CONTEXT OF THE STUDY

From 2004/2005 onwards, first year students in Industrial Management and Engineering program (IME) at the University of Minho have been participating in Project-Led Education (PLE), during the first semester of the course. The main reason for adopting PLE in this context is associated with the importance of fostering interdisciplinary approaches in engineering curricula and student motivation. Interdisciplinarity is a key feature of PLE, in so far as students need to relate different content areas and apply them to a project throughout the semester (Powell & Weenk, 2003).

In Project-Led Education, students work together in teams to solve large-scale open-ended projects related to their (future) professional context. The kind of project selected for each semester draws upon a challenging theme, which requires the development of students' learning outcomes of the Project Supporting Courses (PSC). The competencies that students need to develop within this approach include both technical competencies that students must develop while doing all the PSCs and also the transversal competencies (e.g. project management, problem-solving, oral and written communication, self-regulation of learning, amongst others). In regard to the PSCs that participate in the first year project, they include: General Chemistry (GC); Calculus C (CC); Introduction to Industrial Engineering (IIE) and Computer Programming 1 (CP1) (see Figure 1).

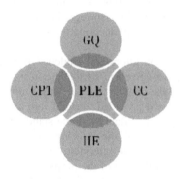

Figure 1. Project-supporting courses involved in the first year of PLE

The student teams are composed of six to eight students and they have a tutor that supports them and monitors the development of the project. The tutor's role is to facilitate student progress and monitor the learning process (Powell & Weenk, 2003).

PLE is coordinated by a team made up of the course coordinator, lecturers, tutors and educational researchers. In the first week of the project, a tutor is randomly assigned to each team of students. The tutors are usually teachers from the department (Department of Production and Systems – DPS), where the program is developed. Occasionally, tutors are selected from other departments, always on a voluntary basis. These are mainly lecturers from PSCs who are willing to take on the tutoring role. The tutors from DPS were PSC lecturers as well as non-PSC lecturers. Tutors were most of the times responsible for one team only.

Findings from previous research carried out in this context have shown that results of PLE are, in general, positive, for both students and lecturers (Fernandes,

Flores, & Lima, 2009a; Lima, Carvalho, Flores, & van Hattum, 2007). By and large, the project has shown an effective contribution to the active involvement of students in their own learning processes and to the development of transversal competencies, enhancing their motivation and helping them improve their performance in the first year of their studies – the year which is generally considered to be critical in terms of early drop out and academic achievement (Fernandes, Flores, & Lima, 2012; Fernandes, Lima, Cardoso, Leão, & Flores, 2009; van Hattum & Mesquita, 2011).

METHODS

This chapter draws upon data from a broader piece of research aimed at evaluating the impact of Project-Led Education (PLE) on students' learning processes and on faculty work (Fernandes, 2011). It aims at analyzing the tutoring process carried out within the context of PLE implemented in the first year of the IME program, and it focuses on the following research questions:
– How do tutors look at their experiences as tutors in PLE?
– What are the students' perspectives in regard to the tutoring process in PLE?
– What are the challenges for implementing tutoring processes in higher education institutions?

Data collection focused on tutors and students' perspectives and experiences. All of the participants have agreed to participate in this study which draws upon the principles and methods of instrumental case study, as suggested by Stake (2003, p. 137), in so far as it provided "insight into an issue." The aim is not to draw a generalization but to facilitate the understanding of the ways in which the different stakeholders experience the tutoring process within PLE. Data were collected through semi-structured interviews to tutors and focus groups and questionnaires to students at the end of the project. The interviews were conducted to nine tutors who participated in tutoring processes within PLE. The main dimensions included in the interview protocol focused on their experiences as tutors in PLE, strategies used during tutorial meetings, tutors' role(s) in PLE, conditions for effective tutoring practices, and skills required for an effective tutor.

In regard to students' perceptions, the questionnaires administered at the end of the project and the focus groups carried out to a group of students who have volunteered to participate in the study aimed at collecting data concerning the overall satisfaction of their experience in PLE. For the purpose of this chapter we will focus only on the dimensions which relate to the tutoring process and the role of the tutor in PLE. As far as data analysis is concerned, content analysis was carried out in order to identify recurring patterns as well as contrasting themes in the participants' accounts (Miles & Huberman, 1994).

FINDINGS

Findings are presented according to the overall perceptions of the stakeholders involved in PLE, namely, tutors and students. From the data analysis, four main categories were identified: the tutoring process in PLE, the role of the tutor, skills for effective tutoring and, finally, the difficulties and challenges of tutoring. These themes will be explored in this section.

The Tutoring Process in PLE

The tutoring process in PLE is developed by a lecturer who is involved in one of the courses lectured in the semester in which the project is carried out. Each tutor is responsible for a team of 6 to 7 students, which is formed at the beginning of the project. Students are free to choose their teammates, but should meet, however, some criteria in order to assure that the groups are heterogeneous, for example, in regard to gender issues and previous technical expertise (undergraduate studies). Typically, each PLE edition consists of six groups and six tutors, respectively.

The tutoring process in PLE can be characterized by a weekly meeting between the tutor and his/her group. During this meeting, which takes about one hour, the tutors discuss with the students several issues related to teamwork and project management. Tutorial meetings are held in the project room of each group, at a pre-scheduled time and date, decided by the tutor and his/her team. Tutorial meetings are not included in students' timetable, they are held in extra-curricular moments.

According to findings from tutors and students participating in PLE, it is possible to identify a number of important characteristics of tutoring which are in line with existing literature (Bordes & Arredondo, 2005; Carrasco Embuena & Lapeña Pérez, 2005; Crisp & Cruz, 2009; Miller, 2002; Roberts, 2000). These include tutoring as a form of academic subject knowledge support aimed at advancing students' knowledge relevant to their chosen field (Crisp & Cruz, 2009; Miller, 2002; Roberts, 2000), tutoring as a form of guidance which is intended to promote and facilitate students' development, in the intellectual, emotional, personal and social dimensions (Carrasco Embuena & Lapeña Pérez, 2005) and tutoring process as an opportunity to develop positive relationship between first year students' and their comfort with the university environment (Bordes & Arredondo, 2005). Data also indicate that tutors in PLE must develop a set of roles, as stated by Powell and Weenk (2003). These roles may include, for instance, being a settler of the exercise, a stimulator of the students or one who monitors the students' learning process and provides feedback throughout the project.

In general, tutors and students describe the tutoring process as the following:

As a tutor, my priority has to do with what I think the main needs of the group are. What I have noticed is that most of the difficulties that students face are problems related to project management and motivation. And these two issues are highly related because sometimes students' motivation drops because no one in the team knows where to go and this is due to the lack of planning and project management skills. (Tutor)

In regard to the topics discussed in the tutorial meetings, what I usually do is to look at where students are in the project. I ask them if they are meeting their planning, I discuss tasks with them. (Tutor)

The tutor tries to gather all the information from the staff coordination team and inform us what we should know. For example, before the milestones, like a midterm presentation, the tutor tells us how much time we have for the presentation and helps us decide what contents we should present and how we should organize/prepare the presentation. (Student)

The tutor was an important element in the group. I don´t think she was the kind of person that would tell us what we had to say/do. In the tutorial meetings, I would see the tutor as a person who was there to try to help you, not only with issues related to the project, but also in things related to your own problems. (Student)

Besides these tasks that characterize the tutors activity, it is important to recognize that in this kind of learning approach students play a more active and critical role in the learning process as they are requested to develop a set of transversal competencies. Therefore the guidance and support of a tutor in dealing with teamwork and project management issues is of great importance. As argued by one of the students in the questionnaire at the end of the year:

The main difference between PLE and traditional learning is the ways in which we work. PLE is more demanding and it forces students to work harder, both individually and in group. I think it is more effective like this as it is learning independently. (Student)

This quote highlights that working with projects is more demanding for students than traditional teaching and learning environments, where students play a more passive role. First year engineering students have little experience in teamwork, project management and other important skills that are required to be developed by today's' engineers. Thus coaching in this field will be of great value for students.

Most tutors who are engaged in PLE experiences state that the tutoring process can make a difference for the successful implementation of project based approaches. They pointed out several advantages of being involved in tutoring processes, such as improving student and teacher relationship, stimulating student motivation and, mainly, supporting and monitoring student learning (Veiga Simão, Flores, Fernandes, & Figueira, 2008). These findings call into question the role of the tutor in the context of project-led education.

The Role of the Tutor

Data from students and tutors' perceptions point out four main roles of the tutor in PLE (see Figure 2). These include monitoring the project, motivating the team, supporting problem solving and assessing the project.

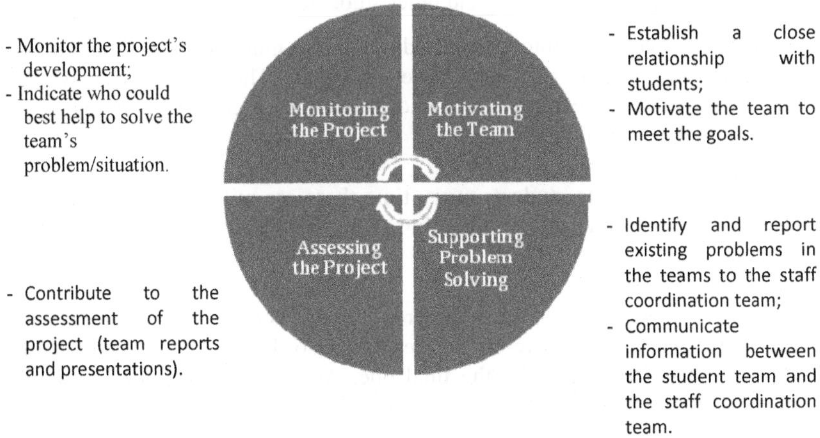

- Monitor the project's development;
- Indicate who could best help to solve the team's problem/situation.

- Contribute to the assessment of the project (team reports and presentations).

Monitoring the Project

Motivating the Team

Assessing the Project

Supporting Problem Solving

- Establish a close relationship with students;
- Motivate the team to meet the goals.

- Identify and report existing problems in the teams to the staff coordination team;
- Communicate information between the student team and the staff coordination team.

Figure 2. Tutor's role in PLE

One of the tutors' main roles is to monitor the development of the project. The tutor should support students in the development of project management skills, as it is of great importance for students to know how to manage tasks, solve problems, set up deadlines, participate in the decision making process, take a leadership role if necessary, etc. Tutors refer that sometimes one of the difficulties that commonly arises relates to knowing what to do next, which sometimes involves making important decisions that will determine the project's direction. The tutor can play an important role in supporting students with formative and timely feedback and he/she may also suggest other available resources which they can use, as the following quotes illustrate:

I try to provide feedback about the project development. At a certain point, I ask them what they want to do. I try to understand when teams need to make decisions. Sometimes the team doesn't go any further because a decision needs to be made. (Tutor)

Being a tutor is like supervising – there are different ways of doing it. In some cases, it is more effective to take a more authoritative stance, in other cases it results better to stimulate students' reflection, ask them questions. There is not just one way to do it. In summary, it means meeting with the students and supporting them in whatever they need. (Tutor)

Also of great importance is student motivation. The tutor can help keep students motivated by setting out challenges related to their work or, in some other cases, just by being there for them and following their work or by helping them on what to do next. Findings showed that some students were concerned with meeting the tutors' expectations and doing a good job in order not to let the tutor down. As one student stated, "as we didn´t want to disappoint our tutor we worked even harder." This is corroborated by the tutors and other students:

> In PLE, the role of the tutor is not to direct but to guide. He/she should make students believe that they can do even better. The tutor also plays an important role in keeping teams motivated and identifying strategies to overcome the difficulties. (Tutor)

> I provide feedback to students every time there are milestones (the students want to know how well they are doing. They want to know tutors' opinion). (Tutor)

> Our tutor was very important in the group. She was always very careful with our work. She usually gave us two deadlines, so that we could send her the report first before delivering the final one. And this way we tried to avoid mistakes in the final report .... (Student)

Formative assessment and continuous feedback processes play an important role in PLE, as students are provided with several opportunities to improve their work and are able to discuss results with teachers and tutors (Powell, 2004; Sadler, 1998; Yorke, 2003). Students recognize the value and benefit of feedback received during the tutorial sessions, group presentations and midterm reports, which allow them to improve their performance and set out new strategies for achieving the learning outcomes in a more effective way (Fernandes, Flores, & Lima, 2012). As the students themselves highlighted,

> In PLE, feedback was very important because we had the opportunity to do better the next time. After submitting the projects' preliminary report, we received corrections of our work by lecturers and tutors and we were able to improve the next report as we had understood our mistakes. I think we learn a lot with our mistakes. (Student)

> The tutor played an important role by providing feedback in regard to the projects' milestones. She tried to make sure that we kept up with the deadlines, so we would first send her our report in order to get a first impression of its quality and only then we would submit it. (Student)

Although tutors agreed that their role could make a positive impact on student motivation, especially with first year undergraduate students, who usually deal with problems concerning academic failure and early drop-out rates, they also recognized that it is very difficult to find strategies to motivate students when they are unmotivated. During the interviews, some tutors shared their experiences on how they tried to motivate their teams:

> At the middle of the semester I had an individual talk with each team member. The goal was to concentrate on each single person in the team and try to motivate them and get a commitment from them. The sense of responsibility is very important. (Tutor)

> At a certain moment, I had to make them believe that the choice they had made was the best one. Even if that decision could limit the project, it was important to support that decision and make them think that this was a great solution. (Tutor)

Students' opinions are also in accordance with these perspectives. They refer that the tutors' role is mainly associated with the tasks related to monitoring the project and facilitating cooperation amongst team members. However, an interesting finding arising from the data concerning the tutors' role in PLE points to difficulties in managing students' expectations in regard to the teachers' role both as a tutor and as a lecturer (van Hattum & Vasconcelos, 2008). Tutors refer that students often show some distrust in regard to the teams in which the tutor is also a course lecturer, as students argue that these groups will benefit in terms of the technical support which the tutor can provide them. This possible bias was also present in some of the students' suggestions for further improvements in PLE experiences, as they stated that no tutor should be a course lecturer in order to guarantee consistency in the tutorial task (Veiga Simão et al., 2008). Similar findings were also presented by a study carried out by Larsson (1983), for instance, as research showed that teachers' acts were sometimes restricted by the students' expectations and conceptions of teaching. This was often the case with students participating in tutorials, as they usually expected teachers to make use of their authority as subject matter experts and "correct" or "clarify" students' doubts (Dahlgren, Castensson & Dahlgren, 1998). Thus, it is possible to assume that students' expectations can somehow influence teachers' performance and the ways in which they look at their own role as a tutor or lecturer.

Skills for Effective Tutoring

In regard to the main skills required of a tutor, the semi-structured interviews carried out with the tutors involved in PLE showed that the kind of attitude to adopt in regard to the team was of key importance. This in is line with earlier work which has pointed to the tutor's perspective as a facilitator of the students' learning process (Das, Mpofu, Hasan, & Stewart, 2002; Groves, Rego, & O'Rourke, 2005; Dolmans, Wolfhagen, Scherpbier, & Van Der Vleuten, 2001). The skills and attitudes include willingness to listen, showing interest and concern, enjoying contact with students, being nice, honest and open with students. Besides these competencies related to the affective domain, which are essential to deal with teamwork, the tutor should also be concerned with challenging students to go further in research and enhance deep learning. Students identified tutor availability, along with project management and interpersonal skills, as the most important skills required to be a good tutor in project-based approaches (Veiga Simão et al., 2008). Evidence shows the importance of the pedagogical and relational dimensions of the teaching and learning process (Hargreaves, 1998), pointing, once again, to the need for specific training.

> Our tutor tried to understand if there were problems in the team. I noticed that concern. I think that a tutor has to be someone who is good at personal relations. (Student)

> Each tutor has his/her own way of working and dealing with the team. It is up to you and your team to try to take the best out of him/her. For example, if a tutor is good at preparing presentations, you should use the best of that and learn from him/her ... If another tutor is good at something else, then use that in the same way, etc. (Student)

> What we expect from a tutor is that he/she gives us ideas, challenges us, and is also demanding. (Student)

According to Johnston and Tinning (2001), the tutor should question, probe, challenge and encourage critical reflection by group members thus creating greater awareness and understanding of individuals' own beliefs, values and assumptions. This requires specific competencies and training for teachers in charge of this role. In fact, when asked about their professional backgrounds and prior experience in group dynamics and facilitation of learning, most of the tutors identified this gap as one of the major weaknesses to develop effective tutorials (Veiga Simão et al., 2008). As one tutor stated:

> My main difficulty as a tutor was the lack of training on what to do. As a tutor, if there had been a meeting at the beginning of the semester discussing a set of topics related to tutorials, I think it would have been very useful. (Tutor)

This quote illustrates the need to foster greater dialogue amongst tutors and create opportunities for them to interact and exchange experiences, focusing upon their own practices. Self-reflection and feedback from peers are important to enhance a better perception of tutors' self-efficacy (Hansen, 2004). For instance, a group of researchers involved in problem-based learning in medical education were interested in knowing when tutors should intervene and contribute appropriately to group discussion (Lee, Lin, Tsou, Shiau, & Lin, 2009). They carried out a study which investigated the specific scenarios during group tutorial sessions that prompted or motivated tutors to participate in the group discussion.

    The authors videotaped tutorial discussions and tutors were later shown the tapes and were asked to explore their intentions and analyze the episodes in which they had intervened in the discussions. These findings provided valuable insights for the improvement of the tutor's role within problem-based learning and also provided important material to build a framework for training future tutors (Lee et al., 2009). Similar activities can be developed amongst tutors in order to develop facilitative skills and to foster personal and professional development.

Difficulties and Challenges of Tutoring

In regard to the difficulties and challenges of tutoring, most tutors feel that they are not well prepared in terms of pedagogical knowledge and practice to face the challenges of the "new" reality of Higher Education (Bireaud, 1995). Greater training and opportunities for professional development are needed in order to work within a student-centered perspective. The tutors' role is one of the issues to be taken into account. Evidence from tutors showed the importance of training for tutorial tasks:

> As an engineering teacher, I think that training in areas such as communication skills, teamwork, project management, problem solving, learning styles, etc. would be very helpful to perform the role of the tutor in a better way. (Tutor)

Along with the need for adequate training, tutors argue that the more active role played by tutors in the project also has strong implications for their workload (Fernandes, Flores, & Lima, 2009b; Alves, Moreira, Lima, & Sousa, 2009). Although the overall evaluation at the end of the project has been considered positive, both by faculty and tutors, the latter are aware that PLE takes a great deal of their time. The project coordination team works as a team project and tasks are distributed amongst faculty and tutors. However, the workload associated with this kind of student-centered approach requires a much more demanding role from the faculty. Some of them only become aware of this when they actually get involved in PLE. This is the case of the lecturer who participated for the first time in PLE:

> I have never thought that PLE would involve so much work! It is a pity that people who usually criticize this kind of approach to learning are not aware of the workload which it entails. People have no idea whatsoever! (Tutor)

The lack of institutional support is also pointed out as a constraint due to all the effort put into the project, especially in regard to tutors' tasks and duties:

> There is no support. It is up to you as a teacher and your good will, otherwise you cannot be a tutor. The tutor's role is not recognized in terms of teaching hours. Besides this, I think PLE approaches are not valued – we spend a lot of time reviewing students' reports and giving feedback and nobody sees that. In order for things to work better, we need more time to prepare and to reflect. (Tutor)

Tutors also mention the problems which they face when trying to keep the balance between their teaching and research activities. In this respect, it is important to note that most of the current performance appraisal models implemented amongst higher education institutions tend to value less the teaching activity in detriment to

289

research (Fernandes & Flores, 2012). In the United Kingdom, for instance, several studies suggest that teaching and learning was undervalued in UK higher education and that promotion policies emphasized performance in research rather than in teaching (Ramsden & Martin, 1996; Parker, 2008). Also, the results of a report developed by the Higher Education Academy (2009), based on information from 104 higher education institutions, demonstrated that the inclusion of teaching in promotion criteria is inconsistent and often absent. By and large, academics believe that teaching is not recognized to the same extent as research. Because the research role is the traditional conception of what academics do, it is most often seen as having greater value and higher status (Parker, 2008; Young, 2006). This perspective emphasizes the products of academic research – published papers, reports, and presentations. Therefore, it is necessary to create and ensure the appropriate conditions for academics' professional development and recognition of their teaching performance. In this sense, performance appraisal should be considered as a strategy to stimulate their professional development rather than an attack to their professionalism (Cousins, 1995; Day, 1992).

CONCLUSION AND DISCUSSION

Findings of this study highlight the importance of the tutors' role to support and monitor student learning and enhance student and teacher motivation. As Powell and Weenk (2003) suggest, making the transition from lecturer to project tutor is not simple. However, students and tutors evaluated PLE, in general, as a positive approach to enhance students' learning and increase their motivation. Most of the tutors in this study were satisfied with PLE and they mentioned that it had encouraged them to be more engaged with students. However, they recognized that their role was, in fact, very demanding. Their practice was mainly based on their own teaching experiences and their ability to "learn by doing," which has been facilitated by their active involvement in several PLE experiences over the past few years.

However, some critical areas were identified such as the need for more training to fulfill the tutors' role as well as the lack of institutional support and recognition of the tutoring process. In regard to training of tutors, the participants addressed the importance of sharing and discussing ideas and practices amongst colleagues as a strategy to overcome some of the difficulties faced during the process. Thus, opportunities for professional development are a key feature for the success of tutoring within PLE and in other settings. However, training itself may not be the answer to all of faculty's uncertainties in order to become effective tutors. As Haith-Cooper (2000) has demonstrated, based on a literature review of the lecturers' role in problem-based learning within health education, no amount of training will change beliefs. Staff development activities must be understood in order to develop a broader understanding of students' learning process, with special focus on the "new" roles and duties that teachers must respond to when involved in project or problem based approaches. Faculty also claimed greater institutional support. They need more time to step back from their teaching tasks and reflect on their professional practice. For instance, more opportunities to do research on teaching and publish can lead to the recognition of improved practice. Besides this, organizational policies and procedures that encourage and reward teaching and continuing education are also required (Johnston & Tinning, 2001).

In regard to the tutors' role, the participants recognized the need for more interaction between tutors and the importance of clarifying and making the tutors' role explicit to students, so that both tutors' and students' expectations can be met. The idea of creating reflective practice groups amongst PLE teachers involved in tutoring seems an interesting and appropriate strategy to implement as they may prepare themselves more effectively through the exchange and reflection based upon their own experience, as suggested by Johnston and Tinning (2001). This strategy is more likely to prepare faculty to meet the demands of problem-based learning than traditional forms of staff development (Johnston &Tinning, 2001). In this sense, collaboration, along with the valorisation of teaching, is an essential strategy for the improvement of tutoring practices in order to foster high quality teaching and learning in higher education.

REFERENCES

Albanese, M. A., & Mitchell, S. (1993). Problem-based learning: A review of literature on its outcomes and implementation issues. *Academic Medicine, 68*, 52-81.

Alves, A. C., Moreira, F., & Sousa, R. (2007). O papel dos tutores na aprendizagem baseada em projectos: três anos de experiência na Escola de Engenharia da Universidade do Minho. In A. Barca, M. Peralbo, A. Porto, B. Duarte da Silva, & L. Almeida (Eds.), *Libro de Actas do Congreso Internacional Galego – Portugués de PsicoPedagoxía* (pp. 1759-1770). A Coruña/Universidade da Coruña: Número extraordinário da Revista Galego-Portuguesa de Psicoloxía e Educación.

Barnett, J. E. (2008). Mentoring, boundaries, and multiple relationships: Opportunities and challenges. *Mentoring & Tutoring: Partnership in Learning, 16* (1), 3-16.

Blackwell, J. E. (1989). Mentoring: An action strategy for increasing minority faculty. *Academe, 75*(5), 8-14.

Bologna Declaration (1999). *The European higher education area, joint declaration of the European Ministers of Education*, Bologna, 19 June, 1999.

Bordes, V., & Arredondo, P. (2005). Mentoring and 1st year Latino/a college students. *Journal of Hispanic Higher Education, 4*(2), 114-133.

Boronat Mundina, J., Castaño Pombo, N., & Ruiz, E. (2007). *Dimensión convergente de la tutoría en la universidad: tutoría entre iguales*. Retrieved from http://www.eduonline.ua.es/jornadas2007/comunicaciones/2G3.pdf.

Boud, D., & Feletti, G. (Eds.). (1997). *Changing problem-based learning. The challenge of problem-based-learning* (pp. 1-14). London: Kogan.

Brown, M. C., Davis, G. L., & McClendon, S. A. (1999). Mentoring graduate students of color: Myths, models, and modes. *Peabody Journal of Education, 74*(2), 105-118.

Campbell, T. A., & Campbell, D. E. (1997). Faculty/student mentor programs: Effects on academic performance and retention. *Research in Higher Education, 38*(6), 727-742.

Carrasco Embuena, V., & Lapeña Pérez, C. (2005). La Acción Tutorial en la Universidad de Alicante. In M. J. Frau & N. Sauleda (Eds.), *Investigar el diseño curricular: Redes de docencia en el Espacio Europeo de Educación Superior* (pp. 329-358). Alicante-Spain: Universidad de Alicante.

Chao, G. T., Walz, P. M., & Gardner, P. D. (1992). Formal and informal mentorships: A comparison on mentoring functions and contrast with non-mentored counterparts. *Personnel Psychology, 45*(3), 619-636.

Cousins, J. (1995). Using collaborative performance appraisal to enhance teacher's professional growth: A review and test of what we know. *Journal of Personnel Evaluation in Education, 9*(3), 199-222.

Crisp, G., & Cruz, I. (2009). Mentoring college students: A critical review of the literature between 1990 and 2007. *Research in Higher Education, 50*(6), 525-545.

Dahlgren, A. M., Castensson, R., & Dahlgren, L. O. (1998). PBL from the teachers' perspective. *Higher Education, 36,* 437-447.

Das M., Mpofu, D. J. S., Hasan, M. Y, & Stewart, T. S. (2002). Student perceptions of tutor skills in problem-based learning tutorials. *Medical Education, 36*(3), 272-278.

Davidson, M., & Foster-Johnson, L. (2001). Mentoring in the preparation of graduate students of color. *Review of Educational Research, 71*(4), 549-574.

Day, C. (1992). Avaliação do Desenvolvimento Profissional dos Professores. In A. Estrela & A. Nóvoa (Orgs.), *Avaliações em Educação: Novas perspectivas* (pp. 89-104). Lisboa: Educa.

De Grave, W. S, Dolmans, D. H, & Van der Vleuten, C. P. (1999). Profiles of effective tutors in problem-based learning: Scaffolding student learning. *Medical Education, 33,* 901-906.

Dickey, C. (1996). *Mentoring women of color at the University of Minnesota: Challenges for organizational transformation.* Minneapolis: University of Minnesota. (ERIC Document Reproduction Service No. ED399838).

Dolmans, D. H., Gijselaers, W.H., Moust, J.H., de Grave, W.S., Wolfhagen, I. H., & van der Vleuten, C. P. (2002). Trends in research on the tutor in problem-based learning: Conclusions and implications for educational practice and research. *Medical Teaching, 24,* 173-180.

Dolmans, D. H., Wolfhagen, I. H., Scherpbier, A. J., & Van Der Vleuten, C. P. (2001). Relationship of tutors' group-dynamics skills to their performance ratings in problem-based learning. *Academic Medicine, 76,* 473-476.

Ehrich, L., Hansford, B., & Tennent, L. (2004). Formal mentoring programs in education and other professions: A review of the literature. *Educational Administration Quarterly, 40*(4), 518-540.

Fernandes, s. (2011). *Aprendizagem baseada em projectos no contexto do ensino superior: Avaliação de um dispositivo pedagógico no ensino de engenharia* (Project-based learning in higher education: A case study in engineering education]. Doctoral Thesis. University of Minho, Braga, Portugal.

Fernandes, S., & Flores, M. A. (2012). A docência no contexto da avaliação do desempenho no Ensino Superior: Reflexões no âmbito de um estudo em curso. *Revista Iberoamericana de Evaluación Educativa, (5)*1.

Fernandes, S., Flores, M. A., & Lima, R. M. (2009a). Using the CIPP Model to Evaluate the Impact of Project-Led Education. A case study of Engineering Education in Portugal. In Xiangyun Du, Erik de Graaff, & Anette Kolmos (Eds.), *Research on PBL Practice in Engineering Education* (pp.45-56). SENSE Publishers.

Fernandes, S., Flores, M. A., & Lima, R. M. (2009b). Engineering Students' Perceptions about Assessment in Project-led Education. In Urbano Dominguez (Ed.), *Proceedings of the International Symposium on Innovation and Assessment of Engineering Curricula* (pp.161-172).Valladolid, Spain.

Fernandes, S., Flores, M. A., & Lima, R. M. (2012). Student's Views of Assessment in Project-Led Engineering Education: Findings from a Case Study in Portugal. As*sessment & Evaluation in Higher Education, 37*(2) 163-178.

Fernandes, S., Lima, R. M., Cardoso, E., Leão, C., & Flores, M. A. (2009). An academic results analysis of a first year interdisciplinary project approach to industrial and management engineering education. In D. Carvalho, N. van Hattum, & R. M. Lima (Eds.), *Proceedings of the First Ibero-American Symposium on Project Approaches in Engineering Education* (PAEE'2009) (pp. 37-43). Guimarães, Portugal.

Flores, M. A., Veiga Simão, A. M., & Carrasco, V. (2012). Tutoring in higher education in Portugal and Spain: Lessons learned from six initiatives in place. In J. O'Meara & M. Spitlle (Eds.), *Internationalising education: Global perspectives on collaboration and change* (pp. 107-124). New York: Nova Science Publishers.

Graaff, E. & Kolmos, A. (2003). Characteristics of problem-based learning. *International Journal of Engineering Education, 17*(5) 657-652.

Graaff, E. & Kolmos, A. (2007). *Management of change implementation of problem-based and project-based learning in engineering.* Rotterdam: Sense Publishers.

Green, S. G., & Bauer, T. N. (1995). Supervisory mentoring by advisers: Relationships with doctoral student potential, productivity and commitment. *Personnel Psychology, 48,* 537-561.

Groves, M., Rego, P., & O'Rourke, P. (2005). Tutoring in PBL medical curricula: The influence of tutor background and style on effectiveness. BMC. *Medical Education, 5,* 1-7.

Haith-Cooper, M. (2000). Problem-based learning within health professional education. What is the role of the lecturer? A review of the literature. *Nurse Education Today, 20*(4), 267-272.

Hansen, S. (2004). The supervisor in the project-organized group work should participate in developing the students' project competencies. *European Journal of Engineering Education, 29* (3), 451-459.

Hargreaves, A. (1998). The emotional practice of teaching. *Teaching and Teacher Education, 14*(8), 835-854.

Helle, L., Tynjälä, P., & Olkinuora, E. (2006). Project-based learning in post-secondary education – theory, practice and rubber slings shots. *Higher Education, 51,* 287-314.

Jacobi, M. (1991). Mentoring and undergraduate academic success: A literature review. *Review of Educational Research, 61,* 505-532.

Johnson, C. S. (1989). Mentoring programs. In M. L. Upcraft & J. Gardner (Eds.), *The freshman year experience: Helping students survive and succeed in college* (pp.118-128). San Francisco, CA: Jossey-Bass.

Johnson, I. H. (1996). Access and retention: Support programs for graduate and professional students. *New Directions for Student Services, 74,* 53-67.

Johnston, A.K. & Tinning, R.S. (2001) Meeting the challenge of problem-based learning: Developing the facilitators Nurse Education Today, *21,* 161-169.

Kahveci, A., Southerland, S. A., & Gilmer, P. J. (2006). Retaining undergraduate women in science, mathematics, and engineering. *Journal of College Science Teaching, 36*(3), 34-38.

Larsson, S. (1983). Paradoxes in teaching. *Instructional Science, 12,* 355-365.

Lee, G., Lin, Y., Tsou, K., Shiau, S., & Lin, C. (2009). When a problem-based learning tutor decides to intervene. *Academic Medicine, 84,* 1406-1411.

Lima, R. M., Carvalho, D., Flores, M. A., & Van Hattum-Janssem, N. (2007). A case study on project led education in engineering: students' and teachers' perceptions. *European Journal of Engineering Education, 32*(3), 337-347.

Mangold, W. D., Bean, L. G., Adams, D. J., Schwab, W. A., & Lynch, S. M. (2003). Who goes who stays: An assessment of the effect of a freshman mentoring and unit registration program on college persistence. *Journal of College Student Retention, 4*(2), 95-122.

Miles, M. B., & Huberman, A. M. (1994). *Qualitative Data Analysis,* 2nd edition. Thousand Oaks, CA: Sage Publications.

Miller, A. (2002). *Mentoring students & young people: A handbook of effective practice.* London: Kogan Page.

Murray, M. (2001). *Beyond the myths and magic of mentoring.* San Francisco, CA: Jossey Bass.

Murray, K., & Macdonald, R. (1997). The disjunction between lecturers conceptions of teaching and their claimed educational practice. *Higher Education, 33,* 331-349.

Neville, A J. (1999). The problem-based learning tutor: Teacher? Facilitator? Evaluator? *Medical Teaching, 21,* 393-401.

Pagan, R., & Edwards-Wilson, R. (2003). A mentoring program for remedial students. *Journal of College Student Retention, 4*(3), 207-225.

Paglis, L. L., Green, S. G., & Bauer, T. N. (2006). Does advisor mentoring add value? A longitudinal study of mentoring and doctoral student outcomes. *Research in Higher Education, 47*(4), 451-476.

Parker, J. (2008). Comparing research and teaching in university promotion criteria. *Higher Education Quarterly, 62*(3), 237-251.

Philip, K., & Hendry, L. B. (2000). Making sense of mentoring of mentoring making sense? Reflections on the mentoring process by adult mentors with young people. *Journal of Community and Applied Social Psychology, 10,* 211-223.

293

Powell, P. C. (2004). Assessment of team-based projects in project-led education. *European Journal of Engineering Education, 29*(2), 221-230.

Powell, P. C., & Weenk, W. (2003). *Project-led engineering education.* Lemma.

Ramsden, P. & Martin, E. (1996). Recognition of good university teaching: Policies from an Australian study. *Studies in Higher Education, 21*(3), 299-315.

Roberts, A. (2000). Mentoring revisited: A phenomenological reading of the literature. *Mentoring and Tutoring, 8*(2), 145-170.

Rodriguez, Y. E. (1995). Mentoring to diversity: A multicultural approach. *New Directions for Adult and Continuing Education, 66*, 69-77.

Sadler, D. R. (1998). Formative assessment: Revisiting the territory. *Assessment in Education: Principles, Policy & Practice, 5*(1), 77-84.

Salinitri, G. (2005). The effects of formal mentoring on the retention rates for first-year, low-achieving students. *Canadian Journal of Education, 28*(4), 853-873.

Silver, M., & Wilkerson, L. (1991). Effects of tutors with subject expertise on the problem-based learning tutorial process. *Academic Medicine, 55*, 298-300.

Stake, R. (2003). Case studies. In N. K. Denzin & Y. S. Lincoln (Eds.), *Strategies of qualitative inquiry* (2nd edition). Thousand Oaks, CA: Sage.

The Higher Education Academy. (2009). *Reward and recognition in higher education institutional policies and their implementation.* Retrieved 7 January 2013, from http://www.heacademy.ac.uk/assets/documents/rewardandrecog/RewardandRecognition_2.pdf.

Thomas, L., & Hixenbaugh, P. (Eds.). (2006). *Personal tutoring in higher education.* Stoke-on-Trent: Trentham Books.

van Hattum, N. & Mesquita, D. (2011). Teacher perception of professional skills in a project-led engineering semester. *European Journal of Engineering Education, 36*(5), 461-472.

van Hattum-Janssen, N., & Vasconcelos, R. M. (2008). The role of the tutor in Project-Led Education: The development of an evaluation instrument. In C. da Rocha Brito & M. M. Ciampi (Eds.), *International Conference on Engineering and Technology Education*, INTERTECH 2008, Peruíbe, Brazil, March 2-5, 2008.

Veiga Simão, A. M., & Flores, M. A. (2006). O aluno universitário: Aprender a auto-regular a aprendizagem sustentada por dispositivos participativos. *Ciências & Letras, 40*, July/December, 229-251.

Veiga Simão, A. M., Flores, M. A., Fernandes, S., & Figueira, C. (2008). Tutoria no ensino superior. Concepções e práticas. *Sísifo. Revista de Ciências da Educação, 7*, 75-88. Retrieved from http://sisifo.fpce.ul.pt.

Wallace, D., Abel, R., & Ropers-Huilman, B. R. (2000). Clearing a path for success: Deconstructing borders through undergraduate mentoring. *The Review of Higher Education, 24*(1), 87-102.

Yorke, M. (2003). Formative assessment in higher education: Moves towards theory and the enhancement of pedagogic practice. *Higher Education, 45*, 477-501.

Young, P. (2006). Out of balance: Lecturers' perceptions of differential status and rewards in relation to teaching and research. *Teaching in Higher Education, 11*(2), 191-202.

Zalaquett, C. P., & Lopez, A. D. (2006). Learning from the stories of successful undergraduate Latina/Latino students: The importance of mentoring. *Mentoring & Tutoring, 14*(3), 337-353.

AFFILIATIONS

Sandra Fernandes
Faculty of Psychology and Education Sciences
University of Coimbra, Portugal

Maria Assunção Flores
Institute of Education
University of Minho, Portugal

RENATA PORTELA RINALDI, MARIA IOLANDA MONTEIRO,
ALINE MARIA DE MEDEIROS RODRIGUES REALI AND ROSA
MARIA MORAES ANUNCIATO DE OLIVEIRA

AN ONLINE PROGRAMME TO PREPARE TEACHER TUTORS: AN EXPERIENCE INVOLVING A UNIVERSITY-SCHOOL PARTNERSHIP

INTRODUCTION

The Universidade Federal de São Carlos (UFSCar) has become a partner with Open University of Brazil (UAB) to offer five undergraduate programmes at a distance,[i] among which is K-4 Teacher Education (LPe-UAB/UFSCar). The overall goal of this online programme is to carry out actions, programmes, projects, and activities related to public policies elaborated so as to expand opportunities of access to quality, tuition-free higher education in Brazil. Its specific goal is to conduct the education of K-4 teachers as established by Law no. 9,394, which instituted on December 20, 1996 the *Diretrizes e Bases da Educação Nacional* (Directives and Foundations for National Education) or LDB 9,394/96, the *Diretrizes Curriculares Nacionais para a Educação Infantil* (National Curricular Directives for Children Education), and Legal Opinion no. 5/2005 of the *Conselho Nacional de Educação* (National Education Commission), which established the *Diretrizes Curriculares Nacionais para o Curso de Pedagogia* (National Curricular Directives for Teacher Education Programmes).

The curricular component known as "Supervised Teacher Practicum" is an integral part of Brazil's teacher education programmes. The objective of this component is to promote the first-hand experiences of student teachers in K-4 school settings and their reflection processes by exposing them to real-life teaching situations.

In view of the specificities of distance education, among which are (a) the physical distance between the faculty in charge of this curricular component (i.e., Supervised Teaching Practicum) and LPe-UAB/UFSCar's students, (b) the latter's geographical dispersion (i.e., they are from different towns and cities throughout Brazil), and (c) the use of information and communication technologies (ICTs), it was necessary to seek ways to establish collaborative partnerships between LPe-UAB/UFSCar and public K-4 schools so as to prepare practicing schoolteachers to act as partners in the education of student teachers, i.e., by taking up the role of face-to-face (as opposed to online) tutors of the same during their practicum activities in the classroom/school. On the other hand, the programme was devised to provide an opportunity for the participating schoolteachers to improve their professional knowledge. In order to achieve these goals and meet the

M.A. Flores et al. (eds.), Back to the Future: Legacies, Continuities and Changes in Educational Policy, Practice and Research, 297–309.

aforementioned challenges, inherent to distance education, a programme was devised: "Preparation of Schoolteacher Tutors for UAB/UFSCar's Teacher Education Program," also offered at a distance. This online MOODLE-based extension programme aims at preparing teachers by means of activities such as an introduction forum, a questions forum, and the production of narratives. As this continued teacher preparation course is offered at a distance via the Internet, it does not require that participants take a leave from their professional duties. One of the programme goals was the involvement of different actors so as to collectively ensure, theoretically as well as methodologically, the supervision of and support for LPe-UAB/UFSCar's students' practicum activities and experiences at the partner schools.

In this context, the purpose of this article is to analyse the development and implementation of a partnership between UFSCar and public schools at which practicing K-4 schoolteachers (considered by the group as having the status of K-4 teacher educators and hereinafter referred to as "teacher tutors" or TTs) follow and support LPe-UAB/UFSCar's students' practicum experiences. Specifically, it is the purpose of this study to answer the following general question: *What are the contributions and limitations of a programme to prepare teacher tutors – involving a U-PS partnership and conducted via the Internet – vis-à-vis the professional development of practicing schoolteachers and university researchers?*

Given the above, this chapter firstly presents a brief discussion of some theoretical and methodological aspects relating to teacher learning and professional development. Furthermore, the structure of the programme to prepare TTs, i.e., the programme aimed at preparing practicing schoolteachers to act as teacher tutors, is outlined and its accordance with this initiative by LPe-UAB/UFSCar is discussed. Subsequently, in order to answer the aforementioned research question some results of this process are described. Finally, this chapter presents an overview of the results from this initiative, with reference to the practicing teachers, partner K-4 schools, and university researchers.

THEORETICAL AND METHODOLOGICAL UNDERPINNINGS

Teaching has always been a complex, multifaceted, and challenging activity (Cochran-Smith & Fries, 2005). This complexity has significantly increased in the past decades, posing even greater challenges to teacher education programmes. These challenges derive especially from the fact that today's teachers practice in a fast-changing world, i.e., in professional contexts permeated by increasing complexity and uncertainty, whose situations and problems cannot be solved by mere application of available technical and theoretical knowledge (Day, 1999). Indeed, according to Schön (1987), today's teachers should be capable of selecting and organizing some aspects based on constant (re)assessment, giving them consistency, and establishing a direction for their actions in order to make decisions and propose solutions to everyday dilemmas.

From this perspective, regardless of the educational modality, i.e., face-to-face or at a distance, during preservice teacher education, it is important that student teachers (a) become acquainted with the historical and cultural characteristics of schools and communities, (b) observe and carry out successful teaching and learning practices, and (c) have the chance to engage in activities and tasks related to teaching and being a teacher. In order to become aware and critical of their beliefs, choices, and practices, it is essential that they are given the opportunity to adopt more experienced and successful teachers as role models before starting their teaching careers. Experiences of this kind are believed to strengthen the social commitment to their career choice. Meeting these demands becomes even more complex and challenging when professional education is conducted at a distance, as is the case of LPe-UAB/UFSCar.

Therefore, it is important to attend to studies indicating that research on teaching and schooling processes has recently undergone conceptual and methodological changes. Research on teachers and teaching has gradually shifted from a positivist perspective to a theoretical framework that enables the characterization and understanding of complex classroom processes and their actors' individual aspects. This shift has implied researchers 'entering' classrooms and schools to observe, participate, and debate about education with its main actors: teachers and students. Conceptual and methodological changes in research have brought forth a set of technical, procedural, ethical, political, personal, and educational aspects.

Moreover, this change has often implied longer 'school stays' of the so-called 'university partners.' This collaborative mode of interaction between researchers and teachers focuses on the importance of establishing multiple interpretations and goals for the construction of new knowledge. Likewise, this knowledge is based on the assumption that teaching is continuously evolving. From this perspective, dilemmas or problems require collective decision-making, which implies, in spite of their having well-defined roles, a non-hierarchized dialogue between researchers and teachers (U-PS), organized in order to construct new knowledge and find solutions to the everyday, concrete, practical problems of schools.

According to Clark, Moss, Goering, Herter, Lamar, Leonard, Robbins, Russell, Templin and Wascha (1996), this type of collaborative investigation is based on action-research and encompasses many specific designs and definitions. Its implementation involves the following elements: collaboration, focus on practical problems, emphasis on professional development, mutual understandings and consensus, democratic decision-making, and shared action.

Through a process of collaboration between the institutions concerned (U-PS), schoolteachers and researchers can critically examine school and classroom contexts as well as the role of the university in such initiatives, develop and implement interventions, and evaluate them with regard to their ability to promote the *construction of new knowledge* and the *professional development* of both parties.

This is so because it is generally assumed that (a) teaching implies life-long learning and continuous professional development, (b) the school should be the locus of teacher learning processes par excellence, (c) partnerships and permanent dialogue between schoolteachers and researchers can better prepare prospective teachers to practice in multifaceted classroom and school situations, and (d) practicing schoolteachers can assist university faculty in supervising and monitoring student teachers' professional development and at the same time pursue their own professional development.

In addition to the paucity of studies on teacher education at the school, the research reported herein has taken into consideration the scarce data on educators in general, which indicate that key aspects of this professional activity, e.g., the educators' own pedagogical knowledge, have been ignored (Messina, 1999 as cited in Vaillant, 2003). This study has also taken into account the lack of public policies for this category of educators – unlike other categories in Brazil, which have to follow pre-established education guidelines (e.g., K-4 teachers) – and of professional teaching requirements (i.e., certification for K-12 teachers). Teacher education programmes do not require that their educators be certified teachers, whether they are university faculty or schoolteachers; apparently, the mastery of specific knowledge suffices to render their actions successful.

Yet, it is well-known that teachers' and teacher educators' performances depend on a number of factors related to objective work conditions, remuneration, incentives, and most of all on their knowledge and teaching competence. Given the current demands of contemporary society on the school, teachers—like their students—should learn how to work in dynamic, ever-changing environments, where (a) knowledge is constructed from different sources and perspectives, (b) understanding what is learned and learning how to learn are essential requirements for both teachers and students, and (c) teachers' changes cannot be understood independently of how their own professional learning is signified.

The programme that was implemented and its corresponding investigation indicated that teacher learning is an on-going process that occurs throughout teachers' professional lives, not limited to formal and traditional educational spaces, since teachers learn by teaching as well as from other teachers and professionals. Teacher education can be understood as being related to different stages of a teacher's career, such as (1) the phase that precedes formal teacher education, (2) the phase corresponding to the first career years, and (3) the phase related to advanced professional development (Cochran-Smith & Fries, 2005; Vaillant, 2003). They also learn by observing their teachers' practices as students throughout their entire schooling processes. Along these lines, teachers' educational demands are seen as ever changing along with their career phases and other more specific characteristics related to school contexts.

Teachers' beliefs (or values, judgments, opinions, ideas, personal theories) play a prominent role in professional teacher learning processes; this is to say that these aspects strongly define their teaching practices. Moreover, it is important to remark that these beliefs are strongly influenced by personal experiences, experiences associated with formal knowledge, and school- and classroom-related experiences.

Other essential aspects to be taken into consideration as regards professional teacher learning processes are those associated with Shulman's (1986, 1987) teaching knowledge base and pedagogical reasoning model.

In this sense, insofar as teachers' knowledge is constructed from and in interaction with their previous and current context-based experiences, educational activities have specific characteristics, e.g., they (a) are situated, (b) involve social interaction processes, and (c) are shared with others, since no one has all the necessary knowledge and skills to teach successfully in isolation.

The literature in the field of teacher education indicates – unambiguously – that teachers must *learn how to learn from practice*, since teaching requires improvisation, guesswork, and experimentation. And, in order to *learn from practice* it appears that teachers need to learn how to adapt their knowledge to each teaching situation, which implies (a) inquiring about what students do and think and how they understand what is taught, (b) using their knowledge to improve their practice, (c) monitoring, assisting, and reviewing their students' assignments, (d) being given time and opportunity for such processes to occur effectively, and (e) being willing to change. *Practice-based learning need* not *occur in real time*; teachers can resort to materials such as multimedia and written cases, observation of teaching situations, and examples of students' tasks. These materials can assist teachers in investigating and analysing their own or the teaching practices of others.

In addition to specific content knowledge, knowledge about work contexts, and pedagogical content knowledge (i.e., knowledge needed by teachers to be able to bridge the distance between the meaning of any given curriculum content and that constructed by their students), an important aspect to be highlighted in the teacher tutors' knowledge base is their students' learning specificity, i.e., adult learning. In this sense, it is also important to emphasize the knowledge related to *teaching other teachers how to teach*.

Another aspect that should be considered refers to societal demands on the school, students' profiles, and the desired teacher profile. The difference between real and desired profiles can often engender paradoxical situations. Notwithstanding the manifest goal of teacher education programmes, i.e., to prepare teachers to practice in a fast-changing world, where the role of schools is to promote students' flexibility and constant adaptation, teachers are prepared according to a whole different logic, i.e., by endowing them with a fixed set of knowledge in the hope that it will have practical application throughout their professional lives.

Some authors, such as Imbernón (1994), emphasize that teacher educators require a range of competencies, such as being able to (a) stimulate groups of adults, (b) design educational projects and strategies, (c) successfully implement and carry out workplace-based action-research practices, (d) make use of and teach how to use methodological tools to investigate and analyse teaching practices, and so forth. Additionally, Rinaldi (2009) points out other fundamental K-4 teacher educators' competencies and knowledge. According to her, teacher educators should: (a) have previous experience as schoolteachers; (b) have mastery of content and know how to explain it to students, (c) be patient; (d) be able to plan collective work experiences; (e) be able to learn by listening to their teachers; (f) take pleasure in teaching; (g) acquire technological knowledge; (h) be able to teach how to do research; (i) value human beings; (j) learn in order to teach; (k) learn about ethics; (l) learn about the school, its students, faculty, and staff; (m) recognize that they cannot know everything; (n) know how to observe the school's everyday procedures, among others. This knowledge strengthens teacher educators' actions and supports them in finding out whatever additional teaching knowledge is required of them to successfully act as educators of prospective K-4 teachers.

In educational terms, many are the strategies that can be adopted to prepare teacher educators, from strategies concerning the first years of this activity to those related to more advanced phases in the professional development of teacher educators.

These assumptions were taken into consideration regarding the education of both the prospective teachers (i.e., LPe-UAB/UFSCar's students) and the practicing schoolteachers to act as educators (teacher tutors), as will be shown in the following section.

TEACHER TUTORS' PROFESSIONAL DEVELOPMENT PROGRAMME
AND ITS INVESTIGATION

The professional development programme "Preparation of Practicing Tutors for UAB/UFSCar's Teacher Education Program," conceived from a collaborative perspective, was carried out online at UFSCar's Teachers Portal (www.portaldosprofessores.ufscar.br) by means of a MOODLE virtual learning environment (VLE), with printed and digital material, and other digital media, such as educational videos and software. It included several interactive tools that enabled synchronous and asynchronous communication, namely forums, journals, electronic messaging, a posting wall, and so forth (see Figure 1).

Figure 1. Virtual Learning Environment (VLE) Moodle.
Source: www.portaldosprofessores.ufscar.br

This initiative involved the university faculty in charge of the practicum curricular component as well as other faculty[ii] responsible for planning and conducting the teacher tutors' preparation. These actors worked collaboratively, as a team, whose composition was: two faculty in charge of LPe-UAB/UFSCar's curricular component "Supervised Teaching Practicum"; one practicum coordinator; one secretary; one faculty in charge of the preparation of teacher tutors; four mentors responsible for assisting the participating schoolteachers (prospective teacher tutors) online and monitoring their VLE activities; and one instructional designer.

Broadly put, the underpinnings for the preparation of teacher tutors to work in partnership with LPe-UAB/UFSCar were the construction of knowledge on teacher learning and distance education and reflection on their own professional practices with the intent of preparing them to act as teacher tutors (TTs).

From this perspective, the educational process was conducted in the same way as a university outreach or extension course, lasting 120 hours divided into two modules as shown in Table 1.

Invitation and previous selection of practicing K-4 schoolteachers were conducted by the practicum coordinator and the coordinator of the UAB student support centres by means of their respective cities/towns' departments of education where there were LPe-UAB/UFSCar's student teachers interested in conducting their practicum activities and schoolteachers willing to join with the university in a partnership to prepare these students as aforementioned.

The criteria for the preliminary selection of schoolteachers were: (a) teaching experience (minimum 5 years); (b) readiness to participate in the teacher preparation course; and (c) willingness to act as a partner teacher tutor of LPe-UAB/UFSCar's student teachers, welcoming them to their classrooms, dialoguing with them, and sharing their experiences with them throughout their practicum activities. The final group of participants was later chosen from this preliminary cohort of schoolteachers. The final selection was based on the evaluation of their resumes and answers to a questionnaire. They were selected according to their (a) professional paths, (b) current professional standing within and without the classroom, (c) professional qualifications, and (d) experience as K-4 teachers.

After this screening process, 45 experienced and successful practicing K-4 schoolteachers were selected to attend the online TT preparation course in the first half of 2010. These teachers worked at partner schools receiving LPe-UAB/UFSCar's student teachers in the towns/cities where the UAB student support centres were or in surrounding towns/cities. In the second semester, about 70 schoolteachers with the same characteristics attended the course.

Once the practicum and teacher preparation activities had begun, in order to improve the communication among UFSCar, partner K-4 schools, and UAB student support centres, LPe-UAB/UFSCar had to select and hire professionals to work at the UAB student support centres, called Face-to-Face Practicum Tutors (FFPTs). These professionals helped the participating schoolteachers to work in a MOODLE VLE, e.g., how to navigate the VLE, access different tools, send reports and perform course activities, participate in web-conferences, communicate with the practicum coordinator and mentors, and so on.

Table 1. Modules of the teacher tutor preparation course

Module	Work Unit
1	*Unit 1: Professional paths: getting to know the group* Goals: (a) explore the VLE and some of its tools; (b) fill in documents that will later enable the team to analyze data concerning this experience and divulge them; (c) learn about each participant's professional path (with data complementing the information on their registration form) and the characteristics of their professional contexts. *Unit 2: Teacher learning and teacher knowledge base* Goals: (a) study teacher learning processes and their characteristics and, especially, (b) understand the concept of teacher knowledge base and its characteristics with respect to professional teaching. *Unit 3: Identity and role of teacher tutors* Goals: (a) learn about the specificities of teacher learning in the first career years; (b) understand the concepts of teacher knowledge base and pedagogical reasoning from a real-life perspective; (b) reflect on the role and identity of TTs at the school, especially in the classroom. *Unit 4: Supervised practicum supervisor: educators of prospective teachers* Goals: (a) reflect on the role of TTs in assisting and monitoring student teachers; (b) systematize and evaluate the contents addressed during Module 1.
2	*Unit 5: TTs at work: construction of a teacher education practice* Goals: (a) construct, collectively and open-endedly, strategies of professional education and action to assist LPe-UAB/UFSCar's student teachers; (b) follow and reflect on the process of becoming a teacher tutor, in charge of practical guidance during supervised practicums; (c) evaluate self and the teacher tutor preparation course.

FFPTs communicated continuously and systematically with the practicum coordinator and programme secretary for guidance about TTs' registration issues and solution to problems encountered. Moreover, they were in constant contact with the course mentors about everyday activities or to share difficulties/dilemmas (e.g., course dropouts or difficulties reported to the coordination of their UAB student support centres). Thus, FFPTs took up the role of mediating work relations between the university, UAB student support centres, and schools, which was fundamental to the LPe-UAB/UFSCar's curricular component "Supervised Teaching Practicum." In addition to this support to TTs, FFPTs helped their corresponding student teachers to fill in the forms needed to be granted entrance into partner schools as defined by their respective cities/towns' departments of education. Moreover, in some cases, these professionals played an active role in finding practical solutions to facilitate the entrance of their student teachers into LPe-UFSCar/UAB's partner schools.

Therefore, the next section presents the results of this experience bearing in mind that prospective teachers need to build a knowledge base, competencies, and skills. Student teachers also have to learn how to reflect on and evaluate their own practices, teach, and become a teacher. It is believed that by promoting the preparation of TTs to follow and assist prospective teachers during their practicum, two immediate benefits will be derived: (1) investment in the professional development of practicing K-4 schoolteachers, which has, as suggested by recent research, direct influence on their students' learning, depending mostly on what teachers know and can do (OECD, 2005; Cochran-Smith & Fries, 2005; Darling-Hammond, 2001), and (2) mitigation of the impact caused by the professional integration process reported by novice teachers, i.e., the "reality shock," (Vieenma & Staring, 1998) in order to decrease the number of early-career teachers who quit the profession within the first year (OECD, 2005; Derry & Potts, 1998).

SOME OUTCOMES FROM THE TEACHER TUTOR PREPARATION COURSE

The outcomes from the first two offers of the teacher tutor preparation course in 2010 point to some positive effects, namely:
- TT's increased familiarity with ICTs, and improved knowledge repertoire about teaching and teacher education;
- Shared reflection and dialogue about teaching practices, i.e., schoolteachers and students – prospective teachers – were able to share classroom challenges and opportunities and had the chance to rethink their practices and (re)learn their profession from new perspectives;
- Collaborative management by the university, UAB student support centres, and partner schools;
- Closer relationship between the university professionals (i.e., faculty in charge of the curricular component "Supervised Teaching Practicum," faculty responsible for the TT preparation course, mentors, practicum coordinator, FFPTs) in order to tailor the education of teachers to the reality of Brazilian K-4 schools;
- Implementation of a professional development programme for professionals from partner schools bearing in mind the specifics of each context.

Given the importance of this arrangement to the successful education of LPe-UAB/UFSCar's student teachers and also the difficulties inherent to innovative/pioneer initiatives (as this initiative is understood to be), a lot of energy was expended to ensure the accomplishment of various aspects of the U-PS partnership, from presenting the proposed initiative at UFSCar's higher administrative levels and negotiating it with the administrations of the UAB student support centres to preparing professionals to run the Supervised Teaching Practicum course and educational process in accordance with the approach proposed by LPe-UAB/UFSCar, selection and preparation of TTs, finding partner schools, and placing student teachers at schools that would best meet their needs/possibilities and those of several stakeholders (e.g., K-4 schools).

Nevertheless, it is important to highlight some limitations and difficulties that permeated this process, which were dealt with and mitigated/dissipated over time, for instance:
- Participating schoolteachers' difficulties in using ICTs and navigating the Internet. This difficulty required that the university professionals in charge of TTs' professional development/preparation (i.e., faculty, mentors, instructional

designer, and practicum coordinator) devise support strategies in order to prevent them from abandoning the course, which would imply LPe-UAB/UFSCar having to select and prepare new schoolteachers to receive its student teachers. In addition, as aforementioned, it was necessary to select and hire a new category of professionals, i.e., FFPTs, to assist TTs at their UAB student support centres;

- Difficulties with regard to working online in the VLE, i.e., MOODLE and its tools, e.g., management of time spent on activities, interaction with other classmates through chat-rooms, and collaborative work by means of wiki;
- Difficulty in aligning LPe-UAB/UFSCar's teacher education proposal (for which the Supervised Teaching Practicum faculty were responsible) with that of the TT preparation programme while seeking to integrate theory and practice into both of them;
- TTs' lengthy absences from the VLE due to personal problems, e.g., sickness, overwork, difficulty in balancing their course homework with professional and familial demands, problems related to access to the Internet, among others;
- Difficulties related to some TTs failure to assist their student teachers, who had to be reassigned to other TTs at the same school. This was a problem in that it overburdened some schoolteachers;
- Difficulties regarding the implications of practicum activities to the school community, which brought forth the need to discuss with the student teachers some ethical issues concerning the profession.

Despite these difficulties and limitations, the overall outcome of the U-PS partnership model adopted was markedly positive. This was attested by the TTs themselves as well as by the student teachers, FFPTs, and coordinators of the UAB student support centres.

For instance, one of the UAB student support centres created a blog with pictures and student teachers' accounts of their practicum activities, which had a positive impact on the partner school's culture and routine. Another positive effect of this experience was that some student teachers remained at their partner schools much longer than the period stipulated by LPe-UAB/UFSCar. In addition, some TTs reported that they had shared the preparation course material with colleagues at HTPCs (teachers' meetings at Brazilian schools during which teaching-related theories and practical issues are studied and discussed collectively). Moreover, other TTs indicated having learned new teaching strategies and contents from the partnership established with their student teachers, even before the latter had given their own trial lessons.

In this sense, it is important to emphasize that the experience has been extremely challenging and rich, indicating that collaborative work and dialogue are central to (a) the successful development of practicum activities at a distance, (b) the establishment of fruitful U-PS partnerships, and (c) the effective coordination of university professionals' efforts toward the advancement of more contextualized and meaningful actions in teacher education.

CONCLUSIONS

The initiative in question addresses a multidimensional educational challenge, i.e., it sought to (a) promote a more situated and significant mode of education for LPe-UAB/UFSCar's students, (b) foster practicing schoolteachers' (as well as the researchers') continued education and professional development by means of U-PS partnerships, (c) direct – from a collaborative perspective – the efforts of multiple professionals (i.e., from the university, schools, UAB student support centres) and students by means of distance education, (d) construct pedagogical strategies to render U-PS partnerships viable, and so forth.

This process points to the need for changes in the way teacher education is conceived at the university as well as to reconsider the way K-4 schools are approached for the placement of student teachers during their required supervised practicum activities, i.e., their first professional experiences. Stated differently, the purpose of this initiative was to promote cultural changes at both loci, i.e., the university and the school, since it does not suffice to merely expose student teachers to theories about their future profession at the university or provide them with practicum opportunities without significant collaboration between the university and the school in order to provide today's world with capable professionals. On the contrary, as mentioned above, these situations may strongly concur to what some studies on teacher education call "reality shock."

Preliminary outcomes from this initiative seem to indicate that the U-PS partnership had a positive impact on the participating K-4 schoolteachers' professional and personal lives, especially because they were able to expand the scope of their learning, beyond the classroom. From personal reflections and materials shared with the researchers and peers throughout the programme, the TTs were able to redirect their practices to favour of their student teachers' learning processes as well as to rethink their own teaching strategies and activities so as to promote their students' learning, e.g., planning lessons according to their students' characteristics and working with groups in order to promote collaboration among children (their role and student teachers' role being that of mediators in the teaching-learning processes).

By expressing doubts, anxieties, fears, certainties, and beliefs through a range of on-line tools that guided their practices as educators of student teachers, TTs were able to establish opportunities to reflect "on" and "about" their practices from multiple perspectives, i.e., theirs and those of the researchers and TTs from other schools. Thus, it was observed that the construction of meaning with respect to becoming a tutor and a university partner is linked to each context of action (local context. i.e., the school; regional context, i.e., city or town; school system, i.e., city and state).

In general, some impacts on the university researchers' professional learning were also observed, especially because the initiative was carried out at a distance. Several challenges were addressed as part of the process, e.g., TT's geographical dispersion, different personal and professional characteristics, diverse professional contexts, singular experiences and repertoires of professional behaviours, and so forth. Moreover, these challenges have attested to the relevance of the theoretical and methodological approach adopted, its emphasis on collaborative, non-hierarchical work, and its consideration of the characteristics of the participating institutions along with their schoolteachers' educational needs in order to assist LPe-UAB/UFSCar's students.

NOTES

[i] Musical Education, Environmental Education, K-4 Teacher Education, Information Systems, and Sugar-Ethanol Technology.
[ii] Among these teachers are faculty from other public universities and experienced and successful K-4 teachers that have acted as mentors in educational processes conducted by the authors of this article since 2004.

REFERENCES

Brasil. Conselho Nacional de Educação. (2005). *Parecer 5/2005 do Conselho Nacional de Educação.* Brasília.

Brasil. Conselho Nacional de Educação. (2006). Resolução Cne/Cp Nº 1, De 15 de Maio de 2006. *Diretrizes curriculares nacionais para o curso de pedagogia.* Diário Oficial da União, Brasília, 16 de Maio de 2006, Seção 1, 11.

Brasil. Ministério da Educação. (1996). *Lei de diretrizes e bases,* No. 9.394, 20 December 1996.

Brasil. Ministério da Educação. (2005). *Escola de gestores da educação básica:* Retrieved on 6 November 2010 from http://www.escoladegestores.inep.gov.br/.

Clark, C., Moss, P. A., Goering, S., Herter, R. J., Lamar, B., Leonard, D., Robbins, S., Russell, M., Templin, M., & Wascha, K. (1996). Collaboration as dialogue: Teacher and researchers engaged in conversation and professional development. *American Educational Research Journal, 33*(1), 193-232.

Cochran-Smith, M., & Fries, K. (2005). Researching teacher education in changing times: Politics and paradigms. In M. Cochran-Smith, K. Fries, & K. Zeichner. (Org.), *Study teacher education: The report of the AERA panel on research and teacher education* (pp. 69-109). Washington: AERA/Lea.

Darling-Hammond, L. (2001). The challenge of staffing our schools. *Educational Leadership, 58*(8), 12-17.

Day, C. (1999). Formar docentes. *Cómo, cuándo e en qué condiciones aprende el professorado.* Madri: Narcea.

Derry, S. J., & Potts, M. K. (1998). How tutors model students: Study of personal constructs in adaptive tutoring. *American Educational Research Journal, 35*(1), 65-99.

Imbernón, F. (1994). *La formación del profesorado.* Barcelona: Paidós, 1994.

OCDE. (2005). *Teachers matter: Attracting, developing and retaining effective teachers.* Paris: OCDE.

Rinaldi, P. R. (2009). *Desenvolvimento profissional de formadores em exercício: contribuições de um programa online.* Thesis (Doutorado Em Educação). Universidade Federal de São Carlos.

Schön, D. (1987). *Educating the reflective practitioner.* San Francisco, CA: Jossey Bass.

Shulman, L. (1986). Those who understand: Knowledge growth in teaching. *Educational Researcher, 15*(2), 4-14.

Shulman, L. (1987). Knowledge and teaching: foundations of the new reform. *Harvard Educational Review, 57*(1), 1-22.

Vaillant, D. (2003). *Formação de Formadores: Estado da prática.* Série Preal Documentos, 25. Rio de Janeiro: PREAL.

Vieenman, S., Laat, H., & Staring, C. (1998). Evaluation of a coaching programme for mentors of beginning teachers. *Journal Of In-Service Education, 24*(3), 411-431.

AFFILIATIONS

Renata Portela Rinaldi
Faculty of Sciences and Technology from "Presidente Prudente"
State University of São Paulo "Júlio de Mesquita Filho"
Brazil

Maria Iolanda Monteiro
Education and Human Sciences Centre
Federal University of São Carlos
Brazil

Aline Maria de Medeiros Rodrigues Reali
Education and Human Sciences Centre
Federal University of São Carlos
Brazil

Rosa Maria Moraes Anunciato de Oliveira
Education and Human Sciences Centre
Federal University of São Carlos
Brazil

CONTRIBUTORS

Aline Maria de Medeiros Rodrigues Reali is Researcher at CNPQ (National Council of Technological and Scientific Development, Brazil). She is graduate in Psychology (FFCL Ribeirão Preto, São Paulo State University, 1979), M.A. in Special Education (Federal University of São Carlos) and Ph.D. in Psychology, São Paulo State University, 1990). She is full professor in the Pedagogical Theories and Practices Department and in the Graduate Education Program of the Education and Human Sciences Center at the Federal University of São Carlos, São Paulo, Brazil. Her research interests are teacher professional development, teachers' continuing education, and online teacher education. Currently she is Secretary of Distance Education of the Federal University of São Carlos.

Ana Amélia A. Carvalho is full Professor at the Faculty of Psychology and Education Sciences, University of Coimbra, Portugal. She received her Master degree at the School of Education, University of Manchester, UK in 1991, and her PhD at the University of Minho, Portugal in 1998. Her research interests include teacher education, Web 2.0, mobile learning, and digital games to learn. She organized conferences about Webquest (2006), Web 2.0 (2008), Podcasts (2009), Games and Mobile Learning (2012), and she participated in the organization of ISATT (2011) and the WCCE (2013) in Poland. She coordinated several research projects, the last one started in 2012 – *From games to mobile-learning interactive activities*. She has published books, chapters, articles in national and international journals. Her recent publications include: Carvalho, A. A. (2010) ICT in teacher education: Developing key competencies in face-to-face and distance learning, in N. Reynolds & M. Turcsányi-Szabó (Eds.), *Key competencies in the knowledge Society – IFIP TC3 International Conference* (pp. 23-34). Berlin: Springer; Kukulska-Hulme, A., Pettit, J., Bradley, L., Carvalho, A. A., Herrington, A., Kennedy, D., & Walker, A. (2011) Mature students using mobile devices in life and learning, *International Journal of Mobile and Blended Learning, 31*(1), 18-52.

Andrea Martin is an Associate Professor in the Faculty of Education, Queen's University, Kingston, Ontario, Canada, where she has taught since 1997. Her background is in education and social work and she has taught and worked with children and youth at the elementary and secondary levels with a particular focus on supporting exceptional learners. Her research interests centre on teacher education, with an emphasis on the quality and impact of practicum learning experiences and on the process of collaboration and school-university partnerships, as well as on differentiating instruction for struggling readers with exceptionalities in regular classrooms. She holds a B.A. degree from Smith College, a B.Ed. from Queen's, an M.A. from the University of Sussex, an M.Sc. from the London School of Economics in Social Administration and Social Work Studies, an M.Ed. in Educational Psychology and a Ph.D. degree in Cognitive Studies and Curriculum Studies from Queen's University.

António Nóvoa is President of the University of Lisbon (Portugal), since 2006. Previously, he was Vice-President from 2002 to 2006. He earned a Ph.D. in History at the Sorbonne University (Paris) and a Ph.D. in Educational Sciences at Geneva University (Switzerland). He has been the main advisor for Education to the President of the Portuguese Republic (1996-1998), and the President of the International Standing Conference for the History of Education (2000-2003). During his academic career, he has been Professor in several international universities (Geneva, Wisconsin-Madison, Oxford, and Columbia-New York), and Visiting Professor for short periods in 20 universities around the world. The work of Antonio Nóvoa has been published in 15 countries. He is the author of more than a dozen books and more than 100 book chapters and journal articles. Additionally, he has edited several other books, mainly in the fields of History of Education and Comparative Education, where the work focuses on educational policies and the teaching profession.

Catherine Mcloughlin is Associate Professor in the faculty of education, Australian Catholic University and Research Coordinator. She is engaged in teacher education and the teaching of research methods at postgraduate level. Catherine publishes in a range of teaching and learning areas, including teacher professional development, student engagement and learning processes; emerging technologies and innovative pedagogies and the impact of digital tools and social media on communication, teaching and learning.

Christopher Day is Emeritus Professor of Education and Senior Fellow at the School of Education, University of Nottingham. He has worked, also, as a schoolteacher, teacher educator and local authority adviser. He has extensive research and consultancy experience in England, Europe, Australia, South East Asia, North America and with the OECD in the fields of teachers' continuing professional development, school leadership and change. He is the Editor of 'Teachers and Teaching: Theory and Practice,' co-editor of 'Educational Action Research'; and Founding Director of the 14 country longitudinal research project, '*Successful School Principalship.*' Recent publications include *The international handbook on continuing professional development* (co-editor and contributor, Open University Press, 2004); *A passion for teaching* (Routledge-Falmer, 2004); *Teachers matter: connecting work, lives and effectiveness* (lead author, Open University Press, 2007); *Successful principal leadership in times of change: International perspectives* (lead-editor and contributor, Springer, 2007); *The new lives of teachers* (Routledge, 2010); *School leadership on pupil outcomes: Building and sustaining success* (Open University Press, 2011); *New understandings of teacher's work: Emotions and educational change* (Springer, 2011) and the editor of the *International handbook on teacher and school development* (Routledge, 2011).

Ciaran Sugrue is Professor of Education at University College Dublin (UCD). He is a former chairperson of ISATT, and is an associate editor of its journal, Teachers and Teaching Theory and Practice. His research interests are wide ranging but primarily focused on School Leadership and Educational Change, as well as connecting these with continuing professional learning within the teaching profession, and on qualitative research methods – their cultural conjunctures and disjunctures across national borders and in the international arena. He was General Editor of Irish Educational Studies from 1998-2008, and is a member of the editorial boards of several international journals. His forthcoming books include: *School leadership unmasked: A longitudinal life history* (Springer) and an edited text (with Tone Dyrdal Solbrekke): *Professional responsibility: New horizons of praxis* (Routledge). Recent publications include: *The future of educational change: International perspectives* (London: Routledge, 2008), while recent journal articles include: Sugrue, C. (2009) From heroes and heroines to hermaphrodites: Emancipation or emasculation of school leaders and leadership? *School Leadership and Management, 29*(4), 361-372.

Colleen Leathley is a Research Officer in the Institute for Advancing Community Engagement, Australian Catholic University, as well as a part time lecturer at the University. She is a registered psychologist who over the past 13 years, has held a number of senior positions within the NSW Health system including within the Clinical Excellence Commission. She has coordinated a statewide program in clinical leadership drawing upon her expertise in personal, social and organisational development.

Els Laroes is Head of the Teacher Education Department of Utrecht University, The Netherlands. She is currently working on her PhD thesis on collaborative processes in professional development schools. After finishing her MA in English Linguistics, she taught English as a foreign language in secondary schools in The Netherlands. She moved to teacher education in 1991. As teacher educator she worked at the Utrecht College of Higher Education for five years, followed by a five year period of being member of the management team for the department of secondary teacher education. In this period she obtained the degree Master of Educational Management. In 2001 she became head of the teacher education department of Utrecht University. As teacher educator and manager in teacher education she is specifically interested in inter-organizational collaboration within partnerships between universities and secondary schools in which boundary crossing and brokers are central concepts.

Fernando Ilídio Ferreira is an Associate Professor at the University of Minho, Portugal. He received his PhD at this University in 2003. His research interests include school organization, educational policies, teacher education, child studies and non-formal education. His publications include Ferreira, F. I. (2009) Education, social mediation and community development: an ethnographic

313

research in a rural area. *Community Development Journal*, *44*(4), 460-469; Flores, Maria Assunção & Ferreira, F. I. (2009) The induction and mentoring of new teachers in Portugal: Contradictions, needs and opportunities. *Research in Comparative and International Education*, *4*(1), 63-73; Ferreira, F. I. (2008) Reformas educativas, formação e subjectividades dos professores. *Revista Brasileira de Educação*, *13*(38), 239-251; Ferreira, F. I. (2007) Transformation de l'école et paradoxes de l'autonomie au Portugal. *Revue internationale d'éducation de Sèvres*, *46*, 45-54; Ferreira, F. I. (2012) A ideologia da adaptação: Tensões entre educação e trabalho no contexto da Aprendizagem ao Longo da Vida, in C. A. V. Estêvão (Org.), *Políticas de formação, ética e profissionalidade* (pp. 145-166). Curitiba: Editora CRV; Sarmento, T., Ferreira, F. I.; Silva, P., & Madeira, R. (2009) *Infância, família e comunidade: As crianças como actores sociais*. Porto: Porto Editora.

Flávia Vieira is full Professor at the University of Minho, Institute of Education, Centre for Research in Education. She works in the areas of pedagogical supervision, pedagogies of teacher education, autonomy in language education, and higher education. She is author or co-author of the books: *No caleidoscópio da supervisão: Imagens da formação e da pedagogia* (2006, 2nd ed. 2010); *Pedagogy for autonomy in language education in Europe – towards a framework for learner and teacher development* (2007, Authentik); *Struggling for autonomy in language education – reflecting, acting and being* (2009, Peter Lang); *Transformar a pedagogia na universidade – Narrativas da prática* (2009, De Facto Editores). She has been actively involved in the scholarship of pedagogy and has coordinated multidisciplinary projects aiming at the constitution of communities of practice in her university.

Geert Kelchtermans (1962) studied educational sciences and philosophy at the University of Leuven in Belgium, where he received his PhD in 1993 with a narrative-biographical study on teacher development. He now works at the same university as a full professor and chair of the Centre for Educational Policy, Innovation and Teacher Education. Geert Kelchtermans has widely published internationally on teacher development, narrative-biographical methodology, micropolitics in schools and, more recently, leadership in schools. As a red thread throughout his work runs his interest in unraveling the complex interplay between on the one hand subjects (teachers, leaders) and their individual and collective sense-making and on the other the structural and cultural conditions constituting teachers' and school leaders' work lives. In Leuven he teaches courses on school development, educational innovation, pedagogy of teacher education and qualitative research methods.

Gerrit Stols holds the degrees HED, BSc Hons (North West University), MSc, and PhD (UNISA). He is currently a senior lecturer in the Department of Science, Mathematics and Technology Education, University of Pretoria specialising in mathematical education. He spent three months as a visiting scholar at the

University of Georgia in the USA. He taught mathematics at various schools for twelve years. His research interests in mathematics education concern the use of technology in the mathematics classroom as well as mathematical conceptual development. He has published several articles in national and international journals and has presented conference papers and workshops locally and abroad. He has authored and co-authored twenty study guides, textbooks and manuals.

Hafdís Guðjónsdóttir is Associate Professor of education at University of Iceland School of Education. She earned her PhD from the University of Oregon in special education. Hafdís worked for 25 years as a general classroom teacher and special educator in elementary and high schools. Her focus is on inclusion, multicultural education, curriculum development, differentiated learning, teaching mixed-ability classes, cooperative learning, authentic assessment, mathematics for all students, teachers; their work, lives and professionalism, school change, and collaboration with families. From the perspective of constant changes, critical theory and pedagogy Hafdís researches with teachers, their students and families and school personnel. Her research methodology is qualitative approaches with a focus on teacher research and self-study of teacher education. Her research interests are in the area of inclusion, multicultural education, pedagogy and educational practices, teacher professionalism and development.

Hirotoshi Yano is Professor of education at Mukogawa Women's University, Japan. He received Ph.D. from Osaka City University in 1997, based on his dissertation on the post-war reform of the upper secondary school curriculum in Japan. Before he joined Mukogawa Women's University in 2011, he worked more than twenty years and became a professor emeritus at Osaka City University. His research interests are in issues on curriculum policy and school-based curriculum design in primary and secondary education. He studies school education mainly from a comparative and historical perspective, and views it as part of lifelong learning, where people teach and learn interactively in learning communities. His latest work published in English is "A shift away from an egalitarian system: where do educational reforms in Japan lead?" (*Journal of Curriculum Studies*, *45*(1), 2013). He is currently responsible for local educational administration as a member of Osaka City Board of Education.

Hisayoshi Mori is Associate Professor of early childhood education and care at Ryukoku University Junior College, Japan. He received Ph.D. from Osaka City University in 2005, based on his dissertation on the curriculum of the University of Chicago Laboratory School (the Dewey's Laboratory School). Before he joined Ryukoku University Junior College in 2011, he worked at Aichi Konan College, Japan. His main research interests include history of curriculum and instruction, and professional development for teachers. His latest work is "A study on the system and the characteristics of learning activities at the Dewey's Laboratory School for the "community-centered" school" (*Research Journal of Educational*

Methods. Vol. 36, 2011. Edited by National Association for the Study of Educational Methods.)

Irene Hazou is Associate Professor and Vice President for Academic Affairs at Bethlehem University. She holds a Ph.D. in Mathematics. Her research interests are in Mathematics and Science Education. She had an oversight over the quality assurance process in academics and international relations at Bethlehem University for more than 11 years.

Jan Vermunt is a Professor of Education at the University of Cambridge, Faculty of Education. He is an educational psychologist whose research interests have evolved from student learning and teacher learning as separate domains to include the way teacher learning and professional development affects processes and outcomes of student learning and vice versa. In 1992 he earned his doctoral degree from Tilburg University with a thesis on student learning entitled 'Learning styles and regulation of learning processes in higher education.' He moved to Leiden University in 1995, where he worked for six years as an associate professor. From 1999 to 2002 he was a Professor of Educational Development and Research at Maastricht University. From 2004 to 2012 he was professor of Teaching and Teacher Education at Utrecht University, The Netherlands. Here, his research interests broadened to include experienced teachers' professional learning processes and outcomes in the context of educational innovations.

Joke Daemen is Teacher Educator at the Centre for Teaching and Learning and at the Freudenthal Institute for Science and Mathematics Education, Utrecht University, The Netherlands. She studied mathematics at Utrecht University and worked as a mathematics teacher in several Dutch secondary schools. After ten years she moved to the Utrecht College of Higher Education, where she worked as mathematics teacher and teacher educator. In 1999 she became a teacher educator at Utrecht University. From 1993 onwards she participated in several educational projects, mostly concerned with curriculum development for teacher education in cooperation with schools for secondary education. She participated in research projects on the professional development of teachers in the context of educational innovations. During the last ten years she was also involved in the development of a new mathematics curriculum for secondary education in collaboration with mathematics teachers and the Freudenthal Institute for Science and Mathematics Education.

Jude Butcher is Director, Institute for Advancing Community Engagement and Professor of Community Engagement at Australian Catholic University. Previously he has been Head of School of Education and Head of Department of Education at the University and its predecessor colleges. He is a member of the Wollongong Diocesan Catholic Schools Council and the Board of Edmund Rice Education Australia as well as being Board Chair, Edmund Rice Centre for Justice and

Community Education. He has been involved in Aboriginal education for more than 25 years and in educational capacity building in Timor Leste for 11 years.

Kristin Johnston is an Honorary Fellow, Institute for Advancing Community Engagement at Australian Catholic University and Research Officer for the Sisters of St Joseph. Kristin was responsible, with Professor Paul Chesterton, for the foundation research "The Poor and Catholic Schools." She is a commissioner of the NSW Catholic Education and chair of the Catholic Education and Social Welfare Co-ordinating Committee. She has also had a long standing commitment to rural ministries in New South Wales. She is currently director of Mary MacKillop research.

Liesbeth Piot (1984) obtained a Master's degree in Educational Sciences at the University of Leuven. Supported by the Research Fund – Flanders, she recently finished her PhD dissertation "Changing times, changing leaders? A description and analysis of leadership practices at the upper-school level." Her research focuses on school leadership, particularly the working relationships between principals in school networks or school clusters. She also has a profound interest in qualitative research methods and develops in-service training for principals at the Centre for Educational Policy, Innovation and Teacher Training (University of Leuven).

Linda Darling-Hammond is Charles E. Ducommun Professor of Education at Stanford University where she has launched the Stanford Center for Opportunity Policy in Education and the School Redesign Network and served as faculty sponsor for the Stanford Teacher Education Program. She is a former president of the American Educational Research Association and member of the National Academy of Education. Her research, teaching, and policy work focus on issues of school reform, teacher quality and educational equity. From 1994-2001, she served as executive director of the National Commission on Teaching and America's Future. Darling-Hammond was named one of the nation's ten most influential people affecting educational policy over the last decade. In 2008-09, she headed President Barack Obama's education policy transition team and continues to serve as a policy advisor to the president. Among Darling-Hammond's more than 300 publications are *Powerful teacher education: Lessons from exemplary programs* (Jossey-Bass, 2006); *Preparing teachers for a changing world: What teachers should learn and be able to do* (with John Bransford; Jossey-Bass, 2005), winner of the AACTE Pomeroy Award; *Teaching as the learning profession* (co-edited with Gary Sykes; Jossey-Bass, 1999), which received the National Staff Development Council's Outstanding Book Award for 2000; and *The right to learn* (Jossey-Bass, 1st edition, 1997), recipient of the American Educational Research Association's Outstanding Book Award for 1998.

Maria Assunção Flores is Associate Professor with qualification at the University of Minho, Portugal. She received her PhD at the University of Nottingham, UK in

2002. Her research interests include teacher professionalism, teacher education, evaluation and professional development, induction, change, and higher education. She has published books, chapters, articles in national and international journals. She is a member of various international associations and currently she is chair-elect of the International Council on Education for Teaching. She was a visiting scholar at the University of Cambridge, UK, from September 2008 to May 2009. Her recent publications include Flores (2012) Teachers' work and lives: A European perspective, in C. Day (Ed.), *The Routledge international handbook of teacher and school development* (pp. 94-107), London: Routledge; Flores, M. A. (2010) School cultures and organizations and teacher induction, in J. Wang, S. J. Odell, & R. T. Clift (Eds.), *Past, present, and future research on teacher induction: An anthology for researchers, policy makers, and practitioners* (pp. 45-56), Lanham, Maryland/ New York: Rowman & Littlefield Education; and Flores, M. A. (2011) Curriculum of initial teacher education in Portugal: New contexts, old problems, *Journal of Education for Teaching, 37*(4), 461-470.

Maria Iolanda Monteiro majored in Education at Universidade Estadual Paulista "Júlio de Mesquita Filho" (UNESP) in 1993, received her M.Ed. from UNESP in 2000 and her Ph.D. in Education from University of São Paulo (USP) in 2006. Her experience in education has focused on teaching methods and techniques, especially regarding the following topics: teacher knowledge and practices, school success and failure, literacy, language variation, environmental education, distance education, education and continuing education of elementary school teachers. Dr. Monteiro conducted postdoctoral studies at the School of Education, University of Campinas (UNICAMP) in 2010. Presently, she is an associate professor at Federal University of São Carlos (UFSCar), acting in both the online and face-to-face teacher education programs offered by this institution.

Maria Teresa Vilaça is Assistant Professor at the University of Minho, Portugal. She received her PhD at the University of Minho, Portugal in 2007. Her research interests include pre-service and in-service science teacher education, health education and sexuality, and education for sustainable development. She has published chapters and articles in international books and journals. She is a member of the leadership team of The Northern Regional Directorate of The Portuguese Biologists Association, a co-chair of the Research and Development Centre 'Culture, Quality of Life and Citizenship' of the Association for Teacher Education in Europe (ATEE), Brussels, and a member of the Schools for Health in Europe (SHE) Research Group, coordinated by the Research Programme for Health and Environmental Education at the Danish School of Education, University of Aarhus and NIGZ as WHO Collaborating Centre for School Health Promotion. She was a visiting scholar for a period of 15 days at the Pedagogical University of Mozambique, Mozambique, in 2010 and 2011, and at the São Paulo State University 'Júlio de Mesquita Filho' (UNESP), Brazil, in 2012. Her recent publications include: Vilaça, T. (2012) Ação, competência para a ação e visibilidade de género na educação em sexualidade nas escolas promotoras de saúde; Vilaça, T. (2011) Supervision and professional development in in-service teacher training regarding sexuality education. In G. Mészáros & I. Falus (Eds.), *Responsibility, challenge and support in teachers' life-long professional development. ATEE 2010 annual conference proceedings* (pp. 181-195). Brussels, Belgium: Association for Teacher Education in Europe, ATEE.

Paulien C. Meijer is Professor in Educational Sciences with focus on teacher educators' professional development at Open University in Heerlen, the Netherlands. She also works as researcher and teacher educator at the Department of Education, Faculty of Social and Behavioral Sciences of Utrecht University, the Netherlands. As teacher educator and former teacher in social sciences, she is specifically interested in identity issues in teacher learning and development in which transformation and defense mechanisms are central concepts. She publishes in various scientific journals about teacher learning throughout their professional career, in primary, secondary and higher education. She supervises a range of PhD students in this area.

Renata Portela Rinaldi is an Associate Professor with the Department of Education at Universidade Estadual Paulista "Júlio de Mesquita Filho" (UNESP) and has been a researcher with CNPq (National Council for Scientific and Technological Development) since 2010. She received her Ph.D. in Education from Federal University of São Carlos (UFSCar), with an emphasis on Teaching Methodology, in 2009. Dr. Rinaldi's work experience has focused on Teacher Education, and her research interests include continuing teacher education, teacher learning and professional development, teacher educators, school inclusion, and distance education.

Rosa Maria M. Anunciato de Oliveira is an Associate Professor at Federal University of São Carlos (UFSCar). She has a bachelor degree in Letters (1985) and Pedagogy (1988) from the School of Philosophy, Sciences, and Letters of Sorocaba, an M.Ed. (1995) and a Ph.D. in Education (2001) from UFSCar. Dr. Oliveira presently coordinates the research group "Studies on Teaching: Theory and Practice." Her work experience in Education has focused on Teacher Education, and her research interests encompass the following topics: teacher education, conceptions about teaching, elementary school education, students' conceptions, and professional learning.

Sandra Fernandes is Assistant Professor at the Faculty of Psychology and Education Sciences of the University of Coimbra, Portugal. She received her PhD in Educational Sciences at the University of Minho in 2011. After she concluded her PhD, she was granted a post-doctoral research grant (ref. SFRH/BPD/68349/2010) by the Science and Technology Foundation (FCT) to develop a project focused on performance appraisal of faculty in higher education, carried out in Portugal (University of Minho) and in the United Kingdom

(University of Nottingham). She has published several papers focusing on areas such as teaching and learning in higher education, performance appraisal of faculty, evaluation of project-based approaches, student assessment, tutoring in higher education, amongst others.

Sarah Howie is a Professor in the Faculty of Education, at the University of Pretoria. She is also the Director of the Centre for Evaluation and Assessment in Education and Training. The CEA has undertaken research, evaluations and training for the National Department of Education, various provincial departments of education, the Japan International Cooperation Agency, UNICEF, the Zenex Foundation, World Bank, Umalusi, Shuttleworth Foundation as well as various other non-government organisations, private corporations and higher education institutions. Her scientific field of interest and areas of work include monitoring, evaluation and assessment, international comparative research in the fields of science and mathematics education, reading literacy and information and communication technology, and learner achievement. Currently she is the co-National Research Coordinator for Progress in Reading Literacy Study (PIRLS 2006 and PIRLS 2011) and was the co-National Research Coordinator for Second Information Technology in Education Study (SITES).

Shawn Michael Bullock is Assistant Professor of science education at Simon Fraser University in British Columbia, Canada. He is interested in how problems of learning science, problems of learning to teach science, and problems of learning to teach science using digital technologies interact with one other. Recently, Dr. Bullock has also adopted a historical approach to understanding how professional knowledge is constructed from experience, using the continuing education of Canadian engineers in the 20th century as a case study for analysis. He is the author of Inside Teacher Education, published in 2011 by Sense.

Shukri Sanber is Associate Professor and lectures in Educational Research and Educational Assessment. His academic interests are in formative and self-assessment, ICT in teacher education, teacher research and program evaluation. He has participated in the review of several school systems in Australia and the evaluation of several social intervention programs in Australia and overseas. He has taken a leading role in the integration of ICT in teacher education programs at the School of Education (NSW).

Sólveig Karvelsdóttir (1940-2011) was assistant professor at University of Iceland School of Education. She earned a BA degree in pedagogy, a BA in Counseling and Career and a M.A. degree in pedagogy all from the University of Iceland. Sólveig worked for many years as a general classroom teacher in elementary schools before she gained further education and began her work at the University of Iceland. Her focus was on teachers' professionalism, collaboration and interaction, counseling, and families. Her research methodology was mostly qualitative approaches with focus on teachers; their lives, work situation and condition, interaction with students and collaboration with families.

Sonja Van Putten has been a Lecturer in Mathematics and Mathematics Education at the University of Pretoria for the last ten years. Prior to that she taught high school Mathematics for seventeen years. Her doctorate was based on an investigation of the professional identity of mathematics education students, and she continues to explore this field in an effort to gain insight into the problems experienced in mathematics education in South Africa. Her passion for Mathematics Education has led her to specialise in the Methodology of Mathematics Education which is her main lecturing platform.

Tom Russell is a Professor in the Faculty of Education at Queen's University, where he has taught since 1977. In the period 2007-2010 he held a Queen's University Chair in Teaching and Learning. His teaching includes a graduate course on action research and a physics curriculum methods course for preservice teachers. His research focuses on how people learn to teach and how teachers improve their teaching, with special reference to learning from experience. He is a co-editor of a number of books, including *Enacting a pedagogy of teacher education* (2007), and the *International handbook of self-study of teaching and teacher education practices* (2004). He is an editor of *Studying Teacher Education,* a Routledge journal commencing publication in 2005. Tom holds an A.B. degree in physics from Cornell University, a Master of Arts in Teaching degree from Harvard University, and a Ph.D. degree in Educational Theory from the University of Toronto.

Toshiyuki Kihara is Professor of practical school education at Osaka Kyoiku University, Japan. He received Ph.D. from Japan Woman University in 2003, based on his dissertation on the teacher development through lesson studies in Japan. Before he belonged to Osaka Kyoiku University in 2007, he had worked at Osaka University, Okayama University and Osaka City University for 16 years. His teaching and research interests span curriculum and instruction, lesson study and teacher education. His current research focus is on exploring the relationships between lesson study and teacher development, especially on developing models for collaborative teacher development and curriculum leadership through school-based practical researches. His latest book is *Lesson study and educational technology* (co-edited with Toshiyuki Mizukoshi, Shizuo Yoshizaki and Mana Taguchi, Minervashobo, 2012).

REVIEWERS

Antonia Aelterman, *Ghent University, Belgium*

Bernardette Charlier, *University of Fribourg, Switzerland*

Cheryl Craig, *University of Houston, USA*

Christopher Day, *University of Nottingham, UK*

Frances Rust, *University of Pennsylvania, USA*

Hafdís Guðjónsdóttir, *University of Iceland, Iceland*

Isabel Rots, *Ghent University, Belgium*

Jan Broeckmans, *Hasselt University, Belgium*

Jude Butcher, *Australian Catholic University, Australia*

Michael Kompf, *Brock University, Canada*

Penny Haworth, *Massey University, New Zealand*